THE CAMBRIDGE COMPANION
OF BINGEN

This specially commissioned collection of thirteen chapters explores the life and works of Hildegard of Bingen (1098–1179), monastic founder, leader of a community of nuns, composer, active correspondent, and writer of religious visions, theological treatises, sermons, and scientific and medical texts. Aimed at advanced university students and new Hildegard researchers, the chapters provide a broad context for Hildegard's life and monastic setting and offer comprehensive discussions on each of the main areas of her output. Engagingly written by experts in medieval history, theology, German literature, musicology, and the history of medicine, the chapters are grounded in Hildegard's twelfth-century context and investigate her output within its monastic and liturgical environments, her reputation during and after her life, and the materiality of the transmission of her works, considering aspects of manuscript layout, illumination, and scribal practices at her Rupertsberg monastery.

JENNIFER BAIN is Professor of Music at Dalhousie University, Nova Scotia. She is the author of *Hildegard of Bingen and Musical Reception: The Modern Revival of a Medieval Composer* (2015) and has published extensively on chant manuscripts, digital tools for chant research, and reception history, as well as on the music of Guillaume de Machaut and Hildegard of Bingen.

THE CAMBRIDGE
COMPANION TO
HILDEGARD OF BINGEN

EDITED BY

JENNIFER BAIN

Dalhousie University, Nova Scotia

CAMBRIDGE
UNIVERSITY PRESS

University Printing House, Cambridge CB2 8BS, United Kingdom

One Liberty Plaza, 20th Floor, New York, NY 10006, USA

477 Williamstown Road, Port Melbourne, VIC 3207, Australia

314–321, 3rd Floor, Plot 3, Splendor Forum, Jasola District Centre, New Delhi – 110025, India

103 Penang Road, #05–06/07, Visioncrest Commercial, Singapore 238467

Cambridge University Press is part of the University of Cambridge.

It furthers the University's mission by disseminating knowledge in the pursuit of education, learning, and research at the highest international levels of excellence.

www.cambridge.org
Information on this title: www.cambridge.org/9781108471350
DOI: 10.1017/9781108573832

© Cambridge University Press 2021

First published 2021

A catalogue record for this publication is available from the British Library.

Library of Congress Cataloging-in-Publication Data
NAMES: Bain, Jennifer, 1967– editor.
TITLE: The Cambridge companion to Hildegard of Bingen / edited by Jennifer Bain, Dalhousie University, Nova Scotia.
DESCRIPTION: Cambridge : Cambridge University Press, 2021.
IDENTIFIERS: LCCN 2021043585 (print) | LCCN 2021043586 (ebook) | ISBN 9781108471350 (hardback) | ISBN 9781108573832 (ebook other)
SUBJECTS: LCSH: Hildegard, Saint, 1098–1179. | BISAC: LITERARY CRITICISM / European / General
CLASSIFICATION: LCC BX4700.H5 C36 2021 (print) | LCC BX4700.H5 (ebook) | DDC 220.6/6–dc23
LC record available at https://lccn.loc.gov/2021043585
LC ebook record available at https://lccn.loc.gov/2021043586

ISBN 978-1-108-47135-0 Hardback
ISBN 978-1-108-45781-1 Paperback

To my daughter, Hannah Docking

Contents

Figures

Tables

Music Examples

Contributors

ALISON ALTSTATT is Associate Professor of Musicology at the University of Northern Iowa. Her research on medieval music and convent ritual has earned awards from the American Musicological Society and the National Endowment for the Humanities. Her book, *Wilton Abbey in Procession: Benedictine Women's Music and Ritual in the Thirteenth-Century Wilton Processional,* is under contract with Liverpool University Press.

WENDY LOVE ANDERSON, Assistant Director of Academic Programs in the Center for the Humanities and Religious Studies Program faculty at Washington University in St. Louis, explores questions of religious identity in medieval Judaism and Christianity. Her first book, *The Discernment of Spirits: Assessing Visions and Visionaries in the Late Middle Ages,* was published in 2011.

JENNIFER BAIN, Professor of Music at Dalhousie University, is author of *Hildegard of Bingen and Musical Reception: The Modern Revival of a Medieval Composer* (2015). She codevelops digital tools for research and has published extensively on chant manuscripts, reception history, and the analysis of music by Guillaume de Machaut and Hildegard of Bingen.

ALISON I. BEACH holds a chair in Mediaeval History at the University of St. Andrews. She has published monographs, translations, and edited collections on monasticism, women, and book production in the twelfth century and recently coedited, with Isabelle Cochelin, *The Cambridge History of Medieval Western Monasticism in the Latin West* (2020).

NATHANIEL M. CAMPBELL is an adjunct history instructor at Union College, Kentucky. He works on twelfth-century texts and their visual traditions, with a focus on Hildegard of Bingen. He has published the first complete English translation of Hildegard's *The Book of Divine Works* (2018).

MICHAEL EMBACH is Director of the Stadtbibliothek and Statdarchiv in Trier. After his degrees in Catholic theology and German literature in Trier and Freiburg im Breisgau, he completed doctoral and habilitation work in new German literature and old German philology. His publications are primarily on the work of Hildegard of Bingen, German and Latin literature of the former archbishopric and electorate of Trier, and the history of the book and libraries in the Middle Ages.

MARGOT FASSLER is the Keough Hesburgh Professor of Music History and Liturgy at the University of Notre Dame and the Robert Tangeman Professor of Music History, Emerita, at Yale University. A fellow of the Radcliffe Institute at Harvard University in 2019–2020, her recent publications include a chapter on the *Liber ordinarus* of Nivelles and an article on women and their sequences in *Speculum*.

CHRISTOPHER D. FLETCHER is Assistant Director of the Newberry Center for Renaissance Studies, where he develops programming and resources highlighting the library's medieval and early modern collections. He holds a PhD in medieval history from the University of Chicago and is pursuing various research projects on the history of public engagement.

JAMES GINTHER is the Sisters of St. Joseph, Toronto, Chair in Theology at the University of St. Michael's College and an associate fellow at the Pontifical Institute of Mediaeval Studies. He has published extensively on theology in the twelfth and thirteenth centuries and is the author of the *Westminster Handbook to Medieval Theology* (2009).

MAGDA HAYTON teaches in the Department of Religious Studies at Missouri State University. She received her PhD from the University of Toronto (2015), for which she was awarded the Leonard Boyle Dissertation Prize. Specializing in premodern prophecy and apocalypticism, she has publications on the reception of Hildegard and Joachim of Fiore in several journals.

LORI KRUCKENBERG is Associate Professor of Musicology at the University of Oregon. Her research focuses on medieval *cantrices* in the German lands, sequences, tropes, and music in narrative. Recent publications have appeared in *The Cambridge History of Medieval Music*

(2018) and *Medieval Cantors and Their Craft* (2017). She received the Bonnie Wheeler Fellowship in 2019.

PETER V. LOEWEN specializes in medieval and Renaissance music at Rice University. He is the author of *Music in Early Franciscan Thought* (2013) and the coeditor of *Mary Magdalene in Medieval Culture: Conflicted Roles* (2014). He has published articles in such journals as *Speculum, Comparative Drama*, and *Franciscan Studies*.

FAITH WALLIS is a historian of medieval Europe at McGill University, specializing in the history of science and medicine. She has published translations and studies of medieval time-reckoning (computus) and medicine, and her current research focuses on medical education and the transmission of medical knowledge in the twelfth century.

Acknowledgments

It is a pleasure to thank the many people and institutions who have helped shape this volume. I am deeply grateful to Kate Brett, who invited me to propose this volume to Cambridge University Press, supported the project at every step, and was an excellent sounding board along the way. To the authors for writing chapters that made me think and for responding so engagingly with all suggestions and queries. To the anonymous reader of the manuscript for a quick turnaround and insightful comments. To my research assistant, Lucia Denk, who enthusiastically devoted many hours in a short space of time at the end stages and provided excellent feedback on drafts of the Introduction and on my chapter (Chapter 10). To Barbara Swanson for her meticulous work creating the index. To the Social Sciences and Humanities Research Council of Canada, which generously provided funds for this project (Ref: 435–2019–0309). To the libraries and institutions that gave us permission to reproduce images: the Biblioteca Statale di Lucca, courtesy of the Ministry of Heritage, Cultural Activities and Tourism; the Rheinisches Bildarchiv Köln; the Benediktinerinnenabtei Sankt Hildegard; and the Biblioteca Vaticana. And, finally, I extend my love and gratitude to Simon and Hannah who support me in countless ways. This book is dedicated to Hannah, my daughter, who selected Hildegard as a grade 8 presentation topic at school while I was preparing this volume; when her teacher warned her that she might have difficulty finding sources, she quipped, "I think I'll be okay."

Introduction

Jennifer Bain

The life of Hildegard of Bingen (1098–1179) has been recounted and her works have been explored in many languages and in many formats: in pamphlets, books, and newspapers; on the radio and in audio recordings; in film and television documentaries; and on countless websites and blogs. Anyone encountering this remarkable historical figure for the first time or wanting to begin research on some aspect of her output and legacy might quickly become overwhelmed by the quantity of material available. Scholars have considered her contributions as a nun, a monastic leader, a preacher, a correspondent, a poet, a theologian, a visionary, a prophet, a composer, a scientist, a medical practitioner, a liturgist, a hagiographer, a cryptographer, and as a founder of her own convent at Rupertsberg. Some authors have studied her works in their historical context and others have investigated the historical reception of her works and ideas through manuscript transmission and the modern reception through printed copies and translations of her written works as well as through performances and recordings of her music. Some writers have focused on the reception of Hildegard herself as a historical figure and as a saint, considering early attempts to secure her canonization, a process that culminated in 2012 with Pope Benedict, who named Hildegard as both a saint and a Doctor of the Church.[1] Given these many and diverse approaches to Hildegard and her output, this volume aims to provide a point of entry for understanding her life and the breadth of her activities and to introduce the reader to primary and secondary sources for further study.

---

[1] "Decrees of the Congregation for the Causes of Saints," May 10, 2012. VIS. Vatican Information Service. Holy See Press Office. http://visnews-en.blogspot.com/2012/05/decrees-of-congregation-for-causes-of_11.html. Pope Benedict XVI, "Apostolic Letter, Proclaiming Saint Hildegard of Bingen, professed nun of the Order of Saint Benedict, a Doctor of the Universal Church," October 7, 2012. www.vatican.va/content/benedict-xvi/en/apost_letters/documents/hf_ben-xvi_apl_20121007_ildegarda-bingen.html.

This collection brings together thirteen chapters, each written by a different scholar, with a variety of disciplines represented. Suitable for advanced university students and for scholars first immersing themselves in Hildegard studies, the chapters provide a broader context for understanding Hildegard's life and monastic setting and offer comprehensive discussions on each of the main areas of Hildegard's output. Two other volumes in English have done something similar: *A Companion to Hildegard of Bingen* (Brill, 2014) and *The Voice of the Living Light* (1998).[2] This new *Companion* complements that by Brill. Denser in style, the Brill *Companion* covers a number of subjects not addressed here, including, for example, chapters on the history of the Disibodenberg (Hildegard's first monastic home), on the influence of the Hirsau reform on Hildegard's own agenda, on Hildegard's "Unknown" language, and on the comparative visionary experiences of Hildegard and her contemporary, Elisabeth of Schönau. This Cambridge *Companion* diverges from the offerings of the Brill volume by providing contextual chapters on life in a medieval convent and on the education of women religious in the twelfth century, as well as in-depth treatments of Hildegard's sermonizing and her correspondence and assessments of the material witnesses of Hildegard's output through examinations of scribal practices at Rupertsberg and the role of illuminations in the Rupertsberg manuscripts.

In style and coverage, this volume is in some ways more like *The Voice of the Living Light*, edited by Barbara Newman. A collection of nine essays, *The Voice of the Living Light* has chapters explicitly addressing Hildegard as a spiritual leader, a religious thinker, a prophet and reformer, a correspondent, an artist, a medical writer, a composer, and a poet. It was published in 1998, the 900th anniversary of Hildegard's birth, an anniversary that inspired the publication of many important editions, studies, and translations and a steady stream since then. This burst of activity warrants an updated introduction to Hildegard's life and works and to the resources available for further study. Recent publications have included English translations of her correspondence (in three volumes: 1994, 1998, and 2004), her homilies on the Gospels (2011), her lives of Saints Rupert and Disibod (2010), and her third and final book of visions (2018), as well as of the early biographical sources of Hildegard and her mentor Jutta (1999).[3] Various editions of her music have appeared as well,

[2] Beverly Kienzle, Debra L. Stoudt, and George Ferzoco, eds, *A Companion to Hildegard of Bingen* (Leiden: Brill, 2014) and Barbara Newman, ed., *The Voice of the Living Light: Hildegard of Bingen and Her World* (Berkeley: University of California Press, 1998).

[3] Hildegard of Bingen, *Liber Divinorum Operum*, trans. Nathaniel M. Campbell (Washington, DC: The Catholic University of America Press, 2018).

including a facsimile edition of her music from the *Riesencodex* (1998) and a number of editions in modern musical notation (1997–1998, 2013, and 2016).[4] Since 1998, hundreds of studies on Hildegard and her output have appeared in English and in German (and in numerous other languages), as well as two new single-authored biographies in English (2001 and 2018)[5] and two major reference works in German: a bibliography of scholarship on Hildegard (1998) and a detailed catalogue of 363 known manuscripts transmitting Hildegard's works (2013).[6] Perhaps most transformative for Hildegard studies in the last two decades (indeed for all pre-1600 scholarship) is the online publication of thousands of manuscripts – including a number of manuscripts of Hildegard's works – made available freely through national and regional digital repositories and libraries; where once scholars either had to travel to see manuscripts or had to rely on black-and-white microfilms, today many manuscripts can be consulted on computer screens – sometimes two or three at a time – with resolutions superior to what is available to the naked eye.

The Cambridge Companion to Hildegard of Bingen not only provides updated scholarship since the publication of the other two volumes in 1998 and 2014 but also brings Hildegard's lived experience in her community of nuns together with her intellectual and creative activities. Divided into three groups, the chapters outline her living and working conditions, as well as her reputation, and provide a twelfth-century context for the kind of education she might have received, as well as for her visionary activity, her theological writing, her medical writings, her correspondence, her sermonizing, and her liturgical activity. The three chapters in Part I, "Life and Monastic Context," introduce the main resources for studying the life of Hildegard but also for understanding what life would be like for women in a monastic environment in the twelfth century and how women religious were educated in medieval German lands. In Chapter 1, Michael Embach presents a biography of Hildegard's life from her early childhood

---

[4] Hildegard of Bingen, *Symphonia Armonie Celestium Revelationum*, 8 vols., ed. and trans. Marianne Richert Pfau (Bryn Mawr, PA: Hildegard Publishing Company, 1997); *Ordo Virtutum: A Comparative Edition*, ed. Vincent Corrigan (Lion's Bay, BC: Institute of Mediaeval Music, 2013) and *Hildegard of Bingen, Symphonia: A Comparative Edition*, ed. Vincent Corrigan (Lion's Bay, BC: Institute of Mediaeval Music, 2016).

[5] Fiona Maddocks, *Hildegard of Bingen: The Woman of Her Age* (London: Headline, 2001) and Honey Meconi, *Hildegard of Bingen* (Urbana: University of Illinois Press, 2018).

[6] Marc-Aeilko Aris, Michael Embach, Werner Lauter, Irmgard Müller, Franz Staab, and Scholastica Steinle, OSB, eds., *Hildegard von Bingen: Internationale Wissenschaftliche Bibliographie* (Mainz: Gesellschaft für Mittelrheinische Kirchengeschichte, 1998), and Michael Embach and Martina Wallner, *Conspectus der Handschriften Hildegards von Bingen* (Münster: Aschendorff, 2013).

to her death in 1179. Translated from German by Florian Hild, the chapter includes an overview of the twelfth-century sources available for reconstructing Hildegard's life. Embach explains some of the difficulties in trying to reconcile seemingly contradictory information and provides multiple theories about certain aspects of her life when the sources have led scholars to different conclusions. In Chapter 2, Alison I. Beach uses a more experiential approach, taking the reader through a "day in the life" of a community of twelfth-century nuns. Using September 30 as a regular day, she tracks hour by hour the activities of the women at Eibingen, a convent across the river from Hildegard's Rupertsberg, her foundation at the confluence of the Rhine and Nahe rivers. To provide us with a context for what Hildegard's daily life might have looked like, Beach starts with the rising of the women two hours before dawn and demonstrates how the religious services of the Divine Office structure the day for the women and interact with their other activities as well as the physicality of the monastic complex. Chapter 3 by Lori Kruckenberg provides a twelfth-century context for Hildegard's demonstrated learnedness, by investigating how women religious acquired knowledge and intellectual skills in medieval German-speaking areas. Kruckenberg draws on a wide variety of evidence about women's education, examining monastic and canonical rules (written regulations that dictate the activities and behavior of nuns and monks), hagiographic literature (specifically the lives of holy women), and material artifacts such as medieval book collections, individual manuscripts, and writing by women. These three chapters together are foundational for the chapters that follow that engage directly with Hildegard's body of work.

Shifting from the life of Hildegard, Part II, "Writings and Reputation," has six chapters that both investigate and contextualize her literary works, focusing on: her theological output, considering her sources, her institutional environment, and her audience; the function and status of her correspondence; her sermonizing through letters, her visionary writings, and her preaching tours; her scientific and medical texts; her reputation as a prophet as developed through the circulation of the *Pentachronon*; and her visionary activity and later reception. In the first chapter in this section (Chapter 4), James Ginther focuses on Hildegard's three major theological and visionary books: *Scivias* (Know the Ways), *Liber vitae meritorum* (Book of Life's Merits), and *Liber divinorum operum* (Book of Divine Works). Ginther considers the authoritative texts that ground Hildegard's theology, the institutional setting of her work, and her implied readers. While acknowledging her wide readership outside of Rupertsberg, he connects her theological writing directly to her role as *magistra* (spiritual leader and teacher of her community). He argues that her nuns were her primary audience and suggests that considering her community as her implied readers raises new questions about her theological program, extending beyond her much-discussed calls for reform and mystical apocalypticism.

Chapters 5 and 6 focus on Hildegard's correspondence and her sermonizing. In Chapter 5, Christopher D. Fletcher considers Hildegard's letter-writing activity within a twelfth-century context. He reveals that, while her letters do not follow the formal structure of most other letters from the period, their intended function was the same: to reach a wider public and to build personal connections. In Chapter 6, Peter V. Loewen provides a context for Hildegard's preaching practices and an overview of what is known about her preaching tours. He identifies a recurring theme of greenness (*viriditas*) in Hildegard's sermons and sermonizing literature and suggests that she adapts ideas from Ambrose, Augustine, and Gregory to present contrasting ideas of *viriditas* and dryness in relation to faith and spiritual gardening.

Of all of Hildegard's writings, her scientific and medical works, known today as *Physica* and *Cause et cure* (Causes and Cures), have the most complicated history as texts. In Chapter 7, Faith Wallis explains that they were compiled after Hildegard's death and drew on materials that Hildegard herself prepared. Wallis situates these books both within the medical culture of the twelfth century and within Hildegard's worldview, offering numerous extracts from the works themselves. She also provides an overview of their reception and Hildegard's reputation as a healer from the early modern to the postmodern period.

The final two chapters in Part II address Hildegard's status as a prophet and as a visionary. In Chapter 8, Magda Hayton discusses the impact of Gebeno of Eberbach's thirteenth-century compilation of excerpts from Hildegard's writings, typically referred to as the *Pentachronon*, shortened from *Speculum futurorum temporum siue Pentachronon sancte Hildegardis* (Mirror of Future Times or the Five Ages of Saint Hildegard). As Hayton explains, the anthology circulated widely in three related but different versions, all presenting Hildegard as both an apocalyptic prophet, who preached about reform and proffered a new theological understanding of the history of salvation, and a spiritual leader, guiding clergy and other monastic members and leaders. In Chapter 9, Wendy Love Anderson distinguishes Hildegard's reputation as a prophet from her reputation as a visionary. She provides a context for Hildegard's visionary activity within the twelfth century and an outline of how Hildegard's visions were received from the twelfth to the early twenty-first century.

The final section of the book, Part III, "Music, Manuscripts, Illuminations, and Scribes," comprises four chapters. It begins with Hildegard's musical activity, considering her music in its liturgical environment, and her *Ordo virtutum* in the context of female Benedictine monasticism, and then turns to the material context of Hildegard's activities. The final chapters consider the didactic elements of the illuminations in manuscript copies of two of her visionary texts, and finally scribal practice at Rupertsberg, gleaned from a study of scribal hands in a number of manuscripts associated with that institution founded by Hildegard. In the first chapter in this section (Chapter 10), I situate Hildegard's musical output within a liturgical framework, providing an overview of the manuscript sources and discussing issues of ordering and layout in relation to other liturgical books in the Middle Ages. I describe Hildegard's musical style, focusing particularly on her use of intertextuality, both literary and musical. In Chapter 11, Alison Altstatt discusses Hildegard's *Ordo virtutum*, the only known sung drama with secure authorship from the Middle Ages. Altstatt describes the drama as theologically and liturgically grounded, drawing on processional rituals, the rite of the Consecration of Virgins, and on the *Rule of St. Benedict*.

The final two chapters turn to materiality, considering the manuscripts that originated in the scriptorium at Rupertsberg. In Chapter 12, Nathaniel M. Campbell focuses on two illustrated manuscripts, Hildegard's *Scivias*, produced during her lifetime (and lost during World War II), and the *Liber divinorum operum* produced forty years or so after her death.[7] He argues that both illuminated manuscripts aim to secure her visionary authority and to integrate her work into wider Christian traditions. In the final chapter (Chapter 13), Margot Fassler addresses the Rupertsberg scriptorium directly, identifying the features of the scribal hands emerging from there. She demonstrates how crucial it is to undertake the painstaking work of tracking the scribal hands in the Rupertsberg manuscripts, because the large number identified thus far suggests the importance of copying at Rupertsberg and the close engagement the nuns would have had with Hildegard's writings of all descriptions.

What should be clear to the reader by the end of the volume is that, despite its breadth of coverage, this collection of chapters offers just

---

[7] *Scivias*, Wiesbaden, Hochschul- und Landesbibliothek RheinMain, MS 1; Jennifer Bain, "History of a Book: Hildegard's 'Riesencodex' and World War II," *Plainsong and Medieval Music* 27, no. 2 (2017): 143–170; and *Liber divinorum operum*, Biblioteca Statale di Lucca, MS 1942, www.wdl.org/en/item/21658/.

a snapshot of the vast multilingual literature that exists on Hildegard, her works, and her reception and that scholarship in German in particular is central to the field. What should be equally clear is that, even given the copious scholarship on Hildegard, there are still many avenues open for research. There are practical, historical questions that have yet to be answered conclusively, such as what exactly Hildegard's relationship was to the monastic community in Eibingen, a question raised by both Michael Embach and Alison I. Beach in their chapters, drawing on recent scholarship by Matthias Schmandt.[8] New research areas also arise by shifting perspective as James Ginther does in his chapter, considering Hildegard's theological trilogy as primarily spiritual texts for Hildegard's nuns at Rupertsberg. Digital methodologies open new possibilities for research, searching, for example, for further evidence of Hildegard's engagement with other medieval works through databases such as the *Patrologia Latina Database*, as Peter V. Loewen demonstrates with Latin text searches in his chapter, and through the *Cantus Database*, as I demonstrate through melody searches in my chapter.[9] As well, the availability of so many digitized manuscripts online makes this the ideal time to delve deeper into issues of paleography, to consider the activities of the scriptorium at Rupertsberg in particular, as Margot Fassler undertakes in her chapter. Secure identification of the Rupertsberg house style and of specific scribal hands in that scriptorium will open up the possibility of finding other manuscripts that originated there and learning more about the monastic environment that Hildegard cultivated.

While readers are certainly welcome to read the chapters in whichever order they choose, the order presented is pedagogical in design: Part II presumes knowledge about Hildegard's monastic life that is provided in Part I; the final two chapters of Part II deal with the medieval and later reception of Hildegard's writings, the main areas of which (theology, letters, sermons, and scientific writings) are presented in the first four chapters of that section; and the chapters in Part III are grounded in the topics presented in Parts I and II: both Hildegard's monastic environment and her literary output. The Select Bibliography provided at the end of the

---

[8] Matthias Schmandt, "Hildegard von Bingen und das Kloster Eibingen: Revision einer historischen Überlieferung," *Nassauische Annalen* 125 (2014): 29–52.

[9] *Patrologia Latina: The Full Text Database.* Includes the complete first edition of: Jacques-Paul Migne, *Patrologia Latina*, 221 vols. (Paris: 1844–1855). http://pld.chadwyck.co.uk/; and *Cantus: A Database for Latin Ecclesiastical Chant – Inventories of Chant Sources*, directed by Debra Lacoste (2011–), Terence Bailey (1997–2010), and Ruth Steiner (1987–1996), web developer, Jan Koláček (2011–), https://cantus.uwaterloo.ca/.

book has four sections, including Latin editions and English translations of Hildegard's works (organized by work); select biographies of Hildegard (in Latin, English, and German); additional resources, such as online databases, bibliographies, and influential collections of essays; and a selection of important manuscripts transmitting Hildegard's works, with URLs provided when available online. Hundreds of other items are cited in the footnotes of the chapters in this volume.

I began research on Hildegard thirty years ago in 1991, when I embarked on graduate study in music theory, and yet from reading the chapters here I still learned much and gained deeper appreciation for Hildegard's creativity and erudition. I hope you do too.

Further Reading

Benedict XVI, Pope. "Decrees of the Congregation for the Causes of Saints." May 10, 2012. VIS. Vatican Information Service. Holy See Press Office. http://visnews-en.blogspot.com/2012/05/decrees-of-congregation-for-causes -of_11.html.

Benedict XVI, Pope. "Apostolic Letter Proclaiming Saint Hildegard of Bingen, Professed Nun of the Order of Saint Benedict, a Doctor of the Universal Church." October 7, 2012. www.vatican.va/content/benedict-xvi/en/apost_ letters/documents/hf_ben-xvi_apl_20121007_ildegarda-bingen.html.

Embach, Michael and Martina Wallner. *Conspectus der Handschriften Hildegards von Bingen*. Münster: Aschendorff, 2013.

Kienzle, Beverly Mayne, Debra L. Stoudt, and George Ferzoco, eds. *A Companion to Hildegard of Bingen*. Leiden: Brill, 2014.

Meconi, Honey. *Hildegard of Bingen*. Urbana: University of Illinois Press, 2018.

Newman, Barbara. *Voice of the Living Light: Hildegard of Bingen and Her World*. Berkeley: University of California Press, 1998.

Silvas, Anna, ed. and trans. *Jutta and Hildegard: The Biographical Sources*. University Park, PA: Pennsylvania State University Press, 1999.

PART I

Life and Monastic Context

CHAPTER I

The Life of Hildegard of Bingen (1098–1179)

Michael Embach

The basic facts of Hildegard of Bingen's life are well established.[1] Born in 1098, she formally entered a female enclosure attached to the male monastery of Disibodenberg on November 1, 1112 along with two other women. The community of women grew, and, in 1136, when her mentor Jutta of Sponheim died, Hildegard was elected *magistra* by the other women. In 1141, she received divine instructions to write down her visions, which resulted in *Scivias* (Know the Ways), the first of three large theological and visionary treatises. Around 1150, she moved her nuns from Disibodenberg to their newly founded monastic complex at Rupertsberg on the Rhine, and for the next three decades she developed a public persona through her prodigious writing in many genres and through her preaching tours. When she died in 1179, she left behind a large body of works, including a corpus of liturgical music, and she left behind a community anxious to see her elevated to sainthood, which in part is why we have as much information about her as we do.

This chapter fills in some of the details of this biographical sketch, while also pointing to the difficulties in doing so. Although many biographies of Hildegard of Bingen are available in a wide variety of formats, there is still no comprehensive, historical-critical biography for researchers.[2] The main difficulty for anyone trying to assess and confirm the details of Hildegard's life is the conflicting evidence that emerges from the documentary material most closely associated with her lifetime. This chapter begins with a description of the sources from which a biography can be generated. It then proceeds chronologically through her life and after her death,

---

[1] This chapter was translated by Florian Hild.

[2] See Franz Staab, "Hildegard von Bingen: Fragmente einer Biographie der Heiligen. Aus dem Nachlass," in Staab, *Die "Heiligsprechung" Hildegards von Bingen*, ed. Georg May, Heimatpflege für den Kreis Mainz-Bingen, Bd. 27 (Bingen: Vereinigung der Heimatfreunde am Mittelrhein, 2012); and Michael Embach, *Hildegard von Bingen (1098–1179): Leben, Werk und Wirkung* (Trier: Paulinus-Verlag, 2014).

describing her earlier years, the beginning of her public activities, the founding of Rupertsberg, her travel and preaching activities, reports about her miracles, her final years, the early reception of her work, and lastly the various canonization attempts.

The Sources of Hildegard's Life History

The most important sources for establishing Hildegard's biography come from her lifetime, or shortly thereafter, including the *Vita sanctae Hildegardis* (Life of Saint Hildegard), the *Vita domnae Juttae inclusae* (Life of Lady Jutta the Anchoress), the *Acta inquisitionis* (Act of Inquisition, a canonization document), the correspondence between Hildegard of Bingen and Guibert of Gembloux, as well as two works written by Hildegard herself: the *Vita sancti Ruperti confessoris* (Life of Saint Rupert, Confessor) and the *Vita sancti Disibodi episcopi* (Life of Saint Disibod, Bishop). There are furthermore documents from Disibodenberg and Rupertsberg, as well as introductory remarks from Hildegard's visionary writings.

Notwithstanding their great significance for a reconstruction of Hildegard's biography, these sources present a series of problems. This is especially true for the documents concerning Hildegard's childhood and youth, which contain sometimes contradictory, hard-to-reconcile information. Moreover, as Sylvain Gougenheim justly complains, Hildegard's life story from age eight to her leadership at the women's enclosure at the abbey of Disibodenberg in 1136 is full of holes.[3] The *Vita Hildegardis*, for example, must be regarded as a posthumously assembled work that combines autobiographical writings of Hildegard with two fragmentary biographies by Gottfried of Disibodenberg (1174–1176) and Guibert of Gembloux (before 1180). These disparate materials, possibly including a now lost "miracle book" of Hildegard's miracles, were synthesized by the monk Theodoric of Echternach between 1182 and 1188. Theodoric, however, did not know Hildegard personally, which explains why the *Octo lectiones in festo sancte Hildegardis legende* (Eight Readings to Be Read on the Feast of St. Hildegard), likely from Theodoric, provides the wrong death year (1181) for Hildegard.

For these reasons, there are still gaps and unresolved aspects of Hildegard's biography, which at this point and time simply cannot be cleared up. The following description of Hildegard's life can therefore only claim to be an approximation.

[3] Sylvain Gougenheim, *La Sibylle du Rhin. Hildegarde de Bingen, abbesse et prophétesse rhénane*, Série Histoire et Médiévale 38 (Paris: Publications de la Sorbonne, 1996), 30.

Family, Birth, and Youth

In the prefatory material to her first visionary and theological work, *Scivias*, Hildegard reports that she received the instruction to write down her visions in the year 1141 and she states explicitly that she was then forty-two years and seven months old.[4] With this information and by consulting further sources, it can be concluded that Hildegard must have been born between August and September 16, 1098. This date should be considered authoritative even though Hildegard herself as well as the last secretary in her retinue, Guibert of Gembloux (ca. 1124–1213), date her birth to the year 1100.[5] The reference to the year 1100 is symbolic, regarded as the beginning of the end of the reign of Emperor Heinrich IV (1084–1105), a catastrophic reign in the church's view. The year 1099 also marks the conquest of Jerusalem and the subsequent rule of the holy city by Godfrey of Bouillon (ca. 1060–1100), as the Christian *princeps* (ruler) and *advocatus sancti sepulchri* (defender of the Holy Sepulchre). Both events, the death of Heinrich IV and the conquest of Jerusalem, were frequently understood in the chronicles of the Middle Ages as symptoms of the birth of a new epoch, to which great meaning was assigned. The *Vita Hildegardis* additionally claims that belief in the doctrine of the Apostles and justice itself began to lose fervor and were doubted at this time. These remarks establish a motive for the necessary reform of the church and the world, and placing Hildegard's birth in that year is a timely coincidence. Against a background of this historical-theological stylization, Hildegard's alleged birth in the year 1100 gains the aura of inaugurating a new spiritual age. Hildegard herself becomes a persona of the new beginning whose historical appearance augured the coming of great events. It is therefore no surprise that the annals of the monastery of Disibodenberg, begun toward the middle of the twelfth century, strongly emphasize the epochal change of the year 1100 by providing a detailed report about the First Crusade and the conquest of Jerusalem.[6]

---

[4] Hildegard of Bingen, *Scivias*, trans. Mother Columba Hart and Jane Bishop (New York: Paulist Press, 1990), 59.

[5] *Vita sanctae Hildegardis*, ed. Monica Klaes, Corpus Christianorum Continuatio Mediaevalis (CCCM) 126 (Turnhout: Brepols, 1993), 22, lines 39–44: "Nam post incarnationem Christi anno millesimo centesimo doctrina apostolorum et ardens iusticia, quam in christianis et spiritualibus constituerat, tardare cepit et in hesitacionem uertebatur. Illis temporibus nata sum" ("Then in the year 1100 AD the teaching of the apostles and the burning justice which He erected in Christians and clerics began to slacken and turned to doubt. That's when I was born").

[6] *Annales sancti Disibodi*, ed. Georg Waitz, Monumenta Germaniae Historica 17 (Hannover: Hahnsche Buchhandlung, 1861), 17–19.

There is only sparse information about the background and the family of Hildegard in the *Vita Hildegardis*.[7] This is bewildering considering that birth and relations were generally of great importance in medieval biographies. It remarks merely that Hildegard's family belonged to the nobility, was wealthy, and that her father's name was Hildebert and her mother's Mechthild. Of Hildegard's father, we know that he belonged to the free nobility, denoting an official position or a feudal relationship but not a formal vassalship. The literature remarks again and again on Hildegard's father's close relationship with the counts of Sponheim, especially Meginhard of Sponheim. The connections between Hildegard's family and the Sponheims, one of the most influential noble families in the mid-Rhine territory, are apparent later when Jutta of Sponheim (ca. 1092–1136), Meginhard's sister, became Hildegard's first teacher in the women's enclosure. There is even less information about Hildegard's mother Mechthild than about her father. Her family's home is supposedly the castle of Merxheim in the Nahe valley.

We know from the sources that Hildegard was the tenth (not necessarily last) child of Hildebert and Mechthild, but knowledge of her siblings is equally sparse. It is at least known that Hildegard's brother Drutwin took over the family home and that another brother, Hugo, was the cantor at the cathedral church of Mainz from 1156 to 1163, which made him one of the three highest-ranking clerics of the diocese. Hugo also worked as a tutor of Rudolf of Zähringen (ca. 1135–1191), the later archbishop of Mainz (from 1160) and bishop of Lüttich (from 1167), and possibly served as a cleric in Hildegard's convent at Rupertsberg from 1175.[8] The next-younger brother, Rorich, is documented together with Drutwin and Hugo as a grantee of property in Bermersheim, although another document only mentions Drutwin and Hugo.[9] Four biological sisters of Hildegard are known by name, although they could also be sisters-in-law, cousins, or nieces: Irmgard, Odilia, Jutta, and Clementia. The latter, Clementia, belonged to the convent at Rupertsberg as a fellow sister of Hildegard. A nephew of Hildegard, named Wezzelin (d. 1185), worked as provost at the St. Andreas monastery in Cologne and helped Hildegard with the compilation of her third book of visions, the *Liber divinorum operum*, after the death of her

---

[7] Marianna Schrader, *Die Herkunft der heiligen Hildegard*, ed. Adelgundis Führkötter, Quellen und Abhandlungen zur mittelrheinischen Kirchengeschichte 43 (Mainz: Selbstverlag der Gesellschaft für mittelrheinische Kirchengeschichte, 1981). Embach, *Hildegard von Bingen*, 8–17.

[8] Guibertus Gemblacensis, *Epistolae quae in codice B. R. Brux. 5527–5534 inveniuntur. P. 2*, ed. Albert Derolez, CCCM 66 A (Turnhout: Brepols, 1989), 346–347.

[9] *Registrum bonorum*, Landeshauptarchiv Koblenz, Abt. 701 A VII 3, Nr. 5 and *Mainzer Urkundenbuch 2. Die Urkunden seit dem Tode Erzbischof Adalberts I. (1137) bis zum Tode Erzbischof Konrads (1200)*, ed. Peter Acht (Darmstadt: Historischer Verein für Hessen, 1968), 1:1137–1175, no. 230, 415.

long-time secretary Volmar in 1173. Hildegard mentions Wezzelin in the opening of this book, calling him a *beatus homo* (blessed man) and a man of noble birth, and Guibert of Gembloux describes him as a nephew and close confidante to Hildegard in a letter to Radulf of Villers.[10] An earlier provost at St. Andreas, Arnold I, archbishop of Trier from 1169 to his death in 1183, calls himself Hildegard's blood relative (*cognate sue*) in a letter to her from 1169 and remembers the close relationship they had maintained since their youth.[11] In reference to this remark, Marianna Schrader and Adelgundis Führkötter claimed that Arnold was in fact Wezzelin's biological brother and thus also a nephew of Hildegard;[12] it is possible, however, that Arnold's reference to Wezzelin as *frater noster* (our brother) describes not a genealogical but only a spiritual relationship in their clerical office.

Finally, there is the possibility that Hildegard was related to the archbishop Philip of Cologne (1167–1191). Josef Heinzelmann considers him to be Hildegard's cousin who communicated with her and Guibert of Gembloux and who repeatedly attempted to meet her.[13] Hildegard did indeed call Philip *fidelis amicus meus* (my faithful friend).[14] In his position as cathedral deacon of Cologne, Philip communicated warmly with Hildegard and expressed his love for her motherly goodness.[15] This amicable relationship continued as Philip became archbishop of Cologne.

It seems remarkable that there is no mention of Hildegard's place of birth in the *Vita Hildegardis*; the text merely claims that it was located "in the territory of Eastern Gaul."[16] Several scholars have suggested possible locations. In 1936, the nun from Eibingen and Hildegard expert Marianna Schrader OSB (1882–1970) identified Bermersheim near Alzey as Hildegard's birthplace; an official document from Sponheim from the year 1127 was signed by a "Hiltebertus of Vermersheim" (Bermersheim) and his son Drutwin.[17] According to Schrader, extensive family holdings from around Bermersheim were granted to the

---

[10] *Guiberti Gemblacensis Epistolae*, Letter 26, 292, lines 828–829. "Reuerende memorie domnus Wescelinus, nepos eius et familiarissimus ei [Hildegardis], sancti Andree Coloniensis prepositus."

[11] Letter 27, in Hildegard of Bingen, *Epistolarium*, ed. Lieven Van Acker, CCCM 91 (Turnhout: Brepols, 1991), part 1, 76.

[12] Marianna Schrader and Adelgundis Führkötter, *Die Echtheit des Schrifttums der heiligen Hildegard von Bingen. Quellenkritische Untersuchungen*. Beihefte zum Archiv für Kulturgeschichte 6 (Cologne: Böhlau, 1956), 83.

[13] Josef Heinzelmann, "Hildegard von Bingen und ihre Verwandten," *Jahrbuch für westdeutsche Landesgeschichte* 23 (1997): 61.

[14] J. Stilting, "De S. Hildegarde Virgine, magistra sororum ord. S. Benedicti in monte S. Ruperti juxta Bingium in dioecesis Moguntina," *Acta sanctorum* 668 (1755): 629–701.

[15] Letter 15, in *Epistolarium*, part 1, 33, line 5: "Quia maternam pietatem uestram diligimus."

[16] *Annales sancti Disibodi*, 6 and 21.

[17] Marianna Schrader, "Zur Heimat- und Familiengeschichte der hl. Hildegard," *Studien und Mitteilungen zur Geschichte des Benediktiner-Ordens und seiner Zweige* 57 (1939): 117–133.

Rupertsberg convent founded by Hildegard, which held power and rights over Bermersheim for centuries. Those ascribing to this theory consider the Romanesque church of Bermersheim to be therefore Hildegard's baptismal chapel. A renewed discussion about Hildegard's birthplace, however, arose in 1997 when Josef Heinzelmann proposed Niederhosenbach in the Hunsrück (near Kirn in the district Birkenfeld) as Hildegard's birthplace instead.[18] Heinzelmann's claim was based on an 1112 document from Disibodenberg that names a Hildebert of Hosenbach, who could be Hildegard's father, but the details of this debate are beyond the scope of this chapter. Finally, it should be mentioned that Johannes Trithemius (1462–1516) suggested another location as Hildegard's birthplace. In the chronicles from Hirsau and Sponheim, he names the castle Böckelheim (Bickelnheim) as her birthplace. Castle Böckelheim belonged to the territory of the county Sponheim.[19] One may assume, however, that Trithemius's ancestral legend was an attempt to paint a close relationship between Hildegard's family and the Sponheims. In his historical writings, Trithemius repeatedly championed the interests of the counts of Sponheim who had, after all, founded his abbey. Certainly his passages should be regarded as pro-Sponheim court historiography rather than historically accurate. Even if the historiographic discussion about Hildegard's birthplace has not yet come to an end, it does not play a decisive role in the evaluation of Hildegard's life and work.

The *Vita Hildegardis* stresses that Hildegard's parents never forgot to be grateful for the gifts of their Creator, despite their wealth and position. This gratitude manifested itself concretely in dedicating Hildegard to the monastic life, a step, according to the *Vita*, that caused much grief for her parents. By handing over their child as an oblate, they followed an old custom of presenting one's own child by paternal fiat as a gift to God, following the Old Testament examples of Samson or Samuel. The *Rule of St. Benedict* includes a passage about oblates (chapter 59), and they were incorporated into the rhythms of monastic life before their eternal profession. Thus, they had the opportunity to receive a high degree of clerical education, liturgical knowledge, and rootedness in a life devoted to God. Offering a child to the church, from the perspective of the parents, was a gesture of the highest gratitude to God by giving up one's most precious possession.

---

[18] Heinzelmann, "Hildegard von Bingen und ihre Verwandten."

[19] Johannes Trithemius, *Chronica Hirsaugiense*, in Trithemius, *Opera historica* 2, ed. Marquard Freher (Frankfurt: Marne & Aubry, 1601), 133: "Fuit autem haec virgo Hildegardis beatissima, oriunda ex comitatu Spanheimensi, in villa qua vocatur Bickelnheim"; and *Chronicon Sponheimense*, in Trithemius, *Opera historica* 2, ed. Freher, 250 (identical text).

Monastic life seemed to correspond to Hildegard's inner disposition and vocation; the *Vita Hildegardis* stresses that she was already remarkably pure, mature, and unworldly as a child. Moreover, she already had visions as a young child, as Hildegard reports in the autobiographical parts of the *Vita*: as a three-year-old she saw such a great light that her soul was shaken. The *Vita* also mentions Hildegard's numerous and long sicknesses. Her later ability to console and heal others thus sprang from her own experience of the transitoriness of being human.

The question of when Hildegard entered the enclosure of Disibodenberg is controversial. The *Vita Hildegardis* states that she was barely eight and thus her entry would have taken place in 1106. There are reasons, though, to doubt this claim. We have two further sources about Hildegard's early life, in addition to the later, posthumously finished *Vita Hildegardis*: the report from Guibert of Gembloux (including the spoken prayers of Hildegard and the two other women during their entrance ceremony),[20] written sixty-six years (1177) after the event of her enclosure, as well as the *Vita domnae Juttae inclusae* (Life of Lady Jutta the Anchoress).[21] The latter text was penned by an unknown monk at Disibodenberg in 1137 and is thus chronologically closer to the described events than either the Hildegard *Vita* or the report of Guibert of Gembloux. We will therefore treat the *Vita Juttae* as the source for Hildegard's youth in what follows.

When she took on Hildegard's spiritual education, Jutta of Sponheim was fourteen years old, the age when, according to medieval law, women were considered adults. Jutta took her eternal vows simultaneously with her entry into the enclosure on November 1, 1112, under Abbot Burchard of Disibodenberg (1108–1113). Hildegard took her eternal vows later under Bishop Otto of Bamberg (ca. 1060–1131), who had also bestowed the dedication of a virgin on Hildegard upon her entry into the women's enclosure on the same day as Jutta. Otto held the office of the incarcerated archbishop Adalbert of Mainz, only from 1112 to 1115, which provides a date range then for when Hildegard took her eternal vows. While the precise date is unknown, it had to have been no later than 1115, when she was sixteen or seventeen, just a few years after her enclosure and dedication at Disibodenberg. According to the autobiographical parts of the *Vita Hildegardis*, the educational program of Jutta of Sponheim included the

[20] Guibert of Gembloux, Letter 38, in *Guiberti Gemblacensis, Epistolae*, 2, 372, lines 201–212.
[21] Franz Staab, *Das Leben der Jutta von Sponheim, Lehrerin der Hildegard von Bingen*, Sponheim-Hefte 21 (Sponheim: Freundeskreis der Burg Sponheim, 1999).

singing of psalms and writing but no work on literature and philosophy; the psalter was Hildegard's central educational, devotional, and song book. Yet Hildegard, in the prefatory remarks to the *Scivias*, specifically mentions the Bible, the church fathers, and unnamed "philosophers" as the basis of interpreting her visions. This suggests that Hildegard continually expanded her educational horizon on her own after the end of Jutta's education,[22] which would not have been unusual in a twelfth-century Germanic context, as Lori Kruckenberg's contribution (Chapter 3) in this volume elucidates.

Jutta of Sponheim, against the will of her parents, had received the dedication of a virgin from Archbishop Ruthard of Mainz and entered into the care of the pious widow Uda of Göllheim, who taught her from the age of twelve or thirteen. Hildegard, too, probably knew or studied with Uda of Göllheim, but where she did so is not mentioned in the *Vita Juttae*; it is likely that Uda taught in the residence of the Sponheims. Hildegard and Jutta went through a lengthy, religious training period prior to Hildegard's regular entry at Disibodenberg.

Jutta of Sponheim originally had serious intentions of pursuing a great pilgrimage, but these plans were in opposition to her brother Meginhard. He and Bishop Otto of Bamberg finally convinced Jutta to found a women's enclosure at Disibodenberg rather than go on a pilgrimage. The Benedictine cloister Disibodenberg (founded in 1108) was considered at the time as the most modern reform cloister in the Mainz diocese. The cloister had originally been built as an Augustinian canonry by Bishop Willigis of Mainz (975–1011). Disibod, whose *vita* Hildegard later wrote, was a seventh-century, Irish-Franconian, itinerant monk.[23] He had settled at an already existing baptismal and missionary church and built a small cloister (*coenobium*) there. When the Benedictines took over from the Augustinians, they built a new

---

[22] Michael Embach, "Hildegard von Bingen (1098–1179) – kryptische Gelehrsamkeit und rhetorischer Sprachgestus," in Edeltraud Klueting T.OCarm and Harm Klueting, eds., *Fromme Frauen als gelehrte Frauen. Bildung, Wissenschaft und Kunst im weiblichen Religiosentum des Mittelalters und der Neuzeit. Öffentliche Internationale Tagung der Diözesan- und Dombibliothek Köln (1. bis 4. April 2009)*, Diözesan- und Dombibliothek, Libelli Rhenani 37 (Cologne: Erzbischöfliche Diözesan- und Dombibliothek, 2010), 128–150.

[23] Latin edition: *Vita sancti Disibodi episcopi, Vita sancti Ruperti confessoris*, in Hildegardis Bingensis, *Opera minora II*, ed. Jeroen Deploige, Michael Embach, Christopher P. Evans, Kurt Gärtner, and Sara Moens, CCCM 226 A (Turnhout: Brepols, 2016), 15–108. English translation: Hildegard of Bingen, *Two Hagiographies: Vita sancti Rupperti confessoris. Vita sancti Dysibodi episcopi*, ed. and English trans. Hugh Feiss; Latin ed. Christopher P. Evans, Dallas Medieval Texts and Translations 11 (Paris: Peeters, 2010). Franz J. Felten, "Disibod und die Geschichte des Disibodenberges bis zum Beginn des 12. Jahrhunderts," in Falko Daim and Antje Kluge-Pinsker, eds., *Als Hildegard noch nicht in Bingen war* (Regensburg: Schnell und Steiner, 2009), 25–34.

and large abbey church on the Disibodenberg, which became the center of the spacious monastic grounds.[24] The numerous building metaphors in Hildegard's *Scivias* are a response to the simultaneous, actual building of the monastery and prepared Hildegard for her own building project on the Rupertsberg.

We can consider as certain that on All Saints' Day (November 1) 1112, Hildegard, together with Jutta – who was to be her *magistra* from then on – as well as a third woman, also named Jutta, was accepted as an oblate and recluse at the Disibodenberg.[25] Where precisely the women's enclosure was located can no longer be determined; however, Eberhard J. Nikitsch assumes that it was housed in the side aisle of the former cemetery chapel.[26] The three recluses could have participated in the celebration of the Eucharist without having to leave the building, since the chapel was used for liturgical purposes.

We have hardly any information about the years that Hildegard lived in the women's enclosure at Disibodenberg.[27] It is certain, though, that she must have undergone a deep spiritual development and earned the special trust of her teacher Jutta. She was one of three chosen sisters who were allowed to prepare the body of their *magistra* for Jutta's funeral. Jutta of Sponheim's spiritual program must have been very demanding: her ascetic and prayer practices exceeded by far those prescribed in the Benedictine rule. Some researchers consider it possible that Hildegard received a vision of the journey of Jutta's soul after her death, which would make it the oldest visionary text of Hildegard that has been transmitted to us (*Vita Juttae*, chapter 10), about ten years older than the earliest vision of the *Scivias*.

Hildegard lived for twenty-four years under the spiritual care of Jutta of Sponheim, who was approached as advisor in many questions concerning faith and life. Chapter 5 of *Vita Juttae* states that "people came from all around, from all social levels – nobles, non-nobles, rich and poor, pilgrims

---

[24] Gabriele Mergenthaler, *Die mittelalterliche Baugeschichte des Benediktiner- und Zisterzienserklosters Disibodenberg zwischen Tradition und Reform*, Heimatkundliche Schriftenreihe des Landkreises Bad Kreuznach 32 (Bad Kreuznach: Kreisverwaltung Bad Kreuznach, 2002).

[25] Trithemius, in *Chronicon Hirsaugiense*, in *Opera historica* 2, ed. Freher, 126: "[Jutta] fuit autem inclusa anno Domini 1112 indictione 5 & aliae tres cum ea, videlicet sancta virgo Hildegardis ... & alia eiusdem nominis virgo."

[26] Eberhard J. Nikitsch, "Wo lebte die heilige Hildegard wirklich? Neue Überlegungen zum ehemaligen Standort der Frauenklause auf dem Disibodenberg," in Rainer Berndt (ed.), *"Im Angesicht Gottes suche der Mensch sich selbst": Hildegard von Bingen (1098–1179)*, Erudiri Sapientia 2 (Berlin: Akademie-Verlag, 2001), 147–155.

[27] Franz J. Felten, "What Do We Know About the Life of Jutta and Hildegard at Disibodenberg and Rupertsberg?" in Beverly Mayne Kienzle, Debra L. Stoudt, and George Ferzoco, eds., *A Companion to Hildegard of Bingen* (Leiden and Boston: Brill, 2014), 15–38.

and guests – who were searching only for Jutta and who looked at her alone as a heavenly oracle ... Many, who lived far away send messengers, often with letters and the request for support in prayer."[28] Guibert of Gembloux refers to Jutta of Sponheim as blessed, a tradition found as well in Trithemius's *Chronicon Hirsaugiense* and maintained today by the Benedictine order in the diocese of Speyer. Trithemius describes Hildegard's teacher further as a *sancta mulier* (holy woman) and ascribes to her the miracles of turning water into wine and walking on the waters of the Glan River.[29]

It is no surprise that Hildegard, at the age of thirty-eight, was elected by her fellow sisters as *magistra* of the community after Jutta's death (December 22, 1136). According to Guibert of Gembloux in a letter to his fellow brother Bovo (letter 38), the election was unanimous; the nuns were certain of Hildegard's *discretio* (discernment) and *temperentia* (restraint), two central virtues of a Benedictine abbess or abbot.[30] The women's enclosure of Disibodenberg had developed into a regular community under Jutta already and many nobles sent their daughters to Disibodenberg for their education. It is assumed that by the time it moved to Rupertsberg (1150/1151), the women's enclosure of Disibodenberg included about nineteen to twenty members. Compared to the ascetic Jutta, Hildegard introduced significant moderations in their way of life, removing the strict rules regarding food and the excessively long prayer and worship times; Jutta sometimes prayed the entire psalter two or three times a day, often kneeling with bare feet in the bitter cold, incurring significant illnesses as a result. Hildegard's changes revealed her as a spiritual authority who also paid attention to the physical and health needs of her community. Her way of life is informed by an attitude that considers the body not as the tomb of the soul but as the temple of the Holy Spirit. While Jutta belongs to the ascetic reform movement of the Benedictine order, Hildegard represents the Benedictine ideal of a middle way between monastic duties and a reasonable moderation of the daily routines. Overall, though, Hildegard observed a great fidelity to the regulations of the Benedictine rule, which she also commented on per the request of an unidentified monastic community.[31]

---

[28] Staab, *Das Leben der Jutta von Sponheim*, 13–15.
[29] Trithemius, *Chronicon Hirsaugiense*, 126, line 28.
[30] Letter 38, in Guiberti Gemblacensis, *Epistolae*, part 2, 375, lines 300–302.
[31] Hildegard of Bingen, *De Regula sancti Benedicti*, in *Hildegardis Bingensis, Opera minora*, Part 1, ed. Hugh Feiss, CCCM 226 (Turnhout: Brepols, 2007), 23–97. English translation in *Hildegard of Bingen: Explanation of the Rule of St. Benedict*, trans. Hugh Feiss (Eugene, OR: Wipf & Stock Publishers, 2005).

The Beginning of Hildegard's Public Activities

The visions and auditions that Hildegard experienced from childhood on became more and more intense and urgent. As she explains in the introduction to *Scivias*, Hildegard received the command to write down what she saw and heard a voice from heaven (*vox de caelo*).[32] Hildegard emphasizes explicitly that her visions were not made up by herself or anyone else. A fruit of her visions was that "the writings of the prophets, of the Gospels, and of other saints and of certain philosophers" were opened up to her.[33] Hildegard viewed all things in the light of God in equally sensuous and spiritual ways. The *Vita Hildegardis* reports on the breadth of her visions: "She saw in spirit the past life and conduct of people, and in the case of some, she could even foresee the way their present life would end, and, according to the character of their conduct and merits, their soul's glory or punishment."[34] The *Vita* reveals as well that Hildegard attempted at first to avoid her prophetic commission by claiming embarrassment and shyness vis-à-vis public opinion.[35] Only after a severe illness, which she considered a divine punishment, did she follow the divine command. Hildegard began by writing down the *Scivias*, an expansive summa of faith, which took about ten years to complete (1141–1151). After five years of work on the book, Hildegard wrote to Bernard of Clairvaux (1090–1153), the greatest clerical authority of the times, for advice on whether she ought to continue to write or remain silent instead.[36] Her letter to Bernard explains that she received her visions in the spirit of mystery (*in spiritu mysterii*) – not with the eyes of the body but with the eyes of the soul: the visions move her heart like a consuming flame and her soul teaches her the depth of interpretation. The famous Cistercian answered Hildegard in a prudent and carefully encouraging way, congratulating her for the mercy of God that reigned within her but also admonishing her to be humble. Bernard further explains that Hildegard had experienced an inner teaching and anointing (*interior eruditio . . . et unctio docens de omnibus*), which made further admonishments unnecessary.[37] While unacknowledged by previous scholarship, the phrase "inner teaching and anointing" elevates the visionary abilities of Hildegard in a special way as almost a verbatim

---

[32] Hildegard of Bingen, *Scivias*, ed. Adelgundis Führkötter and Angela Carlevaris, CCCM 63 (Turnhout: Brepols, 1978), 3.
[33] "The Life of Hildegard," in Anna Silvas, ed. and trans., *Jutta and Hildegard: The Biographical Sources* (University Park: Pennsylvania State University Press, 1999), 160.
[34] Ibid., 163.   [35] Ibid., 159.   [36] Letter 1, in *Epistolarium*, part 1, 3–6.
[37] Letter 1 reply, in *Epistolarium*, part 1, 6–7.

quotation from John's first letter (1 John 2:20): "But you have been anointed by the holy one, and you know everything" (*Sed vos unctionem habetis a Sancto, et nostis omnia*). By quoting from John's first letter, Bernard ascribes to Hildegard the role of a prophetic authority, illumined by the Holy Spirit.

Hildegard's letter to Bernard of Clairvaux from 1146/1147 is the oldest extant writing of the seer and simultaneously a document of great importance for her later work. However, already in the seer's lifetime, the letter exchange with Bernard of Clairvaux received significant editorial attention along with a number of other letters to and from Hildegard, a process described in detail in Christopher D. Fletcher's chapter in this volume (Chapter 5). The edited version from the *Riesencodex*, a kind of "final edition" of Hildegard's works, became determinative for the view of Hildegard in later centuries.[38] Here, Hildegard appears no longer in the role of the insecure and searching suppliant; rather, Bernard merely confirms a seer already on her way to canonical authority of the church.

Hildegard received another confirmation in the years 1147–1148 when Pope Eugene III visited Trier from November 30, 1147 to February 1148 for a synod. Eighteen cardinals as well as numerous bishops from Germany, France, Belgium, England, Lombardy, and Tuscany were present, supposedly even Bernard of Clairvaux.[39] Hildegard used this favorable opportunity to receive approval from the pope regarding her visionary abilities, while paying great attention to church hierarchy. Bishop Heinrich of Mainz, asked by Abbot Kuno of Disibodenberg, made a report of Hildegard's visionary gifts to the pope. An unmediated relationship between Hildegard and the pope was unthinkable.

The pope did show interest in Hildegard's work; he sent Bishop Albero of Verdun, the *primicerius* Adalbert (a presiding officer of the lower clergy, according to Isidore of Seville's definition), and further qualified authorities to Disibodenberg to submit Hildegard's visionary gift to an official investigation. On their return to Trier, they reported back and the *Vita Hildegardis* states that the pope inquired about and began to read from Hildegard's writings, namely parts of the *Scivias*, still a work in progress. Eugene III was so inspired by the reading that he called on those present to praise the Creator in joyous jubilation. According to the *Vita*, Bernard spoke and demanded of the pope not to let such a bright shining light be covered up by silence but

[38] Wiesbaden, Hochschul- und Landesbibliothek RheinMain, MS 2.
[39] "The Life of Hildegard," in Silvas, *Jutta and Hildegard*, 143.

rather that he should confirm such a gift of grace, revealed by the Lord in his time, through his own authority.[40] If one follows the story of the *Vita Hildegardis*, then the pope agreed willingly to this request.

This event made Hildegard an ecclesiastically legitimized, papally confirmed authority, whose words had the approval of the pope, of Bernard of Clairvaux, of an ecclesiastical synod, as well as of the highest levels of secular and monastic clerics. Her writings thus received aspects of orthodoxy and doctrinal affirmation that were of decisive importance for the continued success of Hildegard's work. In times of rising heresies (Catharism) and virulent conflicts in church politics (papal schisms) the success of Hildegard's visionary work would hardly have been possible without papal and ecclesiastical affirmation.

Founding the Convent at Rupertsberg

In the midst of her work on *Scivias*, Hildegard took the initiative to build her own monastic foundation: Rupertsberg, located near Bingen on the left shore of the Nahe. The reasons for Hildegard's move are no longer completely apparent, but it is certain that the enclosure at Disibodenberg had become too small for the greatly increased women's convent. Furthermore, the move to Rupertsberg allowed Hildegard access to the central Rhine axis from which she could more easily connect to other ecclesiastical and secular powers than from the more remote Disibodenberg.[41] Franz J. Felten also considers that Hildegard's founding of a cloister can be viewed as a final emancipatory act from the overpowering mentor Jutta of Sponheim and the omnipresent supervision by the dominant abbey of Disibodenberg.[42] As well, "double cloisters," administered jointly by male and female monastics, were generally under critique, as has been pointed out repeatedly in scholarship.[43] However it may be, the founding and building of Rupertsberg took place in the years 1147 to 1150.[44]

[40] Ibid., 24.
[41] Alfred Haverkamp, "Hildegard von Disibodenberg-Bingen: Von der Peripherie zum Zentrum," in Alfred Haverkamp, ed., *Hildegard von Bingen in ihrem historischen Umfeld. Internationaler wissenschaftlicher Kongreß zum 900jährigen Jubiläum, 13.–19. September 1998, Bingen am Rhein* (Mainz: Verlag von Zabern, 2000), 15–70.
[42] Felten, "What Do We Know About the Life of Jutta and Hildegard at Disibodenberg und Rupertsberg?" 36.
[43] Kaspar Elm and Michel Parisse, eds., *Doppelklöster und andere Formen der Symbiose männlicher und weiblicher Religiosen im Mittelalter*, Berliner Historische Studien 18 (Berlin: Duncker & Humblot, 1992).
[44] "Der Rupertsberg und Eibingen," in Hans-Jürgen Kotzur, ed., *Hildegard von Bingen 1098–1179* (Mainz: Verlag von Zabern, 1998), 73–101.

Hildegard's decision to move into her own foundation was criticized by the men's convent at Disibodenberg. Her spreading fame had contributed to the renown and importance of the institution, and many who were sick, needed counsel, or sought Hildegard for other reasons had come to Disibodenberg. She supposedly conversed with those of the Jewish faith as well, convincing them through their own Jewish writings of the truth of Christianity.[45] Her move, it was feared, would lead to a loss of prestige that was not to be accepted easily. Numerous written protests by monks but also by fellow nuns and their relatives give witness to the great difficulties of the project. For Hildegard, however, the move away from Disibodenberg had almost existential significance. In a letter to Abbot Kuno or Helenger of Disibodenberg (letter 75), Hildegard lays out her reasons for her decisions: "But I know for a fact that God moved me from that place [Disibodenberg] for His own inscrutable purposes, for my soul was so agitated by His words and miracles that I believe I would have died before my time if I had remained there."[46] Hildegard justifies her disobedience to the abbot as well as the disregard of the *stabilitas loci* (stability of place) demanded by the *Rule of St. Benedict* with her duty to obey her visionary message. As so often in Hildegard's life, a long and severe illness followed this crisis. Impressed by this illness, which they considered a divine call to action, the authorities at Disibodenberg relented and gave Hildegard permission to build the new cloister and move to the Rupertsberg. Decisive support came from the margravine Richardis of Stade, the mother of the eponymous fellow nun of Hildegard: she spoke successfully on behalf of Hildegard's plans to Archbishop Heinrich I of Mainz. The *Vita Hildegardis* reports that Hildegard handed over the majority of the endowments that had been given to the sisters of the enclosure and, in addition, "a not inconsiderable sum of money so that there might remain no just cause for complaint."[47]

Probably in the year 1150, Hildegard and twenty noble nuns were able to take possession of the newly founded convent. A more precise date for the move is hard to determine since the *Vita Hildegardis* provides none, but the year 1150 is based on a 1177 letter from Guibert of Gembloux, Hildegard's last secretary, to his fellow brother Bovo. It is probable that the year 1147, mentioned in the *Registrum bonorum* (the Rupertsberg foundation book), is incorrect, because Hildegard was still at

---

[45] "The Life of Hildegard," in Silvas, *Jutta and Hildegard*, 162.
[46] Letter 75, in *The Letters of Hildegard of Bingen*, vol. 1, ed. Joseph L. Baird and Radd K. Ehrman (New York: Oxford University Press, 1994), 163.
[47] "The Life of Hildegard," in Silvas, *Jutta and Hildegard*, 149.

Disibodenberg when a papal commission arrived early in 1148 to examine the *Scivias*.[48] However it may be, on May 1 – at the latest 1151 – the rebuilt chapel on the Rupertsberg was dedicated, as evidenced by a document from Archbishop Heinrich of Mainz from February 15, 1152. The *Vita Hildegardis* also reports that the first years at Rupertsberg were difficult and certainly not without disruptions.[49] Hildegard complained, for example, about the poor furnishings of the settlement, which led to dissatisfaction of some fellow nuns and even the departure of a few of them. The material conditions improved over time due to gifts from wealthy donors who buried their relatives on the convent grounds and donated masses. A wealthy nobleman (*nobilis et dives*) and "philosopher" – assumed by Tilo Altenburg to be Rhine Count Embricho I – is supposed to have supported Hildegard's founding especially strongly, grateful that he could choose Rupertsberg as a final resting place.[50]

The strict dedication to the Benedictine rule caused protest among the sisters and the conflicts with the mother house of Disibodenberg continued for several years. Not until 1158 did a complete resolution take place. On May 22 of that year, Hildegard received two important documents from the archbishop of Mainz, Arnold of Selenhofen (1153–1160), both of which are now in the state archive in Koblenz. The first, which is very important for the economic security of the convent, is a document of ownership in which the grounds – assembled from gifts, exchanges, and purchase – received confirmation from the bishop.[51] The possessions listed include mostly gifts near Bingen from Count Palatine Hermann of Stahleck and his wife Gertrud of Bingen. The second document could be called the "Rupertsberg constitution";[52] it clarifies the legal status of Rupertsberg and regulates the relationship with Disibodenberg. On the basis of these two documents, we know that Rupertsberg was economically independent and exclusively under the archbishop of Mainz. The newly founded cloister received the right to freely choose its spiritual mother (*spiritalis matris*) and was thus excluded from the legal authority and rule of the mother house of Disibodenberg,

---

[48] Landeshauptarchiv Koblenz, Abt. 701 A VII 3, Nr. 5. For *Registrum bonorum* see Schrader and Führkötter, *Die Echtheit des Schrifttums der heiligen Hildegard von Bingen*, 29.

[49] Tilo Altenburg, *Soziale Ordnungsvorstellungen bei Hildegard von Bingen*. Monographien zur Geschichte des Mittelalters 54 (Stuttgart: Hiersemann, 2007), 125–137.

[50] "The Life of Hildegard," in Silvas, *Jutta and Hildegard*, 173; and Altenburg, *Soziale Ordnungsvorstellungen*, 130–131.

[51] Landeshauptarchiv Koblenz, Abt. 164, Nr. 1. Reproduction and commentary by W[infried] W[ilhelmy] in *Hildegard von Bingen 1098–1179*, no. 31, 94–95.

[52] Landeshauptarchiv Koblenz, Abt. 164, Nr. 2. Reproduction and commentary by W[infried] W[ilhelmy] in *Hildegard von Bingen 1098–1179*, no. 32, 96–97.

which only maintained a responsibility to care for the spiritual well-being of
Rupertsberg. This meant that Disibodenberg had to provide celebrants for
the Mass and for spiritual care. It was furthermore determined that the
convent at Rupertsberg would have no secular protector and that protection
and church advocacy would remain exclusively with the archbishop of
Mainz, who had to represent the cloister in its secular matters. The spiritual
supervision excluded, Hildegard had achieved a complete separation of the
new convent from Disibodenberg and secured for herself the greatest possible independence. She remained on alert, though, in her relationship with
Disibodenberg. When the abbey began to withdraw from its duty to provide
a cleric, Hildegard intervened energetically in order to secure the celebration
of the Mass and all liturgical activities. She turned to Pope Alexander III
(1159–1181) and asked him to take care of providing another monk from
Disibodenberg for Rupertsberg after the death of Volmar. Hildegard wrote:

> We are in great distress because the abbot of Mount St. Disibod and his
> brothers have taken away our privileges and the right of election we have
> always had. . . . Therefore, my lord, for God's sake, help us, so that we may
> retain the man we have elected to that office. Or, if not, let us seek out and
> receive others, where we can, who will look after us in accordance with the
> will of God and our own needs.[53]

In his response, directed to Wezzelin the provost in Cologne, the pope
declared that the issue should be decided according to Hildegard's wishes.
Hildegard also went personally to Disibodenberg in order to advocate for
her convent's spiritual needs.

A further provision for Hildegard's newly founded convent was achieved
by a document guaranteeing protection by Emperor Barbarossa from
April 18, 1163.[54] It is assumed that Hildegard personally approached the
emperor in Mainz in order to advocate for her community. She must have
been successful since the document states it was issued on the request of the
honorable abbess Hildegard (*interventu et petitione dominae Hildegardis
venerabilis abbatissae*). This is the only time that Hildegard is officially
referred to as abbess. All other documents call her mother, mistress, lady,
or principal (*mater, magistra, domina, praeposita*). The emperor's document
is based on that from the archbishop of Mainz (May 22, 1158), whose
privileges it repeats and affirms. Additionally, it announces that the convent
does not have to pay taxes, that is, no imperial official has the authority to

---

[53] Letter 10, *The Letters of Hildegard of Bingen* 1, 45–46.
[54] Landeshauptarchiv Koblenz, Abt. 164, no. 3. Reproduction and commentary by W[infried]
W[ilhelmy] in *Hildegard von Bingen 1098–1179*, no. 33:1, 98–101.

demand any payments whatsoever for the possessions of the convent. In the same year (1163), the half-brother of the emperor, Count Palatine Konrad, supplied Rupertsberg with a document of protection for the possessions in his realm. Konrad also appears as witness to a gift of the abbot Ludwig of St. Matthias of Trier after Hildegard's death.[55] Finally, on November 22, 1184 or 1185, only a few years after Hildegard's death, the Rupertsberg convent received a document of protection from Pope Lucius III (also held in the state archive in Koblenz), in which the pope guarantees ecclesiastical and worldly privileges to the convent.[56]

All of this proves that Hildegard secured her convent comprehensively in ecclesiastical and material matters, and indeed, Rupertsberg soon developed well. Guibert of Gembloux reports in his letter to Bovo of Gembloux that Rupertsberg provides room for fifty sisters, several servants, and guests, and he expresses his approval of the spacious buildings that are supplied with running water. Traditional accounts, which probably began in the thirteenth century, state that Hildegard founded a second cloister in 1165 on the right side of the Rhine near Rüdesheim, due to the persistent influx of nuns as well as the recent consideration of non-noble candidates. In this case, it was not a new building but rather Hildegard supposedly took over the Augustinian cloister in Eibingen, which had been founded in 1148 and temporarily destroyed. She is said to have made a prioress the manager of the house but to have kept the dignity and title of abbess for herself. For years, Hildegard apparently ferried across the Rhine from Rupertsberg twice a week in order to manage the obligations of the filial cloister.[57] This tradition, which belongs to the generally accepted literature about Hildegard, was recently evaluated by Matthias Schmandt.[58] His critical investigation of sources found it difficult to prove the claim of Hildegard's founding of the convent at Eibingen. According to Schmandt, neither the founding document of the convent (extant only in a sixteenth-century copy) nor the *Vita Hildegardis* explicitly reports such an act.[59] In addition,

[55] Landeshauptarchiv Koblenz, Großes Privilegienbuch (Privilegien- und Ritenbuch der Klöster Rupertsberg und Eibingen), Abt. 701 A VII 3 Nr. 3, fol. 194.

[56] Reproduction and commentary by W[infried] W[ilhelmy] in *Hildegard von Bingen 1098–1179*, no. 33:2, 98–101.

[57] Matthia Eiden, "Zur Geschichte der Wiedererrichtung der Benediktinerinnenabtei St. Hildegard/ Eibingen 1888–1904," *Archiv für mittelrheinische Kirchengeschichte* 43 (1991): 303–323; and Werner Lauter, "Ansicht des barocken Klosters," in Kotzur (ed.), *Hildegard von Bingen 1098–1179*, 112–113.

[58] Matthias Schmandt, "Hildegard von Bingen und das Kloster Eibingen: Revision einer historischen Überlieferung," *Nassauische Annalen* 125 (2014): 29–52.

[59] The founding document is part of the "großen Privilegienbuchs" (Hauptstaatsarchiv Wiesbaden, Abt. 23, Nr. 135, fol. 1a).

while there are letters from Hildegard to the monasteries at Disibodenberg and Rupertsberg, there are none to Eibingen.

Neither the Rupertsberg nor Eibingen convent buildings have survived. During the Thirty Years War, Rupertsberg was destroyed by the Swedes and disassembled except for parts of the foundation. In place of the destroyed convent buildings at Eibingen, today there is the village church, which houses a shrine containing Hildegard's relics. The present-day St. Hildegard Abbey was opened in 1904 above the village of Eibingen (in the outskirts of Rüdesheim across the Rhine from Bingen) and is the seat of the Benedictines of Eibingen.

Travel and Preaching

Hildegard's letters and the *Vita Hildegardis* (book 3, chapters 17 and 23) reveal that she undertook a number of preaching trips over the course of her life. Hildegard explains that a vision showed her which ecclesiastical communities – men and women – she should visit and that a long disease that tortured her for more than forty days and nights was eased for that purpose. At her destinations, she resolved conflicts. The reasons for Hildegard's travels were her spiritual concern for other monastic institutions as well as the effort to emphasize central aspects of church doctrine and monastic discipline in a new way. The "sermons" given as part of these travels were sermons in the original sense of the word. Hildegard neither preached in the context of the liturgy of the Mass nor would have considered breaking into the realm of the priest's responsibilities. Her strict regard for the Benedictine *discretio*-ideal prohibited that. Furthermore, the sermons pursued no secular or ecclesiastical agendas. It is telling, for example, that Hildegard – contrary to Bernard of Clairvaux – never gave a sermon on behalf of the Crusades. Hildegard's sermons were rather spiritual lectures that she held in front of clerics and the laity and in which she dealt with structural errors or bad developments in church and in the world, described in more detail in Peter V. Loewen's chapter in this volume (Chapter 6).[60] Hildegard stresses that she took on this role not because she wanted to but out of obedience to her divine mission. This attitude expresses itself in her choice of prophetic speech. The *Vita Hildegardis* declares that Hildegard was "not so much led as driven by the Holy Spirit" to her travels,[61] and we know that

---

[60] Letter 15r, in *The Letters of Hildegard of Bingen*, 1, 60.
[61] "The Life of Hildegard," in Silvas, *Jutta and Hildegard*, 191.

she was accompanied by two fellow sisters.[62] The individual journeys still need further investigation; for some, we hardly know more than their destination.

Reports About Miracles, Healings, and Exorcisms

The third book of the *Vita Hildegardis* is mostly dedicated to her miracles, possibly originating in a lost "miracle book." The text indicates that the miracles happened mostly in the close vicinity of Rupertsberg, often in the neighboring village of Bingen. Most were miracles of healing (*miracula sanitatis*) performed overwhelmingly on women. The reports sometimes name the healed persons, their illness and recuperation, and witnesses who experienced the miracles and confirmed them under oath. The means of healing were spoken words, laying of hands, signing the cross, and blessings but also material means such as water, bread, or a braid of Hildegard's hair. Besides Hildegard's biographer, Theodoric of Echternach, miracle reports are also noted by Hildegard's fellow sisters; and finally, her death is accompanied by supernatural signs and events and numerous miracles took place at Hildegard's grave. The *Acta inquisitionis* also includes miracle reports, partially copied from the *Vita Hildegardis*.[63] This last source was not considered sufficient by the Roman authority for canonization, as the several failed attempts at canonization in the thirteenth and fifteenth centuries reveal.

The most important function of the miracle reports is to prove the supernatural gifts of Hildegard as well as to document her particular closeness to Christ, the *medicus coelestis* (heavenly physician). The portrayal of the miracles is based to a high degree on the norms associated with the genre of "miracle reports." Therefore, we have to take into account that the communicated information is of low quality as far as its attention to detail is concerned. Here, in brief, are a few examples of such miracles from the *Vita Hildegardis*:

A girl, sick with a three-day fever, is healed by Hildegard by laying of hands, blessing, and prayer (book 3, chapter 1). Hildegard heals a brother of her order, named Roricus, in a similar way from his fever (book 3, chapter 2). A woman named Sibilla from Lausanne, suffering from bleeding, is healed by Hildegard by means of sending a written directive (book 3,

---

[62] "The Life of Hildegard," in Silvas, *Jutta and Hildegard*, 171.
[63] "Acta Inquisitionis de virtutibus et miraculis sanctae Hildegardis," in Silvas, *Jutta and Hildegard*, 258–272.

chapter 10). The text communicates the specific words sent, an Adam-Christ-typology: "In the blood of Adam, death arose; in the blood of Christ, death was extinguished. Through the same blood of Christ I order you, O blood, to check your flow!"[64] Hildegard heals an epileptic by blessing him (book 3, chapter 19).

The *Vita Hildegardis* gives much space as well to reports of exorcisms and, here too, a typological relationship to Jesus Christ is established. The text reports, for example, how a demon-possessed woman named Sigewize is led to Hildegard in the eighth year of her predicament (book 3, chapter 21). The visit was arranged by the abbot Geldof of Brauweiler, whose intercession with Saint Nicolas could not heal the possessed woman. Hildegard sends an incantation to Geldof, which exorcises the evil spirit at first but it then returns into the woman. In an extensive effort, with the participation of seven priests, Hildegard finally manages to heal the possessed woman permanently. Worth mentioning among the "post-mortem" miracles occurring at Hildegard's grave is the healing of a demon-possessed woman named Mechthild from the village of Laubenheim.[65]

The *Vita Hildegardis* repeatedly stresses that Hildegard ascribed her healings not to her own powers but to the workings of divine mercy, contending that Hildegard did not perform healings grounded in the power of her own personality alone but rather that her miracles are heteronomous, significatory acts pointing to Christ as the cause and the church as the enabling space of the event. Hildegard explains that her actions originate in humility and that she can do nothing by herself. In the same way, she views her illnesses as a thorn against possible arrogance and cites the Apostle Paul: "So that I don't exalt myself, a thorn in the flesh was given me, a messenger of Satan to buffet me" (2 Corinthians 12:7).

Final Years and Death

Hildegard's final years were overshadowed by severe illness and the loss of her long-time secretary Volmar (d. 1173). Nevertheless, Hildegard continued her literary work unwaveringly. When work on the *Liber divinorum operum* halted due to Volmar's death, Hildegard turned to Abbot Ludwig of St. Matthias in Trier.[66] He undertook the final editorial work of the manuscript and sent the monks Gottfried and Otto to Rupertsberg to assist

---

[64] "The Life of Hildegard," in Silvas, *Jutta and Hildegard*, 187.

[65] "Acta inquisitionis," in Silvas, *Jutta and Hildegard*, 259.

[66] Petrus Becker, *Die Benediktinerabtei St. Eucharius-St. Matthias vor Trier*, Germania Sacra NF 34, 8 (Berlin and New York: De Gruyter, 1996), 593–595.

Hildegard in finishing the text. Otto later created a text-only copy of *Scivias* around 1210, which is located today in the St. Nicolas hospital in Kues.[67] In gratitude for Gottfried and Otto's assistance, Hildegard had given early copies of her work to their monastery at Trier (in fact, a number of modern historical-critical editions of Hildegard's works are based on those Trier manuscripts).[68] These interactions show in an exemplary way that the production and distribution of Hildegard's works were supported by a cooperative Benedictine sphere. More than a logistical accomplishment, they show the imprint of a real monastic spirit on Hildegard's work.

After a long illness, Hildegard died in the circle of her fellow sisters at Rupertsberg on September 17, 1179. The *Vita Hildegardis* explains that she received a vision about the day of her death that she communicated to her fellow sisters. Knowing the hour of one's death was considered in the Christian tradition as a special sign of closeness to God, even of having been chosen by grace. According to the *Vita*, her death took place on a Sunday, the day of the resurrection of the Lord, at the beginning of dusk. The text reports that a circular shape appeared in the heavens with a red, shimmering cross in the center. The funeral was also the source of miracles, but such details belong to the usual, typologically determined contents of the genre of medieval legends of saints. The exact location of Hildegard's original burial is unknown, but possibly her grave was on the outside of the convent church at Rupertsberg and then was moved to the inside. She was, however, buried near Rupert, Bertha, and Wigbert, who were worshiped as saints, a clear sign of her saintlike reputation at the time of her death. According to tradition, Hildegard's gravesite quickly became a place to which many came for solace and intercession and where many miracles took place.

Aspects of Her Works' History

Toward the end of Hildegard's life and then after her death, the visionary's written works garnered a high estimation in the monastic *lectio* (readings).[69] In a letter, dated November 1, 1176, by Guibert of Gembloux to the convent at Rupertsberg, he reports that the *Liber vitae meritorum* was used on account of its wonderful teaching (*mirifica doctrina*) in the Cistercian

---

[67] Ibid., 127, no. 92.

[68] Michael Embach and Martina Wallner, *Conspectus der Handschriften Hildegards von Bingen* (Münster: Aschendorff, 2013), 254–270.

[69] Michael Embach, "Hildegard of Bingen (1098–1179): A History of Reception," in Kienzle, Stoudt, and Ferzoco, *A Companion to Hildegard of Bingen*, 273–304.

monastery at Villers as refectory reading and in the Benedictine monastery of Gembloux as evening reading.[70] The inclusion of Hildegard's work into the canon of monastic *lectio* gave the visionary's work a confirmation that placed it side by side with the undisputed authorities of the tradition. The *Rule of St. Benedict* determines in chapter 38 ("The Reader for the Week") that no one should randomly take a book and begin reading.[71] Referring to the evening reading it states in chapter 42 that one should read the "collationes" of Cassian, the *Vitae* of the Fathers, or something else edifying to the hearers.[72] Hildegard's works were also considered as such indisputably elevated reading material for the monastic reading program. Hildegard herself, in her commentary on the *Rule of St. Benedict*, refers to the monastic *lectio* as a sacred service, which had been equated to the sacrament of the alter in the time of Benedict.[73] The reader, as Hildegard follows Benedict's argument, transmits sacred words.

Hildegard's work also gained increasing respect in the field of academic theology. Between 1210 and 1231, the *Liber divinorum operum*, the *Scivias*, and the *Liber vitae meritorum* were subjected to an investigation by theologians at the University of Paris. As part of his pilgrimage to St. Martin of Tours, the Strasbourg *custos* Bruno delivered Hildegard's writings to the bishop of Paris. The bishop directed that all theology teachers should inspect Hildegard's writings between the octave of St. Martin's Day and the octave of the Epiphany (a two-month period). After finalizing this procedure, Hildegard's writings were handed over to Wilhelm of Auxerre (d. 1231), the famous magister at the University of Paris. The *Acta inquisitionis* reports that Wilhelm confirmed the view of the Paris academics. He supposedly claimed with enthusiasm that the words in Hildegard's writings "were not human but divine" and Bruno, guardian of St. Peter in Strasbourg, said that they originated without an earthly teacher and were created exclusively under the influence of the Holy Spirit.[74] The judgments of Wilhelm of Auxerre and the Paris theologians provided the official inquisition mandate for the planned canonization process.

Also with a view to the planned canonization, a description of Hildegard's life and her performed miracles was produced (the *Vita*

---

[70] Guibert of Gembloux, "Letter to the Sisters at the Rupertsberg Convent," in *Guiberti Gemblacensis Epistolae*, part 1, 251–253.
[71] *The Rule of St. Benedict in English*, ed. Timothy Fry (Collegeville, MN: The Liturgical Press, 1982), 60.
[72] Ibid., 64.   [73] Hildegard of Bingen, *Explanation of the Rule*, 58–59.
[74] "Acta inqusitionis," in Silvas, *Jutta and Hildegard*, 268–269.

Hildegardis); from around the year 1000, the Roman authorities required a *vita* of the person who was to be canonized, considering the life, reputation, works, and miracles. This text, produced in three stages by three authors, going back mainly to the years 1181 to 1188, as well as the *Octo lectiones in festo sancte Hildegardis legende* (Eight Readings to Be Read on the Feast of St. Hildegard) prove the desire to support the veneration of Hildegard.[75] Probably written by Theodoric of Echternach, the *Octo lectiones* contain a short version of the *Vita*, full of rhymed prose and compiled together with the letters of Guibert of Gembloux. Meant to be read in the cloister's refectory on Hildegard's Feast Day, they emphasize Hildegard's holiness (*sanctitas*) more strongly than the *Vita*.

Hildegard As "Popular Saint" and Official Canonization

Pope Gregory IX (1227–1241) signed a document to the church of Mainz on January 27, 1228 that became the basis for the planned canonization of Hildegard.[76] It claims that the convent at Rupertsberg had officially requested the canonization of Hildegard in a document that is unfortunately not preserved.[77] The pope's reply was affirmative and he mentioned that he had heard about the laudable and saintly life of Hildegard. Hildegard had already performed numerous miracles in the past, the pope wrote, and would undoubtedly continue to do so in the future. The revelation of the Holy Spirit helped her write many books that were worth being brought to the attention of the Roman church. Based on these accomplishments, the pope now wanted to elevate a person whom the Lord in heaven had already honored, and he wanted to enter Hildegard into the catalogue of saints (*sanctorum catalogum asscribentes*). The pope added a *forma interrogationis*, which regulated the process of Hildegard's canonization by questioning credible witnesses. In addition, three commissioners were appointed to act as delegates of the Holy See and manage

---

[75] *Octo lectiones in festo sanctae Hildegardis legendae, in Vita sanctae Hildegardis*, ed. Monica Klaes, CCCM 126 (Turnhout: Brepols, 1993), 73–80; English translation in Silvas, *Jutta and Hildegard*, 213–219.

[76] Georg May, "Der Kanonisationsprozeß Hildegards im 13. Jahrhundert," in *900 Jahre Hildegard von Bingen: Neuere Untersuchungen und literarische Nachweise*, ed. Wolfgang Podehl, Verzeichnisse und Schriften der Hessischen Landesbibliothek Wiesbaden 12 (Wiesbaden: Hessische Landesbibliothek Wiesbaden, 1998), 27–43. José Carlos Santos Paz, "La 'Santificacion' de Hildegarde en la Edad Media," in Berndt (ed.), *Im Angesicht Gottes suche der Mensch sich selbst*, 561–575.

[77] The documents regarding Hildegard's canonization were collected and published by Peter Bruder, "Acta inquisitionis de virtutibus et miraculis S. Hildegardis, Magistrae Sororum Ord. S. Benedicti in Monte S. Ruperti juxta Bingium ad Rhenum," *Analecta Bollandiana* 2 (1883): 116–129.

the process: Gerhard, provost of the high cathedral church of Mainz; Walther, dean of St. Peter in Mainz; and Arnold, scholastic of St. Peter. They concluded their investigation on December 16, 1233 and the sealed protocol of the witness statements went to the holy seat.

Despite Rome's positive attitude, the 1228 initiative was not concluded because the cardinals tasked with judging the dossier criticized the canonization documents as incomplete in their description of Hildegard's miracles. Consequently, Pope Gregory IX demanded the completion of the documents from the church of Mainz in his reply (*Supplicantibus nobis*) from May 6, 1237.[78] He also appointed new commissioners: the Mainz cathedral dean and cathedral scholastic as well as a cathedral lord named Walter. Since the new commission did not supply Rome with a more extensive protocol by 1243, the successor of Gregory IX, Pope Innocent IV (1243–1254), turned again to the church of Mainz. In his request *Supplicantibus olim*, dated September 24, 1243, the pope asked for the complete dossier.[79] The church of Mainz put together further details that were included in the text version of 1233, but these were not considered as sufficient. The canonization process halted.

According to unconfirmed reports, Popes Clement V (1305–1316) and John XXII (1316–1334) worked for Hildegard's canonization but again without success. This negative result needs to be considered within the general situation of canonization processes in the thirteenth century. Between 1199 and 1276, only twenty-three of forty-eight Roman investigations regarding canonization were concluded positively and of the thirteen women who were considered for canonization between 1198 and 1431 only five achieved the honor. On December 5, 1324, however, the twelve cardinals of Avignon offered indulgences to those who went on a pilgrimage to the Rupertsberg on Hildegard's Feast Day (September 17). On February 18, 1325, the archbishop of Mainz confirmed the indulgence, generally considered as a kind of substitute for the lacking papal canonization of a person regarded as a saint, and added another one.

Hildegard's grave at Rupertsberg was opened twice in the years 1489 and 1498, which can be seen as further, if not strictly formal, attempts at canonization. The archbishop of Mainz, Berthold of Henneberg (1441–1504), was in charge of these exhumations and motivated by the hope of finding a canonization document in Hildegard's coffin. In 1498, a lifting of the

---

[78] Pope Gregory IX, "Supplicantibus nobis," in *Nova subsidia diplomatica* 9 (Heidelberg: Goebhardt, 1788), 12.

[79] Pope Innocent IV, "Supplicantibus olim," in *Nova subsidia diplomatica* 11 (Heidelberg: Goebhardt, 1788), 34–36.

bones (*elevatio*) was performed, which in the Middle Ages was considered an informal canonization. The Benedictine abbot Johannes Trithemius (1462–1516), who was present at this event, composed a multi-strophe sequence for Hildegard, which is an important document for the veneration of Hildegard at the turn of the Middle Ages to the modern era.[80] The text, which unfortunately as transmitted lacks the music, was supposed to be used as part of the liturgy of the Mass in order to intensify the memorial of Hildegard. Numerous similar testimonies prove that Hildegard was considered a popular saint over the centuries and received great estimation and veneration from the clerics of the church and the orders, as well as from the simple faithful.

Only about 800 years after the original initiative did the canonization of Hildegard receive a successful conclusion. After Pope Benedict XVI (2005–2013) restarted the canonization process in the years 2010–2011, Hildegard was officially sainted on May 10, 2012 in Rome. As part of the opening of the thirteenth Roman synod of bishops on October 7, 2012, Hildegard's elevation to Doctor of the Church followed (*doctor ecclesiae universalis*). This honor had to investigate the following points in a strict process: *Orthodoxa doctrina* (right belief of the teaching), *Eminens doctrina* (outstanding character of teaching), *Insignis vitae sanctitatis* (degree of holiness), and *Ecclesiae declaratio* (declaration by the church). Hildegard's elevation to Doctor of the Church declares that the work of the visionary had a decisive influence on the entire Christian theology. Only three other women besides Hildegard have received this honor: Teresa of Avila, Catherine of Siena, and Theresia of Lisieux.

Thus, Hildegard of Bingen, who always called herself a simple woman (*paupercula femina*), has become one of the most highly respected voices of the Christian world.

Further Reading

Latin Editions and English Translations

"Acta Inquisitionis de virtutibus et miraculis sanctae Hildegardis." In Anna Silvas, ed. and trans., *Jutta and Hildegard: The Biographical Sources*. University Park, PA: Pennsylvania State University Press, 1999, 258–272.

Benedict XVI, Pope. "Decrees of the Congregation for the Causes of Saints." May 10, 2012. VIS. Vatican Information Service. Holy See Press Office. http://visnews-en.blogspot.com/2012/05/decrees-of-congregation-for-causes-of_11.html.

---

[80] Michael Embach, "Johannes Trithemius (1462–1516) als Propagator Hildegards von Bingen," in Haverkamp (ed.), *Hildegard von Bingen in ihrem historischen Umfeld*, 561–598.

Benedict XVI, Pope. "Apostolic Letter Proclaiming Saint Hildegard of Bingen, Professed Nun of the Order of Saint Benedict, a Doctor of the Universal Church." October 7, 2012. www.vatican.va/content/benedict-xvi/en/apos t_letters/documents/hf_ben-xvi_apl_20121007_ildegarda-bingen.html.

Hildegard of Bingen. *Explanation of the Rule of Benedict*, trans. Hugh Feiss. Eugene, OR: Wipf & Stock, 2005.

The Letters of Hildegard of Bingen, ed. Joseph L. Baird and Radd K. Ehrman. 3 vols. New York and Oxford: Oxford University Press, 1994–2004.

Two Hagiographies: Vita sancti Rupperti confessoris. Vita sancti Dysibodi episcopi, ed. and English trans. Hugh Feiss; Latin ed. Christopher P. Evans. Dallas Medieval Texts and Translations 11. Paris: Peeters, 2010.

Silvas, Anna, ed. and trans., *Jutta and Hildegard: The Biographical Sources*. University Park, PA: The Pennsylvania State University Press, 1999.

Vita sanctae Hildegardis, ed. Monika Klaes. Corpus Christianorum Continuatio Mediaevalis 126. Turnhout: Brepols, 1993.

Secondary Literature

Embach, Michael. "Hildegard of Bingen (1098–1179): A History of Reception." In Beverly Mayne Kienzle, Debra L. Stoudt, and George Ferzoco, eds., *A Companion to Hildegard of Bingen*. Leiden: Brill, 2014, 273–304.

Embach, Michael and Martina Wallner. *Conspectus der Handschriften Hildegards von Bingen*. Münster: Aschendorff, 2013.

Felten, Franz J. "What Do We Know About the Life of Jutta and Hildegard at Disibodenberg and Rupertsberg?" In Beverly Mayne Kienzle, Debra L. Stoudt, and George Ferzoco, eds., *A Companion to Hildegard of Bingen*. Leiden: Brill, 2014, 15–38.

Kotzur, Hans-Jürgen, ed., *Hildegard von Bingen, 1098–1179*. Mainz: P. von Zabern, 1998.

Schmandt, Matthias. "Hildegard von Bingen und das Kloster Eibingen: Revision einer historischen Überlieferung." *Nassauische Annalen* 125 (2014): 29–52.

CHAPTER 2

Living and Working in a Twelfth-Century Women's Monastic Community

Alison I. Beach

This chapter describes a single day in the life of a community of religious women in the late twelfth century. With so many variations in daily routine based on the liturgical season, seasonally dependent work, and local custom, I have chosen a particular day – September 30 – at a particular community – the monastery of Eibingen, just north of the Rhine near the town of Rüdesheim. The connection between Eibingen and Hildegard's foundation at Rupertsberg, a monastery that lay about seven kilometers to the south, on the opposite side of the Rhine, is unclear. Hildegard may have founded Eibingen in 1165, colonized the new community with nuns from Rupertsberg, and served as *magistra* there until her death in 1179; or she may simply have served as spiritual advisor to a preexisting community of religious women there.[1]

Since no ruins remain to suggest the monastery's physical layout and no textual sources survive to document the community's particular daily practices, I rely heavily here on the sixth-century *Rule of St. Benedict* (*RB*), which established the basic pattern of daily life at Eibingen. I also refer to customs associated with the monastery of Hirsau, an influential reforming community in the Black Forest, to suggest further aspects of everyday life at Eibingen.[2] Both of Hildegard's communities probably used or were influenced by Hirsau's customary, using it either as a source of spiritual inspiration or as a set of guidelines for the proper ordering of their houses.[3] I also draw on material and textual sources from contemporary

---

[1] Matthias Schmandt, "Hildegard von Bingen und das Kloster Eibingen: Revision einer historischen Überlieferung," *Nassauische Annalen* 125 (2014): 29–52.

[2] *Willehelmi abbatis Constitutiones Hirsaugienses*, ed. Candida Elvert and Pius Engelbert, Corpus Consuetudinum Monasticarum (CCM) 15.2, 378.

[3] Isabelle Cochelin, "Customaries As Inspirational Sources," in Carolyn Marino Malone and Clark Maines, eds., *Consuetudines et Regulae: Sources for Monastic Life in the Middle Ages and the Early Modern Period*, vol. 10, Disciplina Monastica (Turnhout: Brepols, 2014), 27–72.

women's communities in German-speaking lands, as well as from similar communities in other parts of Europe.

The last day of September falls within the long period of liturgical Ordinary Time that spans the time between Pentecost (fifty days after Easter Sunday) and the beginning of the new liturgical year marked by Advent (which precedes Christmastide). A weekday with no special ecclesiastical feast to celebrate, September 30 was an ordinary (ferial) day at Eibingen, structured, like every day, around the eight hours of the Divine Office, also known as the Opus Dei or the Liturgy of the Hours. Following ancient tradition and taking Psalm 118 [119]:62 ("I arose at midnight to give praise to thee") and Psalm 118 [119]:164 ("Seven times a day I have given praise to thee") as prescriptive, the *Rule of St. Benedict* (*RB* 16:1–5) establishes eight "offices" of sung communal prayer: Matins (before daybreak), followed by Lauds (at daybreak); the four shorter daytime hours at regular intervals between Lauds and Vespers: Prime, Terce, Sext, None; and, finally, Vespers (at the rise of the evening star) and Compline (as darkness falls). Although the twenty-four-hour clock was not used in medieval Europe, I will adopt it in the following for the sake of clarity. The chanting of the psalms comprises the core of the Divine Office, and the *Rule of St. Benedict* organizes the liturgy so that the nuns sing all 150 psalms in the course of each week, with some of them sung daily.[4] While the *Rule* mandates the basic parameters for the celebration of the Divine Office, Benedict also left the nuns quite a bit of latitude in terms of their own local liturgical practice. Many liturgical details were prescribed in the Hirsau customary, but these could also be modified or augmented by a particular community.

This chapter, like the monastic day, is organized around this daily cycle of sung corporate prayer, recognizing the fundamental role that the liturgy of the hours played in the spirituality and flow of daily life in this twelfth-century women's community. "Let nothing," Benedict exhorts, "be preferred to the Work of God " (*RB* 43).

Matins

The day begins with a bell sounding in the darkness of the dormitory, signaling to the sleeping sisters that it is time to rise and proceed to their church to sing their first prayers of the day. It is around 3 a.m., and the first

---

[4] For an introduction to the history and structure of the Divine Office associated with monastic communities that followed the *Rule of St. Benedict*, see John Harper, *The Forms and Orders of Western Liturgy from the Tenth to the Eighteenth Century: A Historical Introduction and Guide for Students and Musicians* (Oxford: Clarendon Press, 1991), 78–86.

light of dawn is still a good two hours away on this late September morning. The beds from which the women rise, while not much more than simple straw- or hay-filled pallets, were at least not shared, as they would likely have been in the noble homes from which the majority had come.

It is unclear precisely how the women would have moved from dormitory to oratory to sing the day's first liturgical office. Responding to contemporary norms and expectations that dictated that all interaction between religious women and men should be carefully limited and controlled, many religious communities devised elaborate systems for enclosing nuns. At the monastery of Lippoldsberg in Lower Saxony, for example, the nuns' oratory was situated on a raised western gallery, accessed only through a second-floor passage and door. In other communities, night stairs led down from the dormitory into the women's oratory on the ground floor, a space that was partitioned by a long dividing wall running east to west or by a screen that enclosed the women in their choir, between the chancel (the space around the altar) to the east and the nave of the church to the west. Whether confined to a raised gallery or to a carefully bounded space below, the women would have been able to see the main altar and hear the celebration of Mass there on the days when a priest could be present to officiate.

The focus in these predawn hours, however, is on neither priest nor altar but on the nun-cantor (*cantrix*), the individual charged with overseeing the execution of the Divine Office. With the community gathered in silence, at her signal, the very first words of this (and every) monastic day ring out from one side of the oratory: *Domine labia mea aperies* (Oh Lord, open thou my lips); and from the opposite side of the oratory comes the response: *et os meum adnuntiabit laudem tuam* (and my mouth shall show forth thy praise). Matins was the longest of the eight hours of the Divine Office. On this summer (falling between Easter and November 1) ferial day, the nuns sing two nocturns – the first comprising six psalms with antiphons, a versicle and response, and a short lesson from scripture with a respond; and the second comprising six psalms with antiphons, a short reading from the church fathers, and a versicle and response. In her own commentary on the *Rule of St. Benedict*, Hildegard notes that committing the necessary passages from scripture to memory makes it possible for the nuns to recite the lessons even in the darkness of the hour or with no book to read.[5] The office concludes with the nuns chanting the *Kyrie eleison*, the *Pater noster* (the Lord's Prayer), the *Preces* (a series of verses from the psalms

---

[5] Hildegard of Bingen, *Explanation of the Rule of Benedict*, trans. Hugh Feiss (Toronto: Peregrina Publishing, 1990), 24–25.

sung as versicles and responses between the *cantrix* and the choir), a collect
(a prayer), and the closing salutation or blessing *Benedicamus domino* (Let
us bless the Lord).[6]

The *cantrix* was also responsible for overseeing the use and storage of the
numerous books required for the proper execution of the Divine Office:
a Psalter (a book of psalms), a lectionary (containing the necessary readings
from scripture), various books containing patristic and hagiographical
readings, a collectar (containing the collects, or prayers, for the office), as
well as an antiphoner and troper (with the required musical texts in
a format large enough to be seen by a choir).

Lauds

Immediately after Matins, the women have time to leave the oratory to use
the toilet, a break to facilitate what the *Rule of St. Benedict* discreetly refers
to as "seeing to the needs of nature" (*RB* 8). We can imagine the nuns'
latrine (*necessarium*) at Eibingen standing somewhere close to the dormitory, perhaps connected to it by a short passage extending off the western
range. A short walk back to the area of the dormitory, then, leads the nuns
to their toilet, which likely comprised a few cubicles, perhaps separated by
curtains. In wealthier communities, human waste would drop down into
a channel that was fitted with a sluiceway that could be opened periodically
to flush it with a rush of water diverted from a stream or spring, from
wastewater piped in from kitchens and workshops, or from the rainwater
collected from the roofs from the various monastic buildings. Although
archaeological evidence for upper latrine structures, seats and cubicles
made of wood, are scant for both women's and men's communities,
surviving evidence for toilets in women's monasteries suggests that they
were generally not as advanced as those in (often wealthier) male
communities.[7]

At about 5 a.m., as dawn begins to break, the nuns return to the oratory
to sing the office of Lauds. Here, again, their focus is on the *cantrix* as they
chant the invitatory lines of the office, a verse from Psalm 69, sung as
a versicle (a short verse) and response:

---

[6] Psalm 150:17; on the specifics of monastic Matins following the pattern established in the *Rule of St. Benedict*, see Harper, *The Forms and Orders of Western Liturgy*, 90–93.

[7] Roberta Gilchrist, *Gender and Material Culture: The Archaeology of Religious Women* (London and New York: Routledge, 1994), 125–126; on the management of water and wastewater in medieval monasteries more generally, see J. Patrick Greene, *Medieval Monasteries*, Archaeology of Medieval Britain (Leicester and New York: Leicester University Press and St. Martin's Press, 1992), 109–132.

Deus in adiutorium meum intende . . .
Domine ad adjuvandum me festina.

O God, make speed to save me . . .
O Lord, make haste to help me.[8]

Following the versicle are psalms (some with antiphons), a canticle (a hymn or chant based on a biblical text), a short reading from scripture, a short respond, a hymn, a second versicle and the *Benedictus* canticle with antiphon, again the *Kyrie*, *Pater noster* and *preces*, a prayer, and the *Benedicamus domino*. On some weekdays, when a priest can be present to officiate, Mass follows Lauds. Because the women are not permitted to enter the chancel, the area around the altar, the consecrated host is passed into their enclosure through a specially designed turning window.[9]

The nuns next make their way from their oratory to their chapter house in the eastern range along the cloister walk, the covered arcade that encloses the monastery's central green space (cloister garth).[10] They enter and take their respective seats along the stone benches that circle this rectangular room. One of the nuns stands and reads aloud a chapter of the *Rule of St. Benedict* (a practice from which the room takes its name) from the manuscript on the stand at the head of the room. This chapter house book also contains two calendars: a martyrology (which contains the names and brief biographies of prominent and locally important saints on the day of their death) and the necrology (a calendrical list of the names of deceased members of the community, including its patrons, on the day of their death). The day's reading from the martyrology for September 30 recounts the torturing and beheading of Saints Victor and Ursus, surviving members of the legendary fifth-century Theban Legion who had fled to Solothurn (modern Switzerland), and commemorates the death of Saint Jerome (d. 420) in Jerusalem. The names of the more ordinary dead listed in the necrology are next spoken aloud. This communal naming of the dead, a form of liturgical remembering, makes present those sisters, family members, and patrons who had died on that day, allowing them to live on among the living.[11] Evoking the names of the dead also emphasizes their dependence on the prayers of the living for their purification in Purgatory – prayers that are vital to their

---

[8] On the office of Lauds, see Harper, *The Forms and Orders of Western Liturgy*, 97–98.

[9] Gisela Muschiol, "Gender and Monastic Liturgy in the Latin West (High and Late Middle Ages)," in Alison I. Beach and Isabelle Cochelin, eds., *The Cambridge History of Medieval Monasticism in the Latin West*, 2 vols. (Cambridge: Cambridge University Press, 2020), 2:803–815.

[10] Paul Meyvaert, "The Medieval Monastic Claustrum," *Gesta* 12, no. 1/2 (1973): 53–59.

[11] Patrick J. Geary, *Living with the Dead in the Middle Ages* (Ithaca, NY: Cornell University Press, 1994), 87.

eventual salvation. The chapter meeting continues with a short sermon that offers an interpretation of a passage of scripture. The nuns of the double monastery of Admont (in modern Austria) had a small barred window in their chapter house through which their spiritual advisor, a monk from the men's community, delivered this sermon on ferial days. On feast days, when the monks were busy with their own observances, one of the nuns preached.[12] Hildegard may well have developed her own skills as a preacher, which she exercised beyond the monastery walls, in this context. The meeting concludes with a discussion of pressing matters of business relating to the life and functioning of the community, including the distribution of the day's work assignments. Some of the nuns head off into the various workspaces (kitchen, cloister, workshops, etc.) within their monastic precinct during the short interval before Prime, while others step forward to confess faults to the *magistra* and are assigned penalties in accordance with the severity of their sins.

Prime

At approximately 6 a.m., the nuns gather again in their oratory to sing Prime, the first of the day's four short minor offices. Because September 30 is a ferial day in Ordinary Time, all of the minor offices follow the same pattern; following the invitatory (the same one that opened Lauds), the nuns sing a hymn, chant three psalms, read a passage from scripture and from patristic or hagiographic works, and share concluding prayers (*Kyrie, Pater noster*, etc.), always ending with the *Benedicamus domino*.[13]

With Prime over by around 6:15 a.m., the women turn to the day's first period of manual work, just under four hours long and interrupted briefly by the singing of the minor hour of Terce at 9 a.m. Manual labor is central to the spirituality expressed in the *Rule of St. Benedict* and work indeed fills a significant portion of the day, with both economic and spiritual functions. The *Rule* specifies that the nuns work until the fourth hour of the day (at that time of year, around 10 a.m.). At Eibingen, the nuns likely engaged in a number of activities in support of the material, spiritual, and intellectual life of their community. The nature and extent of their manual work depended on the season and the needs of the community, as well as on the availability of the various lay servants who served the monastery, living just

---

[12] Alison I. Beach, *Women As Scribes: Book Production and Monastic Reform in Twelfth-Century Bavaria* (Cambridge: Cambridge University Press, 2004). See also Peter V. Loewen, Chapter 6, this volume.

[13] On the office of Prime, see Harper, *The Forms and Orders of Western Liturgy*, 98–100.

outside the nuns' inner precinct. Customaries from the Carolingian period reflect the common use of lay servants and reveal that manual work in some communities was primarily symbolic, particularly as liturgical obligations expanded to fill more of the monastic day.[14]

Work may have presented the occasion for the nuns to leave the monastery and to interact with various servants, as well as lay sisters and brothers who also carried out some of the work of the monastery and who were a common feature of houses with connections to Hirsau. Some communities also supported one or more *inclusae*, religious women who lived a solitary life in the general orbit of the monastery. *Inclusae* would not have participated in the residential or liturgical life of the monastery, but as members of the monastic community, they would have required a certain amount of upkeep, including the provision of food (presumably sourced in the monastery kitchens).

Twelfth-century religious women were also known for their expert needlework, and periods of work at Eibingen would almost certainly have included cloth work including embroidery, sewing, and perhaps also spinning and weaving. The beautifully embroidered altar cloth produced with Byzantine silk and costly dyes at Rupertsberg in the thirteenth century is a well-known example of the textile work associated with Hildegard's monastic circle, a tradition that surely had roots in the twelfth century. The women of the Swabian monastery of Zwiefalten (f. 1089) were avid embroiderers and donors of liturgical textiles in the twelfth century, and they are known to have sent their work as gifts to other monastic communities in their circle; the Chronicle of Petershausen notes the gift of a chasuble, alb, and stole from Zwiefalten in the aftermath of the devastating fire in 1159.[15] Examples of the needlework of Zwiefalten's nuns are preserved today among the monastery's surviving manuscripts in the form of a decorative and protective silk cover for one of their liturgical books, as well as in the skillful and decorative repairs they made to the parchment in a number of their surviving manuscripts. Embroidery and other textile work were ideally suited to enclosed religious women, as they could do this sort of work in a variety of locations without leaving the monastic enclosure, and the objects that they produced were of practical,

---

[14] Isabelle Cochelin, "Monastic Daily Life (c. 750–1100): A Tight Community Shielded by an Outer Court," in Beach and Cochlin, *Cambridge History of Medieval Monasticism in the Latin West*, 1:542–560.

[15] See Alison I. Beach, Shannon M. T. Li, and Samuel Sutherland, *Monastic Experience in Twelfth-Century Germany: The Chronicle of Petershausen in Translation* (Manchester: Manchester University Press, 2020), A.45, 174.

economic, and spiritual value to the community. Textile work was also closely associated with noble women of the sort enclosed at Rupertsberg and (perhaps to a lesser extent) Eibingen.[16] Religious women were also often charged with the cleaning and maintenance of liturgical textiles. When an altar cloth or priest's vestment needed cleaning, however, a male custodian would have had to pass these out to the nuns from the screened-off chancel, a space from which women were excluded for reasons of ritual purity.[17]

Another important type of manual labor practiced by nuns in many medieval religious communities was the copying and painting of books. At wealthier communities in which book production was extensive, there might be a separate workspace designated as a scriptorium, but book copying, decorating, and binding could also be undertaken in one of the ranges of the cloister walk, which had the advantage of good ventilation, protection from rain, and ample natural lighting.

While some women's communities produced simple, utilitarian manuscripts for devotional reading, nuns in wealthier houses are known to have produced richly illuminated liturgical books and biblical texts. The scribal and artistic talents of some religious women attracted the attention of abbots, priests, and bishops often quite far afield who might send materials and instructions for the production of particular books. Between 1140 and 1168, for example, the monk Sindold of Reinhardsbrunn commissioned a matutinal (a book for the celebration of the night office) from the nuns of Lippoldsberg, providing them with the parchment, pigment, and leather that they would need to produce the volume.[18] The names of some of the female scribes and artists who produced these books in the High Middle Ages are occasionally preserved in booklists, necrologies, and in the prefaces to texts that they helped to take down in dictation and copy. In some rare cases, a nun-scribe identifies herself in a colophon (a copyist's identifying mark) or a female artist paints and labels herself in a self-portrait. The nuns of Rupertsberg produced at least one expertly copied and lavishly

---

[16] Stefanie Seeberg, "Women As Makers of Church Decoration: Illustrated Textiles at the Monasteries of Altenberg/Lahn, Rupertsberg, and Heiningen (13th – 14th c.)," in Therese Martin, ed., *Reassessing the Roles of Women As "Makers" of Medieval Art and Architecture*, 2 vols. (Leiden and Boston: Brill, 2012), 1:375–84.

[17] Muschiol, "Gender and Monastic Liturgy," 806.

[18] See Sindold's Latin letter (including specific instructions for page layout), to the nuns in *Collectio Reinheresbrunnensis*, ed. Friedel Peeck, Monumenta Germaniae Historica Epistolae Selectae 5:34–35, and the letter of an anonymous nun to Sindold giving her explanation for the slight delay in the completion of the volume, 80–81.

illustrated manuscript of Hildegard's visions in her (now lost) visionary text *Scivias* (*Know the Ways*).[19]

While Eibingen's nuns are not likely to have engaged in heavy agricultural labor outside their enclosure, many of them, drawn from local families, would have grown up around the many vineyards that lined the hills along the Rhine, some of which certainly would have belonged to the monastery. Wine was vital to monastic life as well as to the monastic economy. According to the *Rule of St. Benedict*, each nun was to receive approximately a half-liter of wine to drink per day, but wine was also required for liturgical and medical use. Hildegard herself seems to have known quite a bit about wine.[20] She wrote about the difference between "frentsch" and "heunisch" grape varieties and sang the praises of wine as an aid to health, calling it the "blood of the earth" and incorporating it into many of her medical recipes.[21] The participation of Eibingen's twelfth-century nuns is not documented, but it stands to good reason that they would have taken a strong interest in the growing and harvesting of the grapes on their lands and in vinification, which would have included the selection of fruit, fermentation, and storage.[22] The nuns of modern Eibingen, which was refounded in 1904, produce wine under the supervision of a master nun-winemaker, and the nuns do some of the physical labor in the monastery's vineyards.

Terce

Those in a position to set their work aside return to the oratory at 9 a.m. to sing the minor office of Terce; but a nun in the middle of a delicate book illustration, for example, would be permitted to skip Terce and continue working until the fourth hour of the day, when the *Rule of St. Benedict* prescribes the start of a period of devotional reading that ends with the singing of the minor office of Sext.

While the *Rule* does not dictate a fixed location for private devotional reading, a nun might return to her bed in the dormitory to read or sit in the oratory or the cloister. The customary of Hirsau gives specific instructions for proper posture while reading; readers were to keep their arms to themselves and their feet on the ground. One or two nuns were assigned

---

[19] See Campbell, Chapter 12, this volume for further detail.

[20] Victoria Sweet, "Hildegard of Bingen and the Greening of Medieval Medicine," *Bulletin of the History of Medicine* 73, no. 3 (1999): 381–403.

[21] Tom Scott, "Medieval Viticulture in the German-Speaking Lands," *German History* 20, no. 1 (2002): 100. Sweet, "Hildegard of Bingen and the Greening of Medieval Medicine."

[22] Scott, "Medieval Viticulture in the German-Speaking Lands."

the job of circulating among their reading sisters to be sure that nobody was sleeping. These watchful *girones*, also mandated by the *Rule of St. Benedict*, would also have had an aural cue to the diligence of individual readers, as monastic reading was private but not silent. The nuns were expected to pronounce each word quietly in order to build greater understanding of the meaning of the text, and there would have been a certain level of noise when more than a few readers were gathered together.[23]

The type of meditative reading of a biblical text practiced in a monastic setting was sometimes undertaken in conjunction with the reading of a patristic commentary. In this *lectio divina* (sacred reading), the reader reads each verse carefully, sometimes over and over again, considering various points of interpretation with the help of the commentary – a form of prayer that medieval authors compared with a cow ruminating, chewing its cud.[24]

The evidence for the book collections at Admont, Lippoldsberg, and Zwiefalten suggests that religious women in German-speaking lands could have access to extensive book collections well-suited to the practice of *lectio divina*. Surviving book lists from women's houses in German-speaking lands document a number of extraordinary twelfth-century libraries particularly geared toward an extensive and in-depth study of the Bible.[25] The nuns of these three relatively well-documented communities had access to an impressive array of works by patristic standbys like Jerome and Gregory the Great and by more contemporary theologians and exegetes such as Bernard of Clairvaux, Hugh of St. Victor, Gerhoch of Reichersberg, and Rupert of Deutz.[26] The nuns of Admont wrote letters to regional experts in biblical exegesis, including Gerhoch, suggesting that they were engaged readers of many of these books and perhaps composed exegetical works of their own, including some of the sermons that they preached in their chapter house.

Sext

With the morning periods of work and devotional reading over, the nuns again gather in their oratory to sing the minor office of Sext and then head

---

[23] Duncan Robertson, *Lectio Divina: The Medieval Experience of Reading*, Cistercian Studies Series, no. 238 (Collegeville, MN: Cistercian Publications, 2011), xiv and 93–94.

[24] See ibid., 98.   [25] Beach, *Women As Scribes*.

[26] On Lippoldsberg, see Julie Hotchin, "Women's Reading and Monastic Reform in Twelfth-Century Germany: The Library of the Nuns of Lippoldsberg," in Alison I. Beach, ed., *Manuscripts and Monastic Culture: Reform and Renewal in Twelfth-Century Germany* (Turnhout: Brepols, 2007), 139–189. On Zwiefalten, see Constant Mews, "Monastic Educational Culture Revisited: The Witness of Zwiefalten and the Hirsau Reform," in George Ferzoco and Carolyn Muessig, eds., *Medieval Monastic Education* (London and New York: Leicester University Press, 2000), 182–197.

immediately along the cloister walk toward the refectory. Each woman stops at the *lavabo* (the small stone trough supplied with running water) just outside it to wash her hands before entering and taking her seat for the day's single meal. In many contemporary monasteries, lead pipes distributed water to the various parts of the monastic precinct including the *lavabo*, kitchens, and workshops. Another pipe carries the water from the lavabo into a larger drain, where it joins wastewater from other parts of the monastery and is later used to flush the channel under the latrines, carrying the human waste out into the main precinct drain.[27]

Although the *Rule of St. Benedict* stipulates that the nuns should be offered two cooked dishes at their meal, the menu was subject to the discretion of the abbess and to availability based on economics and the season. The *Rule* also provides for a generous pound of bread and about a half-liter of wine per woman per day. If we assume that the hand signals designated in the Hirsau customary for communication during periods when speaking was not permitted reflect the most commonly eaten foods, then we can imagine a menu that often included cheese, bread, milk, eggs, cake, bread fried in a pan, meat (although the *Rule* concedes this only to the ill or elderly), various oils, honey, and *pulmentum*, a simple form of soup or porridge based on vegetables, with the possible addition of legumes, grain, eggs, fish, meat, or cheese – the type of cooked dish (*pulmentaria cocta*) prescribed by Benedict.[28] In her commentary on the *Rule*, Hildegard notes that, when there was sufficient fish, eggs, or cheese for a third dish, this should be considered a special treat.[29]

Bioarcheologists have begun to offer a new window on the monastic diet that is an important complement to this sort of textual evidence for monastic foodways.[30] Techniques such as stable isotope analysis of bone collagen (its main structural protein), the morphological and chemical analysis of teeth and bones, and microanalysis of calcified dental plaque (calculus) offer new ways to reconstruct the monastic diet and to detect nutritional stress. Stable isotope analysis of human remains excavated from the cemetery at the Cistercian Dunes Abbey in Koksijde (on the coast of modern-day Belgium), for example, suggests a diet heavily reliant on

---

[27] Greene, *Medieval Monasteries*, 115.

[28] Massimo Montanari, *Medieval Tastes: Food, Cooking, and the Table* (New York: Columbia University Press, 2015), 33.

[29] Hildegard of Bingen, *Explanation of the Rule of Benedict*, 32.

[30] Clark Spencer Larsen, "Bioarchaeology: The Lives and Lifestyles of Past People," *Journal of Archaeological Research* 10, no. 2 (2002): 119–166.

marine food, a finding supported by the large quantity of fish bone and mollusk shell found within medieval layers of the monastery's medieval garbage.[31] Excavated refuse piles and cooking areas sometimes yield further archaeobotanical evidence for diet, suggesting the consumption of wheat, oat, barley, rye, peas, and beans. Although not frequently excavated and analyzed, deposits of waste from the same sort of latrines that the nuns of Eibingen visited in the interval between Matins and Lauds have the potential to provide further evidence for monastic diet and health. Archaeological finds from toilets and drains include, among other things, seeds and pits, which suggest the consumption of fruit, and whipworm and roundworm eggs, signaling the presence of intestinal parasites resulting from the contamination of food and water supply and populations at risk for malnutrition.[32]

While the nuns eat this single meal of the day, one sister reads aloud to the community, with edifying selections drawn from scripture, patristic writings, or saints' lives. This reading is intended not only to edify but to prevent idle chat as the women sit together to eat.[33] Only the voice of the daily reader was to break the silence in the refectory. At the conclusion of the meal, some of the nuns return to the dormitory to rest on their beds until None. Those who opt to return to their private devotional reading are enjoined to take care not to disturb the rest.

None

After singing None, the last of the day's four minor offices, around 3 p.m., the women return to their assigned work in the cloister walk, gardens, and workshops that lie beyond the north range of the monastery.

Vespers

With the setting of the sun, at about 6 p.m., the nuns gather in their oratory for Vespers. Like Prime, Terce, Sext, and None, Vespers opens with the invitatory:

---

[31] Caroline Polet and M. Anne Katzenberg, "Reconstruction of the Diet in a Mediaeval Monastic Community from the Coast of Belgium," *Journal of Archaeological Science* 30 (2003): 527–528.

[32] Evilena Anastasiou and Piers D. Mitchell, "Human Intestinal Parasites from a Latrine in the 12th Century Frankish Castle of Saranda Kolones in Cyprus," *International Journal of Paleopathology* 3, no. 3 (2013): 218–223.

[33] Teresa Webber, "Reading in the Refectory: Monastic Practice in England, c. 1000-c.1300," London University Annual John Coffin Memorial Palaeography Lecture (February 18, 2010). Unpublished paper.

Make haste, O God, to deliver me . . .
make haste, O Lord, to help me.

Longer and more complex than the preceding minor offices, Vespers has a structure similar to that of Lauds; the nuns chant four psalms with antiphons, followed by a reading from scripture, a hymn, a versicle and response, the *Magnificat* (canticle) with an antiphon, a chanted *Kyrie* and *Pater noster* (Our Father or Lord's Prayer), collect, and the blessing.[34]

After Vespers, the nuns gather in the north cloister walk, where a chest (*armarium*) containing some of the monastery's books is kept. With the lamps lighted, the women sit together for a period of private devotional reading known as Collations.[35] The *Rule of St. Benedict* (*RB* 42) prescribes this period of silent reading after Vespers, specifically mentioning the reading of the Conferences (*Collationes*) of John Cassian, but the women could also choose from a range of patristic and early monastic texts.[36]

Compline

Shortly after Vespers, the nuns return to their oratory one last time for the day and sing the short office of Compline, opening with the versicle and response:

Converte nos deus salutaris noster . . .
et averte iram tuam a nobis

Convert us, O God our savior . . .
and turn your anger from us.[37]

The end of Compline marks the beginning of a long period of silence, prescribed in the *Rule of St. Benedict* (*RB* 42), to be broken only the next day by the opening of Matins, when the daily cycle of the Divine Office begins anew.

The discipline of silence was a central feature of traditional monasticism and its cultivation was thought to lead to the nun's increased ability to hear the voice of God. Restraint in speech reduced the distraction that resulted from idle talk and fostered the monastic virtues of humility and obedience. Even during the great period of silence that began after Compline,

---

[34] On the monastic office of Vespers, see Harper, *The Forms and Orders of Western Liturgy*, 101.
[35] Eva Schlotheuber and John T. McQuillen, "Books and Libraries within Monasteries," in Alison I. Beach and Isabelle Cochelin, eds., *The Cambridge History of Medieval Monasticism in the Latin West*, vol. 2 (Cambridge: Cambridge University Press, 2020), 975–997.
[36] Webber, "Reading in the Refectory," 9.
[37] On the monastic office of Compline, see Harper, *The Forms and Orders of Western Liturgy*, 102–103.

however, the nuns could communicate. The Hirsau customary details an elaborate system of hand gestures that could be used not only in the refectory and during periods of work but also during the silent hours of the night.[38] Like all monastic rules and regulations, however, the rule of silence could be bent and interpreted. For example, Gertrude, the twelfth-century nun who wrote the Life of an anonymous *magistra* of the monastery of Admont, praised her for never speaking in the vernacular (German) during the night silence. Instead, she responded to the requests of the young girls in her charge for short poems by dictating them only in Latin.[39]

As the nuns return to their individual beds (around 7:30 p.m. at the end of September), their day comes to an end. One or two stay awake, of course, keeping the time in order to rouse the community for Matins and the start of the new day.

Further Reading

Latin Editions and English Translations

Hildegard of Bingen. *De Regula sancti Benedicti*. In *Hildegardis Bingensis: Opera minora*, ed. Hugh Feiss. Corpus Christianorum Continuatio Mediaevalis 226. Turnhout: Brepols, 2007, 23–97.

    Explanation of the Rule of Benedict, trans. Hugh Feiss. Toronto: Peregrina Publishing, 1990; rpt. Eugene, OR: Wipf & Stock, 2005. https://monastic matrix.osu.edu/cartularium/explanation-rule-benedict

Secondary Literature

Beach, Alison I., ed. *Manuscripts and Monastic Culture: Reform and Renewal in Twelfth-Century Germany*. Turnhout: Brepols, 2007.

Beach, Alison I. *Women As Scribes: Book Production and Monastic Reform in Twelfth-Century Bavaria*. Cambridge and New York: Cambridge University Press, 2004.

Beach, Alison I. and Isabelle Cochelin, eds. *The Cambridge History of Medieval Monasticism in the Latin West*. 2 vols. Cambridge: Cambridge University Press, 2020.

Bruce, Scott G. *Silence and Sign Language in Medieval Monasticism: The Cluniac Tradition, c.900-1200*. Cambridge: Cambridge University Press, 2010.

---

[38] Scott G. Bruce, *Silence and Sign Language in Medieval Monasticism: The Cluniac Tradition, c.900–1200* (Cambridge: Cambridge University Press, 2010).

[39] Jonathan Reed Lyon, ed., *Noble Society: Five Lives from Twelfth-Century Germany*, Manchester Medieval Sources (Manchester: Manchester University Press, 2017).

Cochelin, Isabelle. "Customaries As Inspirational Sources." In Carolyn Marino Malone and Clark Maines, eds., *Consuetudines et Regulae: Sources for Monastic Life in the Middle Ages and the Early Modern Period*. Disciplina Monastica. Turnhout: Brepols, 2014, 27–72.

Gilchrist, Roberta. *Gender and Material Culture: The Archaeology of Religious Women*. London and New York: Routledge, 1994.

Harper, John. *The Forms and Orders of Western Liturgy from the Tenth to the Eighteenth Century: A Historical Introduction and Guide for Students and Musicians*. Oxford: Clarendon Press, 1991.

Martin, Therese, ed. *Reassessing the Roles of Women As "Makers" of Medieval Art and Architecture*. 2 vols. Leiden and Boston: Brill, 2012.

Polet, Caroline and M. Anne Katzenberg. "Reconstruction of the Diet in a Mediaeval Monastic Community from the Coast of Belgium." *Journal of Archaeological Science* 30 (2003): 525–533.

Robertson, Duncan. *Lectio Divina: The Medieval Experience of Reading*. Cistercian Studies Series, no. 238. Collegeville, MN: Cistercian Publications, 2011.

Schmandt, Matthias. "Hildegard von Bingen und das Kloster Eibingen: Revision einer historischen Überlieferung." *Nassauische Annalen* 125 (2014): 29–52.

CHAPTER 3

Literacy and Learning in the Lives of Women Religious in Medieval Germany

Lori Kruckenberg

Introduction: Hildegard and Formal Learning

When Hildegard of Bingen spoke of her formal education, she frequently underscored the limits of her "earthly" training, stating that the knowledge that flowed through her was divine rather than human in origin. In the opening declaration of *Scivias*, for instance, Hildegard says that, despite not knowing how "to analyze the syntax of words, or to divide their syllables," nor having "any knowledge of their cases or tenses," she had been granted, through heavenly visions and auditions, a sudden understanding of "the meaning of the exposition of the Scriptures, namely the Psalter, the Gospel, and the other catholic volumes of both the Old and New Testament."[1] In a variety of writings, Hildegard refers to herself as *indocta* – "unlearned" or "uneducated" – an adjective that she and others bestow on her teacher Jutta of Sponheim as well.[2] Hildegard also links the limits of her learnedness to her gender, as can be found in the introduction and conclusion to her *Explanation of the Rule of Benedict*, where she refers to herself as a "poor female person and untrained in learning."[3]

Others in Hildegard's sphere – acquaintances, intimates, and *vita* writers – echo similar assessments. Adelbert, prior of Disibodenberg, recalled to her in a letter the narrowness of her literary knowledge, stating:

> We remember how you were educated among us, how you were taught, how you were established in the religious life. For your instruction was

---

[1] Hildegard of Bingen, *Scivias*, trans. Columba Hart and Jane Bishop (New York: Paulist Press, 1990), 59.

[2] See *Vita sanctae Hildegardis*, ed. Monika Klaes, Corpus Christianorum Continuatio Mediaevalis (CCCM) 126 (Turnhout: Brepols, 1993), 24; and Anna Silvas, ed. and trans., *Jutta and Hildegard: The Biographical Sources* (University Park: Pennsylvania State University Press, 1999), 168.

[3] Hildegard of Bingen, *Explanation of the Rule of Benedict*, trans. Hugh Feiss (Eugene, OR: Wipf & Stock, 2005), 48.

that appropriate only to a woman, and a simple psalter was your only schoolbook.[4]

In a discussion of her formative years, the authors of the *Vita sanctae Hildegardis* (Life of Saint Hildegard), Gottfried of Disibodenberg and Theodoric of Echternach, state that, save for having been taught the psalter and simple notation, Hildegard had "received no other teaching in the arts of literature or of music from a human source."[5] The *vita* writers go on to marvel that she was nonetheless able to produce such a prodigious number of writings and books.

Hildegard's meager schooling caused her to enlist the help of more conventionally educated individuals, who could take down dictation. Initially, she turned to nuns under her charge, ones apparently better trained as scribes and more expert in Latin than she. Later the monk Volmar – who served as her secretary and confessor for many years – helped to mediate her mystical experiences, putting her words into more polished and proper Latin. Following Volmar's death in 1173, Hildegard turned to Ludwig of St. Matthias, Gottfried of Disibodenberg, and Guibert of Gembloux for their scribal, literary, and editorial assistantship.

Despite these and other assertions of the deficiencies of both her principal instructor and her own schooling, one finds among contemporary reports small contradictions in the educational background of Hildegard and her teacher. The *Vita domnae Juttae inclusae* (Life of Lady Jutta the Anchoress, ca. 1140), a work likely commissioned by Hildegard, characterizes Jutta quite differently than Hildegard does:

> Once [Jutta] had passed the tender years of her infancy, her mother handed her over to be instructed in the learning of the sacred Scriptures. In these she made good progress; whatever her capacious intelligence could absorb from them she committed to her retentive memory, and thereafter strove to implement with good deeds.[6]

This *vita* also shows Jutta to be a skilled and dedicated teacher who passed on all acquired knowledge, especially with regard to teachings from the Old and New Testament, and who "held back none of her daughters."[7] These depictions of Jutta's learnedness and pedagogical generosity contrast starkly to the epithet *indocta mulier* (uneducated woman) and other statements found in the *Scivias* and the *Vita sanctae Hildegardis*.

---

[4] Hildegard of Bingen, *The Letters of Hildegard of Bingen*, ed. Joseph L. Baird and Radd K. Ehrman, 3 vols. (New York: Oxford University Press, 1994–2004), 1:172.

[5] Gottfried and Theodoric, *Life of Hildegard* (book 1.1.) in Silvas, *Jutta and Hildegard*, 139–140.

[6] Silvas, *Jutta and Hildegard*, 67.   [7] Ibid., 73.

Other discrepancies emerge among medieval reports. While in numerous accounts Hildegard is portrayed as barely literate and in need of scribal assistance, certain passages present her as capable of writing down her visions in her own hand, privately and unaided.[8] She also expressed frustrations with her secretaries when they had introduced changes into her writings.[9] Her dissatisfaction suggests not only that she detected emendations but also that she was competent enough to offer an opinion on both the style and the substance of their scribal interventions. Another inconsistency occurs between books 1 and 2 of the *Vita sanctae Hildegardis*: in the former, she is described as having received rudimentary training in psalm singing and musical notation, while in the latter, she is said to have "never studied neumes or any chant at all."[10] Odo of Soissons also writes to her in a letter: "It is reported . . . that you bring forth the melody of a new song, although you have studied nothing of such things."[11]

Medieval authors are not the only writers to present diverging views on Hildegard's learning. Concerning her literary and musical output, some modern scholars have located traces of influence from specific authors (Plato via Calcidius, Cicero, Augustine, Boethius, William of Hirsau, Honorius Augustodunensis, Rupert of Deutz) and works (i.e. the anonymous *Speculum virginum* [Mirror for Virgins]) as well as familiarity with specific literary and musico-liturgical genres.[12] Others have challenged such conclusions, suggesting instead that her familiarity with specific authors, texts, genres, and schools of thought might be accounted for as knowledge transmitted to her orally rather than her direct engagement with such texts or through any kind of formal instruction.[13]

Scholars today have offered multiple explanations for the meaning and intention behind the assertions on her literary and linguistic competencies. Some suggest taking her and her *vita* writers' words at face value. Others view these remarks as examples of *humilitas* or other rhetorical topoi. Some propose that such protestations belong to larger strategies, ones meant to appease or silence her detractors, legitimize the divine nature of her visions,

---

[8] Silvas, *Jutta and Hildegard*, 159–160, 225.

[9] Joan Ferrante, "'Scribe quae vidis et audis': Hildegard, Her Language, and Her Secretaries," in David Townsend and Andrew Taylor, eds., *The Tongue of the Fathers: Gender and Ideology in Twelfth-Century Latin* (Philadelphia: University of Pennsylvania Press, 1998), 102–135.

[10] Silvas, *Jutta and Hildegard*, 139 and 160.   [11] Hildegard, *Letters*, 1:110.

[12] See chapters in this volume by James Ginther (Chapter 4), Peter V. Loewen (Chapter 6), Faith Wallis (Chapter 7), and Jennifer Bain (Chapter 10), for example, and reference to other scholarship.

[13] For an overview, see Justin A. Stover, "Hildegard, the Schools, and Their Critics," in Beverly Mayne Kienzle, Debra L. Stoudt, and George Ferzoco, eds., *A Companion to Hildegard of Bingen* (Leiden: Brill, 2014), 109–137.

authorize her leadership decisions, add to the force of her legal complaints, or prepare and construct a dossier for canonization. As Joseph Baird and Radd Ehrman put it, "the extent of Hildegard's education is a problem not likely ever to be solved."[14]

It is not the purpose of this chapter, however, to either determine the intent or decide on the meaning of the words of Hildegard or her contemporaries on her education. Neither does this chapter set out to relitigate the trustworthiness of statements made by her and others. Instead, it aims to present more broadly standards and expectations of, as well as contexts for, literacy and learning common to women religious in medieval Germany. The remainder of the chapter proceeds from three vantage points. First, monastic and canonical rules together with a pair of conciliar decrees will be reviewed for information they contain pertaining to learning and literacy in women's communities. This section focuses on early rules, most written or compiled between the fifth and ninth centuries, and which were foundational texts for women's houses in the early medieval period.

Following this survey, relevant hagiographic works will be considered. Hagiographic literature cannot, of course, be read as a set of unassailable facts; even so, *vitae* register through the depiction of their holy protagonists idealized forms of religious life. Just as the *vitae* of Hildegard and Jutta provide information about the educational conditions of their subjects and offer insights into contemporary values on female learning, so too can other *vitae* be inspected for views on and values held for female learning. As spiritual exempla, the women of these *vitae* promote, on the one hand, and reflect, on the other, social, cultural, and institutional norms for the education of women religious. In such accounts, we encounter the exemplary pupil, teacher, reader, and singer as she pursues her sacred duties in her convent, cell, or religious house.

The chapter closes with a short review of important scholarship presenting concrete examples of learnedness and literacies found in and among women's communities in medieval Germany. These various studies examine artifacts from the macro perspective, such as book collections as a whole or scriptoria, and from the micro perspective, such as individual manuscripts, parts of manuscripts, or writings by women. Types of evidence include the remnants of libraries, medieval book inventories, and documents related to book acquisition such as commissions, purchases, donations, in-house copying, and book loans. How women used and engaged

---

[14] Hildegard, *Letters*, 1:6.

their books can be surmised in part through the evidence of glosses, annotations, addenda, and manuscript wear. Illustrations, individual ownership marks, *ex libris* marks, colophons, and names of dedicatees offer clues about the intended readers and owners. The identification of women scribes, information about their scriptoria, and the interaction between female and male agents can shed light on educational matters in ways that rules and *vitae* cannot. Finally, there are numerous examples of female authors from women's communities in medieval Germany, and these will be addressed in relevant cases.

Before continuing, a short explanation on the types of "nuns" considered here as well as the rationale for the chronological scope of the study are warranted. Throughout this chapter, "women religious" (*mulieres religiosae*) and "female religious" will be used to refer collectively to nuns, ruled canonesses, secular canonesses (including *Stiftsdamen*), anchorites, consecrated or holy widows, beguines, and other holy women who dwelled in, formed, established, or took part in religious communities, households, or cells.[15] Some followed a known or authorized rule (e.g. the *Regula Benedicti, Regula ad virgines, Institutio sanctimonialium Aquisgranensis, Regula Augustini*), while others apparently lived according to a discipline set out in a local or hybrid rule that has not survived or according to guidelines and precepts never formalized in writing.[16] Some women religious such as beguines did not observe a rule per se.

By including different types of female religious in this chapter, I hope to present a more representative and balanced picture of the religious landscape of medieval Germany, and one familiar in some measure to Hildegard as well as her forebears and her successors, rather than restricting evidence to professed nuns only. Hildegard was herself, of course, a Benedictine nun who dwelled in the double community at Disibodenberg and later at the convent at Rupertsberg. Yet, while living at the latter, she did not always adhere to the strict regulations of enclosure demanded by the *Regula Benedicti*, and this exemption is one frequently

---

[15] Women religious is a translation of *mulieres religiosae* (or *religiosae*), a term frequently found from the thirteenth century on. Modern scholars also apply this term as a more neutral translation for *sanctimoniales, moniales, monachae, canonissae, canonicae, puellae*, and *ancillae Dei* for the entire Middle Ages. For a discussion of variety of terms in use in the ninth, tenth, and eleventh centuries, see Thomas Schilp, *Norm und Wirklichkeit religiöser Frauengemeinschaften im Frühmittelalter: Die "Institutio sanctimonialium Aquisgranensis" des Jahres 816 und die Problematik der Verfassung von Frauenkommunitäten* (Göttingen: Vandenhoeck & Ruprecht, 1998), 54; and Steven Vanderputten, *Dark Age Nunneries: The Ambiguous Identity of Female Monasticism, 800–1050* (Ithaca, NY: Cornell University Press, 2018).

[16] Vanderputten, *Dark Age Nunneries*, 1–36.

encountered among medieval *religiosae*, especially German noblewomen. Before joining her Benedictine community, however, Hildegard lived as a girl with the anchorite Jutta, and together with another girl Hildegard's age they were "entombed" in a cell. Prior to her life as anchorite, Jutta was educated for three years under the guardianship of Uda, a holy widow. In addition to Hildegard's diverse "monastic" lineage, her exchanges and interactions with the outside world included religious orders different than her own – Augustinians, Premonstratensians, Cistercians, as well as unruled canonesses. Finally, because Hildegard is grouped among the German female mystics especially connected to the twelfth, thirteenth, and fourteenth centuries, I include some later medieval examples – especially from Gertrude of Helfta and from select communities of Dominicans (an order postdating Hildegard's lifetime) – for they provide another witness to education among women religious. Thus, this chapter examines evidence of learning and literacy as reported for and by different types of women religious from the ninth up to the middle of the fifteenth century, with the intent of presenting a wide-angle view of female religious in medieval Germany and the broader cultural, social, and institutional contexts for thinking about their education as well as that of Hildegard.

Education of *Religiosae* According to Rules and Rulings: *Omnes litteras discant*

The numerous extant rules for medieval women religious routinely confirm that Latin literacy was a standard expectation. The *Regula ad virgines*, a set of sixth-century prescriptions for nuns by Caesarius of Arles, puts it most succinctly and explicitly: "Omnes litteras discant" (All shall learn to read).[17] Literacy made possible the primary mission of these communities: performing the daily rounds of lessons, chants, prayers, and other spiritual obligations, at specific times of the day, week, and year. According to several rules, the minimum age for admission was set to six to seven years old so as to ensure that the member was old enough to learn the alphabet and recognize letter forms.[18]

---

[17] Caesarius of Arles, *Oeuvres monastiques I: Oeuvres pour les moniales*, ed. Adalbert de Vogüé and Joël Courreau, Sources Chrétiennes, vol. 345 (Paris: Cerf 1988), 170–272; Maria Caritas McCarthy, trans., *The Rule for Nuns of St. Caesarius of Arles: A Translation with a Critical Introduction in Studies in Mediaeval History* (Washington, DC: Catholic University of America Press, 1960), 175.

[18] Ibid., 173. Albrecht Diem, "New Ideas Expressed in Old Words: *The Regula Donati* on Female Monastic Life and Monastic Spirituality," *Viator* 43, no. 1 (2012): 1–38; Albrecht Diem, "Das Ende des monastischen Experiments. Liebe, Beichte und Schwiegen in der *Regula cuiusdam ad virgines* (mit einer Übersetzung im Anhang)," in Anne Müller and Gert Melville, eds., *Female "vita religiosa"*

Rules say little about educational curricula, but the Book of Psalms was clearly a core text. The *Regula Benedicti* (Rule of St. Benedict), a sixth-century rule written for monks but used by and adapted for nuns, is the most explicit text in this regard. It dictates that the community should sing through the entire psalter weekly, and it lays out in painstaking detail the order of the 150 psalms, the division of their chapters and verses, as well as their distribution throughout the day and week. While in-house solutions for the ordering of the psalms are allowed, the obligation of a weekly reading of the psalter must nevertheless be met (chapter 18).[19]

Scriptures – that is, the rest of the Old Testament together with the New Testament – comprise the other standard text for female religious. The *Regula Augustini* (Rule of St. Augustine), especially widespread from the late eleventh century on, commands all to listen at mealtimes as scriptures are read aloud.[20] The *Regula Benedicti* makes frequent mention of reading and singing from the scriptures during the liturgy, and while it does not prescribe a lectionary schedule akin to that for the psalter, it does give some general guidelines for scriptural choices at Vigils and Matins, respectively, and assigns specific biblical canticles at Vespers, Compline, and Matins. The *Institutio sanctimonialium Aquisgranensis*, a rule for canonesses from 816, provides by far the most comprehensive instructional "program" for women religious. It maps out a course for the study of Holy Writ thusly:

> Let her first study the Psalter. Then let her gather wisdom for life in the Proverbs of Solomon. Let her learn in Ecclesiastes to despise the vanities of the world. Let her follow in Job examples of virtue and patience. Then let her pass onto the Gospels, never to be put aside once taken in hand. Let her also drink in the Acts of the Apostles and the epistles with a totally willing heart, and then the rest of the New and Old Testament in their proper order.[21]

The various rules say little about other appropriate *lectiones*, but the *Regulae* themselves are generally required reading in their respective communities, as

---

between Late Antiquity and the High Middle Ages: Structures, Developments and Spatial Contexts (Münster and Berlin: LIT Verlag, 2011), 81–136.

[19] Because there are many English translations of the *Regula Benedicti* available, I refer the reader to chapters rather than pages. For an excellent Latin–English edition: *The Rule of Saint Benedict*, ed. and trans. Bruce L. Venarde (Cambridge, MA: Harvard University Press, 2011).

[20] Raymond Canning, trans., *The Rule of Saint Augustine: Masculine and Feminine Versions*, intro. Tarsicius J. van Bavel (London: Darton, Longman & Todd, 1984), 28.

[21] Translation from Alison I. Beach, *Women As Scribes: Book Production and Monastic Reform in Twelfth-Century Bavaria* (Cambridge and New York: Cambridge University Press, 2004), 20. This passage from the *Institutio* was inspired by a letter from Jerome to Laeta (Letter 107) concerning the education of her little daughter, Pacatula.

with the anonymous *Regula cuiusdam ad virgines* (Someone's Rule for Virgins), which states that, before mealtime, the abbess can assign multiple chapters of this rule for spiritual nourishment.[22] The *Regula Benedicti* emphasizes the importance of hearing and comprehending the rule read (chapter 58) and advises further it be read aloud routinely so that no one can claim ignorance as an excuse for her disobedience (chapter 66). Other appropriate texts for religious inculcation include biblical commentaries (chapter 9) and the writings of the church fathers and hagiography at Compline (chapter 42). One later exception for supplemental readings occurs in the twelfth-century statutes for Premonstratensians (*Statuta ordinis Praemonstratensis*), which prohibits canonesses from learning anything beyond the psalter, prayers, and the Marian vigils.[23] However, in the event that a particular sister had been educated prior to joining the community, she might, with permission from the abbot, be allowed to read other books on feast days.[24] In the *Regula Benedicti*, supplemental texts are chosen for their ability to edify listeners (chapter 42) and instill monastic virtue (chapter 73), and thus the *Regula Benedicti* warns against reading from nine of the first ten books of the Old Testament before bed (the Book of Ruth is the exception), since such texts are deemed unsuitable for the weak-minded (chapter 42).

Rules generally denote that reading was both a communal and an individual activity. Communal readings took place in the liturgy, at mealtimes, and while sisters performed manual tasks.[25] Connected to these different settings were different modes of reading. Speaking, reciting on discrete pitches, and chanting all constituted ways to read communally, and a premium was placed on listeners remaining attentive and silent. By contrast, individual reading was done quietly, inaudibly, or *sotto voce* (*Regula Benedicti*, chapter 48). Several rules mandate that books be made available to individuals and that time should be set aside every day for private reading.[26] Overall, the various rules warn against the corrosive potential of idleness and gossip and indicate that the *lectio divina* not

---

[22] Diem, "Das Ende," 123. Caesarius' *Regula ad virgines* is also required reading: see McCarthy, *Rule for Nuns of Caesarius*, 189.

[23] Raphaël van Waefelghem, *Les premiers statuts de l'Ordre de Prémontré: Le Clm. 17.174 (XIIᵉ siècle)* (Louvain: P. Smeesters, 1913), 66. For a translation of the books appropriate for sisters and other statutes for Premonstratensian women, see Beach, *Women As Scribes*, 112–116.

[24] Ibid.

[25] See Beach, Chapter 2, this volume, as well as, for instance, the *Regula cuiusdam ad virgines* in Diem, "Das Ende," 123, 125.

[26] Canning, *Rule of Augustine*, 35. McCarthy, *Rule for Nuns of Caesarius*, 175–176. The *Regula Benedicti*, chapters 48 and 49.

only fulfilled the obligation of a *religiosa* but also served to combat moral corruption and torpor in the community.[27]

Expectations for literacy pervade the various rules, and not surprisingly attempts to regulate competency and maintain standards can be found. Carelessness in reading and in singing are met with penalties for adults and corporal punishment for children.[28] According to the *Regula Benedicti*, the selection of a *lectrix hebdomadaria* (weekly reader) was determined not according to her seniority or rank but rather according to her ability to read in a way that edified the listener (chapter 38), a duty reiterated in chapter 47 for singers and readers. Of course, the importance of *lectrices* and *cantrices* to edify as they read and recite presumes aural comprehension. The importance of aural acquisition is reflected in warnings to remain alert during communal readings and safeguard against drowsiness.[29] The rigors of daytime and nighttime rounds must have overwhelmed younger members of the community, however, and Aurelian of Arles's rule, also called *Regula ad virgines*, made some accommodation for the very youngest girls in the convent, exempting them from the most strenuous liturgical duties.[30]

Writing, another dimension of literacy, receives few words in rules, but the *Regula Benedicti* does list a wax tablet and stylus among the items that the abbess must make available to each nun (chapter 55). Moreover, this rule instructs a novice formally entering the community to write her statement of profession; if, however, she is still "unlettered," a surrogate could write the vow for her, and the entrant could enter a mark next to the vow (chapter 58).

Rules also warn against certain educational practices and abuses, and whereas private reading played a role in the formation of women religious, references to supervision of private reading and limiting types of personal communications surface. For instance, oversight of personal letter exchange comes under the purview of the abbess or some other senior member in the community.[31] Caesarius of Arles adjures that neither the daughters of nobility nor those of common folk should be received into a convent for the sole purpose of rearing and teaching them, although there is ample evidence to suggest that this practice continued well into the central Middle Ages.[32]

In general, the various rules give few if any details about material support, learning conditions, instructors, and pedagogy. The presence of libraries can

[27] Ibid.   [28] Canning, *Rule of Augustine*, chapter 2.4, 27. *Regula Benedicti*, chapter 45.
[29] McCarthy, *Rule for Nuns of Caesarius*, 175.
[30] Mayke De Jong, *In Samuel's Image: Child Oblation in the Early Medieval West* (Leiden: Brill, 1996), 33.
[31] McCarthy, *Rule for Nuns of Caesarius*, 188. *Regula Benedicti*, chapter 54.
[32] McCarthy, *Rule for Nuns of Caesarius*, 179.

be assumed, but virtually nothing is said about the management and acquisition of books, though from the twelfth century on, ordinals, customaries, statutes, and so on sometimes offer details on the offices and duties of librarians and scribes in the various monastic and canonical orders.[33] In terms of teaching personnel, Caesarius refers to a "mistress of the novices" in the *Regula ad virgines*, but he does not specify her duties.[34] In ordinals, constitutions, customaries, and other prescriptive texts written after 1100, indications for and definitions of the offices of female cantor (*cantrix*), librarian (*armaria*), and teaching mistress emerge, but such information in the various rules compiled before the twelfth century is scarce. One relatively early statement on educational oversight was issued at the Synod of Chalon-sur-Saône of 813, which directs the abbess to take care that her charges "strenuously apply themselves to reading, to the Office, and to singing the psalms."[35] These Acts also order each female religious to learn to read and sing in order to fulfill her sacred duties. This latter decree, adopted verbatim at the council of Mainz in 847, declares:

> Female religious should apply themselves in their monastery to read and chant, to celebrate or pray the psalms, and celebrate the canonical hours – namely Matins, Prime, Terce, Sext, Nones, Vespers, Compline – all in equal measure.[36]

Thus, while the various rules and legislation governing female religious are often vague on implementation and methods of teaching, collectively these late patristic and early medieval texts make clear that literacy was a basic necessity and one that made possible these communities' fundamental spiritual obligations.

Female Learning and Literacy According to the Hagiographic Tradition

Hagiographic literature presents another perspective of education found in religious communities. As sacred biographies, the lives of saintly women present idealized nuns, canonesses, anchorites, widows, lay sisters, and

---

[33] The office and duties found in Dominican communities in the German-speaking lands are especially well studied: see Gertrud Jaron Lewis, *By Women, for Women, about Women: The Sister-Books of Fourteenth-Century Germany* (Toronto: Pontifical Institute of Mediaeval Studies, 1996), 200–283; Rebecca L. R. Garber, *Feminine Figurae: Representations of Gender in Religious Texts by Medieval German Women Writers, 1100–1375* (New York: Routledge, 2003), 61–104; and Johannes Meyer, *Das Amptbuch*, ed. Sarah Glenn DeMaris. Monumenta Ordinis Fratrum Praedicatorum Historica 31 (Rome: Angelicum University Press, 2015).
[34] McCarthy, *Rule for Nuns of Caesarius*, 182.
[35] Adapted from Vanderputten, *Dark Age Nunneries*, 168.   [36] Ibid., 169 and 171, respectively.

other consecrated women. They commonly impart, furthermore, details about educational standards, literacy requirements, and attitudes toward learning and teaching in their communities.[37] Some two dozen medieval hagiographies of German women religious have been surveyed for this chapter. From these lives, one can gain some understanding about what, when, where, and how exemplary women read and what were the standards and conditions for their education.

Without a doubt the text most commonly cited in the twenty-some hagiographies surveyed is the Book of Psalms. The references to the psalter and to psalmody are so numerous that it is helpful to organize them along thematic and structural lines:

(1) the psalter as primer;
(2) the psalter in the daily rounds of the Divine Office;
(3) the psalter as ubiquitous, enduring *lectio*, including as the last words spoken, recited, or heard in life;
(4) the psalter or psalmody as catalyst for a miracle;
(5) reading and reciting the psalter as demonstration of discipline and asceticism;
(6) reading the psalter as private, interior devotion and a marker of individual piety and chastity.

In what follows, I provide representative examples from each group, though some references to the psalter or psalmody can easily fit more than one category.

That the Book of Psalms frequently functioned as a textbook is already well-known to historians, and this view is abundantly clear in the hagiographic tradition, as with the *Vita Mathildis posterior* (from 1002/1003), which depicts the young girl Mathilda of Saxony being sent to the convent of Herford for the express purposes of learning to read the psalter.[38] The two lives of Wiborada recount how the future anchorite Wiborada acquired basic literacy through learning the psalms.[39] Unlike modern-day primers, which are texts put aside once a child has mastered the content,

---

[37] For an excellent study on representation of female learning and literacy in a hagiography, see Virginia Blanton and Helene Scheck, "Leoba and the Iconography of Learning in the Lives of Anglo-Saxon Women Religious," in Virginia Blanton, Veronica O'Mara, and Patricia Stoop, eds., *Nuns' Literacies in Medieval Europe: The Kansas City Dialogue* (Turnhout: Brepols, 2015), 3–26.

[38] Sean Gilsdorf, trans., *Queenship and Sanctity: The "Lives" of Mathilda and the "Epitaph" of Adelheid* (Washington, DC: Catholic University of America Press, 2004), 90.

[39] Walter Berschin, ed., *Vitae Sanctae Wiboradae. Die ältesten Lebensbeschreibungen der heiligen Wiborada: Einleitung, kritische Edition und Übersetzung.* Mitteilungen zur vaterländischen Geschichte 51 (St. Gall: Historischer Verein des Kantons St. Gallen, 1983), 38–41, and 132–135.

the psalter remains a central text for life, both within the liturgy and without. In a very brief description of the life of the twelfth-century *conversa* Guda of Arnstein, the author encapsulates her anchoritic existence as listening "to the Divine Offices, intent on the Psalms and prayers."[40] For the fourteenth-century Dominican nun Margret Finkin of Töss, the psalter was her constant reader and companion, so that, from the time she had learned the psalter until the moment of her death, not a day passed when she did not recite the psalms.[41]

The importance of the psalter at the end of one's life is found in the ninth-century *vita* of Abbess Hathumoda of Gandersheim. As she approaches death, she and her community found great comfort in singing the songs of David – sometimes in unison, sometimes in a kind of "polyphonic" intermixture of different psalms, and sometimes in a kind of psalmodic troping through the combination of disparate verses:

> And now the body began to fail little by little, and yet Hathumoda's mind remained firmly fixed on heaven. She often sang along with us the same psalms, and often different ones, as well as certain verses from here and there in the Psalter, so linked to one another in conjoined order they could not be doubted to have been inspired to her holy mind by the same spirit through which they had been written. Between the psalmody and the prayers, the Lord was always in her mouth, Christ always in her heart, and unless she closed her eyes for a bit as if sleeping, she always either sang psalms or spoke about the salvation of her soul.[42]

The hagiographic utility of the psalter is frequently conveyed in miracle stories as well. In the *Vita Leobae*, when a certain sister Agatha was falsely accused of fornication and infanticide, her abbess, Leoba of Bischofsheim (d. ca. 782), directed the large community to recite the entire psalter with arms extended in the form of the cross. Through the nuns' aggregate chanting of the psalter, the falsely accused Agatha was proven innocent and the actual wrongdoers discovered.[43] According to the fourteenth-century *Sisterbook of*

---

[40] Jonathan R. Lyon, ed. and trans. *Noble Society: Five Lives from Twelfth-Century Germany* (Manchester: Manchester University Press, 2017), 238.

[41] Margarete Weinhandl, trans. [into modern German], *Deutsches Nonnenleben: Das Leben der Schwestern zu Töss und der Nonne von Engeltal Büchlein von der Gnaden Überlast* (Munich: O.C. Recht Verlag, 1921), 164.

[42] Frederick S. Paxton, trans., *Anchoress and Abbess in Ninth-Century Saxony: The "Lives" of Liutbirga of Wendhausen and Hathumoda of Gandersheim* (Washington, DC: The Catholic University of America Press, 2009), 137, and 136–140.

[43] C. H. Talbot, trans., *The Anglo-Saxon Missionaries in Germany, Being the Lives of SS. Willibrord, Boniface, Leoba and Lebuin, Together with the Hodoepericon of St. Willibald and a Selection from the Correspondence of St. Boniface* (London and New York: Sheed and Ward, 1954), 217–218.

Töss, Gertrud of Winterthur witnessed how, on Good Friday, while her convent recited the psalter, the figure of a wounded Christ appeared before each sister who read, and he uttered gently to each "With these prayers, my wounds are healed." Yet for those sisters who chose not to read or feigned reading, Gertrud saw how Christ neither stood before nor spoke to them. The episode concludes: "Then [Gertrud] understood, how beloved and worthy to him is [psalmodic] prayer in the community."[44]

Striking, too, is how holy women are described as adopting more ascetically demanding regimens of reading and chanting the psalter. Mathilda of Saxony increased her weekly obligation sevenfold when possible, while the Dominican Beli of Winterthur commonly read the entire psalter every day after the early mass.[45] Hildegard's first teacher, Jutta, intensified her own psalmodic practices not only in frequency but also through heightened physical exertion, thus:

> In the course of her rule of life, [Jutta] used to complete the entire Psalter every day, as well as daily reciting other additions for the living and dead, which could not be expected of anyone else. She sometimes added a second and the third Psalter, but never less than one, except when she was prevented by serious weaknesses. On occasion, she went through the entire Psalter standing in one place, adding a prostration between each verse, but she did this rarely because she had not enough strength for it. More often she went right through the Psalter while standing erect crouching on her knees. Sometimes she used to give herself to this work in bare feet even through the hardest and most pressing winters, so that for this labor she became afflicted by a serious debility.[46]

Finally, hagiographers often depict reading the psalter as a solitary act and one that signifies virtue and piety. Returning to the *Vita Mathildis posterior*, when word of Mathilda's goodness had reached the widowed Henry, duke of Saxony, he dispatched his son and noble vassals to observe her in the cloister that they might report back to him:

> After setting up camp in a field near the convent, a few men entered the chapel as if to pray. There they saw the maiden sitting with a psalter in her hand, demonstrating by her bearing and most honorable visage the full extent of her virtue.[47]

It is not then just her noble carriage and beauty that recommend Mathilda as a suitable bride but also her pious learning, denoted by her psalter.

---

[44] Weinhandl, trans., *Deutsches Nonnenleben*, 186–187 (translation mine).
[45] Gilsdorf, *Queenship and Sanctity*, 102 and Weinhandl, *Deutsches Nonnenleben*, 174–175.
[46] Silvas, *Jutta and Hildegard*, 72.
[47] *Vita Mathildis posterior* in Gilsdorf, *Queenship and Sanctity*, 92.

Mathilda marries Henry, and following his death in 936, she resides as a widow in Quedlinburg and Nordhausen, two *Stifte*, or female religious communities, that she had founded. In these years, she is presented deeply engaged in her psalter, "at times ... so engrossed in reading or chanting the psalms, she was unable to notice those who passed by."[48]

Vitae also commonly represent the Bible as standard reading. For instance, the unnamed *magistra* of Admont was reported to have been "thoroughly educated in sacred scripture,"[49] and Leoba of Bischofsheim read carefully "all the Books of the Old and New Testament and learned by heart all the commandments of God."[50] While the ubiquity of biblical reading is nearly on par with the Book of Psalms, hagiographers often make a subtle distinction in showing how their protagonists experienced these texts.

While reading the psalter in private is often connoted as an interior, intimate, quiet spiritual experience, an individual's reading of the Bible in contrast often shows an intensive study requiring robust exposition and interpretation to be ultimately shared with others. Hathumoda of Gandersheim is described thusly:

> She devoted herself zealously to the reading of Scripture ... In hearing, reading, and understanding scripture, almost no one at that time exhibited greater caution, a more lively sense, or a more healthy intellect. If she had to question something as is the custom, she covered minutely and fully all that touched on it, so that her questioning itself seemed to teach rather than to question.[51]

Hathumoda moved her examination of scriptures from the private sphere to her community. The *vita* explains that she goes one step further yet, as she sits with guests at mealtimes to discuss, probe, and teach Holy Writ.[52] Leoba's knowledge of scriptures was so thorough that she was dispatched to other convents as well as at court to discuss religious matters.[53] Already in the widely disseminated sixth-century *Dialogues* of Gregory the Great, a "vita" of Scholastica, the sister of Benedict of Nursia, shows the nun earnestly discussing theology with her brother in their annual meeting and through divine intervention she is able to prove to Benedict the virtue of such discourse.[54]

---

[48] Ibid., 112.   [49] Lyon, *Noble Society*, 158.
[50] Talbot, *Anglo-Saxon Missionaries in Germany*, 215.   [51] Paxton, *Anchoress and Abbess*, 126.
[52] Ibid, 127.   [53] Talbot, *Anglo-Saxon Missionaries in Germany*, 223.
[54] Book 2, chapter 23. Philip Woodward, Edmund G. Gardner, and George Francis Hill, trans., *The Dialogues of Saint Gregory, Surnamed the Great; Pope of Rome & the First of That Name. Divided into Four Books, Wherein He Entreateth of the Lives and Miracles of the Saints in Italy and of the Eternity of Men's Souls* (London: P.L. Warner, 1911).

Thus, the individual reading of scripture does not end there but moves to a more "public," that is, communal, space, where speaking, exegesis, and a kind of preaching take place. By contrast, private reading of the Psalms remains private. Mathilda utterly absorbed in her psalter has echoes in depictions of the Virgin Mary in Annunciation scenes. As recent scholarship has shown, in the Latin West beginning in the ninth century, Mary is presented as reading the psalter at the moment the archangel Gabriel announces that she is with child. The newer literary-iconographic representation – the so-called Reading Mary – takes hold first in the German lands and displaces an older tradition of Mary with spindle or weaving thread.[55] The new tradition of Mary reading specifically the psalter is traced to the mid-ninth century, as found in an ivory carving from Metz (ca. 860–870) and in an Old High German versified version of the Gospel of Pseudo-Matthew by Otfried of Weissenburg who describes Gabriel finding Mary "with her psalter in her hands, singing it through until the end."[56] Laura Saetveit Miles has argued that the depiction of Mary as reader, which first emerged in the late Carolingian period, corresponded with the contemporary religious reforms that "reemphasized exactly her model of solitary, studious prayer."[57] Miles connects these "explicit pictorial and textual references" to male monastic and clerical contexts specifically,[58] but contemporary hagiography of female saints shows that Mary engaging her psalter in quiet seclusion was a model for women religious as well.

In contradistinction to this iconographic tradition, representations of female religious with scripture or biblical books take on decidedly different forms. (Here, scriptures, Holy Writ, and the Bible refer to the New Testament together with the Old Testament *except* for the Book of Psalms, since hagiographers and other writers often treat this biblical book as separate from the rest of the Bible.) A chief attribute for abbesses in the medieval German iconographic tradition is the Gospel, with the abbess depicted holding the book in a frontal stance rather than in profile and meeting the viewer's gaze directly rather than reading or interrupted reading.[59] In a partially extant series of eleventh-century sculptural reliefs from St. Liudger in Werden, the *religiosae* are represented as dynamic discussants.[60] The women are paired: each holds

---

[55] Laura Saetveit Miles, "The Origins and Development of the Virgin Mary's Book at the Annunciation," *Speculum* 89 (2014): 632–669.
[56] Ibid., 643–646.   [57] Ibid., 668.   [58] Ibid., 634.
[59] Karen Blough, "*The Abbatial Effigies* at Quedlinburg: A Convent's Identity Reconfigured," *Gesta* 47, no. 2 (2008): 147–169.
[60] Karen Blough, "Implications for Female Monastic Literacy in the Reliefs from St. Liudger's at Werden," in Blanton, O'Mara, and Stoop, *Nuns' Literacies: The Kansas City Dialogue*, 151–169.

a book, the one inclined toward the other, hands held as deeply engaged in learned disquisition. While the books are generic visually and could intend biblical commentaries, sermons, and so on, the hagiographic tradition and rules for women's communities suggest that the most apt texts for communal interrogation would be the Bible. The iconographic traditions of women with psalter and scriptures, then, might be viewed as visual exempla instructing women religious on how to approach these two fundamental readings.

Besides the Book of Psalms and the Bible more generally, few other religious or theological texts are cited in the surveyed *vitae*. Knowledge of the *Regula Benedicti* or other rules is often implied but not necessarily stated explicitly. Occasionally other texts are mentioned as with the Dominican nun Anna of Klingnau, who spent her day enthusiastically reading the lives of saints and martyrs when not attending to her other duties.[61] Leoba of Bischofsheim was fully conversant in patristic writings, conciliar decrees, and ecclesiastical law,[62] while Mathilda of Saxony undertook the *Dialogues* of Gregory I with her close friend Ricburg, the abbess of Nordhausen.[63]

Several *vitae* identify the liberal arts as a component of the education of female religious. Leoba's training in the liberal arts served as a path "to attain a perfect knowledge of divine things so that through the combination of her reading with her quick intelligence, by natural gifts and hard work, she became extremely learned."[64] Mathilda of Saxony's schooling in literary studies prepared her for both a secular life at court and a contemplative one as conventual.[65] The late twelfth-century *Vita sanctae Cunegundis* describes how Empress Kunigunde saw to it that her niece Uta, the first abbess of Kaufungen, was educated in theological, liturgical, literary, and other secular disciplines, as was befitting the role of the head of a women's community.[66] Adelheid of Vilich's philosophical studies nurtured her "rational soul" and readied her for spiritual learning and pursuit of knowledge of God.[67] The unnamed prioress-teacher of Admont is described as "second to none in religious habits and the liberal arts too," and the characterization of her manner of speech (pleasing, well-ordered, temperate, instructive, informative) is indicative of one steeped in

---

[61] Weinhandl, *Deutsches Nonnenleben*, 170.
[62] Talbot, *Anglo-Saxon Missionaries in Germany*, 215.
[63] *Vita Mathildis posterior* in Gilsdorf, *Queenship and Sanctity*, 110.
[64] Talbot, *Anglo-Saxon Missionaries in Germany*, 215.
[65] *Vita Mathildis posterior* in Gilsdorf, *Queenship and Sanctity*, 110.
[66] *Vita s. Cunegundis*, ed. Georg Waitz, in *Monumenta Germaniae Historica* SS 4 (Hanover, 1841), here 823.
[67] Madelyn Bergen Dick, trans., *Mater Spiritualis: The Life of Adelheid of Vilich* (Toronto: Peregrina Publishing, 1995), 21.

grammar, rhetoric, and dialectic.[68] Furthermore, she put her liberal arts training to good use as she is noted for devoting time to dictating letters and writing prose and verse.[69] However, the importance of striking a balance between the love of (secular) learning and leading a spiritual life is noted in the early biography of Gertrude of Helfta, which characterizes her as devoted to the study of the liberal arts. Still, because of

> her excessive attachment to the secular studies . . . she had neglected to adapt the high point of her mind to the light of spiritual understanding. By attaching herself with such avid enjoyment of the pursuit of human wisdom, she was depriving herself of the sweet taste of true wisdom.[70]

Through divine revelation, Gertrude came to understand that her love of learning must be transformed to a desire to know God.

The *vitae* are sparing in details on how communities learned chant, including on aspects of aural learning, acquisition of basic modal theory, or reading notational scripts. Generalities are common as, for example, in the description of Liutbirga, who was reported to have taught girls "psalmody," a word that implies singing the psalms to specific modal recitation formulae but that might be understood more broadly as singing chant or monophonic liturgical song.[71] One particularly poignant description is found in the Dominican *St. Katharinental Sisterbook*. In one of the *vitae*, Katrin Brümsin, a novitiate, struggles with learning and literacy in general. One night, Katrin dreams that an unknown bishop was singing mass on the feast of John the Evangelist, and as the other sisters joined to sing the sequence *Verbum dei deo natum* (The word of God, born of God), Katrin did not. The bishop – who was in fact John the Evangelist – asked her why she refused to sing. Katrin explained that she was unable though she tried with all her heart. Taking her by the hand, the Evangelist placed her before a large chant book open to the golden lettering of the sequence *Verbum dei deo natum* and said gently, "this you should pray to me."[72] Miraculously she sang the entire chant – all twenty-four verses, as the *vita* stresses. When Katrin awoke from her dream, she exclaimed to a fellow novitiate that she had learned the sequence by heart. Doubting her, the sister told her to sing it, and

---

[68] Lyon, *Noble Society*, 156.   [69] Ibid., 159.

[70] Gertrude of Helfta, *The Herald of Divine Love*, trans. Margaret Winkworth (New York: Paulist Press, 1991), 53.

[71] Paxton, *Anchoress and Abbess*, 116.

[72] Ruth Meyer, *Das "St. Katharinentaler Schwesternbuch": Untersuchung, Edition, Kommentar* (Tübingen: Niemeyer, 1995), 124.

Katrin demonstrated that indeed the saint had taught her well. According to the *vita*, from then on Katrin not only possessed the ability to learn chant but flourished in her other studies. Showing a far less gentle approach, Adelheid of Vilich did not refrain from scolding sisters who sang poorly, even boxing the ears of one sister who chanted out of tune. The *vita* reports, however, that this physical inducement brought forth improvement, for, miraculously, the girl sang with a beautiful voice ever after.[73]

Writing – either as copying text or as text composition and compilation – gets occasional mention in the *vitae*. Margret Finkin was eager to learn to read and write Latin,[74] and the anchorite Wilbirg is described as not only reading and receiving letters from her friends but also writing and sending her own.[75] The *Vita Mathildis virginis* recounts how Mechthild of Diessen worked diligently as a scribe, yet at the moment the bells signaled the start of the Office, she did not hesitate to lay down her quill – even stopping mid letter.[76] On the other hand, when Gertrude of Helfta halted scribal work to attend Mass, John the Evangelist appeared to her, telling her to resume her work. In return, she gained special understanding of the meaning of chant as she combined scribal activities while listening to the liturgy at a distance.[77]

In addition to copying texts, book production and parchment preparation are thematized in the *Life of Mechthild of Diessen*. The author, in a rather grim episode, describes how an unnamed sister in the community suffered a horrible scribal calamity. Though the sister was an experienced scribe, once, while pricking the parchment for ruling, she gouged her eye with an awl. Had it not been for the miraculous intervention of Mechthild, this unnamed *scriptrix* would have lost her eye.[78] Not all book makers met with disasters in the scriptorium: in the tradition of the sister-books, Dominican sisters are remembered, blessed, and lauded for

[73] Dick, *Mater Spiritualis*, 29/31.   [74] Weinhandl, *Deutsches Nonnenleben*, 165.
[75] Lukas Sainitzer, ed. and trans., *Die Vita Wilbirgis des Einwik Weizlan* (Linz: Oberösterreichisches Landesarchiv, 1999), 238 and 345.
[76] Lyon, *Noble Society*, 174.
[77] Gertrude of Helfta, *Le Héraut, (Livre IV) in Œuvres spirituelles*, ed. J.-M. Clément, 5 vols. (Paris: Editions du Cerf, 1968–1986), 4:286–288. For an English translation of the relevant passage and discussion of this episode, see Felix Heinzer, "Explaining the Bread of True Intelligence: John the Evangelist as Mystagogue in the Sequence *Verbum dei deo natum*," in Jeffrey F. Hamburger, ed., *Leaves from Paradise: The Cult of John at the Dominican Convent Paradies bei Soest* (Cambridge, MA: Harvard University Press, 2008), 93–95.
[78] Lyon, *Noble Society*, 210–211.

their skills as copyists, notators, painters, and decorators of beautiful codices.[79]

Record-keeping is mentioned in the *vitae* of Mathilda of Saxony who bequeathed to her granddaughter Mathilda, future abbess of Quedlinburg, a necrology. The elder Mathilda had maintained this list of obituary notices of kin and community for memorial purposes, and, on her death bed, she turned over the duty of entering the obits to her namesake.[80] Other types of writing are noted as well. The unnamed *magistra* of Admont dictated letters,[81] while Gertrude of Helfta compiled several volumes of sayings of the saints.[82] The various contributors to the *Legatus* note their admiration for Gertrude's works, particularly the eloquence of her written prayers, spiritual exercises, and biblical exegesis.[83] According to the *Sisterbook of Töss*, the Dominican Willi of Constance authored a beautiful book of religious materials, while Mechthilt of Wangen, who neither knew Latin nor how to write, was wondrously able to write four passion accounts in German – with her own hand.[84]

Manifestations of literacy and learning in the hagiography are also reported through the descriptions of ideal teachers and learners. Teachers are exemplified as alert, tireless, selfless, generous, and are shown often balancing tenderness, moderation, rewards, and practical discipline. Mathilda listened to her students read aloud, corrected them, and quizzed them on their memorization of texts.[85] Leoba had girls read scripture at her bedside, and though she appeared as if asleep, she was able to recognize mistakes and prompt them if they skipped a word or dropped a syllable.[86] She also urged her pupils "to vie with one that they might achieve perfection."[87] The unnamed *magistra* of Admont, "full of charity and love" toward her nuns, responded to the educational interests, and when they requested to be taught prose and verse, she prepared lessons on wax tablets the night before.[88]

For the model female pupil, two themes emerge: displaying a maturity beyond her years and an eager, industrious disposition. In Guibert's letter to Bovo, Jutta is described as possessing already at a young age a "maturity

[79] Jeanne Ancelet-Hustache, ed., "*Les vitae sororum d'Unterlinden*. Edition critique du manuscrit 508 de la Biblioteque de Colmar," in *Archives d'Histoire Doctrinale et Litteraire du Moyen Age* 5:431; Weinhandl, *Deutsches Nonnenleben*, 181; Lewis, *By Women, for Women, about Women*, 272–277; and Garber, *Feminine Figurae*, 71.

[80] Gilsdorf, *Queenship and Sanctity*, 85–86 and 125.   [81] Lyon, *Noble Society*, 158.

[82] Gertrude of Helfta, *Herald of Divine Love*, 53.   [83] Ibid., 53.

[84] Weinhandl, *Deutsches Nonnenleben*, 185; Meyer, *St. Katharinentaler Schwesternbuch*, 122, 252.

[85] Gilsdorf, *Queenship and Sanctity*, 113.   [86] Talbot, *Anglo-Saxon Missionaries in Germany*, 215.

[87] Ibid., 223.   [88] Lyon, *Noble Society*, 158–159.

of mind."[89] Rejecting material wealth and youthful fancies in favor of learning are common manifestations of such maturity, as in the case of Wiborada who renounced worldly possessions and comforts and shunned children's games and ditties so that she might attend daily masses and learn to read.[90] One does find the occasional exception to the keen learner: Anne of Ramschwag, for instance, disliked learning and avoided books. However, once during a reading lesson, when her teacher opened up a book, Anne saw inside the book the Christ child lying vulnerable, tiny, and unclothed. He spoke to her encouragingly, and from then on, Anne approached her studies wholeheartedly and eagerly learned what was demanded of her.[91] Yet it is far more common for accounts of saintly women to describe their subjects as naturally diligent pupils. As a girl, Mathilda distinguished herself as someone who "excelled mightily in every endeavor, upright beyond her tender years, assiduous both in her study of letters and in her handiwork."[92] Hathumoda perfectly combined the ideal traits:

> The jokes and games, however harmless, that are familiar to children her age, she derided as vain, and scorned as good for nothing. The gold and precious baubles, which children however innocently desire as being pretty, she desired not at all, and did not wish to have ... And letters, which others have to be compelled to learn, even by whippings, she begged for with willing zeal and mastered through tireless study.[93]

These examples stand in stark contrast to Hildegard, who minimizes formal learning and its usefulness. Yet not all mystics found earthly training at odds with divine encounters. Gertrude of Helfta enjoyed a formal education, and indeed, her love of learning as a child dominates the first chapter of book 1 of *The Herald of Divine Love*:

> Even at this tender age, she already possessed the wisdom of the mature person. She was so amiable, clever, and eloquent, and so docile that she was admired by all who heard her. As soon as she was admitted to school, she showed such quickness and intelligence that she soon far surpassed in learning and knowledge all the children of her own age and all her other companions as well. Gladly and eagerly she gave herself to the study of the liberal arts.[94]

For Gertrude, as long as her pursuit of knowledge was regarded as a path to greater spiritual understanding, the broad curriculum of her education

---

[89] Silvas, *Jutta and Hildegard*, 104.　　[90] Berschin, *Vitae Sanctae Wiboradae*, 32–41, and 128–133.
[91] Meyer, *St. Katharinentaler Schwesternbuch*, 128–129.　　[92] Gilsdorf, *Queenship and Sanctity*, 92.
[93] Paxton, *Anchoress and Abbess*, 121.　　[94] Gertrude of Helfta, *Herald of Divine Love*, 52.

was not viewed as an impediment to the divine visions that accompanied her through life.

The Evidence of Libraries, Books, and Texts from Women's Communities

Arguably the best, most direct evidence demonstrating literacy and learning of female religious is located in their books. Thus, historians find it instructive to consider the library holdings once conserved in their communities; to inspect closely individual texts that they read and with which they interacted; and to look at the volumes they favored, collected, commissioned, donated, copied, and authored. Since the late 1990s, numerous scholars have produced full-length studies investigating the education and erudition evinced in women's houses in medieval Germany. Katrinette Bodarwé's comprehensive examination of literary witnesses from Gandersheim, Essen, and Quedlinburg provides a window into traditions of learning in these three communities from roughly 850 to 1100.[95] New perspectives on intellectual culture of female religious during the long twelfth century are found in Alison I. Beach's *Women As Scribes*, Fiona Griffith's *Garden of Delights*, and *Listen, Daughter*, a collection of essays on the *Speculum virginum*, edited by Constant J. Mews.[96] Broader in scope is D. H. Green's immensely helpful overview of female literacy for the entire medieval period, with special attention given to the German lands as well as England and France.[97] Monographs by Marie-Luise Ehrenschwendtner and Eva Schlotheuber, respectively, present different approaches to learning among German women connected to the new religious orders of the central and late Middle Ages.[98] The multiauthored study of Paradies bei Soest undertakes through a series of carefully coordinated essays a thorough investigation of intellectual culture in evidence at this

---

[95] See Katrinette Bodarwé, *Sanctimoniales litteratae. Schriftlichkeit und Bildung in den ottonischen Frauenkommunitäten Gandersheim, Essen und Quedlinburg*, Quellen und Forschungen 10 (Münster: Aschendorff, 2004).

[96] Beach, *Women As Scribes*; Fiona Griffiths, *The Garden of Delights: Reform and Renaissance for Women in the Twelfth Century* (Philadelphia: University of Pennsylvania Press, 2007); and Constant J. Mews, ed. *Listen, Daughter: The "Speculum Virginum" and the Formation of Religious Women in the Middle Ages* (New York: Palgrave, 2001).

[97] D. H. Green, *Women Readers in the Middle Ages* (Cambridge: Cambridge University Press, 2007).

[98] Marie-Luise Ehrenschwendtner, *Die Bildung der Dominikanerinnen in Süddeutschland vom 13. bis 15. Jahrhundert* (Stuttgart: Franz Steiner Verlag, 2004); and Eva Schlotheuber, *Klostereintritt und Bildung. Die Lebenswelt der Nonnen im späten Mittelalter. Mit einer Edition des "Konventstagebuchs" einer Zisterzienserin von Heilig-Kreuz bei Braunschweig (1484–1507)* (Tübingen: Mohr Siebeck, 2004).

Westphalian Dominican convent, particularly as manifested in several of its liturgical books.[99] Finally, the three-volume series entitled *Nuns' Literacies in Medieval Europe* presents collectively more than fifty individual essays examining how women read, wrote, scribed, and illustrated texts in both Latin and vernacular languages.[100] This massive project – representing the work of some four dozen authors – signals a historiographical shift in scholarship on learning among women religious; more than a quarter of the essays consider examples from the German-speaking areas and collectively cover the entire Middle Ages.

During the late Carolingian, Ottonian, and Salian periods, numerous female houses throughout the German lands fostered education among their members. Indeed, many of these places boasted a thriving intellectual culture. That erudition flourished in the more elite communities was no doubt facilitated by their status as imperial *Stifte*, which served as homes for daughters, granddaughters, sisters, nieces, and widows of high-ranking nobility. As Helene Scheck puts it, "[by] virtue of their class, royal women of Carolingian Francia and Ottonian Saxony enjoyed the same privilege, even duty, of becoming educated as their male counterparts."[101]

The reconstructed book holdings of the *Stifte* at Gandersheim, Essen, and Quedlinburg reveal a range of texts available to the sisters.[102] Unsurprisingly, psalters, bibles, and pericopes are ubiquitous as are complementary books of commentaries, sermons, and glosses. Also ever-present in these collections are books supporting the *opus dei*, including a variety of chant books and other liturgical and devotional sources (e.g. sacramentaries, prayer books, calendars, and saints' lives). Beyond writings connected to scripture, liturgy, and formation, texts attached to the study of the liberal arts, philosophy, and theology are found. Thus, the reconstructed libraries reveal the presence of an array of texts by patristic and early medieval Christian authors (e.g. Prudentius, Jerome, Sulpicius Severus, Augustine, Cassiodorus, Gregory, and Bede), more contemporary authors (e.g. Paul the Deacon, Alcuin, Smaragdus of Saint-Mihiel, Haimo of Auxerre, Hrabanus Maurus, and

---

[99] Jeffrey F. Hamburger, Eva Schlotheuber, Susan Marti, and Margot E. Fassler, *Liturgical Life and Latin Learning at Paradies bei Soest, 1300–1425: Inscription and Illumination in the Choir Books of a North German Dominican Convent*, 2 vols. (Münster: Aschendorff Verlag and National Museum of Women in the Arts, 2016).

[100] Virginia Blanton, Veronica O'Mara, and Patricia Stoop, eds., *Nuns' Literacies in Medieval Europe: The Hull Dialogue* (Turnhout: Brepols, 2013); *Nuns' Literacies: The Kansas City Dialogue* (2015); and *Nuns' Literacies in Medieval Europe: The Antwerp Dialogue* (Turnhout: Brepols, 2017).

[101] Helene Scheck, "Reading Women at the Margins of Quedlinburg Codex 74," in Blanton, O'Mara, and Stoop, *Nuns' Literacies: The Hull Dialogue*, 3.

[102] Bodarwé, *Sanctimoniales litteratae*.

Liutprand of Cremona), as well as by classical and secular writers (e.g. Terrence, Virgil, Flavius Josephus, Boethius, and Priscian).

Library holdings offer a bird's-eye view of learning, but the existence alone of a text is not proof of its reception either communally or individually, and examination of sources for indications of their use is important. Helene Scheck catalogues types of reader marks, annotations, marginalia, glosses, and corrections found in a Carolingian copy of Jerome's *Epistulae* once held at St. Servatius in Quedlinburg.[103] Her analysis reveals that the canonesses not only leafed through this codex over several generations but also responded to, revised, and interacted with the particular letters for more than five centuries. The source's physical traces and additions are witness to "the reading practices, level of competence, and intellectual interests of its royal female monastic audiences from the eighth century onwards."[104]

Gandersheim, Essen, and Quedlinburg testify to the high level of education among its inhabitants, but other early medieval communities also served as important sites of learning for German women religious. The Regensburg *Stifte* of Obermünster and Niedermünster are special in their possession of early examples of feminized versions of the *Regula Benedicti*.[105] In a late tenth-century copy from Niedermünster, the feminized version of the rule of Benedict was bound with a copy of Caesarius of Arles's *Regula ad virgines*, and the two rules were provided with four full-page miniatures. One image depicts the then abbess holding a book as her sign of authority, while another illustration presents Caesarius pointing to the opening words of his rule as two sisters look on.[106] Both illustrations reinforce the underlying mission of reading and understanding Latin as central to the community. Another book once belonging to Niedermünster is the extraordinary "Uta Codex" (ca. 1025). Adam Cohen characterizes this luxury evangeliary as "representative of female intellectual and spiritual life," calling attention to ways in which the book engages a range of competencies and levels of its readers, even drawing the *trivium* and *quadrivium* of the liberal arts into its program of education and inculcation.[107]

---

[103] Scheck, "Reading Women at the Margins," 3–18.   [104] Ibid., 8.

[105] See Katrinette Bodarwé, "Eine Männerregel für Frauen. Die Adaption der Benediktsregel im 9. und 10. Jahrhundert," in Anne Müller and Gert Melville, eds., *Female "vita religiosa" between Late Antiquity and the High Middle Ages: Structures, Developments and Spatial Contexts* (Münster: LIT Verlag, 2011), 235–274, esp. 264–268, and Adam S. Cohen, "The Art of Reform in a Bavarian Nunnery around 1000," *Speculum* 74 (1999): 990–1020.

[106] Folios 58v (Abbess Uta) and 65r (Caesarius and two women). Digitized images of the complete manuscript are available online: https://nbn-resolving.org/urn:nbn:de:bvb:22-dtl-0000024890.

[107] Adam Cohen, *The Uta Codex: Art, Philosophy and Reform in Eleventh-Century Germany* (University Park: Pennsylvania State University Press, 2000), here 3, more generally, 1–23.

After 1100, a pronounced interest in more contemporary authors mark the literary pursuits cultivated in numerous female houses. Preferences for late eleventh- and twelfth-century discourses on monastic renewal, church reform, and the *cura monialium* are especially manifest in newly founded convents and reformed monasteries.[108] Beach has explored the makeup of the twelfth-century libraries at Wessobrunn, Admont, and Schäftlarn,[109] while Julie Hotchin has done the same for Lippoldsberg and Lamspringe.[110] A common feature in their reconstructions shows that the women were acquiring not only patristic and early medieval texts but also more recent ones, including works by Anselm of Canterbury, Bruno of Segni, Rupert of Deutz, Honorius Augustodunensis, Hugh of St. Victor, and Bernard of Clairvaux. In some cases, Beach and Hotchin argue, these updated collections put the Benedictine nuns in conversation with the intellectual debates connected to reform movements and the enacting of pastoral care in dual-sex communities.[111]

Case studies on individual manuscripts demonstrate ways in which German women religious found purchase in the wider intellectual culture of ecclesiastical and monastic reforms. For instance, the Admont nuns' copy of Anselm's *Orationes sive meditationes* (Book of Prayers and Meditations) – a manuscript likely made by nuns (or canonesses) in Salzburg – shows originality in the ways in which the scribes, artists, and notators reworked the text by incorporating images with chant fragments into the mise-en-page.[112] Michael Curschmann describes the resulting program in Anselm's book of prayers as "remarkable for its intellectual ambition, its artistic execution, and its demand on the viewer."[113] Curschmann continues, "these prayers had been designated by their author as private and non-liturgical. And yet, their ultimate recipients found a way

---

[108] See Susann El Kholi, *Lektüre in Frauenkonventen des ostfränkisch-deutschen Reiches vom 8. Jahrhundert bis zur Mitte des 13. Jahrhunderts* (Würzburg: Königshausen & Neumann, 1997).

[109] Beach, *Women As Scribes*.

[110] Julie Hotchin, "Women's Reading and Monastic Reform in Twelfth-Century Germany: The Library of the Nuns of Lippoldsberg," in Alison I. Beach, ed., *Manuscripts and Monastic Culture: Reform and Renewal in Twelfth-Century Germany* (Turnhout: Brepols, 2007), 139–189.

[111] Beach, *Women As Scribes*, esp. 79–83, 105–106, 131–133; Hotchin, "Women's Reading and Monastic Reform," 152, 160–163.

[112] Rachel Fulton, "Praying with Anselm at Admont: A Meditation on Practice," *Speculum* 81 (2006): 700–733; Michael Curschmann, "Anselm von Canterbury im Frauenkloster: Text, Bild, Paratext und Musik in einer Handschrift *Orationes sive meditationes* (Admont 289)," *Wolfram-Studien* 23 (2012): 79–130; and Michael Curschmann, "Integrating Anselm: Pictures and the Liturgy in a Twelfth-Century Manuscript of the 'Orationes sive Meditationes,'" in Susan Boynton and Diane Reilly, eds., *Resounding Images: Medieval Intersections of Art, Music and Sound* (Turnhout: Brepols, 2015), 295–312.

[113] Curschmann, "Integrating Anselm," 309.

of assimilating the collection into their own way of life and habits of ritual."[114]

The Admont *Orationes* is an example of a text reworked by nuns, for nuns, but twelfth-century texts were also composed specifically for female religious. The *Speculum virginum* (Mirror for Virgins), an imagined dialogue between Theodora, a nun, and her male spiritual mentor, Peregrinus, is one such case.[115] A didactic text written in the first half of the twelfth century, it focuses on a nun's formation, emphasizing the spiritual value of virginity and enclosure to her vocation. While the *Speculum* may have functioned as a guidebook for monks and confessors serving female communities, the accompanying illustrations and music in the earliest manuscript tradition suggest that nuns also engaged the text more directly.[116] Furthermore, through the exemplum of Theodora, it presents a learned nun fully conversant in scripture and models spiritual and intellectual inquiry for *religiosae*.[117] The lavishly illuminated florilegia *Hortus deliciarum* (Garden of Delights) is another text written for a female audience. This late twelfth-century work – comprised of preexisting theological writings, biblical history, canon law, poetry, and music – was assembled, amplified, and glossed by Herrad of Hohenbourg, with nearly 350 individual images. The fundamental purpose of the *Hortus* was to educate women of the Augustinian community of Hohenbourg. The wide range of materials Herrad culled from included contemporary writings of Rupert of Deutz, Honorius Augustodunensis, Peter Lombard, and Peter Comestor. As a text for women, the *Hortus deliciarum* is a fascinating counterpoint to the slightly older *Speculum virginum*. The latter, transmitted in several dozen sources, apparently served as an aid for male clerics caring for nuns pastorally, and the stylized dialogue reinforced the male–female hierarchy of teacher–pupil. By contrast, the encyclopedic nature of *Hortus deliciarum* with its emphasis on pedagogy and synthesis reduced the Augustinian canonesses' dependency on a *magister*, as it reassigned the responsibilities of teaching to Hohenbourg's *magistrae*.[118]

Scribal contributions of nuns, canonesses, and recluses are another manifestation of intellectual culture in their communities. The twelfth

---

[114] Ibid.   [115] See the various essays in Mews, *Listen, Daughter*.

[116] Morgan Powell, "The *Speculum virginum* and the Audio-Visual Poetics of Women's Religious Instruction," in Mews, *Listen, Daughter*, 111–135; and Catherine Jeffreys, "Listen, Daughters of the Light: The *Epithalalium* and Musical Innovation in Twelfth-Century Germany," in Mews, *Listen, Daughter*, 137–57.

[117] Sabina Flanagan, "The *Speculum virginum* and Traditions of Medieval Dialogue," in Mews, *Listen, Daughter*, 181–200, here esp. 189–194.

[118] Griffiths, *Garden of Delights*, 3.

and thirteenth centuries are marked by a greater pool of evidence attesting to the scribal activities of women religious in the German lands. Certainly, female scribes existed before 1100, but securing the identity, provenance, and context has posed problems for historians. Beach has succeeded in locating numerous female scribes in twelfth-century sources, typically relying on a combination of paleographic analysis, identification of names in colophons and necrologies, and other testimonies.[119] Various scholars have shown that women scribes supplied books for their own communities as well as for other male and female communities. Indeed, scribal work emerges as a significant and even an honorable vocation for women religious during the central and late Middle Ages, and activities included not only copying texts but also illuminating, rubricating, notating, binding, and at times coordinating with male scribes or with scribes from other women's communities.[120]

Scribes did not always act as passive copyists; rather at times they exercised agency as editors and coauthors, engaging with and shaping the content of the final products. Evidence from twelfth-century Admont suggests a collaborative process by which nun-scribes not only took down biblical commentaries, expositions, and sermons dictated and preached by Abbot Irimbert but also practiced a certain degree of autonomy for editing final written versions.[121] Other examples of nuns and sisters determining texts and content as compilers and copyists have been detected in later sermon collections.[122]

In late medieval Germany, conditions for the culture of learning and reading changed with regard to contemporary views on Latin literacy in women's communities. Scholars offer different perspectives on the nature and extent of Latin education in women's communities. Ehrenschwendtner points out the limited use of Latin in Dominican convents of southern Germany, providing evidence that only basic linguistic competence was required for reading the Bible and performing the liturgy.[123] Gone is institutional support (at least officially) for traditional Latin-based study of

---

[119] Beach, *Women As Scribes*; and Alison I. Beach, "'Mathild de Niphin' and the Female Scribes of Twelfth-Century Zwiefalten," in Blanton, O'Mara, and Stoop, *Nuns' Literacies: The Hull Dialogue*, 33–50.

[120] For a general overview, see Cynthia J. Cyrus, *The Scribes for Women's Convents in Late Medieval Germany* (Toronto: University of Toronto Press, 2009).

[121] Beach, *Women As Scribes*, 72–88.

[122] See Regina Dorothea Schiewer, "Books in Texts – Texts in Books: The St. Georgener Predigten as an Example of Nuns' Literacy in Late Medieval Germany," in Blanton, O'Mara, and Stoop, *Nuns' Literacies: The Hull Dialogue*, 223–237.

[123] Ehrenschwendtner, *Die Bildung der Dominikanerinnen*, 78–82.

grammar, the other liberal arts, history, and philosophy, and indeed, novitiates were expected to have received a rudimentary education in reading and music (specifically solmization) before entering the convent.[124] Nevertheless, a wider range of vernacular religious literature flourished in these convents,[125] with some convents boasting large collections of German-language books.[126] Moreover, sisters served as scribes to supply their own collections and as librarians to organize and oversee holdings.[127]

In her study of the northern German convents, Schlotheuber, on the other hand, shows that knowledge of Latin in several convents was considerable.[128] In *Liturgical Life and Latin Learning*, Schlotheuber discusses the modern historiography in greater detail.[129] She and her coauthors demonstrate that the Dominican sisters of Paradies bei Soest must have had extensive literary resources available to them and that their command of Latin must have been quite advanced for them to have produced such elaborate and complex liturgical books.[130]

Prayer books and other devotional texts from northern German convents in the Lüneburg-Heath suggest that some communities operated in a literary-linguistic continuum.[131] Books written contemporaneously in the same scriptorium show a range of employment of language: Latin only, Low German only, or a combination of the two. Collectively these manuscripts point to a range of linguistic levels geared toward the abilities of individual readers, on the one hand, and aimed at facilitating greater Latin comprehension, on the other. It also reveals the learnedness of their creators who skillfully compiled, copied, and translated preexisting materials, while amplifying and connecting with newly composed texts.

---

[124] Ibid., 77–119.
[125] The scholarship on German literature for late medieval women religious is vast; see, for example: Johanna Thali, *Beten – Schreiben – Lesen: literarisches Leben und Marienspiritualität im Kloster Engelthal* (Tübingen: A. Francke, 2003); and Antje Willing, *Literatur und Ordensreform im 15. Jahrhundert. Deutsche Abendmahlsschriften im Nürnberger Katharinenkloster* (Münster: Waxmann, 2004).
[126] Antje Willing, *Die Bibliothek des Klosters St. Katharina zu Nürnberg: Synoptische Darstellung der Bücherverzeichnisse*, 2 vols. (Berlin: Akademie Verlag, 2012), esp. xi–xviii.
[127] Ehrenschwendtner, *Die Bildung der Dominikanerinnen*, 287–289, 302–307.
[128] Schlotheuber, *Klostereintritt und Bildung.*
[129] Schlotheuber, "Chapter 3: Intellectual Horizons," in Hamburger et al., *Liturgical Life and Latin Learning at Paradies*, 43–90.
[130] Hamburger, Schlotheuber, Marti, and Fassler, *Liturgical Life and Latin Learning at Paradies bei Soest.*
[131] Henrike Lähnemann, "Bilingual Devotion: The Relationship of Latin and Low German in Prayer Books from the Lüneburg Convents," in Elizabeth Andersen, Henrike Lähnemann, and Anne Simon, eds., *A Companion to Mysticism and Devotion in Northern Germany in the Late Middle Ages* (Leiden: Brill, 2013), 317–341.

Female authorship is found among German *religiosae* of the entire Middle Ages. Hildegard is, of course, the most celebrated writer today, but other marquee names exist as well: Hrotsvit of Gandersheim, Elisabeth of Schönau, Mechthild of Hackeborn, and Gertrude of Helfta. Texts of lesser known and anonymous female authors have come down to us as well. Especially well represented from the German lands are female hagiographers such as Hugeburc of Heidenheim (*Hodoeporicon/Vita Willibaldi* and *Vita Wynnebaldi*, ca. 778/779), Hrotsvit (*Book of Sacred Stories*, ca. 962), Bertha of Vilich (*Vita Adelheidis*, ca. 1056/1057), and Gerdruot of Admont (*Vita cuiusdam magistrae monialium Admuntensium*, ca. 1170).[132] Female authorship has been argued for the anonymous *Vita Mathildis anterior* (ca. 973/974) and the *Vita Mathildis posterior* (ca. 1002/1003).[133] The tradition of sacred biographies finds a new form in the fourteenth-century sister-books tradition. These compilations of short biographies of Dominican nuns were authored by women from the same communities – some in Latin, most in the vernacular, and sometimes as the work of an individual, sometimes as collaborative or corporate enterprise.[134] Evidence for correspondence has survived too, the style, content, and tone of which range from official, formal, and pragmatic to letters of a more personal and intimate nature.[135] Finally, the musical literacy required for the *opus dei* emerges in extant manuscripts pointing to women religious composing music and managing and choreographing the details of the liturgy for their particular community.[136]

---

[132] For a recent review of Hugeburc, see Pauline Head, "Who Is the Nun from Heidenheim? A Study of Hugeburc's 'Vita Willibaldi,'" *Medium Ævum* 71, no. 1 (2002): 29–46. For a discussion of legends and passions, see Stephen L. Wailes, "The Sacred Stories in Verse," in Phyllis R. Brown and Stephen L. Wailes, ed., *A Companion to Hrotsvit of Gandersheim (fl. 960): Contextual and Interpretive Approaches* (Leiden: Brill, 2013), 85–120. For information on Bertha of Vilich and Gerdruot of Admont, see Dick, *Mater Spiritualis*, 15–19, 94–100, and Lyon, *Noble Society*, 152–153, respectively.

[133] Gilsdorf, *Queenship and Sanctity*, 15–21.

[134] Lewis, *By Women, for Women, about Women*, Garber, *Feminine Figurae*, and Anne Winston-Allen, *Convent Chronicles: Women Writing about Women and Reform in the Late Middle Ages* (University Park, PA: Pennsylvania State University Press, 2004).

[135] Alison I. Beach, "Voices from a Distant Land: Fragments of a Twelfth-Century Nuns' Letter Collection," *Speculum* 77 (2002): 34–54; Eva Schlotheuber, "Daily Life, Amor Dei, and Politics in the Letters of the Benedictine Nuns of Lüne in the Fifteenth and Sixteenth Centuries," in Blanton, O'Mara, and Stoop, *Nuns' Literacies: The Kansas City Dialogue*, 249–267; Antje Willing, "Das sogennante Schwesternbuch aus St. Katharina in St. Gallen: Konzeption und Intention," in Antje Willing, ed., *Das "Konventsbuch" und das "Schwesternbuch" aus St. Katharina in St Gallen* (Berlin: Erich Schmidt Verlag, 2016), 113–132.

[136] For example, Lori Kruckenberg, "Music for John the Evangelist: Virtue and Virtuosity at Paradies," in Hamburger, *Leaves from Paradise*, 152–155; and Alison Noel Altstatt, "The Music and Liturgy of Kloster Preetz: Anna von Buchwald's *Buch im Chor* in Its Fifteenth-century Context" (PhD diss., University of Oregon, 2011), 14–180.

To conclude, literacy and learning of female religious in the medieval German lands are well documented. The rules of their communities supported Latin literacy on a fundamental level, allowing them to fulfill their sacred duties. Saints' lives presenting German women religious reinforced the importance of education to meet their spiritual obligations; indeed, many of these hagiographic examples model learning exceeding the basics, and permitting deeper erudition in the pursuit of divine knowledge. Finally, the books acquired, commissioned, copied, and read by *religiosae* together with the texts they compiled and authored show a rich and dynamic tradition of learning and literacy.

For Hildegard, while we have no inventories of books that she had access to nor record of the library at Rupertsberg, this investigation of rules, of hagiographies of other women religious, and of literary practices at other female institutions in medieval Germany suggests that her demonstrated knowledge of a wide range of literature was not unusual for a professed nun of noble birth, living in a time and place marked by reform and spiritual renewal. What makes Hildegard remarkable is how she mobilized that knowledge to produce a prodigious collection of writings, even as she distanced herself from claims to the normal paths to learning and literacy common to her milieu.

Further Reading

Latin Editions and English Translations

Lyon, Jonathan Reed, ed. and trans. *Noble Society: Five Lives from Twelfth-Century Germany.* Manchester Medieval Sources. Manchester: Manchester University Press, 2017.

McCarthy, Maria Caritas, trans. *The Rule for Nuns of St. Caesarius of Arles: A Translation with a Critical Introduction in Studies in Mediaeval History.* Washington, DC: Catholic University of America Press, 1960.

Silvas, Anna, ed. and trans. *Jutta and Hildegard: The Biographical Sources.* University Park, PA: Pennsylvania State University Press, 1999.

Vita sanctae Hildegardis, ed. Monika Klaes. Corpus Christianorum Continuatio Mediaevalis 126. Turnhout: Brepols, 1993.

Secondary Literature

Beach, Alison I., ed. *Manuscripts and Monastic Culture: Reform and Renewal in Twelfth-Century Germany.* Turnhout: Brepols, 2007.

Beach, Alison I. *Women As Scribes: Book Production and Monastic Reform in Twelfth-Century Bavaria.* Cambridge and New York: Cambridge University Press, 2004.

Blanton, Virginia and Helene Scheck. "Leoba and the Iconography of Learning in the Lives of Anglo-Saxon Women Religious." In Virginia Blanton, Veronica O'Mara, and Patricia Stoop, eds., *Nuns' Literacies in Medieval Europe: The Kansas City Dialogue.* Turnhout: Brepols, 2015, 3–26.

Ferrante, Joan. "'Scribe quae vidis et audis': Hildegard, Her Language, and Her Secretaries." In David Townsend and Andrew Taylor, eds. *The Tongue of the Fathers: Gender and Ideology in Twelfth-Century Latin.* Philadelphia: University of Pennsylvania Press, 1998, 102–135.

Garber, Rebecca L. R. *Feminine Figurae: Representations of Gender in Religious Texts by Medieval German Women Writers, 1100–1375.* New York: Routledge, 2003.

Griffiths, Fiona. *The Garden of Delights: Reform and Renaissance for Women in the Twelfth Century.* Philadelphia: University of Pennsylvania Press, 2007.

Mews, Constant J., ed. *Listen, Daughter: The "Speculum Virginum" and the Formation of Religious Women in the Middle Ages.* New York: Palgrave, 2001.

Stover, Justin A. "Hildegard, the Schools, and Their Critics." In Beverly Mayne Kienzle, Debra L. Stoudt, and George Ferzoco, eds., *A Companion to Hildegard of Bingen,* Leiden: Brill, 2014, 109–137.

Vanderputten, Steven. *Dark Age Nunneries: The Ambiguous Identity of Female Monasticism, 800–1050.* Ithaca, NY: Cornell University Press, 2018.

PART II

Writings and Reputation

CHAPTER 4

Hildegard of Bingen's Theology

James Ginther

The common perception of Hildegard as a theologian is that she generally defies the conventional image of a medieval master. We are unable to trace who shaped her theological outlook, and we can only infer from her writings what books comprised the library (or libraries) that she consulted. She held no formal position that a medieval theologian might inhabit: no episcopal chair was hers, no bishop included her in his household of advisors, and no cathedral school claimed her as a master. Now she did gain the endorsement from a number of monastic theologians, not to mention a pope. Moreover, she was probably the only woman in her century to have gained a license to preach publicly to both men and women outside the monastic cloister.[1] However, these facts often emerge in her biography as indicators of her unique status, that her authority did not originate institutionally but rather came out of a recognition of her status as a mystic whom God had granted the gift of visions and the intelligence to proclaim their meaning in concert with the Christian tradition.

Yet, despite these unique factors, and despite the fact that Hildegard may have been the most unconventional theologian of her century, she shared some common features with the men who would gain the title of master of the sacred page at the nascent universities. For all the varieties of theological method and interests that emerged in the Middle Ages, each should be understood through the triangulation of three common coordinates. The first coordinate is the set of authoritative texts in which a theology is grounded. That above all was scripture itself, but not far behind the sacred page were the writings of early Christianity. What most concerns the historical theologian is understanding how a theologian engages the foundational texts in terms of metaphysics (the relationship between the text and the world) and hermeneutics (the relationship

---

[1] Sabina Flanagan, *Hildegard of Bingen: A Visionary Life* (New York: Routledge, 1998), 131–132.

between the text and its readers). The second coordinate is the institutional setting of the theological discourse. This context informed the values and priorities of the theologian. It often was the source of the questions asked and sometimes also the way in which those questions were answered. The final coordinate is the audience, either as auditors or as readers. It is reasonable to assume that a theologian wrote with a specific audience or reader in mind (which modern scholars often call the implied reader), and this helps us to understand often both the content and the structure of a theological text.[2]

It is worth taking the time to articulate these coordinates particularly in the case of Hildegard because it allows the modern reader to assess and analyze her theological writings in the context of the twelfth century. It is easy to lose sight of these coordinates in the thick of Hildegard's visionary topography that appear at first only to draw the reader far away from her social, intellectual, and cultural contexts. Mystical theologians, however, like Hildegard were successful because they could take the reader with them into a rapturous vision but then return them to the ground without being bereft of the vision's meaning. There is beauty, elegance, and theological sophistication in her visionary texts, but Hildegard also has a pedagogical goal in mind. While Hildegard may have never been a master at a cathedral school, she was in fact the *magistra* of her community and so responsible for the education and formation of the women there. It is in that responsibility that her visions took theological shape.

Granted, Hildegard's community of women religious was not the only context in which she functioned as a theologian. She had gained significant fame from her unrelenting critique of the leaders of the medieval Latin church. She had no hesitation in reprimanding a priest, abbot, bishop, or pope if she considered their actions to be undermining the salvific mission of the church. Her prophetic voice has been analyzed and the connection between her mystical experiences and her calls to moral reform has been well forged in Hildegardian scholarship.[3] The second famous context is her preaching against the Cathars. The Cathars were a growing religious sect (often denoted as heretics in the period) who held doctrinal beliefs, and

---

[2] See James R. Ginther, "There Is a Text in This Classroom: The Bible and Theology in the Medieval University," in James R. Ginther and Carl N. Still, eds., *Essays in Memory of Walter H. Principe: Fortresses and Launching Pads* (Aldershot: Ashgate, 2005), 31–50.

[3] See Kathryn Kerby-Fulton, "Prophet and Reformer," in Barbara Newman, ed., *Voice of the Living Light: Hildegard of Bingen and Her World* (Berkeley: University of California Press, 1998), 70–90. See also the alternative reading of Hildegard as prophet by Constant J. Mews, "From *Scivias* to the *Liber Divinorum Operum*: Hildegard's Apocalyptic Imagination and the Call to Reform," *Journal of Religious History* 24, no. 1 (1999): 44–56.

had embraced religious practices, contrary to the medieval Christian church. The Cathars had been so successful in attracting converts from the landless poor to the nobility that many (including Hildegard) considered them to be an existential threat to Christendom. One could argue that in Hildegard's mind the call to moral reform and her anti-Catharism were two sides of the same coin. If it had not been for immoral clergy and lax prelates, the Cathars would not have made inroads in the German territories. The people were ripe for the taking by the Cathars – heretics in Hildegard's worldview – and reform of the clergy and preaching against Cathar teaching were the solutions that had to go hand in hand.[4]

These motifs of prophet and apocalyptic mystic loom large in the scholarship and they have yielded some substantial research. At the same time, they have also produced some unintended consequences. Conceptually, they have served to assign Hildegard to the category of spirituality where women theologians are often placed. Recently, Andrew Prevot (building on the work of Grace Jantzen, Elizabeth Dryer, and Amy Hollywood) has argued that, in treating Hildegard as yet another woman who wrote classics of Western spirituality rather than theology, scholars have separated her from the mainstream of theological thought. They have perpetuated a "centuries-old sexist assumption that women are not likely to contribute very much (if anything) to conceptually rigorous and communally normative thought about God."[5] Instead, we need to confidently identify women like Hildegard as theologians who can address the gamut of theological topics and not just those that fall under the rubric of spirituality or prophecy. The second unintentional consequence has been to minimize the role that Hildegard's community played in her theological work. Rupertsberg has become an important context for understanding her music and liturgy, as well as her medical knowledge and practice. Beyond Margot Fassler's work connecting the liturgical life of Rupertsberg with Hildegard's *Scivias*, there seems to have been little interest in developing the relationship between Hildegard's theologizing and her work to create a new community of nuns.[6]

---

[4] Philip Timko, "Hildegard of Bingen against the Cathars," *American Benedictine Review* 52, no. 2 (2001): 191–205; Beverly Mayne Kienzle, "Defending the Lord's Vineyard: Hildegard of Bingen's Preaching against the Cathars," in Carolyn Muessig, ed., *Medieval Monastic Preaching* (Leiden: Brill, 1998), 163–181.

[5] Andrew Prevot, "No Mere Spirituality: Recovering a Tradition of Women Theologians," *Journal of Feminist Studies in Religion* 33, no. 1 (2017): 107–117, at 109.

[6] Margot E. Fassler, "Allegorical Architecture in *Scivias*: Hildegard's Setting for the *Ordo Virtutum*," *Journal of the American Musicological Society*, 67, no. 2 (2014): 317–378.

In this chapter, I consider Hildegard's community as the immediate context of her theologizing, yielding some fruitful results. This exploration builds on a twofold premise that all theological work, even with a claim that its subject matter is the intersection of the transcendent and the mundane, is primarily a response to local circumstances and thus it has some pedagogical goal in mind. Theologians like Hildegard may cast a theological vision on a grand – indeed, cosmological – scale but that does not prevent her from having a local audience in mind as she wrote.

I argue that Hildegard's three major theological works – *Scivias, Liber vitae meritorum* (Book of Life's Merits), and *Liber divinorum operum* (Book of Divine Works) – formed a structured program of theological education for her community.[7] It is not without coincidence that Hildegard began to compose *Scivias* only a few years after being elected *magistra* of her community in Disibodenberg. Often described as an elaborate *summa* of Christian theology, this text laid the theological foundation for a formation program for her daughters. The two other works build on the *Scivias* and together they form a putative program of theological education that would benefit her community. I say "putative" because there is no explicit evidence that Hildegard successfully implemented this program at Rupertsberg, but I argue that her writing had a reader in mind. It was not as many have imagined, the universal church of medieval Europe, but rather a more focused group of women bound together by monastic vow under the *Rule of St. Benedict*.

I will begin first by addressing the three coordinates of text, setting, and audience in order to establish what this theological program looked like. I will then examine two major theological topics that were of interest to Hildegard – marriage and creation – to demonstrate how they revealed her theological disposition.

The Coordinates of Hildegard's Theology

When studying the theological vision of a medieval thinker, one must remember that theology, like so many disciplines of these centuries, was centered around a text. The twelfth century was a period in which the

---

[7] Hildegard of Bingen, *Scivias*, ed. Adelgundis Führkötter and Angela Carlevaris, 2 vols., Corpus Christianorum Continuatio Mediaevalis (CCCM) 43–43A (Turnhout: Brepols, 1978); Hildegard of Bingen, *Liber vitae meritorum*, ed. Angela Carlevaris, CCCM 90 (Turnhout: Brepols, 1995), hereafter cited as LVM; Hildegard of Bingen, *Liber divinorum operum*, ed. Albert Derolez and Peter Dronke, CCCM 92 (Turnhout: Brepols, 1996), hereafter cited as LDO. Unless otherwise noted, all translations from the Latin are my own.

textual foundations of the liberal arts, for example, became formalized and uniform. That process yielded opportunities for the practitioner of any liberal art to reflect critically on the relevant methods. Canon law, with the exemplary work of Gratian (d. 1140), also offered an influential model on how to think about the theory and practice of a discipline.[8] Theology soon followed in the footsteps of the divine law as cathedral masters began to articulate how they would read scripture or how they would construct sound theological arguments.[9]

The closest that Hildegard comes to articulating her theological method is in a letter written around 1170. The letter was prompted by two queries from the monk Guibert of Gembloux. He had become an ardent admirer of Hildegard and had finally written to her to inquire about how she received and articulated her visions. Hildegard's response is instructive in terms of both what she says to Guibert and what she does not say. We can therefore speak of an explicit method but also some implicit methods at work in Hildegard's theology.

Humility As an Explicit Method

Hildegard responds to Guibert's questions with a clear assertion that her visions occur in a waking state and not in any state of ecstasy. Furthermore, she does not experience her visions sporadically but rather she had been constantly aware of them since her early childhood. There is variation in what she sees and hears spiritually, however, dependent on the natural elements around her. Moreover, there is a direct connection between the gift of the visions and her bodily suffering, a point to which I will return in a moment. The constant spiritual vision is illuminated by an ever present light, which Hildegard named the "shadow of the living light" (*umbra uiuentis luminis*). It is like a mirror or a body of water that reflects the "writings, words, virtues, and deeds of men."[10] Against the backdrop of this constant spiritual vision, illuminated by the shadow of the Living Light,

---

[8] See Peter Lombard, *The Sentences, Book I: The Mystery of the Trinity*, trans. G. Silano (Toronto: PIMS, 2007), xix–xxii.

[9] This desire to articulate an overall theological method would eventually emerge in the inaugural lecture given by a new master of theology. The earliest example is Stephen Langton around 1180. See Nancy K, Spatz, "Imagery in the University Inception Sermon," in Jacqueline Hamesse, Beverly Mayne Kienzle, Anne T. Thayer, and Debra Stoudt, eds., *Medieval Sermons and Society: Cloister, City, University*, Textes et études du Moyen Âge, 9 (Turnhout: Brepols, 1998), 329–342.

[10] Hildegard of Bingen, *Epistolarium*, ed. Lieven Van Acker, 3 vols., CCCM 90-90B (Turnhout: Brepols, 1991–2001), 103r (2.261); *The Letters of Hildegard von Bingen*, 3 vols, trans. Joseph L. Baird and Radd K. Ehrman (New York and Oxford: Oxford University Press, 1994–2004), 2:23.

a more discrete vision would occur, which Hildegard reports as illuminated by the Living Light directly. This discrete experience was what compelled her to write *Scivias*, and based on this description it appears that this type of vision occurred at least two more times for the other two theological works she composed.

Experiencing these visions, and especially the discrete ones illuminated directly by the Living Light, demanded a specific disposition on Hildegard's part: humility. For Hildegard, the virtue of humility was a recognition of the ontological reality of the human person. The human person existed *in medio* in the sense that she was both celestial because of the soul and terrestrial because of the body. The mediating position, however, became compromised by the act of sin, and so human desire, which would naturally seek God, was now disordered (*confusa*). With echoes of the Apostle Paul in the Book of Romans, chapter 6, Hildegard speaks of the frustration that a person wants to know the good but "still cannot keep himself from sinning repeatedly." Even the most saintly of all Christians failed miserably as in the case of St. Peter denying Christ three times just prior to the Passion. Even in a sinful state, however, the *in medio* status of humanity holds true, for humanity is both wondrous and lamentable in that it is prone to sin and yet "God makes them celestial (*stellata*) by his miracles."[11]

Hildegard believed she had to embrace both aspects of humanity in order to be receptive to God's gifts, but humility must be the starting point: "How could any of this be," she asks Guibert, "if I did not recognize that I am so impoverished?"[12] While it is certainly true that humility was a common trope in medieval religious thought and practice, it had a particular bearing on Hildegard's experience and in three ways. First, there was the fact that her gender placed her in a contemptible position in medieval culture. She had little status in terms of authority despite the fact that she was born into a noble family. Being female in the twelfth century meant being considered far removed from the ideal human being, since women were considered irrational, cold, and more susceptible to corrupt behavior than men. Hildegard did not fight against that perception, and indeed to some degree she accepted the misogyny as properly descriptive of her sex. She wore it almost as a badge of honor, however, since she used her gender as a positive way to frame her theology in her writings.[13] Second,

---

[11] *Epistolarium*, 2.259; *Letters*, 2.22.

[12] *Epistolarium*, 2.260; *Letters*, 2.23: "Et unde hoc esset, si ego paupercula me non cognoscerem?".

[13] Barbara Newman, *Sister of Wisdom: Hildegard of Bingen's Theology of the Feminine*, rev. ed. (Berkeley: University of California Press, 1997), 10–11.

Hildegard directly connected her bodily pain and suffering to humility. In her mind, it was a tool God used to remind her who she really was: her pain was a constant reminder of her imperfections. Her embodied soul was incapable of fully perceiving the meaning of her visions because of the defects of that body. Finally, humility as a value and as a practice was embedded in Benedictine culture. The sixth-century Benedict of Nursia had devoted the seventh chapter of his rule to the virtue of humility, which he described as twelve rungs of a ladder that allowed the soul to be exalted.[14] All those steps find resonance in Hildegard's writings either in her description of humility itself or as related virtues.[15]

Implicit Methods: Memory and Classical Rhetoric

To the explicit account of humility as the point of departure in her theology, we can distinguish two implicit methods. Hildegard repeatedly asserts that she is unlearned and not trained in the way that the philosophers of her time were. She gained an understanding of scripture not through any program of theological education, she claims, but rather as a result of a vision she experienced in 1141: "I knew unexpectedly the meaning of the exposition of the books, namely the Psalter, the Gospel and the other catholic books of the Old and New Testament."[16] And yet, there are indications in her writing that Hildegard is more than just a rote stenographer. The first of these appears in the prologue to *Scivias*, where the divine voice mandates:

> But because you are timid in speaking, simple in your exposition, and unlearned in your writing, speak and write those things not according to a human voice, nor according to the understanding of human invention, nor according to the will of human composition; but according to that which you see and hear from on high in the miraculous works of God. Explain these things in such a way that the hearer as she perceives the words of her instructor may make manifest these things according to the tenor of that speech while she desires, demonstrates and instructs.[17]

---

[14] *RB 1980: The Rule of Benedict in Latin and English*, ed. Timothy Fry, Imogene Baker, Timothy Horner et al. (Collegeville, MN: Liturgical Press, 1981), chapter 7 (190–202).

[15] See *Scivias*, ed. Führkötter and Carlevaris, 1.2.33 (1.37–38), 3.8.1 (2.479–480) and 3.8.18 (2.505–506); *LVM*, ed. Carlevaris, 3.4 (126).

[16] *Scivias*, ed. Führkötter and Carlevaris, protestificatio (3). The "catholic books of the Old and New Testament" is odd phrasing. Perhaps it is a conflation of the sources mentioned in *Rule of Benedict*, ed. Fry, chapter 73.4–5 (294–296): "Que enim pagina aut qui sermo diuinae auctoritatis veteris ac noui testamenti non est rectissima norma uitae humanae? Aut quis liber sanctorum catholicorum patrum hoc non resonat . . . "

[17] *Scivias*, ed. Führkötter and Carlevaris, 3.

There are two contradictory assertions made here. On the one hand, Hildegard is instructed to speak and write what she sees in her vision and not to filter it through any human intellectual capacity – interestingly articulated in terms that betray knowledge of three major topics in classical rhetoric: oral speech, argumentation, and literary style. However, she is also commanded to write in a way that her audience will understand so that they may be able to speak of it to others. The former acts as the guarantor for Hildegard's claim to authority; the latter ensures that whatever she writes is intelligible.

Intelligibility requires some form of artifice, and while Hildegard may be silent on this part of her methodology, it is still apparent. She spent nearly ten years writing *Scivias*, five years composing the *Liber vitae meritorum*, and almost ten years again on the *Liber divinorum operum*. On the second text, she speaks of having labored over it.[18] Another indication of artifice was her reliance on her memory. To Guibert in 1170 she writes: "Whatever I see and learn in a vision, I hold in my memory for a long time and what I have remembered is that what I have seen and heard at one time."[19] Hildegard may not have wanted to admit it, but implicit in her theological writings were the tools and methods of classical rhetoric. She took the mandate of helping her reader seriously and in doing so drew on some standard methods in classical memorial arts. It would seem that she was familiar, either directly or indirectly, with the principles about memory from book 3 of the *Rhetorica ad Herennium*. She certainly breaks some of its cardinal rules (she does not use familiar places as the grounding mnemonic devices for complex memorization), but she captures the central notion that connecting words and ideas to images increased an individual's ability to retain the knowledge and to draw on that knowledge for future analysis.[20]

Hildegard built a world for her reader to inhabit in pictorial terms. Using the rhetorical mode of ekphrasis, she created a memorable text that imparts a comprehensive theological vision for her reader to acquire.[21] Ekphrasis, simply put, is "a verbal representation of a visual representation."[22] However, it is more than just descriptive text but rather

[18] LVM, ed. Carlevaris, prologus (8–9).   [19] *Epistolarium*, 103r (2.261); *Letters*, 2.23.
[20] *Rhetorica ad Herennium*, ed. and trans. Harry Caplan, Loeb Classical Library (Cambridge, MA: Harvard University Press, 1954), 3.16–24 (204–224).
[21] Clare Barbetti, "Secret Designs/Public Shapes: Ekphrastic Tensions in Hildegard's *Scivias*," in Margaret Cotter-Lynch and Brad Herzog, eds., *Reading Memory and Identity in the Texts of Medieval European Holy Women* (New York: Palgrave Macmillan, 2012), 81–104.
[22] James A. W. Heffernan, *Museum of Words: the Poetics of Ekphrasis from Homer to Ashbery* (Chicago: University of Chicago Press, 1993).

it "paints a picture" with words about visual objects that themselves have a semiotic function. Apocalyptic texts and medieval visionary literature drew heavily on this rhetorical mode, and so it should be no surprise that Hildegard would exploit it to its fullest degree.[23]

The whole process can be difficult to appreciate from a modern perspective, but not only because we approach memory in very different ways than medieval thinkers like Hildegard. We also, ironically, do not always see the whole of Hildegard's strategy because of the illustrations that have survived in a few manuscript witnesses of *Scivias* and *Liber divinorum operum*. While there is some evidence that Hildegard had a hand in the design in one of the manuscripts,[24] it is more likely that she wanted the reader herself to imagine the visions. There are two facets of her ekphrastic writing that are not captured in the manuscript illustrations. First, these visions are three-dimensional and many of the objects and persons described are placed in relation to one another in a manner that would allow the reader to wander through the described landscape and visionary scenes – akin to a virtual landscape of a modern video game. This is particularly true of the architectural objects in book 3 of *Scivias*, which is analogous to the strategy that Hugh of St. Victor (ca. 1096–1141) employs in his account of Noah's ark. For Hugh, the ark is a massive mnemonic device on which he writes a complex account of Christian theology. It works as a memorial technique because the reader can "walk around" the virtual ark observing the various locations where specific doctrinal truths are housed.[25] Second, many of these images are dynamic and those movements held meaning, an aspect of the pictorial process not easily captured by a static, two-dimensional illustration.[26]

A second rhetorical mode was commentary as Hildegard's visions were presented in a manner conducive for a monastic readership. Each vision

---

[23] For a further account of ekphrasis, see Niels Koopman, *Ancient Greek Ekphrasis: Between Description and Narration*, Amsterdam Studies in Classical Philology, 26 (Leiden: Brill, 2018), 1–40; and Claire Barbetti, *Ekphrastic Medieval Visions: A New Discussion in Interarts Theory* (New York: Palgrave MacMillan, 2011), esp. 17–37.

[24] Madeline H. Caviness, "Gender, Symbolism, and Text Image Relationships: Hildegard of Bingen's *Scivias*," in Jeanette Beer, ed., *Translation Theory and Practice in the Middle Ages*, Studies in Medieval Culture, 38 (Kalamazoo: Medieval Institute Publications, 1997), 71–111, argues that these images reflect Hildegard's thought processes. See also Campbell, Chapter 12, this volume.

[25] See John A. H. Lewis, "History and Everlastingness in Hugh of St Victor's Figures of Noah's Ark," in Gerhard Jaritz, and Gerson Moreno-Riaño, eds., *Time and Eternity: The Medieval Discourse*, International Medieval Research, 9 (Turnhout: Brepols, 2003); Mary Carruthers, *The Book of Memory: A Study of Memory in Medieval Culture* (Cambridge: Cambridge University Press, 2008), 257–260.

[26] Mews, "From *Scivias* to the *Liber Divinorum Operum*," 46.

invites a meditative approach in which the reader could consider the images, actions, and dialogue in the same way that she would ruminate on scripture. The "glossed" approach of Hildegard's interpretation echoes the literature of biblical commentary that inhabited the *lectio divina* in Benedictine communities. Indeed, Hildegard's implicit claim (as separate from the claims of her authority as a prophet) is that her visions are akin to scripture:[27] they are forms of divine revelation that are worthy of meditative reading, wherein one morsel, one versicle, is taken as the object of study for a day, a week or even a month. The repetitive techniques of meditation are in fact part of the structure of the *Liber vitae meritorum*. Each part begins with an exchange between a vice and the corresponding virtue, followed by a set of teachings that set the context for understanding the vices and virtues. The reader then returns to a more analytical account of the vices as well as what penance each one requires.[28]

Context and Audience

It is one thing for Hildegard's implied reader to be monastic, but it still remains to be seen that she had her own community in mind as she wrote. Despite her fame and the fact that the establishment of her community at Rupertsberg was well known, we actually know very little about the rhythms of community life there specifically, beyond the kind of regular structure evoked in Alison I. Beach's chapter in this volume (Chapter 2). We know that the monastic discipline that Hildegard encouraged was not as severe as the community had experienced under Jutta's leadership at Disibodenberg before 1136. Hildegard had a gentler and more moderate approach to discipline, although she could be severe in punishment when it was fitting.[29] We also know that the divine office and worship in general had the highest priority for her community, and Hildegard devoted considerable time and energy to music and worship. The liturgical life at Rupertsberg had a pedagogical component as it was part of the process of formation for the community.[30]

---

[27] Kevin Hughes, "Visionary Exegesis: Vision, Text, and Interpretation in Hildegard's *Scivias*," *American Benedictine Review* 50, no. 3 (1999): 311–326; see also *Epistolarium*, 14r (1.32); *Letters*, 1.53.

[28] There are multiple structures to this text. See Suzanne Ruge, "The Theology of Penance: Observations on the *Liber vitae meritorum*," in Beverly Mayne Kienzle, Debra L. Stoudt, and George Ferzoco, eds., *A Companion to Hildegard of Bingen* (Leiden: Brill, 2014), 221–248.

[29] Franz J. Felten, "What Do We Know About the Life of Jutta and Hildegard at Disibodenberg and Rupertsberg?" in Kienzle, Stoudt and Ferzoco, *A Companion to Hildegard*, 15–38.

[30] Carolyn Muessig, "Learning and Mentoring in the Twelfth Century: Hildegard of Bingen and Herrad of Landsberg," in George Ferzoco and Carolyn Muessig, eds., *Medieval Monastic Education* (Leicester: Leicester University Press, 1998), 87–104, at 91–93.

Nearly everything Hildegard did at Rupertsberg was for specific ends. She saw an opportunity to build a Benedictine community from scratch and form it in specific ways. She chose those who wished to take vows in a way that contributed to a homogeneous community. This meant asserting an elitist attitude by which Hildegard saw women from noble families as better candidates for her community than those from the lower ranks. This struck some of her contemporaries as disconnected with the reform movement that was sweeping religious communities in the German territories that modern scholars now call the Hirsau reform, as well as at odds with the emergence of new religious orders, such as the Cistercians, who did not prize wealth (such as the dowries given to the community when a woman entered the convent) as an indicator of goodness in a person.[31]

While the dowry was an important resource of the community at Rupertsberg, I would argue that this was not the only reason that Hildegard rejected non-noble women. In the letter to Tengswich, the superior of the canonesses at Andernach who had criticized her community, Hildegard speaks of the need to avoid unrest in the community. Her analogy is contemptible of the poor and she asserts that their presence would lead not only to disharmony but also to violence.[32] It is unclear whether this is based on observation of other communities or drawn from her own experiences at Disibodenberg. One wonders as well if a community of noble women would have a greater facility in reading than those who had admitted women from families of merchants, farmers, and the landless poor. At the very least, it demonstrates that Hildegard was intent on engineering every aspect of the community.[33]

It is unlikely then that she would omit textual resources to help to build that community. In a letter attached to Guibert of Gembloux's *Vitae sanctae Hildegardis* (Life of Saint Hildegard), she reports that:

---

[31] Hildegard's elitism was not necessarily out of step with the Benedictines across Europe. See John Van Engen, "The 'Crisis of Cenobitism' Reconsidered: Benedictine Monasticism in the Years 1050–1150," *Speculum* 61, no. 2 (1986): 269–304, at 291; Muessig, "Hildegard of Bingen and Herrad of Landsberg," 92.

[32] *Epistolarium*, 52r (1.129); *Letters*, 1.129).

[33] It is significant that the model of spiritual perfection presented by Hildegard to her community was the noble woman, Bertha, the mother of St. Rupert. Bertha was the real "hero" of the *Vita sancti Rupperti Confessoris* that Hildegard penned around 1170. It was Bertha's actions and virtue that protected Rupert from making the wrong decisions about his life or falling under the influence of corrupt nobles. See Hildegard of Bingen, *Two Hagiographies: Vita sancti Rupperti Confessoris, Vita sancti Dysibodi Episcopi*, ed. Christopher P. Evans, trans. Hugh Feiss, Dallas Medieval Texts and Translations, 11 (Paris: Peeters, 2010), 44–77.

Thus my mind was set that I had therefore taken on the care of the daughters committed to me in all things necessary for their bodies and their souls, just as it has been established for me by my masters. But because of that, I saw with great anxiety a true vision how airy spirits were fighting against us. I saw that these same malignant spirits entangling some of our more noble daughters with diverse vanities like a net. But I informed these same daughters through a showing of God (*ostensionem Dei*), how the diverse vanity of these malignant spirits through deception would be immersed in their hearts, [and] I fortified and entrenched them as much as I was able with God's help in the words of holy Scripture, the good discipline of the *Rule*, and a holy life.[34]

The last three elements are all attested in the Rupertsberg community: Hildegard expounded scripture to her community (probably in chapter), as evidenced from her surviving sermons on the Gospels.[35] Around 1170, Volmar writes a lament about the impact of Hildegard's death (he was responding to a rumor of her impending demise), as her community will be bereft of anyone who can provide new interpretations of scripture, preach new sermons, offer new songs of praise, and the like.[36] While she did not provide a commentary on the *Rule* for her own community (but did write one for another),[37] she knew it well and drew from it to shape her community; and she constantly sought to model a holy life for her nuns to follow. The only resource unaccounted for in her exposition above of what she provided for her community is that "showing of God." I would argue that this "showing of God" was *Scivias*, which detailed the salvific narrative of the battle between God and the devil and the role human beings played sometimes as unwitting victims and sometimes collaborators with evil when giving into sin.

A Theological Program for Monastic Formation

If Hildegard had the women under her care in mind as she composed *Scivias*, how did this affect what and how she wrote? One of the concerns of most monastic theologians was that both men and women religious not get lost in the minutiae of their daily practices. While it was important that

---

[34] *Vita sanctae Hildegardis*, ed. Monika Klaes, CCCM, 126 (Turnhout: Brepols, 1998), 37.

[35] On the role of the sermons on the Gospels, see Beverly Mayne Kienzle, "Hildegard's Teaching in Her *Expositiones evangeliorum* and *Ordo virtutum*," in Ferzoco and Meussig, *Medieval Monastic Education*, 72–86.

[36] *Epistolarium*, 195 (2.443); *Letters*, 2.168.

[37] Hildegard of Bingen, *Explanation of the Rule of Benedict*, trans. Hugh Feiss (Toronto: Peregrina Press, 1990).

a religious know how to pray and sing the Office, the twelfth century saw a shift toward intentionality in such practices rather than just completing those practices successfully. It is one reason why monastic communities began to move away from child oblation and toward only receiving adult novices. The intentions of adult novices were their own, at least in theory. Hence, monastic literature often focused on the bigger picture, that is, how the spiritual exercises and ascetic practices contributed to their religious life and how that religious life had an impact on the larger Christian community and how their lives as monastics were part of the larger story of cosmic salvation.

That larger picture of salvation history is the overall structure of *Scivias* divided into three books. Book 1 begins with God's work of creation, and in that narrative Hildegard embeds the fall of Lucifer and the fall of humanity.[38] That fall becomes the context for talking of the human embodiment and the challenges that brings to the soul as it seeks to return to God. To that context, Hildegard ends this book by talking about the emergence of the Jews as God's chosen people (the synagogue), who become the context for the incarnation, the solution to humanity's sinful state.

The visions of the second book focus on Christ as Savior, in terms of both his divinity and his humanity. His salvific work is the source of the sacraments that assist in the healing of humanity, but the book ends with Hildegard pointing out how the devil threatens the efficacy of the sacraments. This ending leads to book 3 in which the visions flesh out the edifice of salvation and the reader discovers the connections between Christ the savior, the church, and the virtues that can battle against the vices. All this comes to a head in the last days wherein the salvific narrative ends with the last judgment and all those saved join in a symphony of praise to their Creator.

The Danger of Marriage

Within this grand narrative, Hildegard allows the reader to find herself. Two examples will suffice. Although she talks about the sacraments in book 2 within the context of their saving function, she does not discuss the sacrament of marriage. Instead, she broaches this topic in book 1, as she

---

[38] Rachel Fulton Brown, "Hildegard of Bingen's Theology of Revelation," in E. Ann Matter and Lesley Smith, eds., *From Knowledge to Beatitude: St Victor, Twelfth-Century Scholars and Beyond. Essays in Honor of Grover A. Zinn* (Notre Dame: University of Notre Dame Press, 2013), 300–327, suggests a trinitarian structure to *Scivias*. This is not incommensurate with what I am (as well as many others) are suggesting.

recounts the fall of humanity at the hands of Lucifer. From one perspective, a discussion of marriage in connection to the creation of humanity makes sense, as the Genesis text makes clear that marriage originated during humanity's prelapsarian state. Yet Hildegard is not interested in discussing prelapsarian marriage. What actually brings marriage into focus is the comment that the Devil aimed his sights at Eve not only because she was more susceptible to his temptation but also because Adam "burned so strongly in love for Eve" that he would do whatever she asked.[39] It was not just the weakness of Eve that brought the downfall of humanity but the love that Adam had for his wife.

This observation reflects a common ambiguity about marriage among religious communities in twelfth-century Europe.[40] On the one hand, it was an institution established by God and so was a good in itself. On the other hand, it allowed vice to fester in human relationships and so it could also be the "sleeper agent" in the devil's attack on humanity. On this latter point, Hildegard writes that the heavenly voice says:

> But after Adam and Eve were expelled from the garden, they knew the work of conceiving and giving birth to children. Thus from their disobedience, as they fell into death, they seized upon the sweetness of sin, since they knew they were capable of sinning. But in this manner, turning my right institution [of marriage] into sinful pleasure – although they ought to know that passion in their veins was not due to the sweetness of sin, but due to the love of children – they gave into that desire by diabolical suggestion . . . and so the Devil sent out his darts to this work lest it would be completed without his influence, since he has said: "My strength is in human sexual activity (*in conceptu hominum*) and so humanity belongs to me."[41]

The ultimate solution is the passion and resurrection of the Incarnate Son of God, but Hildegard also includes biblical texts and canon law that governed the practices of marriage in the twelfth century. These proscriptions were focused primarily on suppressing lust and controlling the scope of marital sex. She was hardly a solitary voice on these matters, as most theologians held similar views that marriage was a good (and ultimately a sacrament) but it had inherent dangers that required regulation.[42]

---

[39] *Scivias*, ed. Führkötter and Carlevaris, 1.2.10 (1.19).
[40] See Dylan Elliott, *Spiritual Marriage: Sexual Abstinence in Medieval Wedlock* (Princeton: Princeton University Press, 1993), 132–194.
[41] *Scivias*, ed. Führkötter and Carlevaris, 1.2.15 (1.24).
[42] See Pierre Payer, *Sex and the Penitentials: The Development of a Sexual Code, 550–1150* (Toronto: University of Toronto Press, 1984); and David d'Avray, *Medieval Marriage: Symbolism and Society* (Oxford: Oxford University Press, 2005).

Yet her ambivalent treatment of marriage is not her actual goal. After running through a series of proscriptions that assist in avoiding lust and fornication, Hildegard turns to God's most loving sheep, who have been planted in his heart (*ad amantissimas oues meas quae in corde meo plantatae sunt me conuertam*): virgins. She extols their beauty and their high rank among those who inhabit the palace of the heavenly King. They are subject to no law, no prescriptions are laid on their behavior, because they live and act as the Son of God does. Virginity is the most noble of states, with chaste widowhood behind it. The battles to retain a women's virginity in God's eyes, Hildegard states, are battles of great beauty and yield much fruit. These battles are also brighter than the sun and sweeter than any spice. The struggles of virgins leave angels amazed at these women who avoid the pollution from the mud of the world. "Therefore, rejoice, since you persevered, because I am with you when you faithfully receive me and perform my voice with joy in your heart."[43] The reader has been fully briefed on the theological and even legal understanding of marriage but has also walked away with a comparative understanding of the superiority of either taking the vow of chastity from the beginning or becoming chaste after being widowed.

Virginity, Crowns, Veils

The second example of allowing the reader to see herself within the grand narrative of *Scivias* is found in the fifth vision of book 2, where Hildegard talks of the three orders of the church: clergy (priests, canons, bishops, etc.), religious (monks and nuns), and laity. Her discussion of the first order is brief and perfunctory (2.5.1–5) and is followed by an extensive discussion of the monastic orders (2.5.6–22), before offering even fewer comments about the laity than she had about the clergy (2.5.23–25). Her commentary then shifts to general theological observations about the three orders as a whole (2.5.25–38) before returning again to matters concerning only monks and nuns (2.5.39–54).[44]

In this context, Hildegard speaks once again of the superiority of the chaste life, which was established on apostolic teaching in the primitive church. The importance of virgins is represented by the resplendent maiden in her vision. She is surrounded by a great crowd, including women in white veils who also wore gold crowns adorned with images of

---

[43] *Scivias*, ed. Führkötter and Carlevaris, 1.2.24 (1.30–31).   [44] Ibid, 1.177–220.

the Trinity and the Lamb of God. These symbols show that these women have a strong commitment to the Trinity that is held because of their understanding of love and their chaste stability.[45] The image of the veiled virgins would have been very familiar to the nuns of Rupertsberg as they themselves dressed in white veils and gold crowns for the liturgy of high feast days. It was a feature that had gained attention from outside of Rupertsberg, first by Tengswich of Andernach around 1150 (when *Scivias* was near completion) and later by Guibert in 1170. This vision was the source of the dress and through it Hildegard placed her fellow nuns at the apex of worship of God but also as a vital group for the success of the universal church.

Ignoring Virtue

With such lessons learned, the nuns as readers would have entered book 3 prepared to think about how their individual lives were to play a substantial role in the fulfillment of salvation history. As Hildegard takes her reader around the architectural elements of the edifice of salvation, she embeds descriptions of twenty-seven virtues. These virtues were essential to a holy life and cumulatively were the goal of the formation at Rupertsberg. It would appear that the women under her care, however, did not pay sufficient heed. Despite engineering her community through the careful selection of novices and structuring its daily life with beautiful music and hymns for the Office and the liturgy, her community was not acting as it should. Around 1161, Hildegard wrote a harsh letter to her community about their failures. Their behavior was an abandonment of their vows to God. God had set them a royal banquet, but they had repudiated it in exchange for carnal desires. This behavior had lasted for eight years, and now Hildegard was reporting that God's patience was at an end.[46] Two years later, she completed the *Liber vitae meritorum* (LVM). We know that the nuns of Rupertsberg made copies of this text, and so it is likely that they also read it either as part of the reading at table or as a text for the *lectio divina*.[47]

Not only do the same vices and virtues that are found in *Scivias* appear in the LVM, but their "physical" location is also repeated. As she mapped out the edifice of salvation in her first text, Hildegard had described the buildings and columns in relation to each other using compass coordinates.

---

[45] Ibid, 2.5.7 (1.181-182).   [46] *Epistolarium*, 194, 2.439-442; Letters, 2.165-167.
[47] Ruge, "Theology of Penance," 246.

In *Scivias*, it is unclear how these could be of any use, for why would it matter if the Tower of God's will is located in the northeast corner or that the Pillar of the Word of God is located in the northern corner of the campus? However, the LVM reveals the utility, as the compass coordinates act as a mnemonic device by which the reader can make connections between the accounts of the virtues in the *Scivias* and the LVM. The central vision of the LVM is a man so tall that he extends well into the heavens, with the clouds at his chest. As he looks about, he sees a set of vices and their corresponding virtues. Whereas the movement in *Scivias* is counterclockwise starting from the northeast corner, the pathway in the LVM is not as systematic. Part 1 begins in the southeast, but then part 2 jumps to the northwest. All the same virtues of *Scivias* are found in the LVM, and so their reader of both visionary texts could map out the virtues and vices with some regularity. For the most part, Hildegard is consistent in her compass references, but it is not an exact match. Still, the LVM would have filled out what vice each virtue was seeking to remedy.

Rediscovering the Body in Creation

With LVM complete, Hildegard spent the next ten years working on her final theological text, the *Liber divinorum operum* (LDO). As extraordinary as *Scivias* was, the LDO would exceed it in both breadth and depth. It brings together the themes of creation, salvation, and virtue found in the two earlier works and framed them in a much more explicit apocalyptic vision for Christianity. Methodologically, it also reveals Hildegard's exegetical skills at work, as the text includes a close reading of the prologue to the Gospel of John and a multivalent exposition of the Genesis creation narrative. In the LDO, Hildegard develops theological themes that she has become best known for, such as humanity as a microcosm of the universe and the Neoplatonic concept of emanation and return of all creation.

Of all the themes that are in play in the LDO, the one that comes to the forefront time and time again is the body as an object of meditation. This may sound contrary to the values of someone like Hildegard who spoke often of the need to limit the influence of the body in a person's life and to find ways to control or eradicate bodily desire. Moreover, Hildegard does often speak of the soul as if it were a completely separate entity that must do battle to maintain control over the body.[48] This does not mean, however, that the body is something to be rejected or simply tolerated.

---

[48] LDO, ed. Derolez and Dronke, 1.4 (136–264), where this theme is extensively explored.

By laying out in exacting detail how the body reflects and interacts with all of creation, the reader would come to see that the body was a place to discover the work of God. The body connects to creation through the humors and the winds of the world, which all can provide resources to counter the pollution of sin that the body must endure. This perspective on the body is nascent in *Scivias*, but a decade of preaching against the Cathars sharpened Hildegard's account of embodiment. For the Cathars, contempt for the body was grounded in a general contempt of the material world, which was intrinsically evil. This may have led to behavior that put the lifestyle of most Catholic priests to shame, but it was grounded in error, so Hildegard asserted.[49] The LDO makes the case that not only is the body a good – although marred by sin – it is a good intimately connected to the good of all creation. Thus, a human being is a microcosm of all creation, intimately linked both physically and spiritually (part 1, visions 2–3). A human being does not have a body accidentally, nor as a punishment, but as the means to return to God (part 1, vision 4); and, scripture reveals the goodness of that creation and humanity's central role (part 2). Finally, the embodied person is the primary means by which the church (composed of humanity redeemed by Christ and angels) is perfected in history and then into eternity.

Conclusion

Marriage, creation, the dignity of the body – these are just representative topics of the theological depth of Hildegard's writings. There is more to explore, from the doctrine of the Incarnation (Christology) to theories of salvation (soteriology), to an account of the nature of Christian community (ecclesiology), and to any number of other topics in medieval theology. What I have argued here is that, by placing her work within the context of her community, scholars can discover new opportunities for research. The reframing of her theologizing can allow scholars to ask questions that may not have any direct connection to Hildegard's call to moral reform or her apocalyptic mysticism.

Connecting her three theological works to the context of her religious community, however, does not diminish the fact that these very same works attracted readers beyond the monastery gate of Rupertsberg. Her fame is well attested in her correspondence as many monks and prelates, as well as other women religious, sought her wisdom and advice. *Scivias*

---

[49] See *Epistolarium*, 15r, 1.34; Letters, 1.55.

probably gained the widest readership and its contents were the reason that at least one bishop and one cathedral master wrote to Hildegard seeking her opinion on a complex theological question.[50] Still others sought her exposition of various scriptural passages that monastic readers found difficult to understand.[51] Her readership continued beyond her monastery and well into the next few centuries of the Middle Ages.

Moreover, connecting her theology with her community is not an attempt to marginalize Hildegard, as if her implied reader is her only audience and so her theological voice belongs only to one nunnery in medieval Germany. Locating her theological works within her community context instead raises the profile of her community and helps to clarify her overall intentions: Her desire to create a religious community from the ground up, where the influence of either the abbot of Disibodenberg or the archbishop of Mainz was kept to a minimum, was not some reflex of a brilliant thinker who wanted to establish her independence from ecclesial authority. I would argue that instead her community was a fundamental part of the solution to the moral corruption and institutional problems of her century. The nuns of Rupertsberg were to be the Bertha to the Rupert of the present-day church. That was a significant role and indeed such a calling would require not just virtuous behavior at its center but virtue that was grounded in a theological understanding of God, creation, and the salvation of humanity.

Further Reading

Latin Editions and English Translations

Hildegard of Bingen. *The Book of Divine Works*, trans. Nathaniel M. Campbell. Washington, DC: The Catholic University of America Press, 2018.

The Book of the Rewards of Life (Liber Vitae Meritorum), trans. Bruce W. Hozeski. New York: Garland, 1994.

Hildegardis Bingensis: Liber uite meritorum, ed. Angela Carlevaris. Corpus Christianorum Continuatio Mediaevalis 90. Turnhout: Brepols, 1995.

Liber divinorum operum, ed. Albert Derolez and Peter Dronke. Corpus Christianorum Continuatio Mediaevalis 92. Turnhout: Brepols, 1996.

---

[50] *Epistolarium*, 31r (1.83–88), and 40r (1.103-105). Both questions concern the doctrine of the Trinity and both are addressed in a form of argument that easily coheres with Hildegard's three theological works.

[51] See Hildegard of Bingen, *Solutions to Thirty-Eight Questions*, trans. Beverly Mayne Kienzle, Jenny C. Bledsoe, and Stephen H. Behnke (Collegeville, MN: Liturgical Press, 2014), 1–38.

Scivias, ed. Adelgundis Führkötter and Angela Carlevaris. 2 vols. Corpus Christianorum Continuatio Mediaevalis 43 and 43A. Turnhout: Brepols, 1978.

Scivias, trans. Mother Columba Hart and Jane Bishop. New York: Paulist Press, 1990.

Solutions to Thirty-Eight Questions, trans. Beverly Mayne Kienzle, Jenny C. Bledsoe, and Stephen H. Belmke. Collegeville, MN: Liturgical Press, 2014.

Secondary Literature

Barbetti, Claire. "Secret Designs/Public Shapes: Ekphrastic Tensions in Hildegard's *Scivias*." In Margaret Cotter-Lynch and Brad Herzog, eds., *Reading Memory and Identity in the Texts of Medieval European Holy Women*. New York: Palgrave Macmillan, 2012, 81–104.

Ginther, James R. "There Is a Text in This Classroom: The Bible and Theology in the Medieval University." In James R. Ginther and Carl N. Still, eds., *Essays in Memory of Walter H. Principe: Fortresses and Launching Pads*. Aldershot: Ashgate, 2005, 31–50.

Kienzle, Beverly Mayne. "Hildegard's Teaching in Her *Expositiones evangeliorum* and *Ordo virtutum*." In George Ferzoco and Carolyn Muessig, eds., *Medieval Monastic Education*. Leicester: Leicester University Press, 1998, 72–86.

Meussig, Carolyn. "Learning and Mentoring in the Twelfth Century: Hildegard of Bingen and Herrad of Landsberg." In George Ferzoco and Carolyn Muessig, eds., *Medieval Monastic Education*. Leicester: Leicester University Press, 1998, 87–104.

Mews, Constant J. "From *Scivias* to the *Liber Divinorum Operum*: Hildegard's Apocalyptic Imagination and the Call to Reform." *Journal of Religious History* 24, no. 1 (1999): 44–56.

Newman, Barbara. *Sister of Wisdom: St. Hildegard's Theology of the Feminine*. 2nd ed. Berkeley: University of California Press, 1997.

Prevot, Andrew. "No Mere Spirituality: Recovering a Tradition of Women Theologians." *Journal of Feminist Studies in Religion* 33, no. 1 (2017): 107–117.

Ruge, Suzanne. "The Theology of Penance: Observations on the *Liber vitae meritorum*." In Beverly Mayne Kienzle, Debra L. Stoudt, and George Ferzoco, eds., *A Companion to Hildegard of Bingen*. Leiden: Brill, 2014, 221–248.

CHAPTER 5

Reading Hildegard of Bingen's Letters

Christopher D. Fletcher

By 1173, Hildegard of Bingen was a celebrity. Since the circulation of the *Scivias* (Know the Ways) in the 1140s, her prophetic persona had drawn interest and admiration from across the German lands and beyond. Now firmly ensconced at her convent on the Rupertsberg, Hildegard welcomed a steady stream of visitors seeking counsel, consolation, or some other benefit from her gift. Around this time, she received a letter from one of those visitors, the abbot of the Premonstratensian monastery at Ilbenstadt. According to the abbot, Hildegard had reason to remember him, since "I have often pelted you with many letters and have frequently come before you to deliver my petition face-to-face." Even with all this previous interaction, however, there was still a prize that eluded him: "I have never, as you promised, been able to wrench any letters from you."[1]

This fascinating request casts a spotlight on a particularly rich source for Hildegard's life and work: her letter collection.[2] One of the larger personal letter collections to survive from the twelfth century (the modern edition includes 390 items), it contains correspondence between the visionary and individuals throughout Europe from all walks of life. Collectively, these letters show Hildegard carrying out her role as a divinely inspired prophet and *magistra* to the world by transmitting instruction, comfort, admonition, and illumination to those who needed it.[3]

---

[1] Hildegard of Bingen, Ep. 139, *Epistolarium*, ed. Lieven Van Acker, Corpus Christianorum Continuatio Mediaevalis (CCCM) 91A (Turnhout: Brepols, 1993), 313. Unless otherwise noted, all translations in this chapter are my own.

[2] Hildegard of Bingen, *Epistolarium*, 3 vols., ed. Lieven Van Acker and Monika Klaes-Hachmöller, CCCM 91-91A-91B (Turnhout: Brepols, 1991–2001). This edition has been translated into English as *The Letters of Hildegard of Bingen*, trans. Joseph L. Baird and Radd K. Ehrman, 3 vols. (Oxford: Oxford University Press, 1998–2004). For the remainder of this chapter, Hildegard's letters will be cited with the letter number, the volume of the critical edition, and the page number, e.g. Ep. 139, CCCM 91A, 313. The letter numbers are the same in the Baird and Ehrman translation.

[3] An excellent overview of the content of Hildegard's letters is Joan Ferrante, "Correspondent: 'Blessed Is the Speech of Your Mouth'," in Barbara Newman, ed., *Voice of the Living Light: Hildegard of Bingen and Her World* (Berkeley: University of California Press, 1998), 91–109.

All the evidence indicates that Hildegard and her contemporaries valued these letters quite highly. No less a figure than Hildegard's trusted secretary Volmar of Disibodenberg once ranked her "response to those seeking answers to every kind of question" (i.e. her letters) before any of the other pious services she offered to the world.[4] Accordingly, Hildegard and her collaborators spent decades collecting and editing the correspondence, a process documented by manuscript copies of various editions of the letters held in institutions far removed from the Rupertsberg.[5]

All this suggests that there was something special about reading Hildegard's letters in the twelfth century. The anxious complaint of the abbot of Ilbenstadt even gives the impression that receiving a letter from Hildegard was different from – and perhaps even *superior* to – meeting her in person. The singular appeal of Hildegard's letters has not often been discussed in the scholarship on the seer. To be sure, some individual letters have figured quite prominently, because they provide the most in-depth witness to key aspects of her thought, including the experience of her visions.[6] For the most part, however, there has been fairly little discussion about the significance of Hildegard's letters *as letters* or the unique insights these texts provide on her prophetic career.

To shed more light on these issues, this chapter will examine why Hildegard, her collaborators, and her public were so interested in her letters. Doing so requires looking at the collection through both the wide lens of the place of letter-writing in twelfth-century intellectual culture and the narrow lens of Hildegard's exceptional experience as a recognized prophet. As we will see, both of these perspectives are necessary to grasp why she wanted to write letters, why her secretaries (with her assent) wanted to collect them, and why people like the abbot of Ilbenstadt wanted to receive them. This chapter will serve as an introduction for both how Hildegard's letters, precisely because they were *letters*, were the ideal documentation of her saintly life and how they can help modern readers better understand her intellectual background, her political and spiritual

---

[4] Ep. 145, CCCM 91A, 443.
[5] On the collection's development, see Lieven Van Acker, "Der Briefwechsel der heiligen Hildegard von Bingen: Vorbemerkungen zu einer kritischen Edition," *Revue bénédictine* 98, no. 1–2 (1988): 141–168 and 99 (1989), 118–154; Monika Klaes-Hachmöller, "Von einer Briefsammlung zum literarischen Briefbuch," in Edeltraud Forster, ed., *Hildegard von Bingen: Prophetin durch die Zeiten* (Freiburg: Herder, 1997), 153–170; Marianna Schrader and Adelgundis Führkötter, *Die Echtheit des Schrifttums der hl. Hildegard von Bingen* (Cologne: Böhlau, 1956); and Bernhard Schmeidler, "Bemerkungen zum Corpus der Briefe der hl. Hildegard von Bingen," in *Corona Quernea: Festgabe Karl Strecker*, ed. Paul Lehmann, Monumenta Germaniae Historica 6 (Leipzig: K.W. Hiersemann, 1941), 335–366.
[6] Ep. 109r, CCCM 91A, 269–277.

influence, and her determination to conduct her life as a public prophet on her own terms.

Letter-Writing in the Twelfth Century

Why would Hildegard write letters? This question would hardly have occurred to any modestly educated person in Hildegard's day, to say nothing of the seer herself. Letters were the lifeblood of intellectual culture during the twelfth century, which occupied roughly the latter half of the so-called Golden Age of medieval epistolography, a period when intellectuals of all stripes wrote, received, and collected letters at a rate and volume unseen since late antiquity.[7] Indeed, based on the available evidence, it is no exaggeration to say that anyone who participated in intellectual culture between roughly 1000 and 1200 did so, at least in part, by writing letters.

During this period, letters served as an infinitely flexible genre that facilitated cultural work of all kinds, from the practical (e.g. conducting political business) to the social (e.g. maintaining social relationships over long distances) to the theological (e.g. explaining the meaning of scripture), and beyond.[8] All this epistolary work was recorded in a variety of formats, but perhaps none more important than formal collections of correspondence. The emphasis on collecting letters sharply distinguished the "Golden Age" from earlier periods, as the eleventh and twelfth centuries were marked by "an abundance of important letter collections."[9] Scholars have tended to see these collections primarily as literary monuments to the authors who wrote them, preserving a record

---

[7] The standard overview of medieval letter-writing remains Giles Constable, *Letters and Letter Collections*, Typologie des Sources du Moyen Âge Occidental, fasc. 17 (Turnhout: Brepols, 1976). See also Julian Haseldine, "Epistolography," in Frank A. C. Mantello and Arthur George Rigg, eds., *Medieval Latin: An Introduction and Bibliographical Guide* (Washington, DC: The Catholic University of America Press, 1996), 650–658; Hartmut Hoffman, "Zur mittelalterlichen Brieftechnik," in Konrad Repgen and Stephan Skalweit, eds., *Spiegel der Geschichte: Festgabe für Max Braubach* (Münster: Aschendorff, 1964), 141–170; Jean Leclercq, "Le genre épistolaire au moyen âge," *Revue du moyen âge latin* 2 (1946): 63–70; and Rolf Köhn, "Zur Quellenkritik kopial überlieferter Korrespondenz im lateinischen Mittelalter, zumal in Briefsammlungen," *Mitteilungen des Instituts für Österreichische Geschichtsforschung* 101 (1993): 284–310.

[8] John Van Engen, "Letters, Schools, and Written Culture in the Eleventh and Twelfth Century," in Johannes Fried, ed., *Dialektik und Rhetorik im frühen und hohen Mittelalter: Rezeption, Überlieferung und gesellschaftliche Wirkung antiker Gelehrsamkeit vornehmlich im 9. und 12. Jahrhundert* (Munich: Oldenbourg, 1997), 97–132.

[9] Carl Erdmann, *Studien zur Briefliteratur Deutschlands im elften Jahrhundert* (Leipzig: K.W. Hiersemann, 1938), 1.

of their eloquence, their interests, and (as their authors were usually ecclesiastical) their service to the church for future generations.[10]

Although letter-writing flourished in practically all areas of intellectual culture at this time, it seems to have been particularly important for religious thinkers.[11] To be sure, letter-writing had always been an integral part of Christian intellectual life, but the decades before 1050 saw a veritable explosion of religious thinkers writing letters that lasted for the next century and a half, with examples surviving from practically every such author known to us. These included prominent intellectuals and leaders such as Peter Damian, Anselm of Canterbury, and Bernard of Clairvaux; as well as more obscure authors like Gerhoh of Reichersberg, Hugo Metellus, and Peter of Celle. Women were also active participants in this letter-writing culture; though none besides Hildegard left letter collections under their name, it is clear that women regularly corresponded with religious thinkers, often on religious matters. At times, incoming letters written by women are included in religious thinkers' collections, such as the letters from Matilda, queen of England, to Anselm of Canterbury.[12] In other cases, women letter-writers are alluded to in the correspondence male religious thinkers sent to them. Peter Damian, for instance, corresponded with many women on religious topics and even went so far as to claim that his prodigious and theologically dense letter against clerical celibacy (letter 112) was originally written for Countess Adelaide of Turin.[13] Whatever the circumstances, religious thinkers used letters to accomplish a wide variety of spiritual tasks: doctrinal definition, spiritual instruction, exegetical investigation, pastoral care, moral exhortation, contemplative meditation, and so on.

The great flowering of letter-writing among religious thinkers in the High Middle Ages was rooted in significant changes in the foundations of intellectual culture around the turn of the eleventh century.[14] Together, they created a particular "mental formation" that naturally expressed itself

---

[10] R. W. Southern, *Medieval Humanism and Other Studies* (Oxford: Blackwell, 1970), 116.

[11] Christopher D. Fletcher, "Rhetoric, Reform, and Christian Eloquence: The Letter Form and the Religious Thought of Peter Damian," *Viator* 46, no. 1 (2015): 61–91.

[12] For Matilda's letters to Anselm, cf. Epp. 320, 323, 384, and 400 in *S. Anselmi Cantuariensis Archiepiscopi Opera Omnia*, vols. 3–5, ed. Franciscus Salesius Schmitt (Edinburgh: 1946–1951, repr. Stuttgart-Bad Cannstatt, 1968). For a general overview of women writing letters in the Middle Ages, see Karen Cherewatuk and Ulrike Wiethaus, "Introduction: Women Writing Letters in the Middle Ages," in Karen Cherewatuk and Ulrike Wiethaus, eds., *Dear Sister: Medieval Women and the Epistolary Genre* (Philadelphia: University of Pennsylvania Press, 1993), 1–19.

[13] Peter Damian, Ep. 114, *Die Briefe des Petrus Damiani*, vol. 3, ed. Kurt Reindel, Monumenta Germaniae Historica (MGH) Briefe der deutschen Kaiserzeit 4 (Munich: MGH, 1989), 296–297.

[14] Fletcher, "Rhetoric, Reform, and Christian Eloquence," 66–67.

through letters.[15] The first of these changes was the widespread renewal of interest in classical rhetoric, which reached its high point during the eleventh and twelfth centuries.[16] At this time, intellectuals seized on Cicero's insistence that rhetoric – understood to be a tool for persuading others to take a certain action or agree with a certain idea – was primarily concerned with accomplishing a wide variety of practical tasks in all fields.[17] As a result, rhetoric came to play a formative role in medieval thought until the reintroduction of Aristotle in the thirteenth century.[18] The cultural importance of rhetoric unsurprisingly led to an increase in letters, which were such natural vehicles for rhetorical precepts that few medieval authors made any distinction between letter-writing and spoken oratory, the traditional mode of expression for Ciceronian rhetoric.[19]

The other important change in intellectual culture that facilitated the flowering of letter-writing was the growing number of movements within the church to reform and renew spiritual life throughout medieval society.[20] While classical rhetoric imbued highly educated religious thinkers with the tools to express their ideas convincingly, reform provided them with the urgent spiritual use to which those tools could be put.[21] Accordingly, from the eleventh century on, religious thinkers were increasingly more open about using their work (sermons, treatises, commentaries, etc.) to make some kind of measurable impact on the world at large in a variety of ways: redefining the relationship between the ecclesiastical and secular realms, describing and encouraging the development of good prelates, creating new religious orders to better fulfill the spiritual life, and the like.[22]

Whatever their goal, all medieval spiritual reformers needed to convince their audiences to change their behavior. As natural carriers of persuasive rhetoric, then, letters were vitally important to many reform projects, and it is no coincidence that many of the most ardent eleventh- and twelfth-century

---

[15] Cf. Van Engen, "Letters, Schools, and Written Culture," 132 and Fletcher, "Rhetoric," 66–67.

[16] John O. Ward, *Ciceronian Rhetoric in Treatise, Scholion and Commentary*, Typologie des sources du moyen âge occidental, fasc. 58 (Turnhout: Brepols, 1995).

[17] C. Stephen Jaeger, *The Envy of Angels: Cathedral Schools and Social Ideals in Medieval Europe, 950–1200* (Philadelphia: University of Pennsylvania Press, 1994), 128.

[18] See especially Richard McKeon, "Rhetoric in the Middle Ages," *Speculum* 17 (1942): 1–32.

[19] Cf. John O. Ward, "Rhetorical Theory and the Rise and Decline of *Dictamen* in the Middle Ages and Early Renaissance," *Rhetorica* 19, no. 2 (2001): 175–223 and James J. Murphy, *Rhetoric in the Middle Ages: A History of Rhetorical Theory from Saint Augustine to the Renaissance* (Berkeley: University of California Press, 1974), 194–203.

[20] Gerhart B. Ladner, *The Idea of Reform: Its Impact on Christian Thought and Action in the Age of the Fathers* (Cambridge, MA: Harvard University Press, 1959).

[21] Fletcher, "Rhetoric," 74–80.

[22] Giles Constable, *The Reformation of the Twelfth Century* (Cambridge: Cambridge University Press, 1996).

reformers were also prolific letter-writers. Peter Damian, for instance, saw his letters as "nails and goads" that could be used to prod his fellow Christians to reform their lives, and generations of religious thinkers after him felt the same.[23] The reforming power of letters remained strong more than a century later. Guibert of Gembloux, who played an important role in the formation of Hildegard's collection, once resolved "to correct and incite others to follow everything laudable" by "spread[ing] it abroad as much as I could through letters."[24]

Given the pervasiveness of letter-writing during her lifetime, it would have been surprising if Hildegard had *not* written letters. Practically everyone else interested in using the study of divine truths to reshape human thought and behavior recognized the value of the letter form as a vehicle for religious ideas. Thus, if Hildegard had any notions of using her access to divine wisdom to enact some kind of impact on the world, letter-writing was something she – like any other religious thinker in her day – would have been expected to do.

Hildegard As a Letter-Writer

Within this context of the proliferation of letter-writing, however, Hildegard's letters were unique; the vast majority of them did not even look like conventional medieval letters at all. Unlike her contemporaries', Hildegard's letters usually lacked standard aspects of epistolary form like *salutationes*, and they only rarely followed the standard structure of a Ciceronian oration (*exordium, narratio, petitio, reprehensio, conclusio,* etc.). Rather than a speech, the letters she wrote were "true visions" (*uerae uisiones*) from the Living Light.[25] Generally, the rhetorical structure of her letters consisted of a description of a particular vision followed by a brief exposition and then a word of exhortation. More importantly, Hildegard's letters were not filled with the measured and clear "plain words" (*nudis uerbis*) of Ciceronian oratory but rather with the "parables and similitudes" (*parabolas et similitudines*) typical of prophecy.[26] This type of language made Hildegard's work (including her letters) difficult to understand, which would have been anathema to the typical Ciceronian orator.[27] The contrast

---

[23] Peter Damian, Ep. 21, *Die Briefe des Petrus Damiani*, vol. 1, 203.

[24] Guibert of Gembloux, Ep. 13, *Epistulae*, vol. 1, ed. Albert Derolez, CCCM 66 (Turnhout: Brepols, 1988), 199.

[25] Cf. Ep. 84r, CCCM 91, 201.   [26] Ep. 268, CCCM 91B, 18.

[27] Gebeno of Eberbach, *La Obra de Gebenón de Eberbach*, ed. José Carlos Santos Paz (Florence: SISMEL – Edizioni del Galluzzo, 2004), 6.

between Hildegard and her fellow letter-writers has been so striking that the seer still rarely appears in studies of medieval epistolography.[28] These studies, in general, seem to take Hildegard at her word that her letters should be seen in the context of her visionary corpus rather than the more obviously Ciceronian work of her fellow letter-writers.

If we look past their prophetic language, however, it becomes clear that, when it came to persuasion, Hildegard's letters were intended to work exactly the same as any other twelfth-century letter would.[29] While there was no concrete form of a letter during the Middle Ages, medieval authors seemed to agree that there were certain characteristics – all of which were believed to make the content of a given letter more persuasive – that were most easily, if not exclusively, associated with letter-writing.[30] In particular, the collection indicates that Hildegard and her team looked to take advantage of the letter form's ability to reach a wide, public audience; to build a personal connection with a recipient; and to manifest physical presence.

Given the wide manuscript tradition of the collection, it seems reasonable to assume that reports of Hildegard's fame spreading through her "writings" (*litteris*) likely were referring to her letters as much as her treatises or sermons.[31] Indeed, more manuscripts of Hildegard's letters were produced in the Middle Ages than of any of her other, more famous visionary works.[32] According to the manuscript catalogue compiled by Michael Embach and Martina Wallner, there are fifty-nine known copies of various parts of the letter collection and some individual letters (the letter to Bernard of Clairvaux, letters to the clergy in Cologne and Trier) survive separately in some three dozen copies. Taken together, these manuscripts outnumber all the known manuscript copies of her major visionary treatises (*Scivias*, *Liber vitae meritorum*, and *Liber divinorum operum*) combined. That Hildegard's letters would circulate more widely (and be copied into more manuscripts) than her treatises would not have surprised her; most twelfth-century religious thinkers knew that their contemporaries were more likely to encounter their work in a letter than in a treatise, which reached a much smaller audience.[33]

[28] An exception is Van Engen, "Letters, Schools, and Written Culture."
[29] On the particular rhetorical strategy Hildegard employed in her letters, see Gillian T. Ahlgren, "Visions and Rhetorical Strategy in the Letters of Hildegard of Bingen," in Cherewatuk and Wiethaus, eds., *Dear Sister*, 46–63.
[30] Fletcher, "Rhetoric," 69–74.   [31] Ep. 220, CCCM 91A, 480.
[32] Michael Embach and Martina Wallner, *Conspectus der Handschriften Hildegards von Bingen* (Münster: Aschendorff, 2013).
[33] John Van Engen, "Letters and the Public *Persona* of Hildegard," in Alfred Haverkamp, ed., *Hildegard of Bingen in ihrem historischen Umfeld* (Mainz: Verlag Philipp von Zabern, 2000), 375.

More than any other genre at the time, letters were able to reach a large audience relatively quickly; in fact, it was commonly assumed that anything sent in a letter would become public knowledge as a matter of course.[34] Letters thus offered Hildegard an effective means for projecting her prophetic voice throughout Christendom as quickly and widely as possible. Her readers recognized this as well. When a correspondent asked her to send a written version of a sermon she had delivered in Cologne in the 1160s, she responded with a letter addressed to the "shepherds of the Church," which was designed to bring her powerful admonitions to a European audience.[35] In this, Hildegard was again following a maxim largely taken for granted by many twelfth-century religious thinkers: if one wanted their work to be publicly known, one had to write letters.

Because they directly invoked a particular recipient or group, letters were believed to be able to build personal connections between senders and recipients, and it was widely accepted that this connection made the sender's arguments more convincing.[36] This was certainly of interest for Hildegard, who saw it as her mission to convey the words of the Living Light to a humanity that had lost the ability to hear them.[37] Letters offered Hildegard the chance to make the messages contained in her treatises or sermons – which were by nature fairly general – more directly relevant to individual recipients. That is, her correspondents may well have come across prophetic admonitions in her other treatises, but it would have been more difficult to ignore them in a letter, which could personally warn a recipient to "understand these words spoken to *you*," whatever they might be.[38]

Finally, letters gave weight to this personal connection by manifesting the physical presence of the sender before the recipient.[39] This quality allowed medieval letter-writers to send their physical selves over great distances to interact with their readers for every purpose from conversation to admonition.[40] Hildegard's letters, however, offered something more. Far beyond pleasant conversation, a letter from her allowed the possibility for interacting with nothing less than the Living Light itself by sharing in the presence of "an instrument and receptacle of the Holy Spirit."[41] To that end, Hildegard's readers often expressed a desire to interact physically with her through their letters, usually by hearing her voice or seeing her virtues

---

[34] Constable, *Letters*, 11.   [35] Epp. 15–15r, CCCM 91, 32–47.   [36] Fletcher, "Rhetoric," 69–70.
[37] Hildegard of Bingen, *Scivias*, 1.prol., ed. Adelgundis Führkötter and Angela Carlevaris, CCCM 43 (Turnhout: Brepols, 1978), 8.
[38] Ep. 85r/b, CCCM 91, 207. Emphasis mine.   [39] Fletcher, "Rhetoric," 71–72.
[40] Van Engen, "Letters, Schools, and Written Culture," 114.   [41] Ep. 190, CCCM 91a, 429.

in practice.[42] For her part, Hildegard also emphasized the physicality of her letters; even with their prophetic language, she repeatedly commanded her correspondents to "see" and "hear" the visions she sent them, as if they were being received directly from God.

Other high medieval letter-writers took advantage of these same rhetorical characteristics but, at least according to the evidence in the collection, Hildegard's prophetic status amplified them to the point that a letter from her was potentially more persuasive than one from anyone else. Her letters, in other words, were not simply letters, even if they worked the same way other letters did. Corresponding with Hildegard meant corresponding directly with the Living Light, which elevated them, at least in theory, to "talismans" granting prestige to any institution or individual who was worthy enough to receive one.[43]

This high esteem for Hildegard's letters is borne out in the extraordinary amount (more than forty percent) of incoming correspondence in the collection. If their witness is to be believed, the opportunity to somehow create a physical and lasting relationship with the divine was too enticing to ignore.[44] A typical example is that of Abbot Conrad of Kaisheim, for example, who believed Hildegard was "a certain rivulet emanating from the fount of goodness itself, diffusing your benevolence to all those who desire to see and hear the mighty works of God through you," and he begged her to grant him access to this benevolence through "a little gift" (*munusculum*) – that is, a letter.[45]

The Making of Hildegard's Letters

In part, Hildegard's letters acquired their lofty status by design. Their talismanic potential was rooted in Hildegard's prophetic persona, but it was also the product of years of careful curation by Hildegard and her secretaries. The fruit of their labor was an "official" edition of the letters copied into the *Riesencodex*, the last revision of the letters with which Hildegard had been associated. Not surprisingly, this edition is also the most problematic; over the years, the clear emendations, corrections, and alterations in the *Riesencodex* copy when compared to earlier circulating copies have cast a shadow of doubt on the authenticity of the entire collection (the incoming correspondence in particular), although scholars

---

[42] E.g. Guibert of Gembloux, Ep. 16, CCCM 66, 220.
[43] Van Engen, "Letters and the Public *Persona*," 416–417.   [44] Ibid., 399.
[45] Ep. 144, CCCM 91B, 319.

now generally accept Hildegard's authorship of her own letters.[46] Regardless, the efforts made to transform the letters into a formal collection remain instructive for those who read them today, as they bring what she and her collaborators considered the most important aspects of her public persona into sharper focus.

Hildegard's letter collection developed along the same lines as most other high medieval letter collections, transforming over time from an unorganized series of correspondence to a formal, "quasi-literary" work.[47] As is true of any twelfth-century collection, no original copies of the letters survive.[48] Any letters she wrote or received would most likely have been gathered together or copied into what some scholars have called a *Briefbuch* or *Liber epistolarum*, a collection in seriatim of both incoming and outgoing correspondence.[49] These copybooks were the sole record of the correspondence until the letters within it could be edited and refined into a formal collection. Not all the letters in the copybook would have been saved; it was customary for authors and their editors to select only the letters that fit with the overarching theme the collection addressed.

In Hildegard's case, the collection's objective was unquestionably to support the campaign to elevate her to sainthood. The first attempt to create an edited collection of her letters appears to have taken place by the 1160s at the latest, after Hildegard successfully moved her convent to the Rupertsberg. Several manuscripts of selected letters were produced around this time, quite possibly from copybooks held at the new convent.[50] The surviving manuscripts copied from these lost exemplars contain only part of Hildegard's letters, often leaving out the incoming correspondence.[51] Most likely, Volmar was responsible for beginning the editorial process (almost surely with Hildegard's consent), and his aim seems to have been to preserve Hildegard's by then well-known reputation as a prophet. John Van Engen has argued that the purpose of this first edition was to show Hildegard as "an 'oracle' writing letters," and so it focused primarily on her and her voice, which was at this time less polished.[52] Therefore, manuscripts from this first stage include very few incoming letters and omit the names or other identifying information about her correspondents.[53]

[46] See Schrader and Führkötter, *Die Echtheit des Schrifttums*, 1–6.
[47] Klaes-Hachmöller, "Von einer Briefsammlung."   [48] Köhn, "Zur Quellenkritik," 290.
[49] Bernhard Schmeidler, "Über Briefsammlungen des früheren Mittelalters in Deutschland und ihre kritische Verwertung," *Vetenskaps-Societeten i Lund: Årsbok* (1926): 5–27.
[50] Van Engen, "Letters and the Public *Persona*," 376–377.
[51] For a description of these early manuscripts, see Schrader and Führkötter, *Echtheit*, 59–103.
[52] Van Engen, "Letters and the Public *Persona*," 377.
[53] Schrader and Führkötter, *Echtheit*, 85–103.

The next stage in the collection's development occurred between 1170 and 1173, when Hildegard appeared to be dying.[54] The need to secure Hildegard's status as a saint compelled Volmar to create a new edition of the letters that incorporated, for the first time, many of the editorial principles later seen in the *Riesencodex*.[55] These additions included reinserting the incoming correspondence, arranging the letters hierarchically according to the rank of the addressees, and coordinating incoming letters with their responses from Hildegard. Volmar also invented some letters at this stage. Chief among these inventions was a letter from Eugenius III approving Hildegard's visionary work (Ep. 4), which has played an important role in historical descriptions of her career for centuries. On closer scrutiny, the letter does not match the rhetorical style of authentic letters from Eugenius, but perhaps more importantly, the papal license granted in this letter is never mentioned where one would expect to find it – namely, in the preface of the *Scivias*, as a part of the customary flattery of incoming letters, or in the documentation of her legal disputes with her former home of Disibodenberg – which suggests that it did not exist in the early stages of Hildegard's public career.[56] Similarly, a letter in the *Riesencodex* from Conrad III, the King of the Romans, is dubious, since it does not appear in the earlier manuscript tradition of her letters, when it would have had to have been written.[57] Volmar also altered some of Hildegard's own letters at this point, adjusting their language and, at times, combining multiple missives into a single letter.[58]

Reflecting the sense of urgency behind it, the second edition of Hildegard's letters offered much clearer proof of her saintly status. The reintroduced incoming correspondence played a key role in this effort, as it provided a more comprehensive view of Hildegard's interaction with the public, her activities as a source of divine teaching, and the great public interest in communicating with her. Those responsible for the edition of the letters in the *Riesencodex* continued to follow the editorial course Volmar set.[59]

Beyond tinkering with the language or adjusting addressees, the editors made further changes that maximized Hildegard's prestige and minimized any potential complications, or even effaced them entirely. Some letters

---

[54] Van Acker, "Briefwechsel," 134–137.
[55] Van Engen, "Letters and the Public *Persona*," 377–378.
[56] Paul von Winterfeld, "Die vier Papstbriefe in der Briefsammlung der h. Hildegard," *Neues Archiv* 27 (1902): 237–244, esp. 237–238.
[57] Klaes-Hachmöller, "Von einer Briefsammlung," 163.
[58] Schmeidler, "Bemerkungen," 345–351.   [59] Van Acker, "Briefwechsel," 129–134.

present in earlier compilations were removed from the final edition; for instance, the *Riesencodex* lacks a letter from Hildegard harshly criticizing the archbishop of Cologne, lest posterity see Hildegard condemning a bishop who supported the papacy.[60] Still others had their language adjusted so as to seem less controversial, as was the case with a letter from the regular canoness Tenxwind of Andernach (also referred to as Tengswich) criticizing various practices at the Rupertsberg, such as Hildegard's decision to allow her nuns to wear their hair down and adorn themselves with jewelry on certain feast days, among other things. In the original letter, Tenxwind prefaced a quotation of 1 Timothy 2:9 ("also that the women should dress themselves modestly and decently in suitable clothing, not with their hair braided, or with gold, pearls, or expensive clothes") with a sharp critique: "Indeed, the greatest pastor of the Church objects to such things in his letter." In the *Riesencodex*, the editors replaced this stern admonition with a preemptive note of understanding: "All of these things, we believe, you are led to do out of love for the highest Spouse."[61]

All these changes were made to smooth out the thornier aspects of Hildegard's public career and present her as an unquestioned source of life-changing divine wisdom. The alterations made to the collection over the years created a written testament to both the immense influence she wielded over individuals from all walks of medieval life and the devout and humble manner in which she wielded it. In this way, Hildegard's letters were clearly meant to be a decisive document supporting her case for sainthood after her death, one that confirmed her prophetic persona was as powerful and influential as it seemed to be in her other visionary works. In what follows, we will consider how they did so.

Hildegard's Political and Spiritual Influence in Her Letters

Writing years after the fact, Guibert of Gembloux described the general reaction when Hildegard's prophetic persona became publicly known: "many," he recalled, "drawn in by the sweet odor of her fragrance ... hastened to her, from the fields and villages, and from the cities also. All of them desired her helpful judgments and pronouncements, – some for the sake of devotion, others for curiosity, still others for exhortation."[62] Implied by Guibert's detailed description here was the immense power

---

[60] Ibid., 148.   [61] Ep. 52, CCCM 91, 126. Cf. Van Acker, "Briefwechsel," 145.
[62] Guibert of Gembloux, Ep. 26, CCCM 66A, 275.

that Hildegard's prophetic persona carried; whatever their particular interest, everyone seemed to agree that her "judgments and pronouncements" needed to be heard. All of Hildegard's visionary works ostensibly carried this power, but the letters provide us with the best evidence for measuring it. The key to uncovering the extent and nature of Hildegard's influence in her day lies in the dialogue between what the public (as seen in the incoming correspondence) wanted her to do for them and the ways in which Hildegard responded to their expectations.

Hildegard's epistolary public covered a wide geographic area, stretching as far as Paris to the west, Rome to the south, Denmark to the north, and Jerusalem to the east. Other evidence outside of Hildegard's works suggests that her public reach was even larger than her letters indicate. John of Salisbury, for instance, once asked a colleague in Cologne to report on "the visions and oracles of the most celebrated Hildegard" to him while he was exiled in France.[63] For the most part, however, Hildegard's epistolary public was centered in the German lands and the Low Countries. The highest concentration of letters circulated along the Rhine, with the heart of her correspondence (especially in its earliest stages) taking place within the archbishopric of Mainz, to which the Rupertsberg was subject.[64]

In terms of her social reach, Hildegard's message was eagerly anticipated by people from across the social and ecclesiastical hierarchies. Her secular public reached as high as the imperial court of Frederick Barbarossa and the royal court of Henry II of England, but also included middling members of the nobility in the Holy Roman Empire and elsewhere, and reached as low as unnamed laymen. Her ecclesiastical correspondents encompassed a similar range, from popes, Rhineland archbishops, and prominent abbots down to anonymous clergy. However, the letters indicate that Hildegard's influence may have been strongest with leaders of religious communities like herself (abbots and abbesses, priors and prioresses, etc.), as her correspondence with this group accounts for nearly forty percent of the collection.

The geographic and social contours of Hildegard's epistolary public were similar to that of other prominent letter-writers in the twelfth century like Bernard and Anselm. Unlike these other writers, however, Hildegard was not connected to a seat of spiritual or political power (e.g. the Cistercian system of monasteries or the archbishopric of Canterbury,

---

[63] John of Salisbury, Ep. 185, *The Letters of John of Salisbury*, vol. 2, ed. W. J. Millor and Christopher Nugent Lawrence Brooke (Oxford: Clarendon Press, 1979), 224.

[64] María José Ortúzar Escudero, *Die Sinne in den Schriften Hildegards von Bingen*, Monographien zur Geschichte des Mittelalters 62 (Stuttgart: Hiersemann, 2016), 321–324.

respectively) that would have been linked to a large epistolary network. As Guibert intimated, she commanded her public entirely by virtue of her prophetic persona. It was this persona, and the chance to experience the divine through it, that drove individuals throughout the Holy Roman Empire and beyond to reach out to her by letter.

For the most part, all of Hildegard's correspondents were drawn by the notion that she was a conduit for divine knowledge. Nearly every letter she received made some reference to what one correspondent called "the Spirit of God speaking in and writing through you," although what people hoped to learn from it varied.[65] Many were interested in what Hildegard could tell them about the future, either their own or others'; such inquiries ranged from a nobleman asking whether he would die on crusade to laypeople asking about the spiritual fates of friends and family.[66] Other correspondents had more academic queries. A group of monks from Villers, for instance, were keen on obtaining answers to a series of complicated theological questions and sent a series of letters demanding a reply that, to some scholars, bordered on harassment.[67] Other correspondents had more practical concerns in mind, such as finding a cure for various medical problems, including, in at least one case, barrenness.[68]

The majority of Hildegard's correspondents, however, looked to her as a source of relief. For them, the divine knowledge she offered had the ability to cure them of debilitating anxiety, fear, and distress. No group reached out to Hildegard for help of this kind more than abbots and abbesses, who often found themselves mired in a debilitating state of spiritual despair while attempting to fulfill their spiritual responsibilities.[69] For some, the despair was rooted in their inability, as they described it, to lead their unruly spiritual charges to salvation as they were sworn to do. As a result, their office became, as one abbot put it, "a heavy burden ... which is extremely difficult and laborious for me to carry through to the end, [since] I am unfit for the meritorious life and wise teaching it requires, but it is equally dangerous to put it down."[70] Others were held back by their own spiritual shortcomings, feeling that their sins prevented them from being the virtuous pastors the rule required them to be. One abbot, for example, devoted his thoughts "ardently to the desire for good works," but his mind "deceived" him by

[65] Ep. 228, CCCM 91A, 502.   [66] Cf. Epp. 70, 131, 161, 350, 356, 358, and 364.

[67] Ep. 109r, CCCM 91A, 269–71. Cf. Guibert of Gembloux, Epp. 19–26, CCCM 66–66A, 235–257, 264–269, 291–294; and Barbara Newman, "Sybil of the Rhine," in Newman, *Voice of the Living Light*, 26–27.

[68] Ep. 70, CCCM 91, 153.   [69] Ferrante, "Correspondent," 94–99.

[70] Ep. 240, CCCM 91A, 516.

focusing on the better things he was not presently doing, causing him to lose faith in the good deeds he was doing.[71] Many of these despairing monastic leaders went so far as to inquire whether they might find salvation better by leaving their posts.[72]

No matter what the hopes and intentions of their authors were, the most striking takeaway from the incoming letters is the clear sense that the knowledge Hildegard offered had the power to change the world in which she lived. One abbot went so far as to describe Hildegard's work as a literal divine intervention in the world: "For now He raises us up and places His hand on our ruined world," he wrote, "He who joyfully gave to us [you], who are a gift of such quality to shed light on the wickedness in the midst of the world's darkness in our time; to obtain pardon for our sins, rest for our labors, and consolation for our pain."[73] Her correspondents seemed to share an assumption that writing a letter to Hildegard was the best way to bring this divine power she channeled into their own lives.

Taken together, the incoming correspondence implies that a considerable number of Hildegard's contemporaries invested her with a great deal of power and influence; hers was a voice that could admonish to the most powerful rulers in church and state, console the suffering and confused, and open up divine mysteries to those worthy enough to receive them. Given this, it is not surprising that some letter-writers looked to Hildegard as a great agent of spiritual reform, capable of influencing all kinds of individuals to change their lives according to divine truth. Indeed, according to some, Hildegard could achieve this work better than anyone else. The monks of Amorbach repeatedly admonished their monastic colleagues to amend their spiritual lives, but they were more confident that such people "may incline their minds more attentively to your words than ours, since they know and believe that you pronounce commands through a divine vision."[74] The letters in particular were considered quite useful for this purpose, since they preserved her reforming admonitions in text form, thereby keeping the memory of her divinely backed exhortations alive after the initial encounter was forgotten.[75]

While the incoming letters paint a picture of Hildegard as the wielder of significant political power, her own letters, especially those responding directly to outside requests, show that she did not wield this power in a way her public might have expected. Matters of state rarely appear in the letters,

---

[71] Ep. 190r, CCCM 91A, 430.
[72] Ep. 189, CCCM 91A, 427. See also Epp. 140, 144, 174, 190, 200, 207, 229, 237, and 240.
[73] Ep. 91, CCCM 91A, 243.   [74] Ep. 51, CCCM 91, 125.   [75] Ep. 149, CCCM 91A, 332–333.

and even the illustrious secular and ecclesiastical princes with whom she corresponded seemed more interested in securing prayers or guidance in spiritual matters than help with diplomatic, military, or economic matters. As a *magistra* herself, Hildegard must surely have also dealt with matters of this kind, but the letters do not preserve much of that mundane information. A letter from Frederick Barbarossa, for example, includes a promise to "judge . . . the matter to which you have directed us . . . with respect only to justice and fairness," which could well have been a dispute over property or economic rights of her convent.[76] Beyond this, however, no other details about this affair are to be found in the collection, which indicates that Hildegard and her collaborators were not interested in preserving it.

Instead, their aim was to show that Hildegard's politics were inextricably tied to the project of spiritual reform, especially the series of initiatives advocated by the reforming papacy.[77] Generally speaking, her reform program was rooted firmly in traditional Benedictine monasticism, and she used her work to instill the same values codified in the rule – especially order, obedience, and hierarchy – in all of medieval thought and society.[78] Insofar as Hildegard had a political objective for her prophetic career, it was to convince the entire world to adopt the monastic virtues as a means of guaranteeing their salvation.

Her letters were an important component of this effort. Nearly all of them contain a spiritual admonition of some sort, whether it was requested or not. Abbot Helenger of Disibodenberg, Hildegard's former spiritual home, once wrote a short letter requesting a *vita* for his community's patron and may well have been surprised to receive a long letter back demanding that he improve obedience among his monks.[79] Helenger was not alone; many who came to Hildegard with generic requests were likewise given pointed, personal critiques in response. One community of monks asking simply what needed to be improved in the "monastic order" were told, "the most wicked disease of stubbornness wafts out like the putrid stench of a rotting corpse in your own place first of all."[80]

Hildegard sought to correct anyone whose conduct violated her core reform values. She did not hesitate to condemn leaders whose social standing or institutional position exceeded her own; once she angrily upbraided her ecclesiastical superior, the archbishop of Mainz, for

---

[76] Ep. 314, CCCM 91B, 75.
[77] On Hildegard's reforming ideals, see Kathryn Kerby-Fulton, "Prophet and Reformer," in Newman, *Voice of the Living Light*, 70–90.
[78] See Van Engen, "Abbess: 'Mother and Teacher'," in Newman, *Voice of the Living Light*, 46–47.
[79] Ep. 77r, CCCM 91, 168–174.   [80] Ep. 276r, CCCM 91B, 28.

commanding her to release Richardis of Stade to be installed as an abbess elsewhere, "Ach, you speck of dust, why do you not blush when you attempt to scatter yourself on high when you belong down in the rotting filth?"[81] Not surprisingly, she reserved some of her most severe condemnations for secular leaders who interfered with the spiritual business of the church. Frederick Barbarossa, who had frequently clashed with the papacy, felt Hildegard's epistolary rage multiple times. None, however, were as ominous as Hildegard's final surviving letter to him, which warns: "He who is says: I myself will annihilate the obstinacy and crush the opposition of those who disdain me. . . . Hear this, o king, if you wish to live, or else my sword will smite you."[82]

On the other hand, individuals who fell short of her reform ideals out of spiritual despair or confusion often received compassionate responses to alleviate their suffering. Once again, the personal connection created by letters augmented Hildegard's persuasive power, since the consolations she offered were understood to come directly from the divine. For instance, it was not Hildegard, but the "keen Light" itself that informed one correspondent that "you are weak on account of the doubt in your mind, as if you cannot even stand. And why is this? I see your works; indeed, they touch me."[83] She responded similarly to her secular correspondents. When an unnamed woman asked to know whether she would ever have children, Hildegard (speaking as herself) promised to pray that God would grant the woman's request, though she could not give her a definitive answer.[84]

Still, even in her gentler letters, Hildegard never wavered from her commitment to her reform ideals. This is perhaps most visible in her responses to spiritual leaders asking permission to leave their offices. As a rule, she was compassionate when dealing with these requests but always responded with a resolute refusal.[85] Her reason was simple: these men and women were placed in their positions by God to defend all humanity from spiritual harm. As she reminded one abbot, "those in authority (*in magisterio*) stand just as mountains that exist to defend many against their enemies; through their teaching and obedience to God, one sees in them the defense of many from the snares of their enemies."[86]

In other words, a stable leadership in the ecclesiastical hierarchy (but especially in the monastic life) was essential for Hildegard's reform program to work. In this, Hildegard set herself against many other reform efforts seeking a return to the apostolic life; for her, simply following the

---

[81] Ep. 18r, CCCM 91, 54.   [82] Ep. 315, CCCM 91B, 75.   [83] Ep. 144, CCCM 91A, 320.
[84] Ep. 70r, CCCM 91, 156.   [85] Ferrante, "Correspondent," 94.   [86] Ep. 174r, CCCM 91A, 397.

form of spiritual life laid out in the Benedictine rule was sufficient.[87] Without the sure defense the stability of the rule provided, all of Christendom was at risk of succumbing to the attacks of the vices and slipping into damnation, a situation that the reformer in her could not allow. To emphasize the point, Hildegard insisted that anyone who gave up their office for whatever reason removed themselves from the path to salvation; she matter-of-factly told one abbot that he could only give up his pastoral duties "if you have in yourself no eye for living."[88]

It is impossible to say whether Hildegard of Bingen held as much political and spiritual influence as the witness of her letters attests, but, for her medieval editors at least, it was more important to show the relationship between the seer and her public. The dialogue between the incoming and outgoing correspondence reveals a figure in whom contemporaries invested a great deal of power and respect but who nonetheless exercised that power in an orthodox way that remained true to a moderate program of spiritual reform. Though she had the ability to sway important political decisions, if the letters are to be believed, she refused any sort of worldly glory, preferring instead to remain the unlearned, passive transmitter of the Living Light's commands, admonitions, and consolations.

The letters of Hildegard of Bingen allow us to see the famous visionary from a perspective not as easily found in the rest of her corpus. Precisely because of their epistolary nature, the letters show us a prophet in action, engaging with the diverse public she was charged to instruct and illuminate. As such, the letters provide glimpses into aspects of Hildegard's life and career that reflect back on her other works. For example, they offer proof that her prophetic voice – which spoke so powerfully in the *Scivias*, revealed so much divine and natural knowledge in her other treatises, and admonished sinners so strikingly in her sermons – resonated with contemporary audiences at all levels of society throughout Latin Christendom. Perhaps more importantly for the campaign to canonize her, they also confirm how she remained committed to using her prophetic gifts in the humble service of the divine source of her knowledge, as any true saint would do.

This was, of course, the image of Hildegard that she and her secretaries wanted the letters to show, and we must always approach reading them

---

[87] Giles Constable, "Hildegard's Explanation of the Rule of St. Benedict," in Havercamp, *Hildegard in ihrem historischen Umfeld*, 186–187.

[88] Ep. 145, CCCM 91A, 323.

with a healthy dose of caution. All the same, the letters remain a vital source for understanding Hildegard, her work, and her world. On the one hand, they help us to see how Hildegard fit into the intellectual culture of her day; the very existence of the collection confirms that she shared the same intellectual formation and adopted the same strategies for persuasive public outreach as her fellow high medieval religious thinkers. On the other, the letters highlight her exceptionality, detailing how an author with her unique capabilities acquired, nurtured, and managed intense public interest in a way that remained true to the mission she had received. In this, reading Hildegard's letters can, perhaps better than any other source, bring us deeper into the experience of an allegedly "unlearned" oblate from an unremarkable corner of the German lands who became, and remained, "a lantern burning for the illumination of the Church."[89]

Further Reading

Latin Editions and English Translations

Hildegard of Bingen. *Epistolarium*, ed. Lieven Van Acker and Monika Klaes-Hachmöller. 3 vols. Corpus Christianorum Continuatio Mediaevalis 91, 91A, and 91B. Turnhout: Brepols, 1991–2001.
The Letters of Hildegard of Bingen, ed. Joseph L. Baird and Radd K. Ehrman. 3 vols. New York and Oxford: Oxford University Press, 1994–2004.

Secondary Literature

Ahlgren, Gillian T. W. "Visions and Rhetorical Strategy in the Letters of Hildegard of Bingen." In Karen Cherewatuk and Ulrike Wiethaus, eds., *Dear Sister: Medieval Women and the Epistolary Genre*. Philadelphia: University of Pennsylvania Press, 1993, 46–63.
Constable, Giles. *Letters and Letter Collections*. Typologie des Sources du Moyen Âge Occidental, fasc. 17. Turnhout: Brepols, 1976.
Constable, Giles. *The Reformation of the Twelfth Century*. Cambridge: Cambridge University Press, 1996.
Ferrante, Joan. "Correspondent: 'Blessed Is the Speech of Your Mouth.'" InBarbara Newman, ed., *Voice of the Living Light: Hildegard of Bingen and Her World*. Berkeley: University of California Press, 1998, 91–109.
Fletcher, Christopher D. "Rhetoric, Reform, and Christian Eloquence: The Letter Form and the Religious Thought of Peter Damian." *Viator* 46, no. 1 (2015): 61–91.

---

[89] Ep. 113, CCCM 91A, 279.

Haseldine, Julian. "Epistolography." In Frank A. C. Mantello and Arthur George Rigg, eds., *Medieval Latin: An Introduction and Bibliographical Guide*. Washington, DC: The Catholic University of America Press, 1996, 650–658.

Schrader, Marianne and Adelgundis Führkötter. *Die Echtheit des Schrifttums der heiligen Hildegard von Bingen. Quellenkritische Untersuchungen*. Beihefte zum Archiv für Kulturgeschichte 6. Cologne: Böhlau, 1956.

Van Engen, John. "Letters and the Public *Persona* of Hildegard." In A. Haverkamp, ed., *Hildegard von Bingen in ihrem historischen Umfeld: Internationaler wissenschaftlischer Kongreß zum 900 jährigen Jubiläum, 13.–19. September 1998, Bingen am Rhein* (Mainz: Verlag Philipp von Zabern, 2000), 375–418.

Van Engen, John. "Letters, Schools, and Written Culture in the Eleventh and Twelfth Century." In Johannes Fried, ed., *Dialektik und Rhetorik im frühen und hohen Mittelalter: Rezeption, Überlieferung und gesellschaftliche Wirkung antiker Gelehrsamkeit vornehmlich im 9. und 12. Jahrhundert*, Munich: Oldenbourg, 1997, 97–132.

CHAPTER 6

From the Roots to the Branches: Greenness in the Preaching of Hildegard of Bingen and the Patriarchs

Peter V. Loewen

Although a fact often surprising to readers today, preaching was regularly practiced by the female leaders of religious communities of women in Western Europe in the Middle Ages. Beverly Mayne Kienzle writes that Hildegard of Bingen was unrivaled among women preachers of the High Middle Ages.[1] Following the Benedictine tradition, she likely preached locally before her chapter in Rupertsberg and also for the monks at Disibodenberg; it is probably for her nuns that she conceived her *Expositiones Evangeliorum* (Homilies on the Gospels). Its fifty-eight homilies, composed around 1170, are remarkable works of exegesis on twenty-seven Gospel pericopes. Beverly Kienzle notes that while they bear the impress of patristic Bible commentaries (and their Carolingian glosses), Hildegard's intratextual hermeneutics, or the *Glossa Hildegardiana*, yield a dynamic scriptural narrative.[2] It is an overtly performative style of writing, as though she were capturing in prose the spontaneity of a sermon that seamlessly interpolates her voice with the voices of scripture and the layers of commentary on them.

In addition to the preaching she would have done at Rupertsberg and Disibodenberg, between roughly the late 1150s and 1170 Hildegard traveled away from her convent on no fewer than four occasions for the purposes of preaching. Traveling the local rivers, and overland presumably on horseback, Hildegard traversed the length of western Germany from Kirchheim in the south to Cologne in the north. She offers enough detail in her *Physica* about the region's various waterways to suggest she knew the terrain well.[3] Her scientific observations about the Rhine, Main,

---

[1] Beverly Mayne Kienzle, *Hildegard of Bingen and Her Gospel Homilies: Speaking New Mysteries* (Turnhout: Brepols, 2009), 3.
[2] Kienzle, *Hildegard*, 69–70, and 151–152.
[3] For context about Hildegard's *Physica*, see Wallis, Chapter 7, this volume.

Danube, Mosel, Nahe, and Glan rivers – their navigability, flora and fauna, and the properties of their water – probably derive from her experience journeying by boat from one city or convent to another.[4]

What details remain of Hildegard's travels and her preaching may be gleaned from her extant correspondence, the *Vita sanctae Hildegardis* (Life of Saint Hildegard), and various chronicles. Scholars seem to agree that Hildegard made four "preaching tours," but with little direct evidence of her itineraries. It appears she traveled between 1158 and 1161, to Trier on a separate occasion in 1160, through the Rhineland between 1161 and 1163, and to Swabia between 1167 and 1170.[5] Hildegard's biographer Theodoric of Echternach (d. ca. 1192) identifies twenty-one stops in the course of these tours: the cathedral cities of Cologne, Trier, Mainz, Würzburg, and Bamberg; and Disibodenberg, Siegburg, Eberbach, Hirsau, Zwiefalten, Maulbronn, Rothenkirchen, Kitzingen, Krauftal, Hördt, Hönningen, Werden, Andernach, Marienberg, Klause, and Winkel.[6] The trip to Kirchheim, though not on Theodoric's list, is attested in Hildegard's correspondence.[7] There are few eye-witness accounts of her preaching, though centuries later Johannes Trithemius, the author of *Chronica insignis monasterii Hirsaugiensis*, attests with wonder the miraculous speech she gave the monks of Hirsau in 1160.[8]

Preaching, however, particularly for Hildegard can be thought of more broadly as well, as the kind of teaching, cajoling, and criticizing she undertook through her extensive correspondence and through her theological and visionary works. One theme that recurs in her sermons and other writings is her desire to preach through greenness. While she uses *viriditas* (greenness) in mundane circumstances to describe the freshness of vegetation or the vigor of growth sensible to sight, taste, and smell, her language of greenness reaches heights of virtuosity when she uses *viriditas* in the spiritual sense to uncover the forces of life that unify the natural and spiritual worlds of God's

---

[4] Hildegard of Bingen, *Subtilitatum Diversarum naturarum creaturarum* (i.e. *Physica*), in *Patrologia Latina (PL)* 197, ed. Jacques Paul Migne (Paris: 1855), 1125–1352; *Physica*, trans. Priscilla Throop (Rochester, VT: Healing Arts Press, 1998), 101–102.

[5] Mary Palmquist has arranged most of these locations into four itineraries, in "Chronology of the Life and Works of Hildegard," in *The Life of the Holy Hildegard*, trans. Adelgundis Führkötter and James McGrath; ed. Mary Palmquist and John Kulas OSB (Collegeville, MN: Liturgical Press, 1995), 109–111. Kienzle, *Hildegard*, 55.

[6] *Vita sanctae Hildegardis*, ed. Monika Klaes, Corpus Christianorum Continuatio Mediaevalis (CCCM) 126 (Turnhout: Brepols, 1993), 3.17, 54–55 (references are by book, chapter, and page). Kienzle, *Hildegard*, 48–49.

[7] Palmquist, "Chronology," 109–111. See also Kienzle, *Hildegard*, 47. Hildegard's correspondence with a priest named Werner (149r) indicates she visited Kirchheim in 1170.

[8] Johannes Trithemius, *Chronica insignis monasterii Hirsauiensis*, qtd. in Kienzle, *Hildegard*, 53.

creation. Greenness is palpable everywhere in Hildegard's writing, so much so that her meaning defies perfect understanding.

Christel Meier's concise study of "Grün" in Hildegard's writings shows how broadly she applied the term in cosmology, natural science, and exegesis;[9] but how original was her thinking? Sara Ritchey suggests that Hildegard's use of *viriditas* may have derived from the *Speculum virginum*, particularly when she uses "natural language and imagery to convey the same sense of possibility for divine access in the re-created world."[10] Yet comparing her writings with patristic models strongly suggests the seer's hermeneutics fit into a long tradition of scriptural exegesis. A simple search for *viriditas* in the *Patrologia Latina Database* (*PLD*), using the word stem "viridit," returns 1,034 matches (including all declensions). Further analysis clearly shows that writings of Saints Ambrose (33 iterations), Augustine (16 iterations), and Gregory (72 iterations) were formative, many writers either paraphrasing their words or copying them verbatim. Remarkably, Hildegard's works account for nearly a quarter of all uses of *viriditas*: 232 iterations, which would increase to 339 were one to include works not in the *PLD*, namely *Cause et cure* (49), *Liber vitae meritorum* (38), *Expositiones Evangeliorum* (10), *Symphonia armonie celestium revelationum* (9), and *Ordo virtutum* (1).[11] A broader examination of cognates like *viridis, virere, virescere, revirescere, viror, viredo*, and so on would surely reveal an even more expansive understanding of the "greenness" in Hildegard's usage. Yet one suspects it would confirm what a narrower study of *viriditas* evinces: while she was clearly inspired by writings of the church fathers, Hildegard is seldom derivative. Rather, she subsumes their ideas and terminology into her often ecstatic rhetorical style when she preaches, teaches, and sings about the forces of life bound up together in the natural and spiritual worlds.[12]

---

[9] Christel Meier, "Die Bedeutung der Farben im Werk Hildegards von Bingen," *Frühmittelalterliche Studien* 6 (1972): 280–290. See also Peter Dronke, "Tradition and Innovation in Medieval Western Color-Imagery," *Eranos Jahrbuch* 41 (1972): 82–88.

[10] Sara Ritchey, *Holy Matter: Changing Perceptions of the Material World in Late Medieval Christianity* (Ithaca, NY: Cornell University Press, 2014), 56–57.

[11] These works are published in *Beate Hildegardis Cause et cure*, ed. Laurence Moulinier (Berlin: Akademie-Verlag, 2003); *Liber uite meritorum*, ed. Angela Carlevaris, CCCM 90 (Turnhout: Brepols, 1995); *Hildegardis Bingensis: Opera minora*, ed. Hugh Feiss, Christopher P. Evans, Beverly Mayne Kienzle, Carolyn Muessig, Barbara Newman, and Peter Dronke, CCCM 226 (Turnhout: Brepols, 2007); *Hildegardis Bingensis: Opera minora II*, ed. Christopher P. Evans, Jeroen Deploige, Sara Moens, Michael Embach, and Kurt Gärtner, CCCM 226A (Turnhout: Brepols, 2016); and in *Analecta Sanctae Hildegardis Opera*, ed. Jean Baptiste Pitra, Analecta sacra spicilegio solesmensi parata 8 (Paris: A. Jouby & Roger, 1882).

[12] Kienzle, *Hildegard*, 67, 69, 91. John Dadosky makes a similar point in "The Original Green Campaign: Dr. Hildegard of Bingen's Viriditas as Complement to Laudato Si," *Toronto Journal of Theology* 34, no. 1 (2018): 81.

In what follows, I hope to show that Hildegard's exegesis and sermonizing rely on a method akin to Kienzle's idea of intratextual hermeneutics, where Hildegard seamlessly integrates distinct words or phrases from her models with her own voice.[13] Like the church fathers, she uses her knowledge about natural science to convey a spiritual understanding of scripture, but her exegetic method is more dramatic and visionary. Greenness is unifying, joining faith with reason, virtue, and the office of preaching; but, paradoxically, it is also the force that cleaves Lucifer to God and horseradish to dill. Greenness can even represent the sprouting of sadness when it manifests in the body of an ancient, hairy worm covered with puss.[14] The number of possible connections is myriad. For the purposes of this chapter, however, comparative reading of a selection of examples shall suffice to show how Hildegard adapts notions of *viriditas* from Ambrose, Augustine, and Gregory to teach about the opposition of greenness and dryness in matters of faith and spiritual gardening; how the internal greenness of preachers relates to mental greenness; and to prove that God's presence is manifest in her community of nuns.

Greenness and Dryness

As Christopher D. Fletcher's chapter (Chapter 5) on Hildegard's correspondence in this volume details, several of the letters ascribed to Hildegard include versions of sermons she gave on her journeys, usually written at the behest of clerics who had heard her preach during a stop in their city or convent. Although each of them addresses the particular concerns of the letter-writer, the seer often returns to the same themes: the struggles of the clergy to lead by example, the ruin of the church through the corruption of clerics, and the general weakness of Christian faith; and, like the constant gardener, she almost always frames these conflicts allegorically as a struggle between spiritual *viriditas* and *ariditas*.

In her letter to the provost and clerics of the cathedral of St. Peter's in Trier (223r), Hildegard responds to a request for a copy of the sermon she gave there on Pentecost of 1160. She warns her readers that "a mystical light of a true vision" has cause to upbraid them for their

---

[13] Kienzle, *Hildegard*, 151.

[14] Hildegard of Bingen, *Scivias*, ed. Adelgundis Führkötter and Angela Carlevaris, CCCM 43 (Turnhout: Brepols, 1978), 2.7.7, 313. References are by book, vision, chapter, and page. Hildegard of Bingen, *Scivias*, ed. and trans. Mother Columba Hart and Jane Bishop (New York: Paulist Press, 1990), 296. Hildegard writes that the devil imbues people with sadness as though it were "sprouting green" (*Scivias*, CCCM 43, 2.7.17, 320; *Scivias*, ed. Hart and Bishop, 300).

corruption.[15] She explains the weakness of their faith as a lack of greenness. The Holy Spirit is not in them, she says, because "they have no viridity and are dry and withered."[16] This invective against clerical corruption clearly echoes Gregory's reflections on Job 29:18[17] in book 19 of the *Moralia in Job* (Moral Reflections on the Book of Job).[18] In fact, Gregory might have been thinking of Ambrose's *Hexaemeron* when he expounded the spiritual meaning of greenness in the prophet's reference to a palm tree.[19] Yet rather than standing as a model for the verdure of youth and the grace of the church, as does Ambrose, Gregory recognizes the perpetual greenness of the palm tree as a symbol of spiritual struggle, much as the Holy Church struggles to achieve and maintain a standard of faith.[20] Still, his message is ultimately hopeful. Comparing the lives of the chosen ones to a palm tree, he says that, while they appear dry and shriveled in their lower extremities from bearing the burden of cares, they stretch upward with "abundant greenness," a sign of "abundant rewards."[21]

Like Augustine, Gregory uses the fleeting greenness of grass to represent withering faith. He actually includes a short survey of the many references to grass in scripture and the ways they have been interpreted: as allegory for "temporal glory," "food of the devil," "knowledge and doctrine of eternal life," and for preaching.[22] The decisive turn to preaching occurs when Gregory calls on the authority of Jeremiah 14:6, which talks about the asses whose eyes failed them "because they found no grass." Gregory says this was sometimes understood as the "wisdom and doctrine of eternal verdure

---

[15] Hildegard of Bingen, *Epistolarium*, 3 vols., ed. Lieven Van Acker and Monika Klaes-Hachmöller, CCCM 91, 91A, and 91B (Turnhout: Brepols, 1991–2001), Letter 223r, CCCM 91A, 490; *The Letters of Hildegard of Bingen*, ed. and trans. Joseph L. Baird and Radd K. Ehrman, 3 vols. (Oxford: Oxford University Press, 1994–2004), 3:18.

[16] Letter 223r, CCCM 91A, 490; *Letters*, 3:19.

[17] "I said 'I will die in my little nest, and like a palm tree I will have many days'" (Job 29:18).

[18] Constant Mews counts twenty-four references to *viriditas* in Gregory's *Moralia in Job*, but the *Patrologia Latina Database* (http://pld.chadwyck.co.uk/) reports no fewer than forty-five. See Mews, "Religious Thinker: 'A Frail Human Being' on Fiery Life," in *Voice of the Living Light: Hildegard of Bingen and Her World* (Berkeley: University of California Press, 1998), 58 and 112 n. 28.

[19] St. Ambrose, *Hexaemeron*, 3.17, in *PL* 14, ed. Jacques Paul Migne (Paris: 1945), 167. St. Ambrose, *Hexameron, Paradise, and Cain and Abel*, trans. John S. Savage (New York: Fathers of the Church, 1961), 86–87. Ambrose calls on man to imitate the palm, as it never loses its greenness.

[20] Gregorius Magnus, *Moralia in Job*, ed. M. Adriaen, Corpus Christianorum Series Latina (CCSL) 143A (Turnhout: Brepols, 1979), 19.27.48, 994. Following tradition, CCSL references to Gregory's *Moralia* are by book, division, chapter, and page. *Moral Reflections on the Book of Job*, trans. Brian Kerns, OCSO, 5 vols. (Collegeville, MN: Liturgical Press, 2014), 4:190.

[21] *Moralia*, CCSL 143A, 19.27.48–49, 994–995; *Moral Reflections*, 4:190–191.

[22] *Moralia*, CCSL 143A, 29.26.51–3, 1469–71. *Morals on the Book of Job*, ed. James Bliss, 3 vols. (Oxford: J. Parker, 1844–1850), 3.1:337–339.

[*viriditas*]," a concept he goes on to parse in fine detail. Ranging through scriptural authority, he opines that the want of grass and lack of knowledge of eternity are tantamount, and this occurs when one seeks delight in worldly goods, neglecting the nourishment of the "verdure of inward doctrine" (*viriditatis internae doctrinae*).[23] Yet rain in the desert produced greenery, which should be understood in the spiritual sense as preaching "because when the Gentile world enjoyed the shower of holy preaching, it budded forth with both the works of life, and the herb of doctrine."[24]

Gregory paints a dismal picture of the church in turmoil, using the allegory of aridity and greenness much as Hildegard later would: to attest the struggles of faith and, for Hildegard especially, to decry the effects of corruption among clerics. In at least nine distinct cases in the *Moralia*, Gregory parses aridity to explain the challenges of hypocrisy, temptation, depravity, solitude, and carnality.[25] Yet his most compelling statement about the conflict between *ariditas* and *viriditas* occurs in his *Homilies on Ezekiel*. In homily 2 of book 2, Gregory implores people who have heard the voice of God to speak to their neighbors through the office of preaching.[26] Likening the Beloved in the *Song of Songs* to the Holy Church, he transports the reader to the church's dwelling place in the garden, where each soul is "filled with the verdure [*viriditate*] of hope";[27] but, he warns, using language later echoed in Hildegard's exegesis, "the hope of this age is dry because all the things which are loved here hastily fade."[28]

The dichotomy between *ariditas* and *viriditas* in Hildegard's writing often animates the conflict between withering faith and spiritual vitality. For example, responding to Archbishop Eberhard of Bamberg in a letter written sometime between 1163 and 1164 (31r), the seer uses greenness and dryness to explain the connection (or lack thereof) between the Holy Spirit and the eternity of God. She expounds at length, acknowledging that the Holy Spirit is the fire of life inherent in the living God. "[A]nything devoid of life-force is dead, just as a limb cut off from a tree becomes withered [*aridum est*], because it no longer has the stuff of life [*viriditatem*] in it."[29]

---

[23] *Moralia*, 29.26.51–3, 1470; *Morals*, ed. Bliss, 3.1:336.   [24] Ibid.
[25] *Moralia*, 4.4; 8.42; 11.44; 12.4; 12.53; 14.20; 30.14; 30.23; 33.5. References are by book and chapter.
[26] Gregorius Magnus, *Homiliae in Ezechielem prophetam*, ed. M. Adriaen, CCSL 142 (Turnhout: Brepols, 1971), 2.2.4, 227; Gregory the Great, *Homilies on the Book of the Prophet Ezekiel*, trans. Theodosia Tomkinson (Etna, CA: Center for Traditional Orthodox Studies, 2008), 282. References in CCSL to the *Homilies of Ezekiel* are by book, homily, chapter, and page.
[27] *Homiliae in Ezechielem*, 2.2.4, 227; *Homilies on Ezekiel*, 282.   [28] Ibid.
[29] Letter 31r, CCCM 91, 86; *Letters*, 1:97.

Similar themes obtain elsewhere in Hildegard's correspondence. Writing some time before 1173, an abbot (possibly from Rothenkirchen) beseeches Hildegard for some spiritual consolation (191). In her response (191r), Hildegard frames the abbot's dilemma allegorically as a comparison of different types of clouds. The abbot's mind is muddled like a snow cloud, she says, which cannot nurture wholesome herbs. Nor can the windy cloud, because it is filled with the cold north air: "from it, all viridity withers [*viriditatem arescere*], and flowers fall."[30] The remedy for the abbot's snowy mind is a pure air cloud because it "bestows dew, stable temperature, and rain: vegetation and flowers grow from it."[31] Hildegard offers similar advice to the abbess of Kaufungen who, likewise, asks the seer for spiritual comfort. Writing before 1173 she responds (147r), "you have wandered astray in the winter of the spiritual life. And so run quickly to the viridity of the Holy Spirit, which is summer, by changing your morals."[32]

Hildegard is less comforting to the priest Werner of Kirchheim, who in 1170 requested a copy of the sermon she gave there on the subject of "the priests' negligence of divine service."[33] In her sermon (149r), she interprets a mystical vision to excoriate the clergy of Kirchheim. While on her sickbed, she writes that she perceived a wonderful vision of the Bride of Christ (i.e. the church) whose resplendent garments had been tarnished by the corruption and sins of the clergy – lust, fornication, adultery, and avarice. In this declined state, she says the clergy are unable to care for the souls in their charge, which allows their sins to fester like open wounds. Yet rather than guide them to recovery, the seer, speaking in the voice of the church, calls on God to "rain down all kinds of calamities upon mankind in the vengeance of God, and let a cloud cover the whole earth, so that its viridity withers [*viriditas eius arescat*] and its beauty fades."[34] It is a truly frightening revelation, not unlike the menacing fog Hildegard envisions in the first book of the *Liber divinorum operum* (Book of Divine Works), which descends toward the earth, threatening its greenness with desiccation.[35]

---

[30] Letter 191r, CCCM 91A, 433; *Letters*, 2:158.   [31] Letter 191r, CCCM 91A, 433; *Letters*, 2:158.
[32] Letter 147r, CCCM 91A, 328; *Letters*, 2:88.   [33] Letter 149, CCCM 91A, 333; *Letters*, 2:91.
[34] Letter 149r, CCCM 91A, 335; *Letters*, 2:93.
[35] *Liber divinorum operum*, ed. Albert Derolez and Peter Dronke, CCCM 92 (Turnhout: Brepols, 1996), 1.4.1, 137; Hildegard of Bingen, *The Book of Divine Works*, trans. Nathaniel M. Campbell (Washington, DC: The Catholic University of America Press, 2018), 130. Hildegard repeats her description in *Liber divinorum operum*, 138; *The Book of Divine Works*, 133.

Preaching and Gardening

To appreciate more fully the circumstances under which spiritual viridity struggles to thrive in Hildegard's hermeneutics, it would be useful to return to the exegesis of Augustine and Gregory. Augustine, for example, equates the greenness of grass with sin. More specifically, in his frequently quoted commentary on Psalm 91:8, he draws an analogy between the worldly delight inherent in sin and the ephemeral beauty of grass that quickly wilts in the heat of summer.[36] In his commentary on Psalm 128:6, he illustrates the problem using the grasses that grow on rooftops. Their roots are shallow, and so they are easily pulled up and thrown on the fire; and he says this is so because "they lack the sap needed for any green growth [viriditas]."[37]

The struggle for spiritual greening becomes more complex in Gregory's exegesis of Job 14:7–10, as he parses its meaning relative to preaching in chapters 4 through 6 of book 12 of the *Moralia*.[38] By his reckoning, Job's reference to the tree that sprouts after being felled may be understood as the "just person" who hopes for the "freshness [viriditas] of eternal life."[39] For even if its root should rot and the trunk fall into decay (literally "die in the dust"), he says it may return to life. Moreover, this should give comfort to those who suffer for their faith; although a just person may suffer for truth, like a fallen tree that suffers decay and desiccation in the dust, he will "grow in love" and thereby "receive the freshness [viriditas] of spiritual life."[40]

Gregory refines his metaphor to shed light on the calling of preachers. He asks, "What is the just person's root if not holy preaching?"[41] Evidently the tree signifies the preacher, while dust represents the depraved sinners who kill it (him) through their persecution. Yet there is hope, as he says, for the tree can be rejuvenated with water, which Gregory equates with the

---

[36] St. Augustine, "In Psalmum XCI Ennarratio," in *Enarrationes in Psalmos*, ed. Eligius Dekkers and Jean Fraipont, CCSL 39 (Turnhout: Brepols, 1956; 2nd ed. 1990), 91.9, 1286. References are by Psalm, verse, and page. St. Augustine, *Expositions of the Psalms 73–98*, trans. Maria Boulding, OSB, The Works of Saint Augustine III/18 (Hyde Park, NY: New City Press, 2002), 354.

[37] St. Augustine, "In Psalmum CXXVIII Ennarratio," in *Enarrationes in Psalmos*, ed. Eligius Dekkers and Jean Fraipont, CCSL 40 (Turnhout: Brepols, 1956; 2nd ed. 1990), 128.11, 1887–1888. St. Augustine, *Expositions of the Psalms 121–150*, trans. Maria Boulding, OSB, The Works of Saint Augustine III/20 (Hyde Park, NY: New City Press, 2004), 125.

[38] "There is hope for a tree. If it should be cut down, it might sprout again and put forth new limbs. If its root should rot in the ground, and its trunk die in the dust, it will blossom anew at the touch of water and put forth leaves, just as when it was first planted. When a man dies, however, he is stripped and decomposed. Where is he then, may I ask?" (Job 14:7–10).

[39] *Moralia*, CCSL 143A, 12.4.5, 631; *Moral Reflections*, 3:60.

[40] *Moralia*, 12.4.5, 631; *Moral Reflections*, 3:60.   [41] *Moralia*, 12.5.6, 631; *Moral Reflections*, 3:60.

dew of the Holy Spirit.[42] Having recovered his greenness – in the words of Job, "having put forth leaves, just as when it was first planted" – the just man (i.e. preacher) sees to the spiritual greening of others, imparting to them the "freshness [*viriditas*] of truth by their correct faith."[43] The preacher is a just man, who, because of his faith, is able to overcome the ravages of the mob; and, as he returns to greenness, so he is able to restore the virtue of the masses through his pastoral care.

In book II of the *Moralia*, Gregory considers straw a symbol of dryness in his moral exegesis of Job 13:25. Here, the pursuit of dry straw represents the pursuit of temptation stirred by anger, lust, avarice, and pride. It is as though vice has hollowed out their virtue, and so, he says, humans are rightly called straw. "At their creation they were a tree; in temptation they became leaves of themselves; after that they looked like straw in exile. . . . But it was because they lost the green freshness [*viriditas*] of interior love that they are now dry straw."[44] Presenting greenness here as an expression of spiritual love shows that it is more than a miracle of nature. It is clearly sensible in plant biology, but it also has deep moral implications. Juxtaposing these implications of greenness with the dryness of sin intensifies the conflict between virtue and vice, as one might do when preaching.

Hildegard adapts these themes in her own spiritual gardening, particularly in her letters to Archbishop Arnold of Trier (27r), dated 1169, and to Archbishop Eberhard of Bamberg (31r), of 1163–1164. Hildegard is encouraging when she compares Arnold to a tree and says that Eberhard was planted by God with life-giving sap.[45] However, her letter to Abbot Adam of Ebrach (85rb), dated before 1166, is more fraught. Responding to the abbot's anxiety about his future, the seer takes a cosmological view of the problem, ending with a drama that echoes themes in her *Ordo virtutum*. Speaking in the voice of God (the One Who Is), she explains the nature of plant growth – how the sun gave heat and rain and dew gave moisture and viridity to herbs and flowers.[46] She uses a drama to explain further how a man from the north threatens to desiccate the garden with winter, while a man from the east rebuffs him with his nurturing rain. Although the northern man briefly gets his way, the one from the east at last sets aside his harp playing long enough to restore the garden. Hildegard follows up with an explanation that seems to integrate the wisdom of Ambrose's *Hexaemeron* and aspects of Gregory's second and third homilies from book 2 of his

---

[42] *Moralia*, 12.5.6, 632; *Moral Reflections*, 3:60.   [43] *Moralia*, 12.5.6, 632; *Moral Reflections*, 3:61.
[44] *Moralia*, CCSL 143A, 11.44.60, 620; *Moral Reflections*, 3:46–47.
[45] Letter 27r, CCCM 91, 77–79; *Letters*, 1:90–1. Letter 31r, CCCM 91, 83–88; *Letters*, 1:95–99.
[46] Letter 85rb, CCCM 91, 206; *Letters*, 1:195.

Homilies on Ezekiel. Hildegard notes that, as a representative of Christ, Adam of Ebrach must know that the grace of God "shines like the sun," nurturing like wisdom, viridity, and moisture.[47] "But wisdom can degenerate into grossness, viridity can fall under great labor, and moisture can turn into harsh bitterness."[48] Therefore, she advises the abbot do his duty tending this garden of people, serving as a representative of Christ by planting "many wholesome desires and good works."[49]

Internal and Mental Greenness

Perhaps the clearest evidence of Hildegard's dependence on Gregory occurs in her use of the terms *viriditatem mentis* and *viriditatem interioris*, both in the context of preaching. They appear in successive sentences in her letter to Provost Andrew of Averbode (54), written some time before 1166. In the voice of the "Secret Light," the seer writes, "You are terrified as if by the wind, and the green tree of your mind [*ligno viriditatis mentis*] is dormant. But one who has vitality in his inner heart [*viriditatem interioris*] builds on the height of the wall."[50] Applying these terms allegorically to the shepherd who fails to stand up to fear and protect his flock, it seems clear she is admonishing the priest who lacks the life force of faith to perform the *cura animarum*. She advises that such a shepherd "is not suited for pastoral office."[51]

  Searching the entire *PLD* for the term *viriditas interioris* yields only two matches (including other declensions): in Hildegard's letter to Provost Andrew and in her description of moss in the *Physica*. Searching these terms more broadly in the database for other forms of internal (e.g. *internae*, etc.) yields only nine matches, and all but one follow one of Gregory's two uses: his teaching on the "verdure of inward doctrine," from book 29 of his *Moralia*; or chapter 3 of his sixth homily in book 2 of his *Homilies on Ezekiel*, where he discusses the preacher's love of internal greenness.[52] The one source that does not follow Gregory is the *Tractatus adversus Simoniacos* (a Treatise against the Simoniacs) by Hildegard's contemporary Gerhoh of Reichersberg (1093–1169). Gerhoh's commentary teaches that those living together in Christ have the grace of "internal viridity."[53]

---

[47] Letter 85rb, CCCM 91, 207; *Letters*, 1:195.   [48] Letter 85rb, 207; *Letters*, 1:195.
[49] Letter 85rb, 207; *Letters*, 1:195.   [50] Letter 54r, CCCM 91, 132–3; *Letters*, 1:131.
[51] Letter 54r, 132–3; *Letters*, 1:131.   [52] *Moralia*, 29.26.51–3, 1470; *Morals*, ed. Bliss, 3.1:336.
[53] Haec autem omnia . . . adhaerent catholici sacramentorum celebratores; quandiu enim per unitatem fidei magistro concordant veritatis, unitatis vinculum servantes, id ipsum sentiendo omnes in Christo manent, et singuli de spiritu ejus viventes, internae viriditatis gratiam habent, vivitque in

A close examination of nuances in Hildegard's hermeneutics reveals parallels with Gregory's, suggesting she subsumed Gregory's understanding of *viriditas mentis* and *viriditas interioris* as concepts explicitly applicable to preachers and preaching. Gregory promotes the notion that preachers have greenness. He takes the prophet's text "He came to the gate which looked toward the East" (Ezekiel 40:6) to refer to Jesus, but he complicates his metaphor by adding the preacher, who "can be understood under the name of '*gate*' because whoever opens for us the door of the Heavenly Kingdom through his speech is a gate."[54]

Gregory returns frequently to this theme. In chapter 5, teaching by analogy he uses the example of farming and the harvest. "A man casts seed into the earth when he implants a good intention into his heart. But this same earth produces first the blade, then the ear, and after that the full corn in the ear."[55] To explain his meaning, he calls on the authority of Luke 22:57 to show that the blade represents the apostle Peter who, during the Passion of Christ, denied knowing Him. In Gregory's view, Peter was afraid, too unsteady to accept his duty to Jesus without fear. In his words, "there was a greenness in his mind [*viriditas in mente*], because he believed the Savior of all, but being still exceedingly inconstant he was trodden down by the foot of fear."[56] Later, after Christ's resurrection and ascension, Peter showed his mettle after all when he suffered persecution and his own crucifixion in service to his calling. This seems to be the reason Gregory describes Peter's psychological state at this moment of indecision as "greenness in the mind" – like a formative period before a blade grows into corn. Peter possessed the life-giving force of *viriditas*, but while it was still growing in him, he remained vulnerable to moral failing.

Gregory's allegory about the apostle Peter's greenness of mind corresponds to Hildegard's Provost Andrew: fearful, inconstant, and shirking of duty. Gregory's exegesis was designed to explain the preacher's calling, which strengthens the connection between Gregory's allegory and Hildegard's admonition of Provost Andrew. She similarly alludes to this reading of *viriditas* in *Scivias* 3.8 (Know the Ways), where one is told of how the Son of God "wrought them in the greenness of the blossoming of the virtues in His teachings."[57]

salutem communicantium illis, quodcunque celebrant sacramentum in Ecclesia Christi" (Gerhoh of Reichersberg, *Tractatus adversus Simoniacos*, PL 194, ed. Jacques Paul Migne (Paris: 1855), 1360).

[54] *Homiliae in Ezechielem*, CCSL 142, 2.3.2, 238; *Homilies*, 294.
[55] *Homiliae*, ibid., 240; *Homilies*, 296.   [56] Ibid.; *Homilies*, 297.
[57] *Scivias*, CCCM 43A, 3.8.18, 505; *Scivias*, ed. Hart and Bishop, 442.

Gregory makes "internal greenness" explicitly relevant to preachers in the sixth homily from book 2 of his *Homilies on Ezekiel* when he examines the prophet's spiritual temple (Ezekiel 40:17–19) in light of Isaiah 54:12, which describes the defense of God's kingdom with "bulwarks of jasper."[58] According to Gregory, "God made the bulwarks of jasper, which is a green stone, because He established the minds of His preachers in the love of internal greenness [*mentes interne viriditatis*]."[59] This passage, together with the other considerable evidence in the *Moralia*, gives one a clear impression of the preacher's agency as a remediating force in the struggle between spiritual viridity and aridity. Because pastoral care fills preachers with "internal greenness," they are able to lead the people of God to the pasture of "eternal greenness" (*aeternea viriditatis*).

Similar to Gregory's use of *viriditas interioris* (internal greenness) is Hildegard's adoption of the phrase *viriditas mentis* (mental greenness). Searching the entire *PLD* for other combinations of *viriditas* and *mentis*, in different declensions and word order, yields only ten matches, and all of them follow one or the other of three of Gregory's texts: the third and sixth homilies from book 2 of his *Homilies on Ezekiel*; and chapter 5 of book 33 from the *Moralia*. This combination of terms occurs twice in Hildegard's writing: in her letter to Provost Andrew (54r; see the section "Internal and Mental Greenness"); and in her letter to Monk Godfrey (48r) dated sometime between 1152 and 1153.[60]

Monk Godfrey writes to Hildegard in some distress over his past sins and implores her for words of admonition and to give him solace by interceding with God on his behalf.[61] Hildegard responds in the voice of the "Living Light": "O man, streams of water flow from me to invigorate your mind [*viriditatem mentis tuae*]." She scolds him for his low morals and laments that he has been led astray by his worldly desires. However, she praises Godfrey for turning to her for consolation and assures him there is hope for recovery through God the father, who through the "Word will enlighten your spirit, and the fiery Lover will shed the ointment of salvation and the invigoration of the flower of wisdom upon you."[62] The concept seems cryptic at first. Speaking for the "Secret Light" in letter 54, Hildegard says that the green tree of Provost Andrew's mind has gone dormant for lack of spiritual nourishment. She tells the monk Godfrey that the "Living Light" is a water source that has the power to green his mind.

---

[58] *Homiliae*, CCSL 142, 2.6.3, 296; *Homilies*, 354–355.   [59] *Homiliae*, 296; *Homilies*, 355.
[60] Letter 48r, CCCM 91, 118–9; *Letters*, 1:121.   [61] Letter 48, CCCM 91, 118; *Letters*, 1:121.
[62] Letter 48r, CCCM 91, 119; *Letters*, 1:122.

Yet when one reads *ligno viriditatis mentis* and *viriditatem mentis tuae* through Gregory's exegesis, it seems likely Hildegard knew these concepts had specific meaning for preachers and preaching.[63]

The river source of greenness comes into focus in chapter 5 of book 33 of Gregory's *Moralia*, where he describes the spiritual significance of the willow in Job 40:17. Willows are an excellent example of greenness, he says, because they are nearly impossible to eradicate. Even when torn up by the root they will grow back as bountiful as ever. He extends the metaphor to contrast the withering effect of carnality with the "greenness of mind" among followers of the church. In a clear play for the significance to preaching, Gregory explains that, like willows, church followers flourish along waterways where each of them may perceive the "teaching of Holy Scripture" (*percipit ex doctrina sacri eloquii*).[64]

Hildegard's unusual combination of *ligno* (wood) with *viriditas* and *mentis* also has precedent in Gregory's interpretation of the wood of the fallen tree in Job 14:7. Gregory's exegesis proceeds organically from the preacher (the just man from *Moralia* 12.5.6) to Jesus when he incorporates the notion of the *lignum viride* from Luke 23:31. The connection seems uncanny, and yet Hildegard also uses this verse from Luke in the *Liber divinorum operum*, a product of the same span of years as her letter to Provost Andrew.[65] Like Gregory, Hildegard says that Jesus is the green wood, but then elaborates, "because he bore all the viridity of the virtues" (*viriditatem virtutum protulit*).[66] Conversely, she interprets dry wood (*aridum lignum*) as the Antichrist, "because he crushes underfoot all of justice's viridity and dries out what is green in uprightness" (*arida facit*).[67] In this recension of thinking about Luke 23:31, Hildegard shifts the agency of sin from the human to the Antichrist, making the sinner a victim rather than the perpetrator of the detested dryness. This view of the Antichrist seems even more insidious in light of Hildegard's astounding account of the Antichrist's deceptions in part 3 of the *Scivias* (3.11.27). Here, she

---

[63] I do not dispute Beverly Kienzle and Travis Stevens's assertion that, for Hildegard, Rupert of Deutz was the most influential interpreter of Ezekiel, but this particular usage does not seem to occur in his works. See Beverly Mayne Kienzle and Travis A. Stevens, "Intertextuality in Hildegard's Works: Ezekiel and the Claim to Prophetic Authority," in Beverly Mayne Kienzle, Debra L. Stoudt, and George Ferzoco, eds. *A Companion to Hildegard of Bingen* (Leiden: Brill, 2014), 156.

[64] *Moralia*, CCSL 143B, 33.5.11, 1679; *Morals*, ed. Bliss, 3.2:563–564.

[65] In her introduction to the *Liber divinorum operum*, Hildegard writes that the vision came to her in 1163 and that she labored for seven years to write them down (*Liber divinorum operum*, CCCM 92, *Prologus*, 45; *The Book of Divine Works*, 29).

[66] *Liber divinorum operum*, CCCM 92, 3.5.19, 438; *The Book of Divine Works*, 453.

[67] *Liber divinorum operum*, 438; *The Book of Divine Works*, 453.

conjures the apocalyptic scene of the Antichrist drying up water, replacing whole forests with *his* greenness – that is, "to take the greenness from forests and give it back again. In many parts of Creation he will display his illusions, in moisture and freshness and dryness. And he also will cause unceasing deceptions in people."[68]

Here, then, is an excellent example of Hildegard's modus operandi. Rather than quote directly from her source, she absorbs Gregory's commentary into her own exegetic voice. The fact that she found a practical application for this piece of Gregory's wisdom is also important, because it seems to demonstrate her ability to adapt exegesis to the purposes of her preaching and to the pastoral duties of others who sought her advice. When considering the implications of dry wood, her advice takes on even greater urgency. Imagining the insidious threat of dryness in the guise of an Antichrist who is able to deceive people with his own greenness might have motivated Hildegard to prod the provost into action.

Greenness of Hair

Some instances of greenness in Hildegard's writing seem curiously at odds with their nature or lead to unexpected associations. It is not surprising that the Holy Spirit should have viridity, of course;[69] but Lucifer, the first angel, was also greened by God with precious stones.[70] Although fire is usually a force of aridity, Hildegard combines fire and greenness when she imagines the burning greenness of the Holy Spirit pouring over the apostles.[71] Many plants and animals in Hildegard's *Physica* share a degree of greenness, each with its distinct prophylaxis.[72] For example, eating dill and yarrow will combat lust, radishes help cleanse the brain, and it seems taking rue might correct an affliction of the prostate.[73] Yet the viridity of *Stutgrass* is evil, and in several herbs it is harmful – turnips and mustard, for

---

[68] *Scivias*, CCCM 43A, 3.11.27, 591; *Scivias*, ed. Hart and Bishop, 503.

[69] Letter 101, CCCM 91A, 256–7; *Letters*, 2:16. Letter 147, CCCM 91A, 327–8; *Letters*, 2:88; *Scivias*, CCCM 43, 3.6.33, 256; and 3.7.9, 273; *Liber divinorum operum*, CCCM 92, 1.2.21, 82; *The Book of Divine Works*, 71; and CCCM 92, 3.5.2, 409; *The Book of Divine Works*, 420.

[70] *Liber divinorum operum*, CCCM 1.4.12, 143; *The Book of Divine Works*, 137.

[71] *Scivias*, CCCM 43A, 3.7.9, 473. *Scivias*, ed. Hart and Bishop, 418.

[72] *Subtilitatum Diversarum*, in *PL* 197. *Physica*, trans. Throop: twenty herbs, three elements, eight trees (including moss), two stones, one fish, one bird, and three reptiles (including earthworms).

[73] *Physica*, *PL* 197, 44, 1155; 47, 1157; 89, 1164. References are by chapter and page. *Physica*, trans. Throop, 37–8, 41–42, 48. Jaundice, *gicht*, and eye infections seem to have been the most common ailments.

example.[74] Another unexpected source of viridity, one with precedent in patriarchal writing, turns up in Hildegard's correspondence with the Abbess Tenxwind.

In her famous letter to the Abbess Tenxwind (52r), composed sometime between 1148 and 1150, Hildegard extends the hermeneutic of greenness to defend the extravagant practices of the nuns at Rupertsberg. Her praise of greenness in virginity is panegyric. Hildegard's impression of viridity in married women might come across as sarcasm, though, when read in light of Ambrose's and Augustine's notion of greenness in winter – hidden from view but never lost. In book 7 of Ambrose's *Commentary on Luke*, he elaborates on themes from *Paradise* – blossoms, fruits, and how to nurture them – fashioning them into a spiritual interpretation of the *viriditas* of life in potential.[75] He says that, while aridity causes plants to wither, flowers will hasten into bloom with the introduction of moisture. "Thus, then, ye see that the stem of ripe leaves has withered, yet the nature of the flower comes alive, for the greenness is hidden, not lost."[76] The concept also permeates Ambrose's *Commentary on the Song of Songs*: that greenness can never be lost, only hidden from view.[77] Augustine takes up the same point in his *Homilies on the First Epistle of John* to argue that just as the greenness of a plant remains hidden in the root during winter, so the lost soul of the sinner is hidden and needs to be found by God.[78]

Hildegard's notion of the hidden greenness in married women, however, might be a sign of respect when interpreted through her words in the *Liber divinorum operum* (3.5.18). There, Hildegard uses the same allegorical method as Ambrose and Augustine to explain the life force of the Old Testament: it is like "the winter that keeps all viridity buried within," while the New Testament, like the summer, "brings forth plants and flowers."[79] Accordingly, Hildegard seems to suggest that a married woman should hide her wintery greenness in humility (except to please her husband!).

[74] *Subtilitatum Diversarum, PL* 197, 86, 1164; 88, 1164; 94, 1166. *Physica*, trans. Throop, 47–48, 50.

[75] St. Ambrose, *Expositio evangelii secundum Lucam*, 7.127, in *PL* 15, ed. Jacques Paul Migne (Paris: 1845), 1732. St. Ambrose, *Exposition of the Holy Gospel According to Saint Luke*, trans. Theodosia Tomkinson (Etna, CA: Center for Traditionalist Orthodox Studies, 1998), 283.

[76] St. Ambrose, *Expositio evangelii secundum Lucam*, 7.127, in *PL* 15, 1732. Ambrose, *Exposition of the Holy Gospel According to Saint Luke*, 283.

[77] St. Ambrose, *Commentarius in Cantica Canticorum*, in *PL* 15, 1870, 1871, 1938, and 1942.

[78] St. Augustine, "Sermo 9," *In epistolam joannis ad parthos tractatus decem*, in *PL* 35, ed. Jacques Paul Migne (Paris: 1864), 2050. St. Augustine, *Homilies on the First Epistle of John*, trans. Boniface Ramsey, The Works of Saint Augustine III/14 (New York: New City Press, 1990), 140.

[79] *Liber divinorum operum*, CCCM 92, 3.5.18, 438; *The Book of Divine Works*, 453.

Hildegard continues with her defense of the extravagant practices of her nuns, arguing that God's existence is so thoroughly manifest in the virgins of her cloister that greenness flourishes through their hair and it must therefore be worn unbound. The same rules of humility that apply to a married woman, and by extension to a nun enclosed elsewhere (including Tenxwind's Andernach?), simply do not apply to the virgins of her cloister. According to Hildegard, she is unsullied, lovely, unwithering, and "always remains in the full vitality [*viriditas*] of the budding rod."[80] In Sara Ritchey's view, it is an illustration of Hildegard's theology of virginity, where *viriditas* and *virginitas* are yoked together, standing as an illustration of God's accessibility in the world.[81] Yet the viridity that was manifest in the garden of her cloister was also active in the world, as Ritchey says, participating in divinization itself.[82] One might even extend the metaphor to Hildegard's sermons and other sermonic writings, because the verdure seems to have flowed unbound from Hildegard's cloister into the world through her preaching.

In about 1163, for example, Hildegard appears to have excoriated the clergy of Cologne for neglecting their office, allowing the Cathar heretics to set better examples of moral behavior for the souls of that city. Sometime later (perhaps that year), Hildegard sent them a version of her sermon (15r), written at the behest of Philip of Heinsberg, dean of the Cathedral.[83] Hildegard's sermon is spoken in the voice of God, in a style much like her visionary texts. Addressing "The Shepherds of the Church," she teaches the clergy, again through allegory, that their failure to support the laws of the church is tantamount to the earth surviving without its essence. She explains that when the clergy succumb to avarice and vanity, shirking their duty to lead by example, they fail their subordinates, scattering them like ash, much as the earth and all of creation turns to ash without the life-giving marrow of viridity (*viriditate quasi medullam*).[84] The spiritual language of viridity here is clearly related to the exegesis of Ambrose, Augustine, and Gregory; but, like the *Expositiones Evangelorum*, Hildegard's exegesis is more vivid and dramatic as she reveals the sensible properties of viridity. As she says earlier in the sermon, "[T]hese are the materials for the instruction of mankind, which he comprehends by touching, kissing, and embracing, since they serve him."[85]

---

[80] Letter 52r, CCCM 91, 128; *Letters*, 1:129.   [81] Ritchey, *Holy Matters*, 56.
[82] Ritchey, *Holy Matters*, 56.   [83] Letter 15r, CCCM 91, 33; *Letters*, 1:54.
[84] Letter 15r, CCCM 91, 35; *Letters*, 1:55. See Barbara Newman, *Sister of Wisdom: St. Hildegard's Theology of the Feminine* (Berkeley: University of California Press, 1987), 234 n. 89.
[85] Letter 15r, CCCM 91, 35; *Letters*, 1:55.

Conclusion

In the prologue to her Latin drama, the *Ordo virtutum* (Order of the Virtues), Hildegard draws from Isaiah 60:8 to portray Patriarchs and Prophets in a state of wonder as they gaze upon the female Virtues. "Who are these, who come like clouds?" (line 1), to which the Virtues respond that they shine with man and "edify the members of his glorious body" (line 9).[86] Hildegard then has the Patriarchs and Prophets use the language of nature to expound on their relationship: "We are the roots and you the branches, the fruit of the living bud [eye], and we were the shadow of him" (lines 10–13).[87] Margot Fassler observes that the Patriarchs and Prophets and the Virtues of the new order have a stake in the formation of humankind. They "work to shine with him, 'building up' the body."[88] However, the play goes on to entail the critical work of the new order, struggling against the adversity of sin wrought by the devil on the soul through worldly delights that entice the body. It is a story one encounters time and again in the religious dramas of the late Middle Ages. In the German-Latin dramas composed and compiled between the thirteenth and sixteenth centuries, for example, the devil even dances with those easily tempted by vice, Mary Magdalene above all.[89]

At the end of her discussion of the *Ordo*, Fassler surveys the dramaturgy, noting the transformative dynamics of the play – the old patriarchy replaced by the Virtues as "new agents leading the faithful to God."[90] It is a parody of the transformation one observes also in the exegetic tradition, even here in the use of one significant word. The patriarchs developed the hermeneutics of greenness to explain the force of life inherent in scripture. They tease out passages, turn over phrases and words, combining the testimony of gospel writers with the old prophets to expound the meaning of spiritual greenness, and to advocate for good preachers to

---

[86] *Ordo virtutum*, CCCM 226, 506; *Ordo virtutum*, ed. Audrey Ekdahl Davidson; trans. Marianne Richert Pfau (Bryn Mawr, PA: Hildegard Publishing Co., 2002), 2.

[87] *Ordo virtutum*, CCCM 226, 506; *Ordo virtutum*, ed. Audrey Ekdahl Davidson, 2.

[88] Margot Fassler, "Music for the Love Feast: Hildegard of Bingen and the Song of Songs," in Jane A. Bernstein, ed., *Women's Voices Across Musical Worlds* (Boston: Northeastern University Press, 2004), 111.

[89] Peter V. Loewen, "Mary Magdalene Converts Her Vanities Through Song: Signs of Franciscan Spirituality and Preaching in Late-Medieval German Drama," in Peter V. Loewen and Robin Waugh, eds., *Mary Magdalene in Medieval Culture: Conflicted Roles* (New York: Routledge, 2014), 181–207. Loewen, "The Conversion of Mary Magdalene and the Musical Legacy of Franciscan Piety in the Early German Passion Plays," in Georgiana Donavin, Cary Nederman, and Richard Utz, eds., *Speculum Sermonis: Interdisciplinary Reflections on the Medieval Sermon*, Disputatio Series (Turnhout: Brepols, 2004), 235–259.

[90] Fassler, "Music for the Love Feast," 114.

inculcate virtue among the people of God. Hildegard, like the Virtues of her *Ordo*, took up the mantle of the patriarchs, Gregory the Great in particular, expounding greenness more vividly, and numerously, to preach about the greenness that binds the spiritual sense of scripture with the forces of nature. Straining the metaphor in her *Ordo*, one might even say that the patriarchs are the greenness of the roots and Hildegard the branches. They preached greenness; and, following in their footsteps, Hildegard greened the world.

Further Reading

Latin Editions and English Translations

Gregory the Great. *Homilies on the Book of the Prophet Ezekiel*, trans. Theodosia Tomkinson. Etna, CA: Center for Traditional Orthodox Studies, 2008.

Moral Reflections on the Book of Job. 5 vols, trans. Brian Kerns, OCSO. Collegeville, MN: Liturgical Press, 2014–2019.

Hildegard of Bingen. *The Book of Divine Works*, trans. Nathaniel M. Campbell. Washington, DC: The Catholic University of America Press, 2018.

Epistolarium, ed. Lieven Van Acker and Monika Klaes-Hachmöller. 3 vols. Corpus Christianorum Continuatio Mediaevalis 91, 91A, and 91B. Turnhout: Brepols, 1991–2001.

Expositiones Evangeliorum. In *Hildegardis Bingensis: Opera minora*, ed. Beverly Mayne Kienzle and Carolyn A. Muessig. Corpus Christianorum Continuatio Mediaevalis 226. Turnhout: Brepols, 2007, 187–333.

Homilies on the Gospels, trans. Beverly Mayne Kienzle. Cistercian Studies 241. Collegeville, MN: Liturgical Press, 2011.

The Letters of Hildegard of Bingen, ed. Joseph L. Baird and Radd K. Ehrman. 3 vols. New York and Oxford: Oxford University Press, 1994–2004.

Liber divinorum operum, ed. Albert Derolez and Peter Dronke. Corpus Christianorum Continuatio Mediaevalis 92. Turnhout: Brepols, 1996.

Scivias, trans. Mother Columba Hart and Jane Bishop. New York: Paulist Press, 1990.

Secondary Literature

Kienzle, Beverly Mayne. *Hildegard of Bingen and Her Gospel Homilies: Speaking New Mysteries.* Turnhout: Brepols, 2009.

Palmquist, Mary. "Chronology of the Life and Works of Hildegard." In *The Life of the Holy Hildegard*, trans. Adelgundis Führkötter and James McGrath; ed.

Mary Palmquist and John Kulas OSB. Collegeville, MN: Liturgical Press, 1995, 106–113.

Patrologia Latina Database (*PLD*). Chadwyck-Healey. ProQuest, LLC, 1996–. http://pld.chadwyck.co.uk/.

Sweet, Victoria. "Hildegard of Bingen and the Greening of Medieval Medicine." *Bulletin of the History of Medicine* 73, no. 3 (1999): 381–403.

CHAPTER 7

Hildegard of Bingen: Illness and Healing

Faith Wallis

How did Hildegard of Bingen acquire a reputation for expertise in medicine? This is in some respects a mystery story, because the two works now called *Cause et cure* (Causes and Cures) and *Physica* were neither mentioned by Hildegard nor included in the *Riesencodex* of her *opera* compiled with a view to her canonization. They seem to have been assembled at Rupertsberg shortly after her death, and yet they are by no means "not authentic." To the contrary, Hildegard's medical writings were created from materials prepared by Hildegard herself and compiled by the very people who enabled her during her lifetime to compose and disseminate her other texts. As works about medical science and practice, *Cause et cure* and *Physica* are at once idiosyncratic and rooted in the medical culture of the twelfth century. They are above all strikingly Hildegardian in their vision of the human predicament and the divine remedy. In that respect, they convey a genuine "Hildegard-Medicine" far removed from modern counterfeits.

How the *Liber subtilitatum* Became Two Books about "Medicine"

In 1158, Hildegard of Bingen began the *Liber vitae meritorum* (Book of Life's Merits) by summarizing her writing activity since completing *Scivias* (Know the Ways). The visions of the *Liber vitae meritorum*:

> happened in the ninth year after a true vision had shown me, a simple person, the true visions which I have previously laboured over for ten years. This was the first year after that vision had shown me the subtleties of the various natures of creatures with responses and warnings for greater and lesser people. It had also shown me the symphony of the harmony of heavenly revelations, and an unknown language with letters with certain other explanations.[1]

---

[1] Hildegard of Bingen, *Liber uite meritorum*, ed. Angela Carlevaris, Corpus Christianorum Continuatio Mediaevalis (CCCM) 90 (Turnhout: Brepols, 1995), 8, lines 4–10; *The Book of the Rewards of Life (Liber Vitae Meritorum)*, trans. Bruce W. Hozeski (New York: Garland, 1994), 9.

While the chronology is somewhat obscure, it is clear that between *Scivias* and *Liber vitae meritorum*, Hildegard composed three works: the *Symphonia armonie celestium revelationum* (Symphony of the Harmony of Celestial Revelations), the *Lingua ignota* (the Unknown Language), and a *Liber subtilitatum diuersarum naturarum creaturarum* (Book of Subtleties of Diverse Natural Creatures). The *Riesencodex* of Hildegard's writings (Wiesbaden, Hochschul- und Landesbibliothek RheinMain, MS 2), completed at Rupertsberg shortly after her death, includes *Symphonia* and *Lingua ignota* but no treatise on the "subtleties of diverse natural creatures." This omission is all the more striking because Hildegard's secretary and confidante Volmar (d. 1173), in a letter addressed to Hildegard herself, laments that, were she to die, there would be no one to instruct her community on "the natures of diverse created things."[2] Neither Hildegard nor Volmar connect this aspect of her learning specifically with medicine.

Within a few years of Hildegard's death, however, this had changed. Theodoric of Echternach's *Vita*, composed around 1182, records that "moved by the spirit of prophecy," Hildegard followed up on *Scivias* with "certain *books* on the nature of man, the elements and variety of created things, and *how human beings might derive help from this knowledge*."[3] Theodoric thus claims that Hildegard wrote more than one book and that besides expounding the natures of "created things" she also discussed "the nature of man" and provided practical advice.

Matching Hildegard's and Theodoric's descriptions to surviving manuscripts, however, proves difficult. The two oldest witnesses to Hildegard's output on these topics, both dating from the second half of the thirteenth century, reflect Theodoric's testimony. The first, from the monastery of St. Maximin in Trier, names Hildegard as the author and is the unique manuscript of the work known from its rubric as *Cause et cure* (hereafter *C&C*).[4] The second, originally from the Rhineland, is the oldest and fullest

---

[2] *Epistola* 195, in Hildegard of Bingen, *Epistolarium*, ed. Lieven Van Acker, pars secunda, CCCM 91A (Turnhout: Brepols, 1993), 443–444, lines 23–26; *The Letters of Hildegard of Bingen*, trans. Joseph L. Baird and Radd K. Ehrman (New York and Oxford: Oxford University Press, 1998), 2.168. Laurence Moulinier, *Le manuscrit perdu à Strasbourg: Enquête sur l'oeuvre scientifique de Hildegarde* (Paris: Publications de la Sorbonne and St. Denis and Presses Universitaires de Vincennes, 1995), 21–25.

[3] *Vita sanctae Hildegardis* 2.1, ed. Monika Klaes CCCM 126 (Turnhout: Brepols, 1993), 20, lines 5–8; Anna Silvas, ed. and trans., *Jutta and Hildegard: The Biographical Sources* (University Park: Pennsylvania State University Press, 1999), 155. My emphasis.

[4] Copenhagen, Kongelige Bibliothek, Ny kgl. saml. 90b Fol. (c. 1250–1260). The edition by Laurence Moulinier (*Beate Hildegardis Cause et cure*, ed. Laurence Moulinier [Berlin: Akademie-Verlag, 2003]) replaces the one by Paul Kaiser (*Beatae Hildegardis causae et curae*, ed. Paul Kaiser [Leipzig: Teubner, 1903]).

copy of the text[5] that two later manuscripts identify as *Liber subtilitatum de diuersis creaturis* or *diuersarum creaturarum*,[6] a title that matches Hildegard's. This work survives in five complete manuscripts and eight fragments[7] but only Paris lat. 6952 and the anomalous four-book version printed in Strasbourg by Johannes Schott in 1533 and 1544 ascribe it to Hildegard. Schott entitled the work *Physica*,[8] and as this title has now become conventional, I shall do likewise. I reserve the title *Liber subtilitatum* for the work Hildegard claims she composed but which (as I will discuss in what follows) is no longer visible in the form she left it.

Physica is a catalogue of plants, animals, and mineral substances that functions both as a treatise on materia medica and as an encyclopedia framed around the Creation story. The manuscripts of the complete *Physica* fall into two families: the Florence and Wolfenbüttel pair from the thirteenth or fourteenth century and three fifteenth-century copies from Brussels, the Vatican, and Paris (the manuscript already mentioned),[9] the last of which was the basis for Charles Daremberg and F. A. Reuss's edition in the *Patrologia latina*.[10] Each chapter describes an individual entity's properties according to the elemental qualities of hot, cold, wet, and dry. This is followed by therapeutic applications whose efficacy is explained by these qualities. It is in the area of these applications and explanations that the Florence and Wolfenbüttel manuscripts are fuller

---

[5] Florence, Biblioteca Medicea Laurenziana, Ashburnham 1323 (c. 1300).

[6] Wolfenbüttel Herzog August Bibliothek Cod. 56,2 Aug. 4° (thirteenth to fourteenth centuries) and Paris, BnF lat 6952 (fifteenth century). Hildegard of Bingen, *Physica. Edition der Florentiner Handschrift (Cod. Laur. Ashb. 1323, ca. 1300) im Vergleich mit der Textkonstitution der Patrologia Latina (Migne)*, ed. Irmgard Müller and Christian Schulze (Hildesheim: Olms-Weidmann, 2008).

[7] Manuscripts described in Reiner Hildebrandt and Thomas Gloning's introduction to their critical edition of *Physica: Liber Subtilitatum diversarum naturarum creaturarum*, ed. Reiner Hildebrandt and Thomas Gloning (Berlin: De Gruyter, 2010), 14–21, and by Laurence Moulinier, *Le manuscrit perdu*, 47–62. Melitta Weiss-Adamson, "A Reevaluation of Saint Hildegard's Physica in the Light of the Latest Manuscript Finds," in Margaret R. Schleissner, ed., *Manuscript Sources of Medieval Medicine* (New York: Garland, 1995), 55–80; Laurence Moulinier, "Fragments inédits de la Physica: contribution à l'étude des manuscrits de Hildegarde de Bingen," *Mélanges de l'École française de Rome* 105 (1993): 629–650.

[8] Hildegard of Bingen, *Physica s. Hildegardis. Elementorum, Fluminum aliquot Germaniae, Metallorum, Leguminum, Fructuum et Herbarum: Arborum et Arbustorum: Piscium denique, Volatilium et Animantium terrae naturas et operationes. IV. Libris mirabili experientia posteritati tradens* (Strasbourg: Johannes Schott, 1533); *Experimentarius medicinae continens Trotulae curandarum aegritudinem muliebrium ante, in, et post partum librum unicum … Libros item quatuor Hildegardis, de elementorum, fluminum aliquot Germaniae, metallorum, leguminum, fruticum, herbarum, arborum, arbustorum, piscium, volatilium et animantium terrae naturis et operationibus* (Strasbourg: Johannes Schott, 1544).

[9] Brussels, Bibliothèque royale 2551 (s. XV med.) and Vatican City, Biblioteca Apostolica Vaticana Ferraioli 921 (s. XV).

[10] *Patrologia Latina* 197, ed. Jacques Paul Migne (Paris: 1855), 1118–1352.

than the others. Either these medical passages were added to a foundation text that looked more like an encyclopedia or they were pruned away from the more ample and medically oriented Florence–Wolfenbüttel recension to make the shorter versions.

While no version of *Physica* deals with "the nature of man," this is the principal theme of *C&C*. The first two of its six books situate human physiology and pathology within cosmology and natural science. Books 3– 4 constitute a roughly head-to-toe *receptarium* and books 5–6 a collection of materials on medical semeiology and prognosis. Thus *C&C* matches Theodoric's description of a work on "how human beings derive help" from knowledge about their bodies. *C&C* survives complete only in the Copenhagen manuscript, but the discovery of some excerpts in another thirteenth-century manuscript in Berlin has complicated the picture of the genesis of this text.[11] This manuscript is a compilation of extracts from scientific works. One extract matches a passage in *C&C* and others bear some resemblance to *C&C* or parts of Hildegard's visionary work *Liber divinorum operum* (Book of Divine Works). The fragments were copied by the same early thirteenth-century scribe who transcribed the first three items in the volume, namely Godefrid and Theodoric's biographies of Hildegard, some of Hildegard's letters, and *Lingua ignota*, and who likely copied the Lucca manuscript of the *Liber divinorum operum*, possibly at Rupertsberg.[12] The Berlin fragments thus support the hypothesis that, at her death, Hildegard left writings on natural science and medicine that had not been consolidated into a formal treatise.

By the early thirteenth century, Hildegard's identity as a medical writer was firmly established. In 1222, Prior Gebeno of the Cistercian monastery of Eberbach in his dedicatory letter to his compilation of Hildegard's prophecies *Speculum futurorum temporum* (Mirror of Future Times) claimed that Hildegard wrote two books about medicine: a "book of simple medicine (*librum simplicis medicine*) according to the creation of things, in eight books, and a book of compound medicine (*medicine composite*), concerning the causes, signs and treatments of diseases."[13] The terms "simple" and "compound" when applied to medicine refer to two kinds of drug treatments and two genres of medical literature. Hildegard and her circle might

---

[11] Berlin, Staatsbibliothek Preussischer Kulturbesitz, Lat. qu. 674, fols. 103r–116r (s. XIII). Heinrich Schipperges, "Ein unveröffentliches Hildegard-Fragment," *Sudhoffs Archiv* 40 (1956): 41–77.

[12] Marianna Schrader and Adelgundis Führkötter, *Die Echtheit des Schrifttums der heiligen Hildegard von Bingen. Quellenkritische Untersuchungen* (Cologne and Graz: Böhlau, 1956), 80.

[13] Moulinier, "Introduction" to *Cause et cure*, xiii.

have encountered this ancient distinction in the first chapter of Constantine the African's *Pantegni practica* book 2, which lays out three approaches to writing about therapeutics, dealing respectively with basic ingredients (*simplicis medicine*), compound remedies (*composita*) made from multiple ingredients, and diseases themselves.[14] A "book of simple medicines" (e.g. the immensely popular twelfth-century *Circa instans negotium in simplicibus medicinis*) is a catalogue of materia medica arranged by substance. "Compound" medicines are presented either in collections of recipes (*antidotaria, receptaria*) organized by the name or genre of the compound (e.g. oils, syrups) or in manuals of therapeutics (*practica*), where they are grouped by medical condition, often working downward from the head to the feet. The most famous medieval example, the *Antidotarium Nicolai*, was also a twelfth-century creation. *Physica* is organized by substance category (plants, trees, animals, etc.); and books 3 and 4 of *C&C* discuss treatments and furnish recipes in more or less head-to-toe order. The conclusion is irresistible: Gebeno's *Liber simplicis medicine* is *Physica* and the *Liber composite medicine* is *C&C*.[15] Corroborating evidence comes from the end of the fifteenth century, when Abbot Johannes Trithemius of Sponheim (1462–1516) recorded a book by Hildegard *de causis et remediis* that (he claimed) Hildegard herself called *medicina composita* and whose incipit matches that found in the Copenhagen manuscript.[16]

In short, by the 1220s Hildegard's writings on nature had been organized at Rupertsberg into two books and oriented explicitly toward medicine. In 1233, the commission inquiring into the canonization of Hildegard sent to Rome through Bruno, priest of Strasbourg, the *Liber simplicis medicine* and *Liber composite medicine*.[17]

The Genesis of *Physica* and *Cause et cure*

A closer examination of the two books reveals their origin in a single textual project that has not survived. Both open with invocations of Creation: "Deus ante creationem mundi . . ." (*C&C*) and "In creatione hominis . . ." (*Physica*) and they share many passages.[18] However, the lost parent text was not designed as a work about medicine, at least not in the conventional

---

[14] *Pantegni practica* 2.1 (Lyon, 1515) vol. 2, fol. 65va.   [15] Moulinier, "Introduction," xlv–xlvi.

[16] Moulinier, *Le manuscrit perdu*, 40 and "Introduction," xviii.

[17] Petrus Bruder, ed. "Acta Inquisitionis de virtutibus et miraculis S. Hildegardis, magistrae sororum ord. S. Benedicti in Monte S. Ruperti iuxta Bingium ad Rhenum," *Analecta Bollandiana* 2 (1883): 127.

[18] Moulinier, *Le manuscrit perdu*, 81–109; *Physica*, ed. Hildebrandt and Gloning, 42–45.

sense. *Physica* begins with a catalogue of medicinal plants but spreads out to encompass the elements, trees, stones, fish, birds, animals, reptiles, and metals. The prototype of all medieval books on simple remedies, Dioscorides' *De materia medica*, composed originally in Greek in the first century but widely read in the Middle Ages, also included animal and mineral substances, but *Physica* diverges from this model by including extensive recipes. *C&C* is also anomalous when compared to conventional *antidotaria* or *practicae*. Book 1 is almost entirely about the order of the cosmos and the four elements.[19] Book 2, the longest in *C&C*, dilates on the effects of the Fall on physiology, reproduction, and illness. This is followed by a discussion of the causes of diseases, based on Hippocratic-Galenic humoral theory but in no perceptible order. Books 3–4 are a repertory of treatments that exhibits many parallel passages in *Physica* and like *Physica* includes German terminology.[20] Finally, book 5 is about signs and ends with a *lunare* predicting the state of health of an unborn child based on the time a child is conceived.

The indeterminate character of these works suggests that Hildegard's reputation for medical expertise may have been crafted by the Rupertsberg editors who turned the *Liber subtilitatum* into two books on simple and compound medicine. Why did they do this, and why did they include these books in the canonization dossier? Modern scholarship takes it for granted that Hildegard was famous in her day for the kind of medical knowledge and intervention found in these works. They point first to Hildegard's own experience of illness and secondly to her reputation as a healer. Yet neither *C&C* nor *Physica* support this supposition.

Hildegard's personal experience of illness was indeed closely intertwined with her visionary experiences and her understanding of her mission, but little of what she tells us on this subject relates to the contents of *Physica* or *C&C*. The autobiographical fragments in book 2 of the *Vita* occasionally refer to details of pathology – for example, the drying up of her blood vessels or the effect of the south wind.[21] For Hildegard, however, her "aery

---

[19] Victoria Sweet, "Hildegard of Bingen and the Greening of Medieval Medicine," *Bulletin of the History of Medicine* 73, no. 3 (1999): 381–403; Moulinier, "Introduction," xxx.

[20] Irmgard Müller, "Die Bedeutung der lateinischen Handschrift Ms. Laur. Ashb. 1323 (Florenz, Biblioteca Medicea Laurenziana) für die Rekonstruktion der 'Physica' Hildegards von Bingen und ihre Lehre von den natürlichen Wirkkräften," in Alfred Haverkamp and Alexander Reverchon, eds., *Hildegard von Bingen in ihrem historischen Umfeld* (Mainz: Phillip von Zabern, 2000), 421–440.

[21] *Vita* 2.9 (ed. Klaes, 33, lines 1–7), 2.14 (41, lines 84–90); Sabina Flanagan, "Hildegard and the Humors: Medieval Theories of Illness and Personality," in Andrew D. Weiner and Leonard V. Kaplan, eds., *Madness, Melancholy, and the Limits of the Self: Studies in Culture, Law and the Sacred* (Madison: University of Wisconsin Law School, 1996), 20.

pains" indicated demonic assault (demons being located in the atmosphere) rather than a natural pathology connected to corrupt air.[22]
A century ago, the physician-historian Charles Singer concluded that
Hildegard suffered from migraine, based on similarities between the illuminations in the Rupertsberg *Scivias* manuscript and the distinctive visual
features that had recently come to define the condition.[23] Like many of his
contemporaries, Singer associated migraine scotoma with (male) scientists
and intellectuals. The diagnosis thus supported his claim that Hildegard
was a genuine scientific thinker. Singer therefore rejected the authenticity
of *C&C*, where the discussion of migraine is impersonal, conventional, and
mentions only headache.[24] Singer's views on *C&C* have not stood the test
of time, but his migraine diagnosis has assumed the status of fact. Much of
this is due to its popularization by Oliver Sachs;[25] but medievalists accept it
uncritically, though some doubt its significance for understanding
Hildegard's message or achievements.[26]

During her lifetime, Hildegard certainly had a reputation as a healer, but
her documented acts of healing, notably in book 3 of Theodoric's *Vita*,
were always of a religious character. It was as an exorcist, not as a physician,
that she intervened in the case of the possessed woman Sigewize of
Brauweiler. Hildegard also relieved the sick by the laying on of hands
(e.g. *Vita* 3.1, 3.4, 3.15) or making the sign of the cross (e.g. *Vita* 3.2) or by
prayer (e.g. Vita 3.5) or blessed water (*Vita* 3.6–8) or bread (*Vita* 3.9). She
occasionally provides a "textual amulet" (*Vita* 3.10), and a plait of her hair
helps women in childbirth and other situations of distress (*Vita* 3.11–13). In
at least two letters (nos. 287 and 293), she offers medical explanations for
mental turmoil and bad dreams but no recipes or advice apart from
reassurance and prayer. In addressing some more evidently physical ailments, such as the loss of sensory powers of an abbot (letter 112), or the

---

[22] Klaus-Dietrich Fischer, "Hildegard von Bingen: Kranke und Heilerin," *Das Mittelalter* 10 (2005): 32–34.

[23] Charles Singer, "The Scientific Views and Visions of Saint Hildegard (1098–1180 [*sic*])," in Singer, *Studies in the History and Method of Science* (Oxford: Clarendon Press, 1917), 1–55.

[24] Katherine Foxhall, "Making Modern Migraine Medieval: Men of Science, Hildegard of Bingen and the Life of a Retrospective Diagnosis," *Medical History* 58, no. 3 (2014): 354–374; *Cause et cure*, ed. Moulinier, 130 and 208.

[25] Oliver Sachs, *Migraine: Understanding a Common Disorder*, rev. ed. (Berkeley: University of California Press, 1985), 299–301.

[26] Proponents: Sabina Flanagan, *Hildegard of Bingen, 1098–1179: A Visionary Life* (London: Routledge, 1989), chapter 10; Madeline Caviness, "Artist: 'To See, Hear and Know All at Once,'" in Barbara Newman, ed., *Voice of the Living Light* (Berkeley: University of California Press, 1998), 110–124. Sceptics: Barbara Newman, "Hildegard of Bingen: Visions and Validation," *Church History* 52, no. 4 (1985): 163–175; Fischer, "Hildegard von Bingen," 24–25.

sterility of the noble Burgundian lady (letter 70), even such explanations are wanting.[27] To be sure, Christian "charms" and amulet-like remedies are found in both *C&C* and *Physica*, so Hildegard and her circle were not inclined to make sharp distinctions between secular medicine and the styles of religious healing for which she was better known.[28] Yet neither Hildegard nor the religious houses where she lived had any exceptional reputation for the secular medical learning or expertise found in *Physica* and *C&C*. It can be assumed that Hildegard provided Rupertsberg's nuns with material and textual resources for their medical needs, but beyond that lies only speculation.[29] *C&C* does not resemble a conventional collection of recipes or a therapeutic manual that could be used by a monastic infirmarian, as it is not organized for reference or instruction.[30]

So neither migraines nor miracles made Hildegard into a "medical writer"; rather, it was the two books that appeared after her death. How one evaluates Hildegard's interest in medicine and the motivation of her community in repackaging the *Liber subtilitatum* as medicine depends on how one explains the genesis of *C&C* and *Physica*. Two solutions have been proposed by the editors of these works. Laurence Moulinier argues that Hildegard's original *Liber subtilitatum* was an "open text" but resembled the Florence manuscript of *Physica*, though it was not organized in the same manner.[31] *C&C* is based in part, but not entirely, on these unconsolidated materials. Books 3–4 were extracted from the *Liber subtilitatum* (hence the parallel passages), but books 1–2 originated elsewhere, as they resemble parts of the *Liber divinorum operum*.[32] Finally, books 5–6 are not by Hildegard, though they represent materials available to her. Moulinier thus sees *C&C* as authentic in the sense that its materials can be traced to Hildegard; but in its surviving form, it is the creation of editors working after her death.[33]

---

[27] Fischer, "Hildegard von Bingen," 26–31.

[28] Debra L. Stoudt, "The Medical, the Magical, and the Miraculous in the Healing Arts of Hildegard of Bingen," in Beverly Mayne Kienzle, Debra L. Stoudt, and George Ferzoco, eds., *A Companion to Hildegard of Bingen* (Leiden: Brill, 2014), 267–268.

[29] Florence Eliza Glaze, "Medical Writer: 'Behold the Human Creature,'" in Newman, *Voice of the Living Light*, 126–128; Moulinier, "Introduction," xc.

[30] As posited by Victoria Sweet, *Rooted in the Earth, Rooted in the Sky. Hildegard of Bingen and Premodern Medicine* (New York and London: Routledge, 2006), 11, and "Greening," 397.

[31] Moulinier, "Introduction," xxxiv; *Le manuscrit perdu*, 61–109.

[32] Hans Liebeschütz, *Das allegorische Weltbild der heiligen Hildegard von Bingen* (Leipzig: Teubner 1930), 86–107.

[33] Moulinier, "Introduction," lvii–lxiii; *Le manuscrit perdu*, 25–35 and 102–104; "Hildegard ou Pseudo-Hildegard? Réflections sur l'authenticité du traité 'Cause et cure,'" *'Im Angesicht Gottes suche der Mensch sich selbst': Hildegard von Bingen (1980–1179)*, ed. Rainer Berndt (Berlin: De Gruyter, 2001), 115–146; Glaze, "Medical Writer," 147.

Berndt Hildebrand and Thomas Gloning, who produced the critical edition of *Physica*, propose a different scenario. A key role is played here by Hildegard's confidante and secretary, Volmar. Hildebrandt and Gloning argue that Hildegard composed the foundational text (*Grundtext*) of *Physica* as the *Liber subtilitatum*. This foundational text corresponds to the expository sections on the nature of each creature in *Physica*. It was essentially an encyclopedia and drew on the *Summarium Heinrici*, an abbreviation of Isidore's *Etymologiae* made ca. 1020–1100,[34] as well as texts on natural history such as the *Physiologus* and treatises on agriculture.[35] Volmar not only furnished Latin equivalents for Hildegard's German names[36] but also added supplementary textual material (*Zusatztext*) about medical applications from other Hildegardian materials. Volmar's enlarged *Physica* survives in the Florence and Wolfenbüttel manuscripts; but the fullest version of the *Zusatztext* is found in *C&C* itself.[37]

In sum, what Hildebrandt and Gloning see as a supplementary *addition* to the base text of *Liber subtilitatum*, Moulinier regards as something that was later *extracted* from the *Liber subtilitatum*.[38] Hildebrandt and Gloning argue that *C&C* substantially existed during Hildegard's lifetime, ready to be used as *Zusatz* to "medicalize" the *Liber subtilitatum*, presumably with Hildegard's consent. Moulinier argues that *C&C* was confected after her death, using materials extracted from an already "medicalized" *Liber subtilitatum* for books 3 and 4. Both scenarios imply that Hildegard herself was interested in medicine, though neither explains why this was not a subject she claimed to write about.

---

[34] For parallels, see Hildebrandt and Gloning, "Einleitung," 29–41. See also Reiner Hildebrandt, "Summarium Heinrici, das Lehrbuch der Hildegard von Bingen," in Ernst Bremer and Reiner Hildebrandt, eds., *Stand und Aufgaben der deutschen Dialektlexikographie* (Berlin: De Gruyter, 1996), 89–110. A twelfth-century MS of this work originated in the monastery of St. Eucharius (now Trier, Stadtbibliothek 1124/2058); Moulinier, "Introduction," xl–xli.

[35] Laurence Moulinier, "Une encyclopédiste sans précédent? Le cas de Hildegarde de Bingen," in Michelangelo Picone, ed., *L'enciclopedismo medievale* (Ravenna: Longo Editore, 1994), 119–134; Moulinier, "Ein Präzedenzfall der Kompendien-Literatur: Die Quellen der natur- und heilkundlichen Schriften Hildegards von Bingen," in Edeltraut Forster, ed., *Hildegard von Bingen: Prophetin durch die Zeiten* (Freiburg: Herder, 1997), 431–447; and Moulinier, "Abbesse et agronome," 135–156.

[36] Reiner Hildebrandt, "Latein statt Deutsch in der 'Physica' Hildegards von Bingen als Reflex einer Kooperation mit ihrem Sakretär Volmar," in Gisela Brandt, ed., *Bausteine zu einer Geschichte des weiblichen Sprachgebrauchs*, vol. 7 (Stuttgart: H.-D. Heinz, 2006), 5–16.

[37] Hildebrandt and Gloning, "Einleitung," 4–11; Hildebrandt, "Die Bedeutung der Florentiner Physica-Handschrift für die authentische Textgewinnung," in Forster, *Hildegard von Bingen: Prophetin*, 448–457 and "Hildegard von Bingen – 16 Jahre nach der Entdeckung der Florentiner 'Physica' Handschrift," in Rudolf Bentinger, Damaris Nübling, and Rudolf Steffens, eds., *Sprachgeschichte – Dialektologie – Onomastik – Volkskunde. Beiträge zum Kolloquium am 3./4. Dezember 1999 an der Johannes Gutenberg-Universität Mainz. Wolfgang Kleiber zum 70. Geburtstag* (Stuttgart: Franz Steiner, 2001), 45–53.

[38] Moulinier, *Le manuscrit perdu*, 94–99.

Prophecy and Healing: A False Dichotomy

Both scenarios also explain why these works are not in the *Riesencodex*: they did not exist in any final form at the time the volume was assembled. It was not because they were considered incompatible with a prophetic and visionary vocation.[39] Indeed, the abrupt appearance of the *liber simplicis medicine* and *liber composite medicine* at the time of the canonization process suggests an intention to use these works to enlarge the scope of Hildegard's claims as a visionary and mystic. The colophon of the Copenhagen manuscript reads "Expliciunt *prophecie* sancte Hildegardis," and the sole copy of *Physica* traced to a library outside the western German lands belonged to an English Augustinian friar of York who collected books about prophecy.[40] Trithemius claimed that Hildegard's medical lore was yet another revelation from the Holy Spirit.[41] In short, writing about medicine, at least the way Hildegard writes about medicine in *Physica* and *C&C*, seemed to her community and her medieval readers to be consistent with her visionary identity.

It did not seem to have mattered to Hildegard's medieval readers that these medical writings are not presented as visions; however, it is precisely this stylistic difference that has caused scholars to doubt their authenticity.[42] *Physica* and *C&C* show evident influence of encyclopedic and medical texts, so to accept them as authentic is to accept that Hildegard was a woman of learning. Even for modern scholars, this is a stumbling block. For example, Peter Dronke's defense of Hildegard's learned attainments leads him to rationalize her visions as a literary strategy for conveying her views,[43] while on the other hand Sylvain Gouguenheim downplays Hildegard's book learning as not only historically unlikely but denigrating her originality.[44] To put it another way, if Hildegard was a mystic, she could not have written a learned work on medicine and natural science; if she wrote learned works, she was not a mystic.

---

[39] As argued by Michael Embach, "Hildegard of Bingen (1098–1179): A History of Reception," in Kienzle, Stoudt, and Ferzoco, *A Companion to Hildegard of Bingen*, 278.

[40] Kathryn Kerby-Fulton, "Hildegard and the Male Reader: A Study in Insular Reception," in Rosalynn Voaden, ed., *Prophets Abroad: The Reception of Continental Holy Women in Late Medieval England* (Woodbridge: D.S. Brewer, 1996), 1–18.

[41] Moulinier, "Introduction," lv–lvi.

[42] Moulinier, *Le Manuscrit perdu*, chapter 6; Glaze, "Medical Writer," 132.

[43] Peter Dronke, "Hildegard of Bingen," in Dronke, *Women Writers of the Middle Ages: A Critical Study of Texts from Perpetua to Marguerite Porete* (Cambridge: Cambridge University Press, 1984), 144–201.

[44] Sylvain Gouguenheim, *La sibylle du Rhin: Hiledgarde de Bingen, Abbesse et prophétesse rhénane* (Paris: Publications de la Sorbonne, 1996).

The aim of the analysis of *Physica* and *C&C* in what follows is to suggest a way out of this impasse. If the Rupertsberg community thought that reframing *Liber subtilitatum* as medicine was consistent with their *magistra*'s religious message, and an asset in their quest to see her canonized, then we must take *Physica* and *C&C* as authentic in the sense her contemporaries understood this. The evidently learned and natural style of medicinal science and therapeutics found in these works was to be celebrated as part of Hildegard's spiritual gift. The shape of these works indicates that their intention was not to support medical practice but to enlarge the scope of Hildegard's teaching. The contents of *Physica* and *C&C* bear this out.

Physica: The Macrocosm in the Service of the Microcosm

That *Physica* hovers between a manual of simple medicine and a natural history encyclopedia is a clue that Hildegard and her editors were alert to distinctive trends in twelfth-century culture. Philosophers like William of Conches emphasized the common ground between medicine and natural science, while the commentaries on the new medical teaching anthology later called *Articella* claimed that medicine was embedded in natural science. Both natural science and medicine were called *physica*.[45] Hildegard's preface to the first book of *Physica* on plants, which serves to introduce the entire work, articulates this theme in her own idiom. She begins by pointing out that the human being was created from earth, and thus "all the elements served him, because they sensed that he was alive, and they cooperated with him in all his activities, and he with them."[46] What makes this relationship possible is the correspondence between macrocosm and microcosm. Every creature has a certain complexional quality – airy, watery, and so on – and these qualities are also found in the composition of the human body. In consequence, a plant can be useful, useless, or harmful, depending on how its qualities align with those of the human body. A moral and spiritual dynamic is also at play: useful herbs display the spiritual side of humanity, while useless or harmful plants

[45] Jerome J. Bylebyl, "The Medical Meaning of *Physica*," *Osiris*, 2nd ser. 6 (1990): 16–41; Édouard Jeauneau, "Quand un médecin commente Jouvenal," in Barbara Obrist and Irene Caiazzo, eds., *Guillaume de Conches: Philosophie et science au XII* siècle (Florence: SISMEL – Edizione del Galluzzo, 2011), 111–121; Mark D. Jordan, "Medicine as Science in the Early Commentaries on 'Johannitius,'" *Traditio* 43 (1987): 121–145; Faith Wallis, "The *Articella* Commentaries of Master Bartholomaeus," in Agostino Paravicini Bagliani, ed., *La Scuola medica salernitana: gli autori e i testi* (Florence: SISMEL, 2007), 125–164.
[46] *Physica*, ed. Hildebrandt and Gloning, 49; my translation.

display man's futile and diabolical mores.[47] Both soul and body mirror the larger creation.

Some creatures are mainly useful for therapy (e.g. plants and stones), while others are considered from the perspective of nutrition (e.g. fish). Within each book, however, an implicit system of spiritual values controls the arrangement of the material. Quadrupeds (book 7) are arranged by size; the elephant comes first (and not, as was usual in bestiaries, the lion) and the ant last. This order is also a moral one, for the elephant is exceptionally chaste.[48] The book on fish (book 5) opens with the whale, the marine equivalent of the elephant, and ends with the serpent-like and poisonous lamprey. The first of the creatures of the air (book 6) is the splendid griffon; bringing up the rear are the noxious flying insects. The order of the books themselves reflects not only the sequence of creation from Genesis but also an ethical perspective. Fish are "purer" than other animals because they mate without physical contact; birds come after fish because they touch when mating but rank above terrestrial animals because they live in the more transparent element of air. Reptiles come last, because they alone among animals were punished at Adam's fall, and their poison is the equivalent of mankind's postlapsarian disordered humors.[49]

Camphor, Salmon, and Sapphires: Exemplary Moments in the *Physica*

The dimensions and scope of the *Physica* make it difficult to survey its medical teachings concisely. Instead, I will compare exemplary chapters on each of the three kingdoms from book 1 on plants, book 4 on stones, and book 5 on fish, to show how Hildegard weaves science and spirituality into a single vision.

In chapter 40 of book 1, Hildegard discusses camphor, an exotic and a relatively new drug in European medicine.

> Camphor that is, "gum" which comes out of a tree has in it pure cold and pungent power like the power in a stone. But the tree from which camphor

---

[47] Ibid.

[48] Ibid., 339. Laurence Moulinier, "Les merveilles de la nature vues par Hildegarde de Bingen," in *Miracles, prodiges et merveilles au Moyen Âge* (Paris: Publications de la Sorbonne, 1995), 115–131.

[49] Laurence Moulinier, "Plantes toxiques et humeurs peccantes: la pensée du poison chez Hildegarde de Bingen," in *Le corps à l'épreuve. Poisons, remèdes et chirurgie: aspects des pratiques médicales dans l'Antiquité et au Moyen Âge* (Langres: Dominique Guéniot, 2002), 71–101; Moulinier, "L'Ordre du monde animal selon Hildegard de Bingen," in R. Durant, ed., *L'Homme, l'animal domestique, et l'environnement du moyen âge au XVIIIᵉ siècle* (Nantes: Ouest Editions, 1993), 119–134; and Moulinier, "Une encyclopédiste," 128–132.

sweats has in it pungent and clean cold, and its nature is clean. Hence wherever its wood or leaves or gum is found, magical arts and witchcraft and fantasies of aerial spirits cannot prevail, but vanish from its presence just as snow melts before the sun, for the same spirit abhors its clean nature, and therefore is not able to lead its powers to accomplish what it would there. And if a person should have and carry upon himself anything from this tree, the good nature of this tree cherishes the tranquillity of his mind, and holds it within ... Take equal weights of aloes and myrrh, and a little less of camphor than of either of these, and assemble them in a pan, that is *zelaz* and add a little *wilde laticha* [wild lettuce] and together with flour, make little cakes and dry them in the sun or on a stone heated in the fire, and when they are dry grind them to powder and from this powder in hot *honchwirz* (hydromel) take a little while fasting, and if you are healthy and strong, you will be wonderfully healthier and stronger, and your powers will be consti-tuted in the proper way; and if you are sick, it will lift you up and strengthen you in a wonderful way, just as the sun brightens a dark day. The heat and cold of the aforementioned spices and herbs with sweetness and of honey has such great powers that healthy things are elevated into more healthy things, and what is sick is made healthy.[50]

Hildegard's distinctive voice is evident in the first part of this chapter, with its concern for spiritual protection and health, but it is important to note that she is following the conventions of a herbal or treatise on materia medica. The primal quality of the plant (in this case, cold) indicates its benefits and dangers (camphor should not be taken uncompounded). Moreover, she explains why the medication works in terms of the primal qualities of the ingredients. The tonic made from camphor is effective because it combines hot and cold ingredients (camphor providing the cold and myrrh the hot).[51] This is the logic of contemporary herbals like Macer's, or pharmacological writings like that of the Salernitan writer Platearius, both of which she may have used.[52]

The anomalous second book of the *Physica* is devoted to the elements, but in fact the only elements discussed are air, water, and earth. "Earth" means particular kinds of earth with medical applications, such as clay and calamine, and "water" denotes specific rivers.[53] The chapters on the German rivers focus on the qualities of the fish that live in them, and

---

[50] *Physica*, ed. Hildebrandt and Gloning, 80; my translation.
[51] *Physica*, ed. Hildebrandt and Gloning 1.176, 150.
[52] Moulinier, "Abbesse et agronome," 139–143.
[53] Laurence Moulinier, "La terre vue par Hildegarde de Bingen (1098–1179)," in Claude Thomasset, Joëlle Ducos, and Jean-Pierre Chambon, eds., *Aux origines de la géologie, de l'Antiquité au Moyen Âge, Actes du colloque international 10–12 mars 2005, Paris Sorbonne (Paris IV)* (Paris: Honoré Champion, 2010), 205–230.

when we turn to book 5 on fish, we learn that it is precisely their aquatic environment that determines their nature. Salmon, for instance (book 5, chapter 5), are cold, nocturnal bottom feeders; hence their flesh "is soft and weak and not good for anyone to eat, because it stirs up all the bad humours in human beings." However, salmon bones have a medical use.

> Someone whose gums are rotting and whose teeth are ailing and fragile should pound the bones of this fish into a powder, and add a small amount of salt and apply this powder around the teeth at night and let the saliva run over it, and he will be healed. The bone of a salmon is somewhat watery, and it loses its watery humours when it is reduced to a powder. And this powder, when tempered with salt (which is hot and moist) draws off the noxious and fetid humours of the teeth.[54]

Hildegard seems to anticipate an objection: How could a cold, moist, and not very healthy fish be an effective remedy? The answer is that pulverizing the salmon bones dries them out. The explanation is not entirely satisfactory (the salt is also moist), but Hildegard's intention to furnish a rationale expressed in the terminology of learned medicine is typical.

The effect of stones[55] depends not only on primal quality but on the time of day. The sapphire for example (book 4, chapter 6) is hot in quality and waxes at midday. Otherwise, though, stones obey Galenic laws. Hildegard describes how to cure a web over the eye by warming a sapphire in one's hand, wetting it with a drop of wine, and applying the stone to the eye: "For the heat of this stone, tempered with the heat of the person ... and with the sharpness of wine added, will dislodge the membrane."[56] Because stones are used almost exclusively for external application, the book on stones contains a high number of prescriptions for Christian amulets. Even here, though, Hildegard explains her treatment in terms of sapphire's natural heat.

> And if a person is possessed by an evil spirit, put a sapphire into wax, and sew this wax into leather, and hang it around his neck, and say: "O you foul spirit, get you away from this person in haste, just as the glory of your splendour fell swiftly away from you at your first fall." And that malign spirit

---

[54] *Physica*, ed. Hildebrandt and Gloning, 269–270.
[55] Moulinier, "La terre," 211–213; Peter Riethe, "Die medizinische Lithologie der Hildegard von Bingen," in Anton Ph. Brück, ed., *Hildegard von Bingen 1179–1979. Festschrift zum 800. Todestag der Heiligen* (Mainz: Gesellschaft für mittelrheinische Kirchengeschichte, 1979), 351–370, and Riethe "Zur Quellengeschichte des 'Steinkatalogs' der Hildegard von Bingen: Die Abhängichkeit des IV. Buch der Brüsseler Handschrift von Bartholomaeus Anglicus," *Scriptorium* 64 (2010): 95–108.
[56] *Physica*, ed. Hildebrandt and Gloning, 237.

will be greatly twisted about and will depart from the person, unless it is
a very vigorous and evil spirit and it will get stronger unless God does not
wish to expel him. For in every creature which proceeds from God, there is
some utility, however useless it may seem, though people may not know it.
But in the sapphire there is almost nothing useless, and the fire within it is so
pure that the Devil disdains and shuns it.[57]

God's power and the power of sacred words are fused with but not
confused with the efficacy of sapphire's natural heat.

Cause et cure: The Roots of Human Suffering and Its Remedy

Compared to *Physica*, *C&C* is more repetitious and meandering, but it too
is guided by a typically Hildegardian theme: humanity's grandeur and
misery, fall, and redemption.[58] Like the opening chapters of Genesis, book
1 focuses on the macrocosm and the elements, while book 2, on the
microcosm of the human body, emphasizes the consequences of the Fall.
Books 3–4 are a sort of salvation history, providing treatments for diseases
by compound medicines, while books 5–6 on prognosis, concentrate on
the future.

Book 1 begins with the creation of the universe, God's plan for humanity, and the four elements, underscoring their role as the link between
macrocosm and microcosm.[59] Like Isidore's or Bede's *De natura rerum*
(On the Nature of Things), *C&C* surveys the cosmos vertically, beginning
with the celestial bodies. Only after Adam's fall did the firmament begin to
revolve and the planets adopt their contrary movements, and this motion
triggers another analogy between macrocosm and microcosm:

> As the soul vivifies and solidifies the body, so too the Sun, the Moon and the
> other planets foster and strengthen the firmament with their fire. For the
> firmament is like the head of a human being. Sun, Moon and stars are like
> the eyes. The air is like hearing. The winds are like smell . . . The firmament
> is also held together by the stars so that it does not collapse, just as humans
> are supported by blood vessels so that they may not melt away or fall apart.
> As the blood vessels pervade the entire human body, from foot to head, so
> the stars pervade the firmament. As blood is moved in the vessels and as it
> moves them in turn and causes them to leap and thrust, so fire is moved in
> the stars and causes them to move and to emit sparks similar to those leaps
> and thrusts.[60]

[57] Ibid., 238.   [58] Glaze, "Medical Writer," 131–132.   [59] *Cause et cure*, ed. Moulinier, 22.
[60] Ibid., 32–33; Hildegard of Bingen, *On Natural Philosophy and Medicine*, trans. Margaret Berger
(Cambridge: D. S. Brewer, 1999), 30–33.

So close is the bond between the cosmos and humanity that the stars receive messages about human deeds and proclaim them – a sort of astrology in reverse. The influence of the Moon on earth and over the human body is especially strong.[61] Beneath the Moon lies the realm of the four elements, which offers Hildegard yet another microcosmic corres-pondence (e.g. air corresponds to the soul).[62] Yet air and water are also the site of the primal creation, for the Spirit of God hovered in the air over the waters at creation. From the earth spring fruitful trees, moistened by the waters of the rain. Thus book 1 ends, so to speak, in the Garden of Eden.

Book 2 opens with the Fall as the starting point of history, of disease, and of sexual generation. Adam's sin turned his pure blood into a poisonous "foam of semen" that boils in the fire of lust; and it is from "thin and unconcocted" semen that offspring are engendered that are "full of ulcers and putridity."[63] This draws Hildegard into a highly original discussion of how the sex, health, and character of children are determined by the degree of conjugal affection between the partners, as well as the strength of the seed.[64]

The consequences of the Fall for the human body are most conspicuous in the disorder of the humors. Here, Hildegard picks up on a prominent theme in twelfth-century philosophy and theology[65] but develops it in an original way. The Fall transformed Adam's pure humors – the classic quaternity of blood, phlegm, choler, and melancholy – into what she calls *flegmata* and *livores*. These two terms are peculiar to Hildegard and are best left untrans-lated. The *flegmata/livores* retain their connection to the four qualities – they are described as "the dry," "the moist," "the foamy," and "the cool"[66] – but they are not equals joined by reciprocal bonds of shared qualities. Instead, their relationship is hierarchical. In each person or physiological type there are two superior qualities and two inferior ones. Whichever two are domin-ant are *flegmata*; the remaining two subordinate humors are *livores*. *Flegmata* is a neutral term, but *livores* has a negative connotation: *livor* means both "livid" and "hatred." Hildegard implies that the *livores* are envious of the

---

[61] *Cause et cure*, ed. Moulinier, 39–42.   [62] Ibid., 44, 46.

[63] Ibid., 59–60; *On Natural Philosophy*, trans. Berger, 39, 51. Laurence Moulinier-Brogi, "La pomme d'Ève et le corps d'Adam," in Agostino Paravicini Bagliani, ed., *Adam, le premier homme*, Micrologus Library 45 (Florence: SISMEL – Edizioni del Galluzzo, 2012), 147–149.

[64] Laurence Moulinier, "Aspects de la maternité selon Hildegarde de Bingen (1098–1179)," *Micrologus* 17 (2009): 215–234.

[65] Irven M. Resnick, "Humoralism and Adam's Body: Twelfth Century Debates and Petrus Alfonsi's *Dialogus contra Judaeos*," *Viator* 36 (2005): 181–195.

[66] *Cause et cure*, ed. Moulinier, 50; Flanagan, "Hildegard and the Humors," 16.

ruling *phlegmata* and potentially rebellious. A healthy relationship among humors is therefore not one of balance or harmony but of proper subordination, where the dominant govern and restrain the others.[67]

Hildegard's understanding of the connection of sin and disease is subtle and original. Humoral disorder causes disease in all its forms – insanity, deformity, stupidity, paralysis, cancer, and gout – but also character flaws like harshness and stubbornness.[68] Disease is but one component of the global misery precipitated by the Fall; hence humans should repent when the elements of the world are disrupted, as well as when their own bodily humors are disordered. They are at once victims and perpetrators of these calamities. As Glaze observes, this reading of the problem of disease "dignifies the art and the tools of medicine" as an analogue to prayer or penance.[69]

Procreation and Pathology

The Fall and its consequences also signal Hildegard's turn from divine Creation to human procreation.[70] Hildegard's treatment of these subjects is exceptional for its depth and detail, and occasionally for its novel ideas, notably about humors, gender, and character. For men, humoral temperament is expressed in libido. Choleric men cannot resist women, melancholic men despise them, and phlegmatic men are indifferent to them. Only sanguine men display moderation in their sexual desires. A second axis of analysis is intelligence: phlegmatic men are good-natured but dull-witted; melancholy men smart but sour-tempered.[71] Compared to men, women's sexual responses are more diffuse and stable. Their humoral types are expressed mainly in physiognomy, personality, menstrual history, and fertility. Moreover, the female types often (though not consistently) seem to be the inverse of the corresponding male type. For example, choleric women are pale, intelligent, and kind – a stark contrast to their ruddy and reckless male counterparts.[72] There are many loose ends in this analysis,

---

[67] Harald Derschka, *Die Viersäftelehre als Persönlichkeitstheorie. Zur Weiterentwicklung eines antiken Konzepts im 12. Jahrhundert* (Ostfildern: Jan Thorbecke Verlag, 2013); Sweet, *Rooted*, chapter 4; Flanagan, "Humors," 16–17.

[68] *Cause et cure*, ed. Moulinier, 87–90; Laurence Moulinier, "Magie, médecine et maux de l'âme dans l'oeuvre scientifique de Hildegarde," in Rainer Berndt, ed., *"Im Angesicht Gottes suche der Mensch sich selbst": Hildegard von Bingen (1098–1179)* (Berlin: Akademie Verlag, 2001), 545–559.

[69] Glaze, "Medical Writer," 136–137.   [70] *Cause et cure*, ed. Moulinier, 92–106.

[71] *Cause et cure*, ed. Moulinier, 106–114.

[72] *Cause et cure*, ed. Moulinier, 126–128; Laurence Moulinier, "Conception et corps féminin selon Hildegarde de Bingen," *Storia delle donne* 1 (2005): 139–157.

but what is impressive is Hildegard's treatment of women on their own terms, not simply as lesser versions or negative reflections of men.[73] The remainder of book 2 covers pathology, reproduction, and regimen. Apart from humoral disorder, diseases can be caused by congenital factors, such as season of conception, but also by the anatomical structure of the internal organs. The stomach, for instance, is wrinkled on the inside to retain food, but in consequence food can harden and putrefy in the stomach.[74] The discussion of menstruation leads into a description of conception. The key figure here is Eve, traditionally despised as the agent of the Fall but here presented as "the first mother of humankind," similar to the ether in her purity and filled with the entire human race, as the heaven is filled with stars.[75] In conception and childbirth, on the other hand, woman is like the earth that is plowed and broken open. Conception takes place when semen attracts the menstrual blood like a cupping glass and coagulates it like cheese.

A chapter on breast milk and weaning announces the transition to Hildegard's third theme, regimen. Hildegard explains the rules for healthy eating and drinking by attending to the seasons and choosing temperate foods and wines.[76] Bloodletting repairs the effects of eating an excessive amount or variety of foods. Overheating of blood can produce nightmares, and in general poor health can take a toll on one's psychological well-being. Thus Hildegard circles back to the story of Adam's fall and its deleterious effects on the human body and soul. Humoral disorder causes sad and bitter thoughts, but emotional instability can also affect the functioning of the organs and even bring on leprosy.

The collection of remedies in books 3 and 4 of *C&C*[77] starts in book 3 with the head (hair loss, headache, insanity, eye problems, etc.) and then moves downward to the lungs, liver, stomach and spleen, the intestines, kidneys and genitalia, and bladder.[78] Problems of male and female infertility are dealt with, as are gout, fistula, ulcers, and insomnia. Book 3 ends with a short appendix on veterinary remedies. By contrast, book 4 is organized into large thematic blocks. The first concerns problems of menstruation in women and libido in men.[79] The second focuses on

---

[73] Joan Cadden, "It Takes All Kinds: Sexuality and Gender Differences in Hildegard of Bingen's *Book of Compound Medicines*," *Traditio* 40 (1984), 149–74, esp. 166; Derschka, *Die Viersäftelehre*, 182–202.
[74] *Cause et cure*, ed. Moulinier, 138–139; *On Natural Philosophy*, trans. Berger, 76.
[75] *Cause et cure*, ed. Moulinier, 144.   [76] Ibid., 153–159.
[77] Surveyed in Irmgard Müller, "Krankheit und Heilmittel im Werk Hildegards von Bingen," in Brück, *Hildegard von Bingen 1179–1979*, 311–349.
[78] *Cause et cure*, ed. Moulinier, 207–235.   [79] Ibid., 231–240.

mental conditions such as diabolical fantasies, enchantments, anger or sadness, excessive grief and laughter, and drunkenness.[80] The third block deals with internal ailments such as nausea, dysentery, vomiting, and dropsy.[81]

Hildegard's Therapeutics: Echoes of "Salerno"

Hildegard's therapeutics include dietary regulation, the ingestion or topical application of prepared medications, external treatments like fumigation, and surgical procedures such as cupping and bloodletting. As in *Physica*, many treatments are accompanied by an explanation couched in humoral terms. For example, her chapter on urinary incontinence identifies the problem as one of cold in the stomach. The remedy is partly dietetic (drink hot wine and mix vinegar with one's food) and partly pharmaceutical (an infusion of sage, a warm plant).[82] Moulinier's edition tracks parallels between these remedies and those found in Salernitan compilations like the *Tractatus de aegritudinum curatione* (Treatise on the Treatment of Illness).[83] It is possibly through the *Tractatus* that Hildegard may have encountered the *Trotula*,[84] a composite work, one section of which was composed by a female practitioner, Trota. As Hildegard is particularly concerned with women's health, it is worth comparing her remedies to those found in this work. Difficult childbirth furnishes an interesting example. The first segment of the *Trotula* ensemble, *Liber de sinthomatibus mulierum* (Book on the Conditions of Women), was written by a man. It explains difficult childbirth as the result of constriction of the cervix and birth canal but provides only preventive measures, particularly diets and baths during pregnancy.[85] By contrast, the section in *C&C* entitled *De curis mulierum* (On the Treatments for

---

[80] Ibid., 240–246.   [81] Ibid., 246–262.

[82] Ibid., 225; *On Natural Philosophy*, trans. Berger, 110.

[83] The term "Salernitan" is used here to denote those medical writings produced in the late eleventh through early thirteenth centuries that are conventionally associated with the region of Salerno in central Italy. Some writers and texts are unquestionably Salernitan, but others are deemed Salernitan because they reflect the style and content of Salernitan thinking. The fact that many of the earliest manuscripts of "Salernitan" writings were made and owned in northern Europe suggests that the term should not be construed too literally. Monica Green is preparing a history of Salernitan medicine; pending its appearance, readers should consult the various volumes of the Edizione nazionale "La Scuola Medica Salernitana," notably Danielle Jacquart and Agostino Paravicini Bagliani, eds., *La Scuola Medica Salernitana. Gli autori e i testi* (Florence: SISMEL – Edizioni del Galluzzo, 2007).

[84] Moulinier, "Introduction," lxxvi–lxxviii.

[85] *The Trotula: A Medieval Compendium of Women's Medicine*, ed. and trans. Monica H. Green (Philadelphia: University of Pennsylvania Press, 2001), 104–105.

Women) has been identified by Monica Green as from the pen of Trota. Trota also prescribes a bath, but during labor, along with sternutatives (to cause sneezing) "for strengthening and opening [the birth canal] ... For ... the organs are shaken and the cotyledons ruptured and thus the fetus is brought out."[86] Hildegard's treatment is also designed for the hour of childbirth. Mild herbs like fennel are cooked in water, wrung out, and bandaged to the woman's thighs and back. The aim is to counteract woman's innate cold, which causes constriction in these regions.[87] Thus Hildegard seems equally aligned to the constriction theory of *De sinthomatibus* and to the practical orientation of *De curis mulierum*.

Few recipes involve multiple ingredients, and not all that do specify quantities or give detailed instructions for preparation. At the higher end of the scale of complexity is the recipe for a purgative potion in book 4. This requires one part ginger, half that amount of licorice, and one-third that amount of zedoary. These are pounded, sieved, and mixed with an equal measure of sugar. Half a hazelnut shell of flour is mixed with as much of the milk of the purgative herb citocacia as can be picked up on the nib of a pen. The paste is divided in four parts and dried in spring sunshine. As in *Physica*, Hildegard explains in terms of elemental qualities how the different ingredients in this compound work to bolster good humors or expel evil ones.[88] It is instructive to place her recipe beside a similar one found in the *Practica* of the "Salernitan" author Bartholomeus (fl. 1150–1170). Bartholomeus's recipe for a laxative uses exact measures rather than proportional amounts but is otherwise very similar. Spices (cinnamon, cloves, spikenard) are pounded together with sugar and mixed with the active ingredient, in this case scammony. The powder is cooked in water until thick and then spread on an oiled marble slab to harden before being cut into tablets.[89] Thus, while Hildegard's compounded medicines have been interpreted as evidence of a specifically female approach to healing, with analogies to cooking,[90] it seems more likely that she was drawing on the abundant literature of pre-Salernitan and Salernitan therapeutics.[91]

Hildegard never cites sources, and the fact that medical literature, especially pre-Salernitan literature, is often conveyed through compilations

---

[86] *Trotula*, 118–119.   [87] *Cause et cure*, ed. Moulinier, 233.   [88] Ibid., 236–237.
[89] *Practica Bartholomei*, ed. Salvatore De Renzi, Collectio salernitana 4 (Naples: Filiatri, 1856), 337–338.
[90] Marcia Kathleen Chamberlain, "Hildegard of Bingen's *Causes and Cures*: A Radical Feminist Response to the Doctor-Cook Binary," in Maud Burnett McInerney, ed., *Hildegard of Bingen: A Book of Essays* (New York: Garland, 1998), 53–73.
[91] Moulinier, "Introduction", lxxvi–lxxxii, lxxxvii–xc.

makes it difficult to pin down what exactly she might have read.[92] Glaze therefore perceptively elects to compare Hildegard's materials to typical genres found in pre-twelfth-century medical manuscripts: summaries of humoral physiology, catalogues of diseases, recipes, instructions on blood-letting, and occasionally, vernacular glosses.[93] Nonetheless, more precise comparisons are possible. Hildegard's preoccupation with the elements, their combinations and transformations, seems to echo authors such as the elusive "Marius Salernitanus," with whom she shares the term *viriditas*.[94] Hildegard's interest in the effects of the Fall on human physiology finds parallels in the *Prose Salernitan Questions* and the *Aphorisms* of Urso of Calabria.[95] She appears to be acquainted with parts of the corpus of writings translated from Arabic into Latin by Constantine the African, notably *De coitu* and the pseudo-Galenic *De spermate*,[96] *De melancholia*,[97] *Pantegni*,[98] and possibly Isaac Judaeus on diets;[99] but she shows no famil-iarity with Arabic medical terminology.[100]

Ultimately, while Hildegard's medical ideas and treatments are not incom-patible with the learned medicine of her age, she is not merely reproducing her sources. As Glaze observes, her scientific learning is undeniable, but it never drives her project; indeed, the reverse is the case. Hildegard's cognitive pro-cesses are subordinate to her visionary imagination. She "thinks with" her medical learning by selecting ideas that suit her overarching preoccupations.[101] In the case of both *Physica* and *C&C*, these preoccupations revolve around a vibrant appreciation of the unity of all Creation, the centrality of human beings as microcosmic reflections of the whole, the effects of the Fall, and the profound religious resonance of the idea of healing and health.

---

[92] Joan Cadden, *The Meanings of Sex Difference in the Middle Ages: Medicine, Science, and Culture* (Cambridge: Cambridge University Press, 1992), 82; Glaze, "Medical Writer," 125.

[93] Glaze, "Medical Writer," 129–130.

[94] Moulinier, "Introduction," lxxxv. See Loewen, Chapter 6, this volume for other ways in which Hildegard draws on the term "viriditas."

[95] Moulinier, "La pomme d'Ève," 147–149, and "Magie, médecine et maux de l'âme," 550–555.

[96] Moulinier, "Conception," 141–142.

[97] Danielle Jacquart, "Hildegarde et la physiologie de son temps," in Charles Barnett and Peter Dronke, eds., *Hildegard of Bingen: The Context of Her Thought and Art* (London: University of London Press, 1998), 121–134.

[98] Moulinier, "Introduction," lxxvii, xcii.   [99] Ibid., xxxiv, lxxviii–lxxxii, xciii–xcv.

[100] Ibid., xcvii–xcviii, refuting Glaze, "Medical Writer," 139–141.

[101] Glaze, "Medical Writer, " 133, 138–139; cf. Laurence Moulinier, "Naturkunde und Mystik bei Hildegard von Bingen: der Blick und die Vision," in P. Pinzelbacher, ed., *Mystik und Natur. Zur Geschichte ihres Verhältnisses vom Altertum bis zur Gegenwart* (Berlin: De Gruyter, 2009), 39–60; Benedikt Conrad Vollmann, "Hildegard von Bingen: Theologische versus naturkundliche Schriften?" Benedikt Conrad Vollmann, ed., *Geistliche Aspekte mittelalterlicher Naturlehre* (Wiesbaden: Dr. Ludwig Reichert, 1993), 40–47 and 128–31; Stoudt, "The Medical, the Magical, and the Miraculous," 249–272.

Reception: Early Modern to Postmodern

Hildegard's Rupertsberg community consolidated her writings for inclusion in the canonization dossier because it understood the integrity of body and health to her vision. It is thus ironic that the reception of Hildegard's medical works from the later Middle Ages until the middle of the twentieth century tended in the opposite direction. The manuscripts of *Physica* and *C&C* rarely circulated beyond the western German lands, where they were housed in monasteries such as St. Maximin in Trier but also in the libraries of individuals, particularly medical practitioners. For example, the Florence manuscript of *Physica* was owned by a German surgeon named Wydonius who sold it in 1385 to another surgeon, Wilhelmus de Reit.[102] These readers mined *Physica* to extract practical information and edited it to make it more usable as a reference work.[103] *Physica* was also excerpted for various kinds of technical writing, such as Master Eberhard's cookbook,[104] and as a source of vernacular science, for example the *Speyerer Kräuterbuch* (the Speyer Herbal).[105] Schott's printed edition of *Physica* (1533) was marketed to a medical audience; when it was reissued in 1544, it was accompanied by the *Trotula*. In sum, late medieval readers of Hildegard's medical writing showed a lively interest in the positive knowledge to be harvested from these works but indifference to their religious and metaphysical messages. Not coincidentally, the appearance of the *Physica* in print led Konrad Gessner to speculate that the Hildegard who wrote the medical works was not the same Hildegard who was famous for visions and prophecies.[106]

The rediscovery of Hildegard's medico-scientific writings in the nineteenth century coincided with the upsurge of German Romanticism and

---

[102] Weiss-Adamson, *Reevaluation*, 56–57.

[103] Ibid., 65–72; Melitta Weiss-Adamson, "Der deutsche Anhang zu Hildegard von Bingens 'Liber simplicis medicinae' in Codex 6952 der Bibliothèque nationale in Paris (f. 232v-238v)," *Sudhoffs Archiv* 79 (1995): 174–191; Irmgard Müller, "Wie 'authentisch' ist die Hildegardmedizin? Zur Rezeption des 'Liber simplicis medicinae' Hildegards von Bingen im Codex Bernensis 525," in Forster, *Hildegard von Bingen: Prophetin*, 420–429.

[104] Melitta Weiss-Adamson, "Die 'Physica' Hildegards von Bingen als Quelle das 'Kochbuch Meister Eberhards'," *Sudhoffs Archiv* 76 (1992), 87–96.

[105] Barbara Fehringer, *Das Speyerer Kräuterbuch mit den Heilpflanzen Hildegards von Bingen: eine Studie zur mittelhochdeutschen Physica-Rezeption mit kritischer Ausgabe des Textes* (Würzburg: Königshausan & Neumann, 1994); Annette Müller. *Krankheitsbilder im Liber de plantis der Hildegard von Bingen (1098–1179) und im Speyerer Kräuterbuch (1456): ein Beitrag zur medizinisch-pharmazeutischen Terminologie im Mittelalter* (Hürtgenwald: Guido Pressler, 1997); Irmgard Müller, "Zur Verfasserfrage der medizinisch-naturkundlichen Schriften Hildegards von Bingen," *Tiefe de Gotteswissens – Schönheit der Sprachgestalt bei Hildegard von Bingen*, ed. Margot Schmidt (Stuttgart and Bad Cannstatt: Frommann-Holzboog, 1995), 1–17.

[106] Moulinier, *Le manuscrit perdu*, 170–175.

nationalism. The first scholarly study, F. A. Reuss, *De libris physicis s. Hildegardis commentatio historico-medica* (Würzburg, 1835), was based on Schott's edition of *Physica* and hailed Hildegard's medicine as an expression of the native folk medicine of the German people. The discovery of the *C&C* in Copenhagen cemented this trend.[107] Casting Hildegard as a folk healer also fed into German enthusiasm for alternative and nature-based medicine, itself a product of Romantic philosophy.

Unlike some kinds of folk medicine and naturopathy, Hildegard avoided being tainted by association with Nazi *Neue deutsche Heilkunde* ("new German medicine").[108] Thus she was available to physicians and laity alike coping with the spiritual trauma of postwar Germany and Austria. At one end of this response lies the work of the neurologist and medical historian Heinrich Schipperges (1918–2003). Schipperges wrote his 1951 Bonn medical doctoral dissertation on Hildegard, and over his career published prolifically on the relationship of medicine and theology, notably in *Artzt und Christ* (now *Zeitschift für medizinische Ethik*). His reading of *C&C*, which he translated into German,[109] emphasizes the spiritual dimension of healing – a dimension much more self-evident in German, where *heilen* means both "to heal" and "to save" (in the religious sense). For Schipperges, Hildegard's medicine is not so much a medical system or record of practice as a Christian vision of reintegration within the divinely created cosmos and an ethical model relevant to the modern world.[110]

The Austrian physician Gottfried Hertzka (1913–1997) claimed that it was imprisonment by the Nazis that sealed his conversion to an alternative health belief system he came to call "Hildegard-Medizin." Hertzka's Hildegard-Medizin was always emphatically religious and unflinching in its faith that Hildegard's healing advice came directly from God,[111] but

---

[107] Sue Spencer Cannon, "The Medicine of Hildegard of Bingen: Her Twelfth-Century Theories and Their Twentieth-Century Appeal As a Form of Alternative Medicine" (PhD diss., University of California, Los Angeles, 1993), 69–72.

[108] Robert Jütte, "The Historiography of Nonconventional Medicine in Germany: A Concise Overview," *Medical History* 43 (1999), 352–353.

[109] *Heilkunde: Das Buch von dem Grund und Wesen und der Heilung der Krankheiten* (Salzburg: Otto Müller, 1957).

[110] Heinrich Schipperges, "Menschenkunde und Heilkunst bei Hildegard von Bingen," in Brück, *Hildegard von Bingen 1179–1979*, 295–310; Schipperges, *Hildegard of Bingen: Healing and the Nature of the Cosmos* (Princeton, NJ: Markus Wiener Publishers, 1997); Schipperges, "Heil und Heilkunst: Hildegards Entwurf einer ganzheitlichen Lebensordnung," Forster, *Hildegard von Bingen: Prophetin*, 476–484.

[111] See his *So heilt Gott. Die Medizin der hl. Hildegard von Bingen als neues Naturheilverfahren* (Stein am Rhein: Christiana Verlag: [1970] 2006); Brenda Lynne Sanders, "Discourse and Device: The Power Strategies of Hildegard Medicine" (PhD diss., University of Illinois at Urbana-Champaign, 2003).

more recent articulations of the movement have shifted closer to secular naturopathy, with a heavily commercial emphasis. Dr. Wighard Strehlow, Hertzka's collaborator and director of the Hildegard-Zentrum spa on the Bodensee as well as the now-defunct online "virtual Hildegard University" aligns Hildegard-Medizin more with postmodern "wellness culture" than traditional Catholicism.[112] Hildegard-Medizin is definitely a business. The Zentrum sells "Virita" remedies, and another line of products is marketed online by JURA Naturheilmittel, a company connected to the Praxis für Naturheilkunde in Constance, which claims Hertzka as a "scientific collaborator."[113] While chided by scientists as unproven,[114] and by historians as inauthentic,[115] Hildegard-Medizin is now an established, if minor, player on the German and eastern European alternative medical scene.

In the Anglo-American sphere, the public interest in Hildegard that emerged in the 1980s and 1990s coincided with the apogee of New Age culture and Matthew Fox's Christian version of New Age, "creation spirituality." Neither granted a large place to the medical writings,[116] or spawned a phenomenon comparable to Hildegard-Medizin, other than a handful of translations of Hertzka's works.[117] English-language websites devoted to Hildegard's medicine, like Healthy Hildegard are nonetheless profoundly derivative of German Hildegard-Medizin, though without the commercial element.[118]

On the other hand, Hildegard's medicine has exerted an appeal for Anglo-American practitioners of medicine, particularly women. Rehabilitating Hildegard as proof of women's long history in the healing profession began in Europe in the early twentieth century, migrated to America

---

[112] Internationale Hildegard von Bingen Stiftung, St-Hildegard.com: www.st-hildegard.com/en/.

[113] JURA Naturheilmettel: https://shop.hildegard.de/); Praxis für Naturheilkunde in Constance: www.tcm-amsee.de/hildegard.htm.

[114] E.g. O. Miche and J. Hübner, "Traditional European Medicine: After All, Is Hildegard von Bingen Really Right?" *European Journal of Integrative Medicine* 1, no. 4 (2009): 226, and Bernhard Uehleke, Werner Hopfenmueller, Rainer Stange, and Reinhard Saller, "Are the Correct Herbal Claims by Hildegard von Bingen only Lucky Strikes? A New Statistical Approach," *Forschende Komplementärmedizin* 19 (2012): 187–190.

[115] Müller, "Wie 'authentisch,'" 420, 428.

[116] Sabina Flanagan, "Zwischen New Age und Wissenschaftlicher Forschung: Die Rezeption Hildegards von Bingen in der englischsprachigen Welt," in Forster, *Hildegard von Bingen: Prophetin*, 476–484.

[117] Gottfried Hertzka's and Wighard Strehlow 's *Handbuch der Hildegard-Medizin* (Stein am Rhein: Christiana Verlag, 1987) was translated into English as *Hildegard of Bingen's Medicine* by Karin Strehlow (Rochester, VT: Bear and Co., 1988).

[118] See the section "About Hildegard" on the Healthy Hildegard website: www.healthyhildegard.com/about-hildegard/.

between the world wars,[119] and enjoyed a brief revival under second-wave feminism.[120] This appeal to physicians reaches back to Schipperges's promotion of Hildegard as an ethical and spiritual model for the modern practitioner and has spawned a handful of specialist studies, largely in the field of psychiatry.[121] It is also the wellspring of the work of Victoria Sweet, a physician-historian with considerable gifts of insight and communication. Besides her published scholarship on Hildegard,[122] Dr. Sweet's evocative memoir and critique of modern medical practice *God's Hotel* weaves Hildegard's medical writing into an appeal for "slow medicine."[123] As a physician, she gravitates toward a vision of Hildegard as a practitioner whose writings were intended for use and instruction. This vision frequently relies less on documentation than on sympathy and imagination, but regardless of its methodological limitations, the result is the special kind of respect and relevance for Hildegard's medicine.

Conclusion

The story of how Hildegard came to be a "medical writer" is bound up with the efforts of generations of people, from the nuns of Rupertsberg to the acolytes of New Age spirituality, to own a piece of the saint's charisma. Yet it is also a story about how texts were composed, put into manuscripts, read, used, and reused in the Middle Ages. Hildegard herself was part of this complex ecology of text production, both as a "consumer" of the scientific and medical knowledge of her milieu and as an exceptional writer. The *Physica* and *C&C* allow us to glimpse something of the enabling infrastructure of her enterprise – the editorial work of Volmar, the silent compilation (or decompilation) of the *Liber subtilitatum* by secretaries and nuns, and the confidence of her biographers and promoters that her spiritual meaning was enhanced, and not diminished, by what she had to say about the relationship of the natural world to humanity's bodily nature and needs. In the midst of this network, Hildegard appears as a woman not only of visions but of vision.

---

[119] Monica Green, "In Search of an 'Authentic' Women's Medicine: The Strange Fates of Trota of Salerno and Hildegard of Bingen," *Dynamis* 19 (1999): 45–46.

[120] Debra L. Stoudt, "Medieval German Women and the Power of Healing," in Lilian R. Furst, ed., *Women Healers and Physicians: Climbing a Long Hill* (Lexington: University Press of Kentucky, 1997), 13–42.

[121] E.g. Monique D. Boivin and Suzanne M. Phillips, "Medieval Holism: Hildegard of Bingen on Mental Disorder," *Philosophy, Psychiatry, and Psychology*, 14, no. 4 (2007): 359–368.

[122] See Notes 19 and 30 in this chapter.

[123] Victoria Sweet, *God's Hotel: A Doctor, a Hospital, and a Pilgrimage to the Heart of Medicine* (New York: Riverhead Books, 2012), chapter 6.

Further Reading

Latin Editions and English Translations

Hildegard of Bingen. *Beate Hildegardis Cause et cure*, ed. Laurence Moulinier. Berlin: Akademie-Verlag, 2003.

Hildegard von Bingen's Physica: The Complete English Translation of Her Classic Work on Health and Healing, trans. Throop, Priscilla. Illustrations by Mary Elder Jacobsen. Rochester, VT: Healing Arts Press, 1998.

On Natural Philosophy and Medicine, trans. Margaret Berger. Cambridge: D. S. Brewer, 1999.

Physica. Liber Subtilitatum diversarum naturarum creaturarum, ed. Reiner Hildebrandt and Thomas Gloning. Berlin: De Gruyter, 2010.

Subtilitatum diuersarum naturarum creaturarum libri nouem, ed. Charles Daremberg and F. A. Reuss. In *Patrologia Latina* 197, ed. Jacques Paul Migne. Turnhout: Brepols, 1855, 1117–1352.

The Trotula: A Medieval Compendium of Women's Medicine, ed. and trans. Monica H. Green. Philadelphia: University of Pennsylvania Press, 2001.

Secondary Literature

Cadden, Joan. "It Takes All Kinds: Sexuality and Gender Differences in Hildegard of Bingen's *Book of Compound Medicine*." *Traditio* 40 (1984): 149–174.

Foxhall, Katherine. "Making Modern Migraine Medieval: Men of Science, Hildegard of Bingen and the Life of a Retrospective Diagnosis." *Medical History* 58, no. 3 (2014): 354–374.

Glaze, Florence Eliza. "Medical Writer: 'Behold the Human Creature.'" In Barbara Newman, ed., *Voice of the Living Light: Hildegard of Bingen and Her World*. Berkeley: University of California Press, 1998, 125–148.

Moulinier, Laurence. *Le manuscrit perdu à Strasbourg: Enquête sur l'oeuvre scientifique de Hildegarde*. Paris: Publications de la Sorbonne and St. Denis and Presses Universitaires de Vincennes, 1995.

Stoudt, Debra L. "The Medical, the Magical, and the Miraculous in the Healing Arts of Hildegard of Bingen." In Beverly Mayne Kienzle, Debra L. Stoudt, and George Ferzoco, eds., *A Companion to Hildegard of Bingen*. Leiden: Brill, 2014, 249–272.

Sweet, Victoria. "Hildegard of Bingen and the Greening of Medieval Medicine." *Bulletin of the History of Medicine* 73, no. 3 (1999): 381–403.

Weiss-Adamson, Melitta. "A Reevaluation of Saint Hildegard's Physica in the Light of the Latest Manuscript Finds." In Margaret R. Schleissner, ed., *Manuscript Sources of Medieval Medicine*. New York: Garland, 1995, 55–80.

CHAPTER 8

The Pentachronon *and Hildegard of Bingen's Reputation As a Prophet*

Magda Hayton

> Therefore, from that time and thereafter she was held in such veneration by all that her words and her writings were received as if the words of God himself.
>
> Gebeno of Eberbach[1]

One of Hildegard of Bingen's many reputations today is that of a prophet of the End Times. Fresh interpretations of her prophecies can be found on numerous websites, in YouTube videos, and in TV documentaries where one finds claims that Hildegard foretold the destruction of the United States (or perhaps the United Kingdom) by a comet or the return of Protestant Christians to the Catholic Church, to name just two examples.[2] Prophetic discourse lends itself to diverse and divergent readings and Hildegard's highly symbolic and at times cryptic prophecies have never been an exception. In her own day, Hildegard was well-known for her prophetically charged calls for reform in which she decried clerical abuses, monastic laxity, lack of adequate leadership in the church, and the Cathar heresy.[3] Contemporaries also solicited Hildegard for the personal advice and direction she could provide through her prophetic gift.[4] Both of these aspects of Hildegard's prophetic reputation continued through the seventeenth century thanks to the publication of an anthology of excerpts

---

[1] "Igitur, ab illo tempore et deinceps ab omnibus in tanta ueneratione habita est, ut uerba eius et scripta eius quasi uerba ipsius Dei reciperentur." Gebeno of Eberbach, *La Obra de Gebenón*, ed. José Carlos Santos Paz, Millennio Medievale 46 Testi 12 La tradizione profetica 2 (Florence: SISMEL, 2004), 98. All translations are my own.

[2] See, for example, the Catholic Prophecy website section on "St. Hildegard" at http://catholicprophecy.org/st-hildegard/ and Brian Kopp, "Apocalyptic Prophecies of Hildegard of Bingen, the Next Doctor of the Church," Sancte Pater (blog), December 20, 2011, www.sanctepater.com/2011/12/apocalyptic-prophecies-of-hildegard-of.html.

[3] On Hildegard's reputation as a prophet during her lifetime, see Kathryn Kerby-Fulton, "Prophet and Reformer: 'Smoke in the Vineyard,'" in Barbara Newman, ed., *Voice of the Living Light: Hildegard of Bingen and Her World* (Berkeley: University of California Press, 1998), 70–90.

[4] See Fletcher, Chapter 5, this volume.

from her writings compiled between 1217 and 1222 by one of her Cistercian devotees, Gebeno of Eberbach (fl. 1220).[5]

Gebeno's anthology, the *Speculum futurorum temporum siue Pentachronon sancte Hildegardis* (Mirror of Future Times or the Five Ages of Saint Hildegard, referred to hereafter as *Pentachronon*), was popular throughout Europe from the thirteenth to the seventeenth century; Michael Embach and Martina Wallner list 102 copies in their catalogue of manuscripts of the works of Hildegard.[6] The *Pentachronon* includes Hildegard's prophecies of present and future history up to and including the life and demise of the Antichrist; it also includes a selection of excerpts from her correspondence in which she responded to the requests of her contemporaries for the spiritual direction and counsel she could offer through her gift of prophetic vision. The purpose of this chapter is to introduce readers to the *Pentachronon*, paying particular attention to how Hildegard and her apocalyptic teachings were presented in the three major versions of the anthology. As we will see, the Hildegard of the *Pentachronon* was both an apocalyptic prophet preaching the need for widespread reform and a new theology of salvation history and an inspired spiritual leader providing guidance to clergy and monastics of all ranks.

The Creation of the *Pentachronon*

In the prologue to the *Pentachronon*, Gebeno recounts when he decided to compile his anthology of Hildegard's writings. It was after a Cistercian abbot from Calabria named John visited Eberbach Abbey in 1217 and privately shared with Gebeno some important news: a hermit in southern Italy had revealed that the Antichrist had just been born.[7] Shortly afterwards, Gebeno heard another "religious and literate man" affirm the same

---

[5] Other Hildegardian prophecies (authentic excerpts from her writings and pseudonymous works) also circulated in the centuries after her death and contributed to her reputation; see Michael Embach, "Hildegard of Bingen (1098–1179): A History of Reception," in Beverly Mayne Kienzle, Debra L. Stoudt, and George Ferzoco, eds., *A Companion to Hildegard of Bingen* (Leiden: Brill, 2014), 273–304.

[6] Michael Embach and Martina Wallner, *Conspectus der handschriften Hildegards von Bingen* (Münster: Aschendorff, 2013), 332–33. This far outnumbers the extant copies of Hildegard's complete works (e.g. ten of the *Scivias* and four of the *Book of Divine Works*). A critical edition of redaction I of the *Pentachronon* is in Gebeno of Eberbach, *La Obra de Gebenón*, edited by Santos Paz, and all citations are taken from this edition. An English translation based on a new semi-critical edition of the "Cum peccata" version of the *Pentachronon* is in preparation by myself and Jonathan M. Newman and will be published with the Dallas Medieval Texts and Translations series (Peeters Press).

[7] Gebeno of Eberbach, *La Obra*, 5. On this episode, see Marco Rainini, *Il profeta del Papa. Vita e memoria di Raniero da Ponza eremita di curia*, Ricerche. Storia – Dies Nova, 2 (Milan, 2016), 81–6.

rumor.[8] Gebeno knew, however, that Hildegard had described five future ages both in her first major theological text, the *Scivias* (Know the Ways), and in her third, the *Liber divinorum operum* (Book of Divine Works), during which there would be a series of tribulations alternating with peaceful periods of renewal, and that the Antichrist would not arrive until the fifth and final age.[9] Although Hildegard provided no dates for when these ages would begin or end beyond stating that the first had begun in her own lifetime, there was clearly much that had yet to happen before the final enemy's arrival. Gebeno also knew that in the *Liber divinorum operum* and in her sermons and letters Hildegard had described a more immediate threat: a soon-to-come tribulation at the hands of the forerun-ners of the Antichrist. Most often, Hildegard described this as a tribulation to befall secular clergy for their failure to carry out their priestly duties; however, she also spoke of both clergy and monastics being evicted from their churches and monasteries and put to flight. So, in order to "refute" and "overcome" the kind of false prophecies concerning the Antichrist being spread by Abbot John from Calabria and others, to warn his contemporaries of more pressing dangers and to make Hildegard's reform-ist teachings on religious life more widely available, Gebeno compiled the *Pentachronon*.[10]

The centrality of Hildegard's teachings on the five ages and the near-future tribulation are reflected in the title that Gebeno gave his work. He called it the *Mirror of Future Times* because "one will see the present miserable state of the church and all future dangers and the advent of the Antichrist as if in some mirror"; he also called it *The Five Ages of Saint Hildegard*, because "in it she prophesies concerning five ages."[11] Gebeno included in his anthology three groups of excerpts: the first group com-prises the visions from both the *Scivias* (3.10.32) and the *Liber divinorum operum* (3.5.15–38) in which Hildegard describes these five ages, associating

---

[8] Gebeno of Eberbach, *La Obra*, 5: "religiosus et letteratus me et aliis audientibus quod iam natus esset constanter affirmabat" / "a religious and literate man was resolutely affirming to me that [the Antichrist] was already born."

[9] Gebeno of Eberbach, *La Obra*, 5–6. Hildegard's five ages are found in *Scivias* 3.11 and *Book of Divine Works* 3.5. For a more detailed account of these five ages, see Kathryn Kerby-Fulton, *Reformist Apocalypticism and Piers Plowman* (Cambridge: Cambridge University Press, 1990), 45–50.

[10] Gebeno of Eberbach, *La Obra*, 5: "Igitur ad confutandos et conuincendos huiusmodi pseudopro-phetas libellum hunc compliaui" / "Therefore, in order to refute and overcome pseudoprophets of this kind, I compiled this little book."

[11] Gebeno of Eberbach, *La Obra*, 4: "Que quinque tempora qui diligenter legere et studiose distinguere uoluerit, et presentem miserum statum ecclesie et omnia futura pericula et aduentum Antichristi quasi in quodam speculo peruidebit. Unde si placet uobis, uocetur ipse liber *Speculum futurorum temporum siue Pentachronon sancte Hildegardis*, . . . quia in eo de quinque prophetat temporibus."

each with a particular animal (fiery dog, tawny lion, pale horse, gray wolf, and black pig). The second group includes excerpts from those letters in which she described further details about what was to come in the imme-diate future, including the epistolary versions of the sermons she preached to laity and clergy (a rare accomplishment for a woman at that time) in Trier (1160–1161), Cologne (ca. 1163), and Kirchheim (1170).[12] To this collection of Hildegard's apocalyptic prophecies, Gebeno added a third group of writings taken predominantly from her correspondence. These are the letters in which she responded to the requests of fellow spiritual leaders, including bishops, abbesses, abbots, and priors, as well as priests, monks, and nuns of lesser ranks, and offered her spiritual guidance and counsel.[13] While the "Sybil of the Rhine" could no longer be directly consulted, Gebeno ensured that some of the guidance she had provided, including her commentary on the *Rule of St. Benedict*, remained available through his compilation.[14]

In order to gather together this material, Gebeno consulted copies of Hildegard's works available in the library of Eberbach Abbey and in the libraries of neighboring monasteries, completing his first, provisional draft (redaction I) in 1220. That same year Gebeno visited Hildegard's own convent at Rupertsberg where he consulted the well-known *Riesencodex* (a manuscript containing a massive collection of Hildegard's works that was begun during her lifetime in an effort to preserve all of her writings) before completing a revised draft (redaction II) in 1222.[15] Despite its provisional nature, by the end of the thirteenth century redaction I had quickly spread through Cistercian houses situated in the northern parts of the Kingdom of

---

[12] On these sermons, see Kerby-Fulton, "Prophet and Reformer," esp. 78, 88–89 and Kathryn Kerby-Fulton, "When Women Preached: An Introduction to Female Homiletic, Sacramental, and Liturgical Roles in the Later Middle Ages," in Kathryn Kerby-Fulton and Linda Olson, eds., *Voices in Dialogue: Reading Women in the Middle Ages* (Notre Dame: University of Notre Dame Press, 2005) 31–55, esp. 39–42.

[13] See Sabina Flanagan, *Hildegard of Bingen: A Visionary Life*, 2nd ed. (London: Routledge, 1998), 152–171.

[14] Santos Paz does not consider all of the texts of spiritual guidance to be part of the *Pentachronon* proper, but rather to be part of what he has called the "compilacio eberbacense" and so these texts are not included in his edition in *La Obra*. See his "Aspetti della ricezione dell'opera di Ildegarda nel Duecento," in Charles Barnett and Peter Dronke, eds., *Hildegard of Bingen: The Context of Her Thought and Art* (London: University of London Press, 1998), 211–223. For my argument that these texts were included by Gebeno as part of the *Pentachronon* itself, see Magda Hayton, "Prophets, Prophecy, and Cistercians: A Study of the Most Popular Version of the Hildegardian *Pentachronon*," *The Journal of Medieval Latin* 29 (2019): 127–128. On the phrase "Sybil of the Rhine" to describe Hildegard, see Barbara Newman, "'Sibyl of the Rhine': Hildegard's Life and Times," in Newman, *Voice of the Living Light*, 1 n. 1.

[15] On the manuscripts Gebeno consulted, see Santos Paz, "Introduccíon," in *La Obra*, xxx–xxxvii.

France and the territories of the Holy Roman Empire north of the Alps; redaction II, in contrast, is currently known to survive in just one thirteenth-century continental manuscript (also of Cistercian provenance) but found its way to England and is the only version known to have circulated there.[16] Neither of Gebeno's redactions bear the marks of a polished final text and this could account for the creation of the "Cum peccata" version or *PentachrononCp*, likely by one of Gebeno's fellow Cistercians, sometime before 1250, which is a better organized and more polished anthology than either of Gebeno's redactions.[17] The *PentachrononCp* circulated widely beyond monastic circles with thirteenth-century copies attributed to Dominicans, cathedral canons, and theologians at the University of Paris; it survives in more complete copies than either redactions I or II.[18] The majority of the texts in these three major versions are the same but differ in organization, and the *PentachrononCp* includes fewer of the texts of spiritual instruction included by Gebeno (discussed further in the section "The Letters of Spiritual Guidance in the Three Major Versions of the *Pentachronon*").[19]

The Presentation of Hildegard As a Prophet in the *Pentachronon*

Gebeno took his provisional draft of the *Pentachronon* with him when he visited Rupertsberg in 1220 and, after showing his work to the nuns, he was confronted by one who was able to cite from memory Hildegard's warning at the end of the *Liber divinorum operum*: "Let no person be so bold as to add anything to the words of this writing by increasing them or to remove anything by decreasing them, lest they be deleted from the book of life and from all blessedness."[20] This injunction is modeled on the final words of the biblical *Apocalypse*, revealing the affinity Hildegard felt with John of

---

[16] The thirteenth-century continental witness of redaction II is Munich, Bayerische Staatsbibliothek, clm. 2619. On the reception of the *Pentachronon* in England, see Kathryn Kerby-Fulton, "Prophecy and Suspicion: Closet Radicalism, Reformist Politics, and the Vogue for Hildegardiana in Ricardian England," *Speculum* 75 (2000): 318–341.

[17] Hayton, "Prophets, Prophecy, and Cistercians" offers a detailed study of the *PentachrononCp*.

[18] On the thirteenth-century witnesses see Hayton, "Prophets, Prophecy and Cistercians," 124 n. 4. There are currently fourteen known complete copies of the *PentachrononCp*, nine of redaction I and ten of redaction II, with numerous other manuscripts containing partial copies or short excerpts.

[19] For further discussion of the different redactions and versions, see Santos Paz, "Introduccíon," in *La Obra*, lii–xcv.

[20] As recounted by Gebeno of Eberbach in his *Epistola Gebenonis prioris de Eberbach ad filias sancte Hildegardis*. Gebeno of Eberbach, *La Obra*, 82.

Patmos.[21] Such affinity between John and Hildegard was not lost on Gebeno.

After Gebeno's visit to Rupertsberg, he wrote a letter to the nuns and included with it a work in which he interpreted the seven trumpeting angels from the biblical *Apocalypse* (8–11) entitled, *Item on the same heretics from the Apocalypse and concerning the seven ages from the preaching of Christ to the end of time* (henceforth *On the same heretics*).[22] In this work, Gebeno makes a lengthy comparison between St. John and Hildegard and boldly claims not only that Hildegard was like a second John but that she herself had been prophesied by John, or, in Gebeno's words, Hildegard was "mystically announced in advance and designated" in the *Apocalypse* "more than one thousand years earlier."[23] Gebeno equates Hildegard with the eagle crying three woes that John describes in *Apocalypse* 8.13: "I looked and I heard an eagle that was flying in midair call out in a great voice: 'Woe! Woe! Woe to the inhabitants of the earth, because of the trumpet blasts about to be sounded by the three other angels!'" According to Gebeno, only Hildegard can be equated with this eagle because, like John of Patmos, "she was always in the contemplation and in the vision of God"; she preached the three woes, which can be found in the *Liber divinorum operum*; she flew through midheaven for she "flourished within the church"; and finally, Hildegard cried out with a great voice, for she "scarcely rested from writing and preaching at God's command."[24] Gebeno also writes that Hildegard received papal approval from Eugenius (1145–1153) at the Synod of Trier (1148) – an account also found in the prologue to the *Pentachronon* and often repeated by later writers – although the authenticity of this claim has been questioned.[25] Gebeno concludes his comparison of Hildegard and the eagle with the

---

[21] Kerby-Fulton, "Prophet and Reformer," 90. Cf. *Apoc.* 22.18–19.

[22] *Item de eisdem hereticis ex Apocalypsi et de VII temporibus a predicatione Christi usque ad finem seculi.* Gebeno of Eberbach, *La Obra*, 88–106. Gebeno's letter to the nuns of Rupertsberg can be found in *La Obra*, 82–7. These two works are not found in redaction II.

[23] Gebeno of Eberbach, *La Obra*, 99: " ... que [i.e., Hildegard] ante mille annos a beato Iohanne apostolo et euangelista in spiritu Dei mystice est prenuntiata et presignata."

[24] "[S]emper in contemplatione et in uisione Dei fuit ... tres plagas trium adhuc futurorum temporum ... in libro *Diuinorum operum* ita manifeste predixit ... in sancta ecclesia ualde sublimi et admirabili uita flouit ... Deo enim iubente ... uix acquiesuit scribere et predicare." Gebeno of Eberbach, *La Obra*, 97–98.

[25] Gebeno of Eberbach, *La Obra*, 98 and 6 (Prologue). John Van Engen has argued that Eugenius did not approve of Hildegard's writings in an official letter ("Letters and the Public *Persona* of Hildegard" in Alfred Haverkamp, ed., *Hildegard von Bingen in ihrem historischen Umfeld* [Mainz: Verlag Philipp von Zabern, 2000], 375–418), but it is possible that Eugenius sent some kind of verbal "blessing" or encouragement (see Kathryn Kerby-Fulton, "Hildegard of Bingen," in Alastair Minnis and Rosalynn Voaden, eds., *Medieval Holy Women in the Christian Tradition, c. 1100–c.1500*

claim that ever since Eugenius approved of Hildegard's visionary writings and encouraged her to keep recording what God revealed to her, "her words and her writings were received as if the words of God himself."[26] According to Gebeno, then, Hildegard's prophecies were further revelations of what had been shown to John and so, in *On the same heretics*, he integrates them with the biblical text, thus creating a new narrative. Gebeno's belief that Hildegard was the fulfillment of John's prophecy and that her visions supplement the biblical text is at the heart of his presentation of Hildegard in the *Pentachronon*.[27]

Gebeno also argued for Hildegard's prophetic authority in the introductory group of texts that open all three major versions of the *Pentachronon*. Here, he reiterates Hildegard's well-known claim that she had received only a minimal education and that the source of her knowledge was divine illumination. He also wrote a short chapter explaining that Hildegard's "obscure and unusual style" of Latin was a further indication that the source of her prophecies was divine, even though it caused many to be "squeamish" and "shrink away" from reading her books.[28] Gebeno also included among these introductory texts Hildegard's own account of her visionary experience from the opening of the *Scivias*, an excerpt the "Cum peccata" editor chose to exclude.

Tribulation and Renewal: The Apocalyptic Narrative of the *Pentachronon*

Over the course of Hildegard's life, her calls for reform became more urgent and, by the end of her life, she had integrated them into a sophisticated theology of salvation history that broke with tradition by claiming that there would be not only periods of spiritual decline and

---

[Turnhout: Brepols, 2010], 343–369). See also Fletcher, Chapter 5, this volume, and Laurence Moulinier, "'Et Papa libros eius canonizavit': Reflexions sur l'orthodoxie des ecrits de Hildegarde de Bingen," in Susanna Elm, Éric Rebillard, and Antonella Romano, eds., *Orthodoxie, christianisme, histoire-Orthodoxy, Christianity, History*. Collection de l'École française de Rome 270 (Rome: École française de Rome, 2000), 177–198.

[26] See Note 1 in this chapter.

[27] On Gebeno's presentation of Hildegard as a prophet within the context of her reputation in the late-twelfth and early-thirteenth century, see José Carlos Santos Paz, "Hildegarde Profetisa: la interpretación de Gebenón de Eberbach," in Sofia Boesch Gajano and Alessandra Bartolomei Romagnoli, eds., "*Speculum futurorum temporum.*" *Ildegarda di Bingen tra agiografia e memoria. Atti del Convegno di Studio (Roma, 5–6- aprile 2017)* (Rome: Istituto Storico Italiano per il Medioevo, 2019), 117–148.

[28] "Libros sancte Hildegardis plerique legere fastidiunt et horrent, pro eo quod obscure et inusitato stylo loquitur, non intelligunt quod hoc est argumentum uere prophetie." Gebeno of Eberbach, *La Obra*, 6.

tribulation before the Last Judgment (a well-established belief) but also periods of widespread renewal, peace, and improvement in ecclesiastical institutions (a striking break with tradition and something that Joachim of Fiore, the other great twelfth-century apocalyptic thinker, developed independently).[29] Hildegard's later writings were her more radical, teaching that the ecclesiastical reforms she and others had long advocated would only be realized if God himself intervened. Hildegard's belief in the effectiveness of human agency had diminished in light of the continuing abuses of the sacerdotal office, the success of the Cathar heresy, and the papal schism that began in 1159 and ended only in 1177, just two years before her death.[30]

The main apocalyptic message of the *Pentachronon* is a continuation of the message that Hildegard herself was proclaiming in the last two decades of her life: a divinely appointed time of punishment would be coming because of priestly (and to a lesser degree monastic) failures, a time during which clerical and monastic wealth would be taken away and many priests and monastics of all ranks would be banished and even killed. It was to be a great purging that would result in widespread renewal and a proliferation of divine justice, with a reformed priesthood entering into a time that Hildegard referred to as a return to "the first dawn of justice."[31] Spiritual leadership, however, would then be within the purview of "strong and wise men," that is, prophets – an unspecified group identified not with any particular religious or ecclesiastical order but only with a gift of divine inspiration and wisdom by which they will lead the faithful.[32] This message was most clearly articulated in the *Liber divinorum operum* (completed by 1174) and in the abovementioned sermons that Hildegard preached in the 1160s and 1170s.

In the *Liber divinorum operum*, Hildegard situated the start of this tribulation within the first of her five ages, which encompassed her present and was represented by the fiery dog. According to Gebeno, this tribulation was the first of the apocalyptic woes that Hildegard had preached as the eagle flying through midheaven, and so, when he copied the final vision from the *Liber divinorum operum* into the *Pentachronon*, he added rubrics

---

[29] Kathryn Kerby-Fulton, *Books Under Suspicion: Censorship and Tolerance of Revelatory Writing in Late Medieval England* (Notre Dame: University of Notre Dame Press, 2006), 45–50.

[30] Kerby-Fulton, "Prophet and Reformer," 73 and 80–90.

[31] Kathryn Kerby-Fulton, "A Return to 'The First Dawn of Justice': Hildegard's Visions of Clerical Reform and the Eremitical Life," *American Benedictine Review* 40 (1989): 383–407.

[32] Gebeno of Eberbach, *La Obra*, 105–106. On the presentation of prophets and prophecy and their significance within the apocalyptic narrative of the *Pentachronon*, see Hayton, "Prophets, Prophecy, and Cistercians," 128–129, 151–160.

stating "Here the first woe of the *Apocalypse* begins" and "The first woe ends here" as guides to his readers.[33] In her narration of the age of the fiery dog, Hildegard describes how divine justice had been declining since the rise of a "secular judge," most likely Emperor Henry IV (r. 1084–1185) of the Holy Roman Empire, making the present moment one of "womanly weakness" – a description she used on numerous occasions to describe the current spiritual state of society.[34] Hildegard placed responsibility for this decline on the shoulders of the clergy – particularly those in positions of oversight – and described them as "rapacious wolves," "ferocious beasts," and "adulterers," who were not providing proper leadership because "they do not shout out what is just and they destroy the law."[35]

Divine intervention comes through the "cruel and oppressive rule of [the clergy's] enemies," that is, of the laity, who insist that the clergy carry out their office as constituted by the church fathers or remove themselves from office.[36] While the clergy will at first resist, they eventually see the error of their ways and agree to reform measures, including the reallocation of ecclesiastical wealth so that they possess no more than what is necessary for them to carry out their office. Even while this clerical reform is happening, however, Hildegard predicts that the events which signal the start of the second age, represented by the tawny lion, will begin: "harsh and even cruel wars will arise, many people will die and many cities will be demolished."[37] It is only when these wars have purged the sins of the people – religious and lay – that justice fully returns and widespread renewal encompassing the whole of society flourishes.

In this second age of the tawny lion, there will be "new and unheard of arrangements of justice and peace," Hildegard writes, "so that people will

---

[33] "Hic primum ue Apocalypsis incipit," "Hic finitur primum ue." Gebeno of Eberbach, *La Obra*, 14 and 17, respectively. See ibid. 22 and 27 for the rubrics indicating where the second and third woes begin.

[34] Gebeno of Eberbach, *La Obra*, 13. On the identification of Henry IV as the "secular judge," see Kerby-Fulton, *Reformist Apocalypticism*, 47. On Hildegard's description of the present as a "womanly time" (*muliebre tempus*) see ibid., 46 and Babara Newman, *Sister of Wisdom: St. Hildegard's Theology of the Feminine* (Berkeley: University of California Press, 1989), 238–240; on the later reception of this idea through the *Pentachronon*, see Nancy Caciola, *Discerning Spirits: Divine and Demonic Possession in the Middle Ages* (Ithaca, NY: Cornell University Press, 2003).

[35] "[R]apaces lupos," "ferocissime bestie," "adulteria quam plurima perpetrant," "quod iustum est non clamant et legem destruunt." Gebeno of Eberbach, *La Obra*, 14.

[36] "[T]yrannidem inimicorum eorum super ipsos [i.e., the clergy] crassari permittet." Gebeno of Eberbach, *La Obra*, 14. On the reformist role of the laity within Hildegard's apocalypticism, see Kerby-Fulton, *Reformist Apocalypticism*, 36–39.

[37] "Sed tamen inter hec omnia, uelut leo in libro *Sciuias* ostendit, dura etiam et crudelia bella . . . exurgent et plurimi hominum in occisione cadent et plurime ciuitates per destructionem ruent." Gebeno of Eberbach, *La Obra*, 17.

wonder, saying they have never known or heard of such things before, because peace has been given to them before the day of judgment."[38] This peace, moreover, will be the fulfillment of the peace that preceded the Incarnation, "because strong men in great prophecy will then rise up and as a result every seed of justice in the sons and daughters of humanity will then flourish."[39] Here, we see Hildegard's break with tradition as she forecasts not only a time of peace before the Last Judgment but also widespread improvement of society and religion.

Hildegard describes two subsequent moments of tribulation and renewal over the course of the remaining three ages, which Gebeno equates with the second and third woes of the Apocalypse (again adding rubrics to indicate where they begin and end). Hildegard's narrative of the second tribulation includes the bold prediction that both the Holy Roman Empire and the papacy would cease to exist as "universal" institutions, being replaced by localized arrangements of lay and ecclesiastical jurisdictions – a prediction that was of great interest to readers of the *Pentachronon* during the Great Western Schism (1378–1417) and likely explains, at least in part, interest in the *Pentachronon* among emergent Lutherans in the sixteenth century.[40] The third and final tribulation (or third woe) within Hildegard's five ages encompasses the period of decline preceding the advent of the Antichrist and the traditional events of the Last Days. In the *Scivias* (3.2.25–41), Hildegard included a description of the life and times of the Antichrist based predominantly on a tenth-century text composed by Adso of Montier-en-Der.[41] Gebeno included this account as well as her later, more developed account from the *Book of Divine Works* in the *Pentachronon*.

---

[38] "Sed et tam noue et incognite ordinationes iusticie et pacis tunc aduenient, ut homines inde admirentur, dicentes quoniam talia prius nec audierint nec cognouerint et quia pax ante diem iudicii ipsis data sit." Gebeno of Eberbach, *La Obra*, 18.

[39] "[Q]uoniam fortes uiri in magna prophetia tunc surgent, ita ut etiam omne germen iusticie in filiis et in filiabus hominum tunc florebit." Gebeno of Eberbach, *La Obra*, 18. On Hildegard's parallel of pre-Incarnation peace with that after the tribulation, see Kerby-Fulton, *Reformist Apocalypticism*, 47–48.

[40] Hildegard wrote that this tribulation, like the first, would be followed by a dramatic increase in prophetic knowledge (*La Obra*, 27). On readings of this passage during the Western Schism, see Magda Hayton, "Hildegardian Prophecy and French Prophecy Collections 1378–1455: A Study and Critical Edition of the 'Schism Extracts'," *Traditio* 72 (2017): 462–3 and Magda Hayton and Robert L. J. Shaw, "Communicating Solutions to the Great Western Schism in 1380s France," *Mediaeval Studies* 80 (2018): 297–338, at 314. On the reception of the *Pentachronon* during the Reformation, see Embach, "Hildegard of Bingen," 273–304.

[41] *Scivias* 3.11.25–41; Gebeno of Eberbach, *La Obra*, 42–52. Cf. Adso of Montier-en-Der, *Letter on the Origin and Time of the Antichrist, in Apocalyptic Spirituality: Treatises and Letters of Lactantius, Adso of Montier-en-Der, Joachim of Fiore, the Franciscan Spirituals, Savonarola*, ed. and trans. Bernard McGinn (New York: Paulist Press, 1979), 81–96.

This first group of texts lays out Hildegard's complete narrative of future history, but Gebeno's primary concern was on the near future and he knew that the *Liber divinorum operum* was not the only place in which Hildegard had described what was soon to come. To ensure that his readers were well informed about what Hildegard had taught, Gebeno gathered together a second group of excerpts from her writings, including another excerpt from the *Liber divinorum operum* (3.5.7), selections from the epistolary copies of the sermons Hildegard had preached in Cologne, Trier, and Kirchheim, and her letter to King Conrad, among others. To these, Gebeno added rubrics indicating how each excerpt aligned with Hildegard's five ages.[42] There is a great deal of overlap between the descriptions in these excerpts and the narrative of the first two ages in the *Liber divinorum operum*, but each adds further detail, allowing a fuller picture to emerge when all of Hildegard's accounts are taken together.

One of the key elements of the soon-to-come tribulation (i.e. the tribulation of the first woe) as presented in the *Pentachronon* is the central involvement of heretics as pseudo-religious or pseudo-prophets. Heretics do not play an active role in Hildegard's description of the first age of the fiery dog in either the *Scivias* or the *Liber divinorum operum*, but she had described at length the role they would play in her letter to the clergy of Cologne. In this prophecy, she identifies the Cathars as forerunners of the Antichrist and describes how they would be allowed to perpetrate a divinely sanctioned chastisement of the clergy. Hildegard depicts the advent of a group of heretical pseudo-religious who, feigning sanctity, would seduce lay princes into following them so that together they could overthrow and disendow the clergy. After this divine correction had been accomplished, the lay lords would realize their seduction, turn on the pseudo-religious and "kill them like rabid wolves," thus retaining the status they have in the *Liber divinorum operum* as positive agents of reform.[43]

It is worth noting that the Cologne letter was highly influential in the centuries after Hildegard's death, often circulating on its own; Embach and Wallner list sixteen individual copies in their catalogue of manuscripts.[44] Through its inclusion in the *Pentachronon*, the letter became the basis of

---

[42] E.g. "Ex Libro dinuinorum operum de primo tempore" and "Ex Epistola sancte Hildegardis ad Colonienses de futura tribulatione clericorum." Gebeno of Eberbach, *La Obra*, 54 and 58, respectively.
[43] "uelut rabidos lupos eos occident ubicumque eos inuenerint." Gebeno of Eberbach, *La Obra*, 62.
[44] Konrad Bund, "Die 'Prophetin', ein Dichter und die Niederlassung der Bettelorden in Köln. Der Brief der Hildegard von Bingen an den Kölner Klerus und das Gedicht, 'Prophetia Sancte Hyldegardis de Novis Fratribus' des Magisters Heinrich von Avranches," *Mittellateinisches Jahrbuch* 23 (1988): 171–260.

Hildegard's reputation as an anti-mendicant prophet that originated within the apocalyptically charged secular-mendicant controversy at the University of Paris that began in the 1250s. The leader of the secular masters at this time, William of St. Amour, launched Hildegard's "anti-mendicant career" when he composed the pseudo-Hildegardian prophecy "Insurgent gentes," essentially a rewrite of the Cologne letter that obviously attacks the Dominicans and Franciscans by identifying them as the heretical pseudo-religious described by Hildegard.[45] "Insurgent gentes" circulated widely throughout Europe, and in the fourteenth century it was read not only as an anti-mendicant prophecy but also as a polemic against Wycliffites and Hussites.[46]

Two other key features of the near-future tribulation are clarified in the excerpt from Hildegard's letter to Trier that immediately follows the excerpt from the Cologne letter in the *Pentachronon*. The first is that the tribulation will affect not only clergy, as presented in the *Liber divinorum operum*, but also monastics. The letter describes how both clergy and monastics will be put to flight and many monasteries destroyed along with cities because members of both groups "have turned aside from obedience and other precepts of the law."[47] The second embellishment offered by this letter is an elaboration of the means by which prophets will provide leadership during the time of peace after the tribulation:

> And then strong men will rise up and prophesy and all the old and new things of the scriptures and all the teachings effused by the Holy Spirit they will gather together and they will ornament the understanding of them like a necklace with precious stones. Through these and through other wise ones many seculars will become good and live in a holy way. This pursuit of sanctity will not dry up quickly, but will last for a long time.[48]

---

[45] Kerby-Fulton, *Books Under Suspicion*, 190–196; Kathryn Kerby-Fulton, "Hildegard of Bingen and Anti-Mendicant Propaganda," *Traditio* 43 (1987): 386–399; Kathryn Kerby-Fulton, Magda Hayton, and Kenna Olsen, "Pseudo-Hildegardian Prophecy and Antimendicant Propaganda in Late-Medieval England: An Edition of the Most Popular Insular Text of 'Insurgent Gentes'" in Nigel Morgan, ed., *Prophecy, Apocalypse and the Day of Doom: Proceedings of the 2000 Harlaxton Symposium*, Harlaxton Medieval Studies vol. 12 (Donington, Shaun Tyas Publishing, 2004), 160–194 ; José Carlos Santos Paz, "Guillermo de Saint-Amour y la Versión Original de la Profecía Antimendicante *Insurgent Gentes*," *Studi Medievali* 57, no. 2 (2016): 649–687.

[46] Pavlína Cermanová, "Constructing the Apocalypse: Connections Between English and Bohemian Apocalyptic Thinking," in J. Patrick Hornbeck, II and Michael Van Dussen, eds., *Europe after Wyclif* (New York: Fordham University Press, 2017), 66–88. On a fourteenth-century Italian translation by fraticelli, see José Carlos Santos Paz, "Propaganda antifranciscana en Florencia a finales del siglo XIV: una traducción italiana inédita de la profecía *Insurgent gentes*," *Studi Medievali* 60, no. 1 (2019): 143–160.

[47] "[P]ropter preuaricationem obedientie et aliorum preceptorum legalium institutionum occurrent." Gebeno of Eberbach, *La Obra*, 63.

[48] "Et tunc fortes uiri surgent et prophetabunt et omnia uetera et noua scripturarum ac omnes sermones per Spiritum sanctum effusos colligent et intellectum eorum sicut monile cum pretiosis

It seems that Gebeno understood his own work of gathering together Hildegard's inspired writings and the ornamentation he provided within his anthology to be something akin to the work of these future prophets. At the end of *On the same heretics*, Gebeno writes that he will leave discussion of the final two woes to these future prophets and then concludes his treatise by saying, "Moreover, I leave behind to their [i.e. the future prophets'] arbitration and judgment the things that were composed by me or compiled from the books of saint Hildegard, so that they can weed out what they judge to need weeding and put into a better order, if there are things that are not so well ordered."[49]

In addition to fleshing out the tribulation and renewal narrative, Hildegard's letter to Trier was also used by Gebeno to calculate when the tribulation would begin in a short tract he included in the *Pentachronon*: *When the great future schism will be from the letter of saint Hildegard to Trier* (written in 1222). Here, Gebeno calculates that the tribulation will start no later than thirty-four years from the time he is writing, that is, by 1256.[50] To accompany this tract, Gebeno also included a short excerpt from the *Liber divinorum operum* under the rubric: *These signs will be given before that schism during which bishops and clergy will be expelled from their places.*[51]

Among the signs are the sins of "hate, homicide and sodomy," but the most significant indication that the tribulation is near will be a proliferation of spiritual novelties.[52] According to the Hildegardian text, it is "when the ancient serpent hisses a variety of customs and a variety of vestments in the people" that "the princes and the nobles and the rich will be expelled from their places by their peers and subordinates and will flee from city to city."[53] This concern with innovation was taken up by Gebeno when choosing texts for the third part of his anthology. As we will see, the third and final group of texts included in the *Pentachronon* move beyond the apocalyptic narrative of tribulation and renewal and focus instead on spiritual instruction for readers on a more personal level.

---

lapidibus ornabunt. Per hos et per alios sapientes plurimi seculares boni fient et sancte uiuent. Hoc autem studium sanctitatis cito non arescet, sed diu durabit." Gebeno of Eberbach, *La Obra*, 64.

[49] Gebeno of Eberbach, *La Obra*, 106. For further discussion of this passage, see Hayton, "Prophets, Prophecy, and Cistercians," 129.

[50] *Item quando magnum scisma futurum sit, ex epistola sancte Hildegardis ad Treuerenses.* Gebeno of Eberbach, *La Obra*, 108–109.

[51] *Ista dabuntur indicia ante scisma illud sub quo episcopi et clerici de locis suis expellentur.* Gebeno of Eberbach, *La Obra*, 107. Cf. Hildegard of Bingen, *Liber divinorum operum*, 2.1.9.

[52] Gebeno of Eberbach, *La Obra*, 107 and 121.

[53] "Et principes et nobiles et diuites per consimiles atque per suos minores de locis suis expellentur et de ciuitate in ciuitatem fugabuntur . . . . Ista omnia tunc fient, cum antiquus serpens uarietatem morum et uarietatem uestimentorum in populos sibilabit." Gebeno of Eberbach, *La Obra*, 122, see also 107. Cf. Hildegard of Bingen, *Liber divinorum operum*, 2.1.9.

The Letters of Spiritual Guidance in the Three Major Versions of the *Pentachronon*

As we have seen, in the first two groups of texts included in the *Pentachronon* Hildegard is presented as an apocalyptic prophet of present and future history with a harsh message of reform for the church as a whole. The remaining texts are of a different sort. Here, Hildegard is seen in action as a spiritual leader – a prophetic leader – whose guidance was sought even by the prelates of her day. As Gebeno's revised version, redaction II gives us the clearest picture of how he conceived of the place of these writings within the overall purpose of the *Pentachronon*. In redaction II, which is divided into three parts (*pars*), these letters of spiritual guidance are contained separately within part three, which is introduced by a brief prologue: "Part three contains the requests for advice that some prelates sent to blessed Hildegard and her replies and some visions about new rites and indiscriminate discipline."[54] The shift in focus is immediately clear: in part three, the underlying causes of the coming tribulation (spiritual novelties, improper discipline, and poor spiritual oversight) will be addressed.

Part three opens with an excerpt from the letter that Hildegard sent to Pope Eugenius while he was holding the Synod of Trier in 1148. In this letter, Hildegard delivers a bold message to the highest ecclesiastical prelate of her day on behalf of the Living Light – a message of both instruction and warning:

> Now again He, who is the Living Light shining in the heavens and in the abyss and lying in the hidden place of listening hearts, says to you: Prepare this writing for the hearing of those who receive me and make it fruitful with pleasant-tasting sap and make it the root of the branches and a leaf flying against the devil and you will have eternal life. Beware lest you spurn these mysteries of God because they are necessary in that necessity that lies hidden and that has not yet appeared openly.[55]

---

[54] "Pars tercia quorundam prelatorum consultationes ad beatam Hildegardim factas eiusque rescripta continet ac quasdam uisiones de nouis ritibus et disciplina indiscreta." Gebeno of Eberbach, *La Obra*, 123.

[55] "Nunc iterum dicit tibi qui est lux uiuens in supernis et in abysso lucens ac latens in abscondito audientium cordium: Prepara scripturam hanc ad auditum me suscipientium et fac illam uiridem in suco suauis gustus et radicem ramorum et uolans folium contra diabolum et uiues in eternum. Caue ne spernas hec mystica Dei, quia sunt necessaria in illa necessitate que abscondite latet et que nondum aperte apparet." Gebeno of Eberbach, *La Obra*, 71. Cf. Hildegard of Bingen, *Epistolarium*, ed. Lieven Van Acker, Corpus Christianorum Continuatio Mediaevalis (CCCM) 91 (Turnhout: Brepols, 1991), Letter 2 and *The Letters of Hildegard of Bingen*, vol. 1, trans. Joseph L. Baird and Radd K. Ehrman (Oxford: Oxford University Press, 1998), 33.

Excerpted from its original context, Hildegard's injunction that her teach-ings be shared among the faithful and her warning that they are to be heeded by even the pope himself now apply to all of the writings that follow in part three.

These writings focus on the correction of clerical and monastic laxity and on the reform of ineffective leadership, both within the secular church and within monastic houses. The excerpts range from a letter sent to Archbishop Philip of Cologne on how to properly discipline subordinates to a letter on the discernment of spirits originally sent to an unknown priest who had sought Hildegard's help with the unclean spirits plaguing him. They also include some of Hildegard's epistolary exchanges with Cistercians, including Gebeno's own monastery of Eberbach, in which she offers instruction on monastic discipline, and the versions of her correspondence with Bernard of Clairvaux that had been edited to embellish Bernard's support of her prophetic gifting.[56] These Cistercian texts are the only works included in the "Cum peccata" version, but Gebeno's longer anthologies (redactions I and II) also include the advice Hildegard offered the nun Jutta on avoiding excessive abstinence and even Hildegard's commentary on the *Rule of St. Benedict* – itself an epistolary work written in response to the request of monks at an unidentified monastery.

In some of these letters, Hildegard herself had contextualized her reformist teachings within a tribulation narrative, such as her letter to a Cistercian prior composed in 1169: "Therefore, you who fear God . . . remove the aforementioned evils from yourselves and purge yourselves before the day of those tribulations when the enemies of God and you make you flee and turn you to the right place of humility and poverty."[57] As we have seen, clerical and monastic laxity together with ineffective leadership are the main roots of contemporary troubles and the ultimate cause of the coming tribulation. By including these teachings along with Hildegard's historically oriented prophecies, Gebeno created an anthology that countered false prophecies about the coming of the Antichrist by teaching the more real and present danger of a pre-Antichrist purging tribulation and offered instruction

---

[56] On Hildegard's correspondence with Bernard, see Van Engen, "Letters," 381–382.

[57] "Uos ergo, qui Deum timetis . . . hec supradicta mala a uobis auferte et uosmetipsos ante diem tribulationum illarum purgate, cum inimici Dei et uestri uos fugabunt et in rectum locum humilitatis et paupertatis uos conuertent." Gebeno of Eberbach, *La Obra*, 74. Cf., *The Letters of Hildegard of Bingen*, ed. Baird and Ehrman, 187.

to clergy, monks, and their leaders on how they might effect reform and properly live out their vocations.

Responding to the Message

Gebeno, it seemed, hoped that the tribulation might be avoided if Hildegard's reformist teachings were heeded. After calculating when the tribulation will begin in *When the great future schism will be*, he concludes with an invocation of the biblical example of the Ninevites, who were able to avoid God's punishment by heeding the warnings of the prophet Jonah and repenting. Gebeno writes, "not even 34 years remain . . . unless perchance [the tribulation] is put off by a grave repentance of humanity, for when the Lord threatened through the prophet [i.e. Jonah] saying *There are still 40 days and then Nineveh will be overthrown* [Jonah 3.4], he was turned from the furor of his wrath by their great penitence."[58] Where Gebeno hoped that readers would heed Hildegard's warnings of tribulation and learn from her spiritual instruction, the medieval editor of the "Cum peccata" version of the *Pentachronon* feared it was already too late. This editor moved *When the great future schism will be* to the end of the anthology and added their own conclusion, which effectively became concluding words for the *PentachrononCp* as a whole. It reads:

> We know without any doubt that blessed Hildegard truly spoke from God and God through her. But still we have hearts of stone because right up to the present day we have repented only a little or not at all, and because of this I fear that soon everything that was written in this book will overcome us.[59]

Decades had passed since Hildegard first wrote and preached about the need for reform and the danger of a coming tribulation, but she had been so effective at getting her message out that it was still on people's minds.

Another example can be found in the *Life of St. Englebert* where Caesarius of Heisterbach recounts how the clergy and people of

---

[58] "[N]on adhuc durabit XXXIIII annos . . . . nisi forte graui penitentia hominum proteletur, cum enim comminatus esset Dominus per prophetam dicens: *Adhuc XL dies et Ninive subuertetur*, graui penitentia eorum auersus est a furore ire sue." Gebeno of Eberbach, *La Obra*, 109.

[59] "Nos autem absque omni dubietate scimus quod beata Hildegardis ueraciter a Deo locuta est et Deus per eam. Et tamen ita lapidea corda habemus, quod usque in hodiernum diem aut parum aut nichil penituimus et propter ea timeo quod in breui ueniant super nos omnia que scripta sunt in libro isto." Gebeno of Eberbach, *La Obra*, 109.

Cologne panicked when the first Dominicans and Franciscans arrived in 1220 and 1222, respectively. The people came running to their bishop, Englebert (1185/6–1225), saying "We fear that these are those about whom the Holy Spirit prophesied through the mouth of blessed Hildegard, the ones by whom the clergy will be overthrown and the city endangered!"[60] People had not forgotten the sermon Hildegard had preached almost sixty years earlier, and with the sudden appearance of the friars they were convinced that what they were witnessing was the fulfillment of her prophecy.

This same prophecy was also on the minds of the nuns at Rupertsberg when Gebeno visited there around 1220. The reason that he composed his exegetical treatise, *On the same heretics*, was because they had asked him to "write especially some things about those heretics our blessed mother had prophesied and warned us about in the letter to Cologne."[61] Whether the nuns were already thinking about the Cologne heretics, or if Gebeno had roused their concern by sharing his own fears, Hildegard's prophetic-apocalyptic message of a coming tribulation continued to resonate well into the thirteenth century.

Conclusion

Interest in the *Pentachronon* was immediate and far-reaching because it rode on the coattails of the reputation as a prophet that Hildegard had established for herself. The *Pentachronon* quickly became one of the most influential works of apocalyptic prophecy and Hildegard one of the most widely read medieval prophets: within thirty years of its publication, the work was being cited by chroniclers, biblical commentators, theologians, and polemicists. As the *Pentachronon* continued to circulate in the follow-ing centuries, future readers likewise saw a reflection of their own times in Hildegard's prophecies and, through this continued engagement, her teachings – as they were presented by Gebeno – shaped debates on reform and responses to crises through the seventeenth century. Through the publication of the *Pentachronon*, Gebeno's desire that both contemporaries

---

[60] "Timemus, ne isti sint illi, de quibus Spiritus sanctus per os beate Hildegardis prophetauit, per quos clerus affligetur et ciuitas periclitabitur." Caesarius of Heisterbach, *Vita, passio et miracula b. Engelberti Coloniensis archiepiscopi*, ed. F. Zschaeck, in *Die Wundergeschichten des Caesarius von Heisterbach, 3: Die beiden ersten Bücher der Libri VIII miraculorum. Leben, Leiden und Wunder des heiligen Engelbert, Erzbischofs von Köln. Die Schriften über die heilige Elisabeth von Thüringen*, ed. Alfons Hilka, Gesellschaft für Rheinische Geschichtskunde 43.3 (Bonn: Hanstein, 1937): 245.

[61] "Preterea monuistis ut de illis hereticis aliqua specialiter scriberem, de quibus prophetat et premonit nos in epistola ad Colonienses beata mater nostra." Gebeno of Eberbach, *La Obra*, 83.

and future generations look to Hildegard for direction was fulfilled and Hildegard's reputation as a prophet of reform, tribulation, and renewal endured.

Further Reading

Latin Editions and English Translations

Adso of Montier-en-Der. *Letter on the Origin and Time of the Antichrist.* In *Apocalyptic Spirituality: Treatises and Letters of Lactantius, Adso of Montier-en-Der, Joachim of Fiore, the Franciscan Spirituals, Savonarola,* ed. and trans. Bernard McGinn. New York: Paulist Press, 1979.

Gebeno of Eberbach. *La Obra de Gebenón de Eberbach,* ed. José Carlos Santos Paz. Florence: SISMEL - Edizioni del Galluzzo, 2004.

Hayton, Magda. "Hildegardian Prophecy and French Prophecy Collections 1378–1455: A Study and Critical Edition of the 'Schism Extracts.'" *Traditio* 72 (2017): 453–491.

Kerby-Fulton, Kathryn, Magda Hayton, and Kenna Olsen. "Pseudo-Hildegardian Prophecy and Antimendicant Propaganda in Late-Medieval England: An Edition of the Most Popular Insular Text of 'Insurgent Gentes.'" In Nigel Morgan, ed., *Prophecy, Apocalypse and the Day of Doom: Proceedings of the 2000 Harlaxton Symposium.* Harlaxton Medieval Studies vol. 12. Donington: Shaun Tyas Publishing, 2004, 160–194.

Secondary Literature

Caciola, Nancy. *Discerning Spirits: Divine and Demonic Possession in the Middle Ages.* Ithaca, NY: Cornell University Press, 2003.

Embach, Michael and Martina Wallner. *Conspectus der Handschriften Hildegards von Bingen.* Münster: Aschendorff, 2013.

Embach, Michael. "Hildegard of Bingen (1098–1179): A History of Reception." In Beverly Mayne Kienzle, Debra L. Stoudt, and George Ferzoco, eds., *A Companion to Hildegard of Bingen.* Leiden: Brill, 2014, 273–304.

Hayton, Magda. "Prophets, Prophecy, and Cistercians: A Study of the Most Popular Version of the Hildegardian *Pentachronon.*" *The Journal of Medieval Latin* 29 (2019): 123–162.

Kerby-Fulton, Kathryn. "Prophecy and Suspicion: Closet Radicalism, Reformist Politics, and the Vogue for Hildegardiana in Ricardian England." *Speculum* 75 (2000): 318–341.

Kerby-Fulton, Kathryn. "Prophet and Reformer: 'Smoke in the Vineyard.'" In Barbara Newman, ed., *Voice of the Living Light: Hildegard of Bingen and Her World.* Berkeley: University of California Press, 1998, 70–90.

Kerby-Fulton, Kathryn. "When Women Preached: An Introduction to Female Homiletic, Sacramental, and Liturgical Roles in the Later Middle Ages." In Kathryn Kerby-Fulton and Linda Olson, eds., *Voices in Dialogue: Reading Women in the Middle Ages*. Notre Dame: University of Notre Dame Press, 2005, 31–55.

Santos Paz, José Carlos. "Hildegarde Profetisa: la interpretación de Gebenón de Eberbach." In Sofia Boesch Gajano and Alessandra Bartolomei Romagnoli, eds., *"Speculum futurorum temporum": Ildegarda di Bingen tra agiografia e memoria. Atti del Convegno di Studio (Roma, 5-6- aprile 2017)*. Rome: Istituto Storico Italiano per il Medioevo, 2019, 117–148.

CHAPTER 9

The Context and Reception of Hildegard of Bingen's Visions

Wendy Love Anderson

When Hildegard of Bingen described her own visions, she and her twelfth-century contemporaries found their best precedents in the Holy Scriptures. Toward the end of Hildegard's life, the Flemish Benedictine Guibert of Gembloux wrote her a letter asking about her visions and comparing her access to God favorably to various Old Testament female prophets – Miriam, Deborah, and Judith – as well as male prophets like Nathan and Elijah.[1] Hildegard replied with a description of her visions but first countered Guibert's flattery by comparing herself not to prophets but to visionary apostles. She immediately identified with the apostles Paul and John, "those who ascended in soul and thirsted for divine wisdom, counting themselves as nothing, they became the pillars of heaven . . . . nor can I [understand] perfectly everything that I see in my body, and in my invisible soul – for in these, human beings are defective."[2] In a subsequent missive to Guibert, who had asked her permission to render her visions in better Latin, she pointed out that here too she was in excellent visionary company: since Moses, Jeremiah, and Paul had all testified to their inability to speak skillfully, Hildegard's readers should not be scandalized "because I am not given the faculty or competency of setting forth in Latin those things which are revealed to me or are commanded divinely to be put forth to be manifested through me."[3]

---

[1] Guibert of Gembloux, first letter to Hildegard of Bingen, in *Guiberti Gemblacensis Epistolae* 1, ed. Albert Derolez, Corpus Christianorum Continuatio Mediaevalis (CCCM) 66 (Turnhout, Brepols, 1988), 216–20.

[2] Hildegard of Bingen, first letter to Guibert of Gembloux, in *Epistolarium* 1, ed. Lieven Van Acker, CCCM 91 (Turnhout: Brepols, 1991), 55–56: "Sed qui in ascentione anime sapientiam a deo hauserunt, et se pro nichilo comptaverunt, hii columpne celi facte sunt . . . . Nec ea que video perfecte possum, quamdiu in corporali officio sum et in anima invisibili, quoniam in his duobus homini defectus est."

[3] Hildegard of Bingen, *Visio ad Guibertum missa*, in *Hildegardis Bingensis Opera Minora II*, ed. J. Deploige and S. Moens, CCCM 226A (Turnhout: Brepols, 2016), 27:433: "Nec vero te, seu quempiam mea legentium, iste latini eloquii quem patior defectus, scandalizet, quod ad ea quae mihi revelantur vel per me manifestari divinitus imperantur proferenda, simul etiam mihi facultas aut competens latine proferendi non datur . . . ."

Neither Hildegard nor Guibert chose to compare Hildegard's visions to those of postbiblical Christian figures, even though both must surely have been acquainted with, for instance, the light-filled vision in which St. Benedict of Nursia saw a bishop's soul carried away to heaven.[4] (Bernard McGinn describes this episode from Gregory the Great's *Dialogues* as "perhaps the most famous nonbiblical vision of the early Middle Ages.")[5] In fact, by the time of Hildegard and Guibert's correspondence in the late 1170s, other visionaries were already beginning to use *Hildegard* as their standard for comparison – and this trend did not end with the twelfth century. This chapter places Hildegard and her visions into the larger context of twelfth-century visionary activity and attitudes, and then sketches out Hildegard's increasingly distinctive position in later visionary history.

Twelfth-Century Visionaries and Their Authorizers

The twelfth century represented a watershed for visionary activity in Latin Christendom. A Christian movement of *reformatio* that had begun in the previous century – extending outward from monasteries to regular priests and bishops to, eventually, lay Christians – was institutionalized with a series of reforming popes, the rise of new "reformed" religious communities and orders, and a new emphasis on living an apostolic life – including visionary activity. Of course, early Christian visionaries were not confined to the apostolic figures of Paul, who was "caught up to the third heaven" (2 Corinthians 12:2), and John, whose apocalyptic visions of judgment, battle, and a new Jerusalem make up the New Testament book of Revelation. They also included martyrs such as Vibia Perpetua, whose early third-century visions included a ladder into a heavenly garden, a battle with a serpent, and two encounters with a young brother who had predeceased her and whose posthumous suffering she ended through her own prayers.[6] Early Christian monastic traditions also produced their share of visionaries: according to his hagiographer Athanasius of Alexandria, the famous

---

[4] Gregory the Great, *Dialogues* 2.35, ed. and trans. by Adalbert de Vogüé as *Grégoire le Grand: Dialogues*, Sources Chrétiennes 251, 260, and 265 (Paris: Cerf, 1978–80). See, among others, V. Recchia, "La visione di S. Benedetto e la 'compositio' del secondo libro dei 'Dialoghi' di Gregorio Magno," *Revue Bénédictine* 82 (1972): 140–155.

[5] Bernard McGinn, *The Growth of Mysticism: Gregory the Great Through The Twelfth Century* (New York: Crossroad, 1994), 71.

[6] See Peter Dronke, *Women Writers of the Middle Ages: A Critical Study of Texts from Perpetua to Marguerite Porete* (Cambridge: Cambridge University Press, 1984), and more recently Petr Kitzler, *From* Passio Perpetuae *to* Acta Perpetuae: *Recontextualizing a Martyr Story in the Literature of the Early Church* (Berlin: De Gruyter, 2015).

fourth-century monk Antony engaged in regular combat with demons, whom he saw as a sequence of wild beasts, and with the devil, who appeared to him in various human guises and tried to trick him; Antony also saw the soul of his monastic colleague Amun ascending into heaven, along with the judgment of many other souls.[7] In subsequent centuries, many Christian martyrs, monks, and saints were described as following similar visionary patterns. For instance, when the sixth-century Irish missionary abbot Columba (or Colmcille) had his life rewritten in three books by a seventh-century cousin, Adomnán, the third book consisted entirely of visions by and about Columba. Adomnán included visions in which Columba defeated a host of demons wielding iron darts, saw various individuals' souls being carried up to heaven, and encountered an angel carrying a book of glass who instructed Columba to consecrate a new king of Iona.[8] As this last vision suggests, early medieval Christian visions featured explicitly political as well as theological messages, both of which would find their place in Hildegard's *oeuvre*.

Beginning in the twelfth century, however, and continuing into the thirteenth and fourteenth centuries, visions in the Christian West were recorded more frequently, were more personal in content, and were experienced by a wider range of visionaries (especially laypeople and members of various "new" religious orders) than their predecessors.[9] Dozens, if not hundreds, of twelfth-century Christians experienced visions featuring emotional engagement between the visionary and the subjects of the vision; buoyed by the rising tide of church reform, these visions often addressed the problems of Christian life in the present, ranging from interpersonal disputes to doctrinal quandaries and political crises. The monastic and miraculous visionary traditions of early Christianity never entirely vanished – after all, many of the twelfth-century's major visionary figures are associated with monastic life, including Hildegard – but even monastic visions started to become more current, as well as more controversial. Hildegard's own visions are a case in point: they included detailed practical instructions about the location of her new monastic institution at

---

[7] See Pascal Bertrand, *Die Evagriusübersetzung der Vita Antonii: Rezeption – Überlieferung – Edition: Unter besonderer Berücksichtigung der Vitas Patrum-Tradition* (Utrecht: Proefschrift Universiteit Utrecht, 2006).

[8] Adomnán of Iona, *Vita Sancti Columbae*, ed. and trans. A. O. Anderson and M. O. Anderson as *Adomnan's Life of Columba* (Oxford: Clarendon Press, 1991), esp. 3.5.

[9] See McGinn, *The Growth of Mysticism*, 149–157, for the argument that twelfth-century visionaries looked both back to a monastic past and forward into a reform-driven future; many other histories of Christian mysticism – e.g. Steven Fanning, *Mystics of the Christian Tradition* (New York: Routledge, 2006), 85 – similarly remark on the "'new mysticism' that emerged in the twelfth century."

Rupertsberg and the design of her nuns' headdresses, elaborate allegories depicting the nature of the Trinity and the history of salvation, and pointed warnings to the current Holy Roman Emperor against installing a series of antipopes. Of course, visions of demons or the afterlife – often reported safely after the death of all interested parties – did not demand the burden of proof that Hildegard's more immediate visions did. Financial and logistical repercussions were one obvious source of concern: when Hildegard's visions urged her to move her community of women from Disibodenberg to Rupertsberg at considerable trouble and expense, her *Vita* claims that "many were wondering about the revelation, whether it was from God or from the dryness of airy spirits, which misleads many."[10] As Barbara Newman pointed out, Hildegard's visions in fact "provided both the material and the authority for her teaching," countering any possible claim of error or spiritual seduction.[11] In Hildegard's correspondence with Guibert and with an earlier series of powerful clergymen, including the Cistercian leader Bernard of Clairvaux and his pupil Pope Eugenius III, she demonstrated another twelfth-century visionary innovation: finding ways to authorize her visions as truly coming from God. The construction of Hildegard's visionary persona – the woman who could compare herself to the apostles Paul and John – was, in many ways, just as important as the content of her visions, because without the former, the latter would go unheard.

Hildegard was prominent, but not unique, among the "new" self-authorizing visionaries of the twelfth century. Toward the end of his commentary on the Gospel of Matthew, the Benedictine theologian Rupert of Deutz (1075–1129) included an extended autobiographical account in which he described two different sequences of visions he had experienced as a young man, beginning with the crucified Christ appearing to him on the altar and continuing through visions of the Trinity lifting Rupert up onto a book, the Ancient of Days embracing and kissing him, the Holy Spirit greeting him as a recently baptized "child," and multiple erotic encounters between Rupert and Christ, couched in the language of the Song of Songs.[12] These visions, the much older Rupert insisted, had

---

[10] "Multi enim de reuelatione admirabantur, utrum a Deo esset an de inaquositate aeriorum spirituum, qui multos seducunt." *Vita Sanctae Hildegardis*, ed. M. Klaes, CCCM 126 (Turnhout: Brepols, 1993), 2.2.5.

[11] Barbara Newman, "Hildegard of Bingen: Visions and Validation," *Church History* 54 (1985): 164.

[12] On Rupert, see John Van Engen, *Rupert of Deutz* (Berkeley: University of California Press, 1983), especially 67–72, and McGinn, *The Growth of Mysticism*, 328–333. On Rupert's self-presentation and claims to authority, see also Karl Fredrick Fabrizius, "Rupert of Deutz on Matthew: A Study in Exegetical Method" (PhD diss., Marquette University, 1994) and Jay Diehl, "The Grace of

inspired his entire life's output of scriptural commentaries and monastic treatises: "from that time on 'I have opened my mouth' (Ps. 119:131) and I have never been able to stop writing."[13] Although Rupert's theological reputation was never predicated on his visionary experiences, his visions served as a way to authorize and even authenticate his interpretation of scripture. Similarly, the Cistercian Joachim of Fiore (ca. 1135–1202) attributed his revolutionary understanding of salvation history and its reflection in scripture to divine inspiration, including a vision of a ten-stringed psaltery that enabled him to understand the mystery of the Trinity as it manifested itself in the three stages of history.[14] Joachim, however, saw himself not as a visionary but as a divinely inspired interpreter of scripture; one chronicler quotes him as saying, "God ... has given me the spirit of understanding, so that I may very clearly understand all the mysteries of holy Scripture in God's Spirit, just as the holy prophets understood who once recorded it in God's Spirit."[15] Still, when Joachim's followers wanted to improve his theological reputation shortly after his death, they began to claim that his spiritual life had begun with an early vision of God the Father on Mount Tabor during a pilgrimage to the Holy Land.[16] For both Joachim and Rupert, visions could authorize new interpretations of scripture, but their scriptural teachings could also justify their visions within the church.

Hildegard was also not unique in her role as a twelfth-century visionary *woman*, but she may have been unusual in how little she needed Guibert's approval. Detailed, personal visions were becoming more and more common in twelfth-century saints' lives; for example, the unfinished *vita* of the English recluse Christina of Markyate (ca. 1097–1156) punctuates its

---

Learning: Visions, Education, and Rupert of Deutz's View of Twelfth-Century Intellectual Culture," *Journal of Medieval History* 39 (2013): 20–47.

[13] Rupert, *De Gloria et Honore Filii Hominis super Mattheum*, book 12, ed. H. Haacke, CCCM 29 (Turnhout: Brepols, 1979), 394: "ego autem extunc 'os meum aperui,' et cessare quin scriberem nequaquam potui." As McGinn points out (*Growth of Mysticism*, 564 n. 33), Rupert's final work, *De Incendio*, implies that his visionary experiences continued throughout his life.

[14] On Joachim and his heirs, see Marjorie Reeves, *The Influence of Prophecy in the Later Middle Ages: A Study in Joachism* (Oxford: Oxford University Press, 1969), and G. L. Potestà, *Il tempo dell'Apocalisse, Vita di Gioacchino da Fiore* (Rome: Laterza, 2004). Joachim's vision of the psaltery appears in his *Psalterium decem chordatum*.

[15] Ralph of Coggeshall, *Chronicon Anglicanum* 1195: *Radulphi de Coggeshall Chronicon Anglicanum*, ed. J. Stevenson (London: Longman, 1875; rprt. Cambridge: Cambridge University Press, 2012), 68: "Sed deus, inquit, qui olim dedit prophetis spiritum prophetiae, mihi dedit spiritum intelligentiae, ut in Dei spiritu omnia mysteria sacrae Scripturae clarissime intelligam, sicut sancti prophetae intellexerunt qui eam olim in Dei spiritu ediderunt."

[16] See Bernard McGinn, *Visions of the End: Apocalyptic Traditions in the Middle Ages* (New York: Columbia University Press, 1979), 315 n. 26.

narrative with its protagonist's visionary experiences. The Virgin Mary promises that Christina will escape her unwanted husband, Jesus brings her a cross of gold to comfort her in the tiny enclosure where she is hiding in a local hermit's cell, deceased members of the nearby monastery pass along messages for their abbot, and ultimately Christina and the abbot pray on either side of Christ at the altar.[17] Still, compared to the breadth and ambition of Hildegard's visions, Christina's recorded visions seem personal, almost domestic – perhaps because they were filtered through the perceptions of her anonymous monastic hagiographer. More comparable were the visions of Hildegard's younger contemporary, Elisabeth of Schönau (1129–1165). Elisabeth seems to have been directly inspired by Hildegard's *Scivias* (Know the Ways), but her earliest visions – like Christina's – provided reassurance about her own spiritual struggles or offered pastoral advice to her immediate community. After an apocalyptic vision of the coming wrath of God, however, the abbot of Schönau shared Elisabeth's vision with a much wider audience, and from that point forward Elisabeth was a public visionary much like Hildegard: in fact, Elisabeth and Hildegard exchanged a series of letters, in which Hildegard commiserated about the challenges of predicting the future and advised care in claiming any authority apart from God.[18] This was also around the time that Elisabeth's brother Ekbert, an educated canon turned priest and monk, moved permanently to Schönau, and they began a process of recording and editing Elisabeth's visions that was continued by Ekbert after her death. John Coakley has pointed out how Elisabeth's visions were often shaped by requests transmitted through Ekbert, so that she sought visionary answers to everything from the assignment of guardian angels to the martyrdom of local saints to the whereabouts of a piece of consecrated Host that a child had sneezed out of his mouth; in a few cases, however, Elisabeth's visionary subjects pushed back, exhibiting offense or refusing to answer some of Ekbert's questions, and in other cases Ekbert consciously edited or even censored Elisabeth's visions.[19] Although Elisabeth's visions

---

[17] These episodes are described in the *Vita* of Christina of Markyate, *Vie de Christina de Markyate*, ed. Paulette L'Hermite-Leclerq and Anne-Marie Legras (Paris: CNRS Éditions, 2007), and translated by Charles Talbot, *The Life of Christina of Markyate: A Twelfth-Century Recluse*, rev. ed. (Toronto: Medieval Academy Reprints for Teaching, 1998). See also S. Fanous and H. Leyser, eds., *Christina of Markyate: A Twelfth-Century Holy Woman* (London: Routledge, 2004).

[18] See *Elisabeth of Schönau: The Complete Works*, ed. and trans. Anne Clark (Mahwah, NJ: Paulist Press, 2000), 139. See also Barbara Newman's reading of this episode in "Hildegard," 174–175.

[19] John Coakley, *Women, Men, and Spiritual Power: Female Saints and Their Male Collaborators* (New York: Columbia University Press, 2006), 24–44.

were hers alone, the two siblings worked together to construct Elisabeth's public visionary persona.

Hildegard's Legacy: Visionaries after the Twelfth Century

Elisabeth and Ekbert's partnership represented a future trend: later medieval visionaries (especially, but not invariably, those who were female) found themselves appealing for ecclesiastical authorization from men who were often their amanuenses, editors, or hagiographers.[20] However, Elisabeth's appeal to Hildegard represented another trend: Hildegard's enduringly positive reputation throughout the Middle Ages meant that later visionaries *and* their authorizers could cite her as an example. While her scientific, linguistic, and musical works languished, her visions were translated into most of the vernacular languages of western Europe.[21] Especially in the Holy Roman Empire, female visionaries could plausibly be assumed to have read some Hildegard. After all, she had addressed a letter to the Cistercian nuns of St. Thomas an der Kyll, so it was no surprise that the thirteenth-century visions that emerged from that same nunnery bear traces of her influence.[22] Moreover, while there is no direct textual or bibliographic link between Hildegard and the thirteenth-century visionaries associated with the nunnery of Helfta, that has not stopped scholars from drawing conclusions about similarities in form, content, and tone.[23]

Less ambiguously, the fourteenth-century Dominican preacher and visionary Johannes Tauler describes several of Hildegard's *Scivias* visions and identifies her as a model for how contemporary visionaries in his day

[20] On these types of appeals see, among others, Dyan Elliott, *Proving Woman: Female Spirituality and Inquisitional Culture in the Later Middle Ages* (Princeton: Princeton University Press, 2004) and Wendy Love Anderson, *The Discernment of Spirits: Assessing Visions and Visionaries in the Late Middle Ages* (Tübingen: Mohr Siebeck, 2011).

[21] As Michael Embach notes, these vernacular translations were primarily drawing from Gebeno's *Pentachronon* during the thirteenth and fourteenth centuries (Michael Embach, "Hildegard of Bingen (1098–1179): A History of Reception," in Beverly Mayne Kienzle, Debra L. Stoudt, and George Ferzoco, eds., *A Companion to Hildegard of Bingen* (Leiden: Brill, 2014), 277. See Hayton, Chapter 8, this volume, for more on the *Pentrachronon*.

[22] On Hildegard's correspondence, see Hiltrud Rissel, "Hildegard von Bingen und Elisabeth St. Thomas an der Kyll," *Citeaux* 41 (1990): 5–43. The St. Thomas visions are discussed more fully in Rissel's "Ein Zeugnis vom geistlichen Leben in der Frühzeit: Die sogenannten 'Visionen' von St. Thomas," in Ludwig Nollmeyer, ed., *St. Thomas an der Kyll. Zeit und Geist. Beiträge zu der Geschichte der ehemaligen Zisterzienserinnenabtei* (Trier: St. Thomas, 1980): 55–84.

[23] See, for instance, the commentary of Margot Schmidt in *Mechthild von Magdeburg: Das fließende Licht der Gottheit. Zweite, neubearbeitete Übersetzung* (Stuttgart: Frommann-Holzboog Verlag, 1995).

should see God: he compares her to "our [Dominican] sister up in the country" who "saw with her bodily eyes."[24] In another sermon, Tauler notes that the nuns whom he is addressing have a copy of some of Hildegard's visions (perhaps the *Scivias*) in their own library,[25] and in a third sermon, one of Tauler's central images is clearly Hildegard's vision of the enthroned Godhead from the beginning of the *Scivias*.[26] Later in the fourteenth century, Hildegard's influence as a visionary proponent of church reform seems clear in the similarly visionary and reformist works of Birgitta of Sweden, even though Birgitta never cites her by name (Birgitta's fifteenth-century compiler Johannes Tortsch did, claiming that Hildegard's visions supported Birgitta's).[27]

Still, there is a reason why, as Kathryn Kerby-Fulton writes, "even when we turn to internal evidence, Hildegard's influence in the visionary and mystical spheres of the later Middle Ages is disappointingly oblique."[28] As Kerby-Fulton observes, Hildegard's most enthusiastic readers were not necessarily visionaries but church reformers, ecclesiastical polemicists, and apocalyptic preachers – although these categories frequently overlapped in the late Middle Ages, so that these centuries drew few distinctions between Hildegard as visionary and Hildegard as prophet. In fact, Hildegard's visions were the most popular and enduring of her works, although often not in the format in which she originally wrote them. Out of approximately 360 codices containing some of Hildegard's works, more than 150 include complete or partial copies of the *Pentachronon*, a collection of Hildegard's visions compiled by the Cistercian Gebeno of Eberbach in the 1220s that focused on apocalyptic material.[29] Indeed,

---

[24] Johannes Tauler, Sermon 31 (following the numbering by Théry Hugueny and A. L. Corin, in *Sermons de Tauler*, 3 vols. (Paris: Librarie Desclée et Cie, 1927); in Ferdinand Vetter, *Die Predigten Taulers* (Berlin: Weidmannsche Buchhandlung, 1910), as Sermon 60 f on 311: "ein unser swester oben im lande . . . . Dis sach si mit iren liplichen ögen."

[25] See Tauler, Sermon 31 (Vetter 60–61, 311) and Sermon 68 (Vetter 69, 379).

[26] Jeffrey Hamburger, "The 'Various Writings of Humanity': Johannes Tauler on Hildegard of Bingen's *Liber Scivias*," in Kathryn Starkey and Horst Wenzel, eds., *Visual Culture and the German Middle Ages* (London: Palgrave Macmillan, 2005), 161–205.

[27] See the edition of Tortsch's *Opus mundi*, by Ulrich Montag: *Das Werk der heiligen Birgitta von Schweden in oberdeutscher Überlieferung*, ed. Ulrich Montag (Munich: C.H. Beck, 1968).

[28] Kathryn Kerby-Fulton, "Hildegard and the Male Reader: A Study in Insular Reception," in Rosalynn Voaden, ed., *Prophets Abroad: The Reception of Continental Holy Women in Late-Medieval England* (Woodbridge: D.S. Brewer, 1996), 2.

[29] These numbers come from Embach, "Hildegard of Bingen," 273–304. See also Hayton, Chapter 8, this volume. For a fuller history of Hildegardian manuscript reception and transmission, see Embach's *Die Schriften Hildegards von Bingen: Studien zu ihrer Überlieferung im Mittelalter und in der Frühen Neuzeit* (Berlin: De Gruyter, 2010). For a detailed catalogue of manuscripts, see Michael Embach and Martina Wallner, *Conspectus der Handschriften Hildegards von Bingen* (Munich: Aschendorff, 2013).

Hildegard's reputation as an apocalyptic visionary was so strong that new visions in this genre could easily be modeled after hers. A late fourteenth-century German visionary text called the *Auffahrtabend* or "Ascension Eve," for example, was adapted from the thirteenth-century Latin *Visio fratris Iohannis* (Vision of Brother John), probably between 1386 and 1396, by an author who decided to "introduce, or ground, the prophecy in the visionary authority of the great twelfth-century Teutonic sybil."³⁰ Where the Latin "Brother John" has his vision on an island, much like John of Patmos, the German visionary of the *Auffahrtabend* has his vision begin as he lies in bed, just as in Hildegard's famous vision of the suffering church.³¹ By the end of the fifteenth century, the *Auffahrtabend* vision was even attributed to Hildegard.³² Other non-visionary apocalyptic prophecies were also attributed to Hildegard between the thirteenth and fifteenth centuries, and occasionally Hildegard's visions were collected or even printed together with those of much more strident prognosticators. Her posthumous reputation (along with the claim that her *Scivias* visions had been papally approved) helped to legitimize what were often scathing critiques of the church.³³

It was no surprise that Hildegard's name was used to promote other people's visions: she was increasingly every late medieval theologian's favorite example of a reliably predictive, divinely inspired, and ecclesiastically authorized visionary. In the early years of the so-called Great Western Schism (1378–1417), when two and then three "legitimately" elected popes divided Latin Christendom for almost four decades, Hildegard was among the figures credited with predicting this calamity, but she escaped any of the opprobrium that fell on the late fourteenth-century visionaries who had advocated for the return of the papacy from Rome to Avignon in the 1360s and 1370s.³⁴ Instead, the Great Western Schism cemented Hildegard's

---

³⁰ In Jennifer Deane, "The 'Auffahrtabend' Prophecy and Henry of Langenstein: Adaptation and Transmission of the 'Visio fratris Johannis'," *Viator* 40, no. 1 (2009): 355–386 (quote from 366).

³¹ This parallel is discussed in more detail by Frances Courtney Kneupper, *The Empire at the End of Time: Identity and Reform in Late Medieval German Prophecy* (Oxford: Oxford University Press, 2016), especially 91–92.

³² After first being attributed to Henry of Langenstein (mentioned later in this section). See Kneupper, *Empire at the End of Time*, 106.

³³ See, for instance, Kerby-Fulton, "Hildegard and the Male Reader," on the English reception of *Insurgent gentes*, or Embach, "Hildegard of Bingen," on the German reception of *Quamvis hominis*, both widely attributed to Hildegard. On Hildegard in early modern anthologies, see Jonathan Green, *Printing and Prophecy: Prognostication and Media Change, 1450–1550* (Ann Arbor: University of Michigan Press, 2012).

³⁴ See Renate Blumenfeld-Kosinski, *Poets, Saints, and Visionaries of the Great Schism, 1378–1417* (University Park, PA: Penn State Press, 2016), especially 23–26 on Hildegard and 33–46 on pre-Schism visionaries.

reputation for prophetic accuracy. To pick only one example, Cardinal Pierre d'Ailly, a Paris-trained theologian who spent most of his career trying to end the Schism, preached a 1380 sermon in which he drew extensively on Hildegard's visions to explain the Schism's role in the chronology of the book of Revelation (d'Ailly placed the Schism at the end of the fourth persecution).[35] He subsequently wrote two treatises in the 1380s about how false prophets – a category including not only visionaries and miracle-workers but also "false teachers" (*pseudodoctores*) – had led to the Schism; Hildegard, however, was described as a true prophetess, saint, and authority in both treatises.[36] In a much later work from 1414, as the Schism was coming to a close, d'Ailly repeated his earlier claim that both Joachim and Hildegard were useful guides to the End Times, "since [their] authority is proven by many doctors."[37] As late medieval visionaries increasingly had to fight for their authority (and sometimes, as in the case of Joan of Arc, their lives), Hildegard's enduring reputation left her with a degree of universal respect that no other postbiblical visionary or prophetic figure seemed to enjoy.

The Great Schism even prompted readers to explore Hildegard's visionary works outside the *Pentachronon* anthology. During the early years of the Great Western Schism, the German theologian Henry of Langenstein was forced to leave the University of Paris due to his papal allegiance; before moving on to Vienna, he spent a productive year at the Cistercian monastery of Eberbach, where Gebeno had anthologized Hildegard's works and where a resident visionary, Wilhelm, had inaccurately predicted the Schism would end in a few months.[38] At Eberbach, Langenstein read widely, including Hildegard's visions,[39] and then wrote a treatise (*On the Discernment of*

---

[35] See Laura Ackerman Smoller, *History, Prophecy, and the Stars: The Christian Astrology of Pierre d'Ailly* (Princeton: Princeton University Press, 1994), 96–97, and Louis Pascoe, *Church and Reform: Bishops, Theologians, and Canon Lawyers in the Thought of Pierre d'Ailly* (Leiden: Brill, 2005), 18–19.

[36] Pierre d'Ailly, *De falsis prophetis*, published in Louis Ellies du Pin, *Joannes Gersonii Opera Omnia* (Antwerp: Sumptibus Societatis, 1706; rprt. Hildesheim, NY: Olms, 1987), 1.489–604, and especially 496, 500, and 519. On the dates and titles of the two treatises, see Anderson, *The Discernment of Spirits*, 162.

[37] Pierre d'Ailly, *Tractatus de materia*, ed. Francis Oakley, in *The Political Thought of Pierre d'Ailly* (New Haven, CT: Yale University Press, 1964), 315–316. See Reeves, *Influence*, 422 n. 3. The quote is from 316: "quorundam magnorum doctorum probat auctoritas."

[38] Henry would criticize Wilhelm by name a decade later, in his 1392 *Invectiva* or *Liber contra vaticinia Telesphori*, 516 (as printed in H. Pez, *Thesaurus anecdotorum novissimus* (Augsburg: Veith, 1721–1729), 1, part 2:505–564).

[39] In Henry's 1383 *Epistola de schismate*, he emphasizes that a "vir doctus venerabilis Gebeno" had carefully examined Hildegard's writings and revelations and found them truthful. See the edition of José Carlos Santos Paz, *Cisma y Profecía: Estudio y Edición de la Carta de Enrique de Langenstein a Ecardo de Ders sobre el Gran Cisma* (La Coruña: Universidade da Coruña Servicio de Publicacións, 2000), 92.

Spirits) in which he tried to identify criteria for true and false visions. "When it is therefore doubted whether certain visions or miracles come from a good spirit," Langenstein wrote, "it must be considered what state or grade in the ecclesiastical hierarchy [the visionary] has or used to have ... And he is required to teach about his mission either through authentic letters or evident miracles or numerous outcomes from his prophecies."[40] Wilhelm of Eberbach and Joachim of Fiore did not meet Langenstein's standards, but it seems that Hildegard did; Langenstein drew on her visionary letters and on her *Scivias* in a number of subsequent treatises and sermons about the Schism, even entitling one work *Letter on the Future Dangers to the Church, From the Words of St. Hildegard.*[41] A very different use for Hildegard's visions emerged later in the Schism, in the works of Dietrich of Nieheim, a churchman and conciliarist (alongside d'Ailly), who visited Hildegard's grave in 1408–1409 and subsequently cited a wide range of Hildegard's visions as proof for his historical argument that the Holy Roman Emperor needed to reform both the empire and the church: "St. Hildegard the German nun had previously preached, inspired by the Holy Spirit, about why such long and dangerous schisms thrive in modern times."[42] Even though the Schism inaugurated a period of suspicion of visionaries, Hildegard's own reputation held firm.

The Reformations of the sixteenth century brought Hildegard yet another new set of readers, but now they were reading her visions for their critique of ecclesiastical corruption and viewing her predictions of schism as applying to their own era. Andreas Osiander, a Catholic priest and scholar turned Lutheran university professor and theologian, had read some of Hildegard's works at a monastery before he became a Protestant. In 1527, he published a German pamphlet entitled *Saint Hildegard's Prophecy About the Papists and the So-Called Clergy*, in which he described "Saint Hildegard's" allegorical

---

[40] Thomas Hohmann, *Heinrichs von Langenstein 'Unterscheidung der Geister' Lateinisch und Deutsch: Texte und Untersuchungen zu Übersetzungsliteratur aus der Wiener Schule* (Munich: Artemis Verlag, 1997), 114: "Cum ergo de visionibus alicuius aut miraculis dubitatur, an a spiritu bono sint, considerandum est, quem statum aut gradum in ecclesiastica hierarchia habeat vel habuerit ... Et tenetur ille docere de sua missione vel per litteras authenticas, vel miraculis evidentibus vel prophetiarum suarum crebris eventibus."

[41] This is the 1383 *Epistola de futuris periculis ecclesiae ex dictis sanctae Hildegardis*, edited in Gustav Sommerfeldt, "Die Prophetien der hl. Hildegard von Bingen in einem Schreiben des Magisters Heinrich v. Langenstein (1383) und Langensteins Trostbrief über den Tod eines Bruders des Wormser Bischofs Eckard von Ders (um 1384)," *Historisches Jahrbuch* 30 (1909): 43–61.

[42] In his *Privilegia aut iura imperii circa investituras episcoporum et abbatum*, published by Simon Schard[ius] in *Sylloge de jurisdictione, autoritate, et praeeminentia imperiali* (Basel, 1566), 834: "quare autem tam diuturna schismata et periculosa in modernis temporibus vigent ... S. Hildegardis monialis, de Germania nata, dudum Spiritu sancto inspirante predixit." See Embach, "Hildegard of Bingen," 285.

vision of a begrimed and disheveled Church (originally from her *Liber divinorum operum* [Book of Divine Works]) and applied its moral of clerical wrongdoing and oncoming apocalyptic change to the Protestant Reformation.[43] Only two years later, the Catholic humanist Hieronymus Gebuilerus published a slightly longer treatise in which he reproduced a series of Hildegard's visions to argue that the Catholic Church had become corrupt but could still be reformed with sufficient penance. Like Osiander, Gebuilerus applied Hildegard's visions to the Reformation, but unlike Osiander, Gebuilerus emphasized Hildegard's status as a papally authorized visionary and described her revelations as "presenting the orthodox faith of the Christian Church."[44] Hildegard continued to be popular on both sides of the Reformation, even where many other visionaries were not: by the middle of the sixteenth century, Matthias Flacius Illyricus – another early Protestant theologian, who spent much of the 1550s in furious debate with Osiander about the source of justification by faith – had not only gotten into the now-thriving Protestant business of citing Hildegardian visions to anticipate the downfall of the Catholic Church but also included Hildegard in his *Catalogue of the Witnesses of Truth*, a massive historical compilation of proto-Protestants beginning with St. Peter.[45] Catholic authors responded by pointedly including Hildegard in their lists of Catholic saints and printing her works under a series of ecclesiastical endorsements; her letters, printed in Cologne in the 1550s, were described by the priestly editor Justus Blanckwald as "for the confirmation and stabilization of our Catholic faith and Christian religion."[46] Whether Protestant or Catholic, it seemed, each reader felt Hildegard's visionary critique of the church was on his side.

Hildegard's Visions in the Modern Era

Perhaps thanks to the end of the Wars of Religion, or perhaps due to a rationalist desire to downplay the supernatural, Hildegard's visions were

---

[43] See Embach, "Hildegard of Bingen," 290–291, and Green, *Printing and Prophecy*, 96–99 and 179–180. The pamphlet's German title is *Sant Hildegardten Weissagung uber die Papisten und genanten Geystlichen.*

[44] Hieronymus Gebuilerus, *De praesenti clericorum tribulatione* (Hagenau: Wilhelm Setz, 1529), 2: "Dunc igitur Hildegardis prophetiarum fragmenta quaedam lectu non iniucunda, praesentes orthodoxe fidei christianae ecclesiae."

[45] On Illyricus, see I. Dingel, J. Hund, and L. Ilić, *Matthias Flacius Illyricus: Biographical Contexts, Theological Impact, Historical Reception* (Göttingen: Vandenhoeck & Ruprecht, 2019). Hildegard is described, along with details from her visions, on 650–651 of Illyricus's *Catalogus Testium Veritatis* (Basel: Oporinus, 1556).

[46] Hildegard's *Epistolarum liber*, ed. Justus Blanckwald (Cologne: Johann Quentel and Gerwin Calenius, 1566) features the following on its title page: "Ad confirmandam et stabiliendam Catholicam nostram fidem et religionem Christianam."

much less discussed in the late seventeenth and eighteenth centuries, despite the seemingly endless applicability of their anti-corruption message. Hildegard's visionary works were printed and reprinted in the seventeenth and eighteenth centuries, and she herself continued to be recognized as a local Catholic saint and even (by the nineteenth century) a sort of German folk hero, but the details of her visions seemed not to be of interest to a wider readership.[47] It was only with the early twentieth-century recurrence of interest in "mysticism" as a psychological phenomenon that Hildegard's visions became interesting again, especially outside German Catholic circles: Evelyn Underhill's 1930 edition of *Mysticism* featured "St. Hildegarde" as a "great prophetic mystic" and "a woman of powerful character, apparently possessed of abnormal psychic gifts, [who] was driven by that Living Light which was her inspiration to denounce the corruptions of Church and State."[48] Also in the early twentieth century, Hildegard's visions became famous for a different reason: physician and amateur historian of science Charles Singer diagnosed the long-dead visionary with migraine, a "functional nervous disorder," and this diagnosis moved into popular culture when it was reproduced in Oliver Sacks's 1970 *Migraine: Understanding the Common Disorder*, making Hildegard the unofficial patron saint of migraine sufferers and setting off an extended scholarly debate over the utility of pathologizing twelfth-century religious experience.[49]

Sacks's popular book also combined with spiritualist and New Age teachings in the 1980s to generate new interest in the theology and spirituality of Hildegard's visions along very different lines from their past. Matthew Fox, a popular theologian of "creation spirituality," saw Hildegard as a key precursor. In 1985, he published *The Illuminations of Hildegard of Bingen*, in which he commented on his own selection of Hildegard's visions, giving them titles such as "Viriditas: Greening Power," "Cultivating the Cosmic Tree," "Sophia: Mother Wisdom, Mother Church," and "The Red Head of God Zealous for Erotic Justice."[50] In vision after vision, however, Fox

[47] See Jennifer Bain, "Was Hildegard Forgotten?" *Journal of Musicological Research* 34, no. 1 (2015): 1–30 and Jennifer Bain, *Hildegard of Bingen and Musical Reception: The Modern Revival of a Medieval Composer* (Cambridge: Cambridge University Press, 2015).

[48] Evelyn Underhill, *Mysticism: A Study in the Nature and Development of Man's Spiritual Consciousness* (New York: E. P. Dutton and Co., 1961), 311 and 459.

[49] See Katherine Foxhall, "Making Modern Migraine Medieval: Men of Science, Hildegard of Bingen, and the Life of a Retrospective Diagnosis," *Medical History* 58, no. 3 (2014): 354–374, and Charles Singer, *Studies in the History and Method of Science*, vol. 1 (Oxford: Clarendon Press, 1917), 53. See also Wallis, Chapter 7, this volume.

[50] Matthew Fox, *The Illuminations of Hildegard of Bingen* (Santa Fe: Bear and Company, 1985), table of contents.

deliberately deleted the biblical and patristic references Hildegard had considered crucial to her visionary project; as Fox explained in his preface, "What is most useful to us in these visions of Hildegard is her immense respect for the whole, for the interconnections of parts, for the harmony of humanity and cosmos."[51] In a very different vein, Barbara Newman's path-breaking Hildegard scholarship in the 1980s – especially her 1987 monograph *Sister of Wisdom: St. Hildegard's Theology of the Feminine*, noting the ways in which Hildegard's visions empowered her to present God in the feminine roles of knowledge, justice, and wisdom – also found many readers outside the academy; as Newman notes in a preface to the 1997 revised edition, she was surprised and impressed by Hildegard's appeal to "contemporary spiritual feminists, both within and beyond the Christian churches, as new brands of Sophia theology and Goddess worship were sweeping the land."[52] Although Fox and Newman disagreed on many points,[53] their impact combined to ensure that Hildegard's supposedly countercultural visions came to be cited by a range of feminist thinkers, ecotheologians, New Age spiritualists, and even neopagans from the 1980s forward. Hildegard has been recently described as a gynocentric, feminist philosopher, despite the "problem" of her "inconsistent and incoherent" visionary influence,[54] and a "brash and brilliant medieval abbess, author, herbalist, composer, prophetess, and visionary who . . . . used her visions and supposed mystical powers to buck tradition."[55]

At the same time, the Catholic Church also found new appreciation for Hildegard's visions. In 1979, on the 800th anniversary of Hildegard's death, Catholic interest in expanding her cult outside Germany and completing her long-delayed formal canonization process reignited when the German Episcopal Conference petitioned Pope John Paul II to name Hildegard a Doctor of the Church, only nine years after women had first been granted that honor. Like many earlier theologians, the German bishops emphasized not only Hildegard's visions but also her papal authorization; unlike earlier

---

[51] Ibid., xxvii.

[52] Barbara Newman, *Sister of Wisdom: St. Hildegard's Theology of the Feminine, with a New Preface, Bibliography, and Discography* (Berkeley: University of California Press, 1997), xvii.

[53] Newman castigates Fox for his selective and ahistorical use of Hildegard's visions in her "Romancing the Past: A Critical Look at Matthew Fox and the Medieval 'Creation Mystics'," *Touchstone* (Summer 1992), at www.touchstonemag.com/archives/article.php?id=05-03-005-f.

[54] Jane Duran, "Hildegard of Bingen: A Feminist Ontology," *European Journal for the Philosophy of Religion* 6 (2014): 155–167, with quotes from 156–157.

[55] Hadley Meares, "The Medieval Prophetess Who Used Her Visions to Criticize the Church," *Atlas Obscura*, July 13, 2016, www.atlasobscura.com/articles/the-medieval-prophetess-who-used-her-visions-to-criticize-the-church.

generations, they also mentioned her scientific expertise.[56] John Paul II responded politely but noncommittally, praising Hildegard as a "prophet of Germany" but not as a Doctor of the Church. However, the next pope, Benedict XVI, had been a signatory to the 1979 bishops' petition: he promptly set Hildegard's formal canonization into motion while disseminating his own view of Hildegard as an eminently orthodox Catholic visionary theologian. In a September 2010 audience, Benedict explained that "Hildegard's mystical visions have a rich theological content. They refer to the principal events of salvation history, and use a language for the most part poetic and symbolic."[57] A few months later, Benedict connected Hildegard's vision of the begrimed church to the ongoing scandal involving Catholic priests who had sexually abused children: "In the vision of Saint Hildegard, the face of the Church is stained with dust, and this is how we have seen it. Her garment is torn – by the sins of priests. The way she saw and expressed it is the way we have experienced it this year."[58] Hildegard was formally canonized in May 2012, and in October, Benedict announced that he would declare her a Doctor of the Church. The resulting Apostolic Letter reiterated the importance of Hildegard's visions for her identity as a Catholic theologian: "Hildegard's teaching is considered eminent both for its depth, the correctness of its interpretation, and the originality of its views . . . in her visions and her subsequent reflections she presents a compendium of the history of salvation from the beginning of the universe until its eschatological consummation."[59] In the aftermath of Benedict's resounding assertion of her orthodoxy, Hildegard's visions have become an increasingly important source for Catholic theology on, among other things, the environment: as John Dadosky wrote in 2018, "Hildegard's influence is only beginning. She *is* the original green campaign."[60]

For a good part of Hildegard's own life and for many of the centuries since her death, she was widely known as a visionary. Yet it can be

---

[56] See George Ferzoco, "The Canonization and Doctorization of Hildegard of Bingen," in Kienzle, Stoudt, and Ferzoco, *A Companion to Hildegard*, esp. 310–311.

[57] Benedict XVI, "General Audience," September 8, 2010, in English at http://w2.vatican.va/content/ benedict-xvi/en/audiences/2010/documents/hf_ben-xvi_aud_20100908.html.

[58] "Address of His Holiness Benedict XVI on the Occasion of Christmas Greetings to the Roman Curia," December 20, 2010, in English at http://w2.vatican.va/content/benedict-xvi/en/speeches/ 2010/december/documents/hf_ben-xvi_spe_20101220_curia-auguri.html.

[59] Benedict XVI, "Apostolic Letter Proclaiming Saint Hildegard of Bingen, professed nun of the Order of Saint Benedict, a Doctor of the Universal Church," October 7, 2012, in English at http://w2 .vatican.va/content/benedict-xvi/en/apost_letters/documents/hf_ben-xvi_apl_20121007_ildegarda-bingen.html.

[60] John Dadosky, "The Original Green Campaign: Dr. Hildegard of Bingen's *Viriditas* as Complement to *Laudato Si*," *Toronto Journal of Theology* 34 (2018): 79–95.

challenging to place Hildegard back into a medieval visionary context, especially in a time and place when divinely inspired visions are much less well understood than ocular migraines. A well-received 2009 German film about Hildegard's life, entitled *Vision*, only once attempted to depict Hildegard's "living light" on screen; the *New York Times* movie reviewer complained that it "resembles the CBS logo without the letters."[61] As well, for both medieval and modern readers Hildegard's visionary works have proved challenging, partly because of their length; it is no accident that figures from Gebeno of Eberbach to Matthew Fox opted to select their favorite assortment, despite Hildegard's explicit warnings against doing so. Finally, even aficionados of Hildegard's visions – from Henry of Langenstein forward – have tended to praise her by separating her from other medieval visionaries, whether they view her as more prophetically reliable, more proto-Protestant, more theologically sophisticated, or more environmentally conscious. Hildegard's visions, however, must be read to appreciate the many ways in which she was indeed unique and the many ways in which she drew from and creatively transformed her tradition – much like the apostolic predecessors she claimed.

Further Reading

Latin Editions and English Translations

Elisabeth of Schönau. *Elisabeth of Schönau: The Complete Works*, trans. Anne L. Clark. The Classics of Western Spirituality. Mahwah, NJ: Paulist Press, 2000.
Gebeno of Eberbach. *La Obra de Gebenón de Eberbach*. ed. José Carlos Santos Paz. Florence: SISMEL - Edizioni del Galluzzo, 2004.

Secondary Literature

Anderson, Wendy Love. *The Discernment of Spirits: Assessing Visions and Visionaries in the Late Middle Ages*. Tübingen: Mohr Siebeck, 2011.
Bain, Jennifer. "Was Hildegard Forgotten?" *Journal of Musicological Research*, 34, no. 1 (2015): 1–30.
Coakley, John W. *Women, Men, and Spiritual Power: Female Saints and Their Male Collaborators*. New York: Columbia University Press, 2006.

---

[61] Stephen Holden, "A Multitasking Nun in Medieval Germany," *The New York Times*, October 12, 2010, C6. The film was originally titled *Vision: Aus dem Leben der Hildegard von Bingen* [From the Life of Hildegard of Bingen].

Diehl, Jay. "The Grace of Learning: Visions, Education and Rupert of Deutz's View of Twelfth-Century Intellectual Culture." *Journal of Medieval History* 39, no. 1 (2013): 20–47.

Embach, Michael. "Hildegard of Bingen (1098–1179): a History of Reception." In Beverly Mayne Kienzle, Debra L. Stoudt, and George Ferzoco, eds., *A Companion to Hildegard of Bingen*. Leiden: Brill, 2014, 273–304.

Hamburger, Jeffrey F. "The 'Various Writings of Humanity': Johannes Tauler on Hildegard of Bingen's *Liber Scivias*." In Kathryn Starkey and Horst Wenzel, eds., *Visual Culture and the German Middle Ages*. New York: Palgrave Macmillan, 2005, 161–205.

Kerby-Fulton, Kathryn. "Hildegard and the Male Reader: A Study in Insular Reception." In Rosalynn Voaden, ed., *Prophets Abroad: The Reception of the Continental Holy Women in Late-Medieval England*. Woodbridge: D.S. Brewer, 1996, 1–18.

Kneupper, Frances Courtney. *The Empire at the End of Time: Identity and Reform in Late Medieval German Prophecy*. Oxford: Oxford University Press, 2016.

McGinn, Bernard. "Hildegard of Bingen as Visionary and Exegete." In Alfred Haverkamp. ed., *Hildegard von Bingen in ihrem historischen Umfeld*. Mainz: Trierer Historische Forschungen, 2000, 321–350.

Newman, Barbara. "Hildegard of Bingen: Visions and Validation." *Church History* 54 (1985): 163–175.

PART III

Music, Manuscripts, Illuminations, and Scribes

CHAPTER 10

Music, Liturgy, and Intertextuality in Hildegard of Bingen's Chant Repertory

Jennifer Bain

> She also heard heavenly songs the words and melodies of which she
> wrote down and sang.
>
> Ludwig Schneider, 1857[1]

Among the many areas of Hildegard of Bingen's creative output, her
musical compositions are today probably the best known, because of the
many and varied successful musical recordings that began to circulate in
the late twentieth century. Hildegard is a fixture now in music history
courses, and with the largest output of chant that can be ascribed to
a Western medieval composer – male or female – so she should be.[2]
There is no other female composer of either sacred or secular music from
the medieval period to whom she could be compared; the others we know
of, such as Beatriz de Dia and Herrad of Hohenbourg, have only one or
two surviving melodies attributed to them, while Hildegard has seventy-
seven Latin liturgical chants and a substantial liturgical drama, the *Ordo
virtutum* (Order of the Virtues).

Hildegard's musical compositions relate in many ways to the wider
practice of the liturgy in the Western medieval church and thematically
relate as well to many of her own written works, practicing in her musical
repertory what today literary theorists would describe as intertextuality,
through citation and reference to her own work and to the work of others.
As a process first defined in literary works involving citation and allusion to
other literary sources, the term intertextuality can be more broadly

---

[1] [Ludwig Schneider], *Die heilige Hildegardis, Jungfrau und Abtissin* (Mainz: Lith. v. J. P. Haas, [1857]),
back side of leaflet. I am deeply grateful for the close reading and discussion of an earlier version of
this chapter by faculty and graduate students in the Department of History at Dalhousie University
at the Stokes seminar and for the more recent careful reading and comments from my MA student,
Lucia Denk.

[2] See Jennifer Bain, *Hildegard of Bingen and Musical Reception: The Modern Revival of a Medieval
Composer* (Cambridge: Cambridge University Press, 2015).

understood to include many kinds of media and the arts such as film, dance, the visual arts, and music. Although a twentieth-century term developed by Julia Kristeva and Roland Barthes, this process of adaptation and resonance among groups of works was a fundamental feature within medieval creative practices. Composers of plainchant, for example, borrowed texts from biblical sources, from other liturgical chant texts, and from the lives of saints for whom particular offices were written.[3] Hildegard participated in this common medieval practice of borrowing and reuse in her musical compositions as well as in her written output.

In this chapter, I demonstrate the ways in which Hildegard's music relates to liturgical practice more broadly and interconnects with her other output. I first contextualize the manuscript presentation of her music in relation to general medieval practice, considering the content of the manuscripts in which her music appears as well as the ordering of her chant repertory. I then discuss the ways in which she writes about music, focusing on the role of liturgy in the doctrine of salvation, particularly in her frequently cited Letter 23 and in the culminating, final vision of *Scivias* (Know the Ways), the first of her three large theological treatises. Finally, I trace the kinds of intertextuality with which Hildegard engaged by considering her musical style and borrowing practices, specifically through the use of her own melodies and those from the plainchant repertory and borrowed texts from biblical sources as well as her own written output. I focus on her corpus of seventy-seven chants, often referred to collectively as the *Symphonia*, and touch only briefly on the liturgical drama, the *Ordo virtutum*, which is the subject of another chapter.[4]

Manuscript Presentation of Liturgical Music

Most cathedrals and monasteries in the Middle Ages had standard liturgical books including text and music, such as antiphonals, graduals, processionals, missals, sequentiaries, and troparies for the clergy, the cantors, the cantrices, the monks, and the nuns to follow the liturgy according to the church calendar. In the Middle Ages in these kinds of liturgical books, no authors or composers are indicated for either the texts or the music. Newly composed offices to celebrate saints or occasions added to the church calendar, of which there were many, would have circulated

[3] Marianne Richert Pfau and Stefan Morent, *Hildegard von Bingen: Der Klang des Himmels* (Cologne: Böhlau Verlag, 2005), 54–55.
[4] See Altstatt, Chapter 11, this volume.

initially in independent gatherings or fascicles before being incorporated into new books. Hildegard's own music, however, did not circulate in standard monastic or cathedral books, with only a single exception; her *Alleluia* verse *O virga mediatrix* (O branch and mediator) appears in a sixteenth-century sequentiary and tropary made at the abbey of Saint Gall.[5] Rather, the two main sources preserving her music include other kinds of written material not found in standard chant books, primarily transmitting nonliturgical text. The late twelfth-century Wiesbaden codex (often referred to as the *Riesencodex*) is housed at the Hochschul- und Landesbibliothek RheinMain in Wiesbaden (MS 2) and includes seventy-five of her chants and her liturgical drama, the *Ordo virtutum*. The Dendermonde codex, dating from before 1173 and formerly housed in the St.-Pieters en Paulusabdij in Dendermonde, Belgium (MS 9) (and as of 2017 held at the Katholieke Universiteit in Leuven with no shelf number), has only fifty-seven of her chants, including two that are not found in the Wiesbaden manuscript.[6] The first 465 folios of the *Riesencodex* comprise a collection of Hildegard's writing (her visionary texts and letters, etc.) with her music making up only the last 15 folios, while the Dendermonde codex includes in its 173 folios two texts (Hildegard's *Liber vitae meritorum* [Book of Life's Merits] and Elisabeth of Schönau's *Liber viarum dei* [Book of the Ways of God]) before Hildegard's musical collection, with a final textual work, an unascribed dialogue between a priest and an evil spirit, following the 18 folios of Hildegard's music. As well, in the Wiesbaden manuscript there are clear physical indications (dirty folios and differences in the trimming of the parchment) that her collection of music circulated on its own and was added to the rest of the manuscript before binding. The remaining manuscripts that include individual musical works of Hildegard are also otherwise text manuscripts, most of which involve written works by or about Hildegard as well. A single notated responsory, *O vos imitatores* (O you imitators), appears

---

[5] Stiftsbibliothek, Cod. 546, fol. 369r copied between 1507 and 1514 (Klaper, "Kommentar," 31 in Hildegard of Bingen, *Lieder: Faksimile Riesencodex (Hs.2) der Hessischen Landesbibliothek Wiesbaden, fol. 466–481v*, ed. Lorenz Welker and commentary by Michael Klaper, Elementa musicae 1 [Wiesbaden: Ludwig Reichert Verlag, 1998]).

[6] The musical portions of both of these manuscripts are available in facsimile (Hildegard of Bingen, *Lieder*, 1998 and Hildegard of Bingen, *Symphonia Harmoniae Caelestium Revelationum: Dendermonde: St.-Pieters & Paulusabdij, Ms. Cod. 9*, ed. Peter van Poucke [Peer: Alamire, 1991]) and both manuscripts in their entirety are accessible as high-resolution digital images online: the *Riesencodex* is found on the Hochschul- und Landesbibliothek RheinMain website (http://hlbrm.digitale-sammlungen.hebis.de/handschriften-hlbrm/content/titleinfo/449618), and the Dendermonde manuscript is on the Integrated Database for Early Music (IDEM) of the Alamire Foundation website (www.idemdatabase.org/items/show/160/).

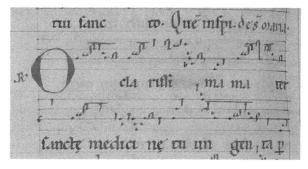

Figure 10.1 Beginning of *O clarissima mater*, Wiesbaden, Hochschul- und
Landesbibliothek, RheinMain, MS 2 [*Riesencodex*], fol. 467v, extract from column 2

along with some of her correspondence in a Stuttgart manuscript (which
includes texts by other authors such as Bernard of Clairvaux and Isidore of
Seville), compiled between 1154 and the 1170s.[7] Notated versions of
Hildegard's Kyrie and her *Alleluia* verse *O virga mediatrix* appear in the
twelfth-century section of a manuscript held in Vienna that chiefly transmits her *Liber vitae meritorum*,[8] and her *Ordo virtutum* appears notated in
a manuscript of a number of her works dating from 1487, a collection
associated with the abbot Trithemius.[9]

Despite this less typical presentation, there are many features in the
musical sections of the two main repositories of Hildegard's music, the
Riesencodex and Dendermonde, that signal that the music was liturgical,
including rubric designations for saints' feasts and for standard liturgical
genres, such as antiphons, responsories, hymns, and sequences. Figure 10.1,
for example, shows the opening of the responsory *O clarissima mater* (O
most radiant mother) from the *Riesencodex* and clearly includes the feast
rubric, "de s[ancta] Maria" (for holy Mary) in the upper right of the image,
and the genre rubric "R" for responsory to the left of the initial "O."

---

[7] Stuttgart, Württembergische Landesbibliothek, Cod.theol.et.phil.qt.253, fol. 40v (described in
Klaper, "Kommentar," 30–31 and reproduced on 25). Tova Leigh-Choate, William T. Flynn, and
Margot E. Fassler suggest, though, that it could have been copied into the manuscript at a later date
because "the leaf containing it served as the unbound cover sheet for a gathering": Tova Leigh-
Choate, William T. Flynn, and Margot E. Fassler, "Hearing the Heavenly Symphony: An Overview
of Hildegard's Musical Oeuvre with Case Studies," in Beverly Mayne Kienzle, Debra L. Stoudt, and
George Ferzoco, eds., *A Companion to Hildegard of Bingen* (Leiden: Brill, 2014), 172.

[8] Vienna, Österreichische Nationalbibliothek, Cod. 1016, f.118v (reproduced in Klaper, "Kommentar,"
25); a repetition of the second "Kyrie" in the chant follows on f.119r. For issues of dating, see
Michael Embach and Martina Wallner, *Conspectus der Handschriften Hildegards von Bingen*
(Münster: Aschendorff, 2013), 290–291.

[9] British Library, Add. MS 15102 (Klaper, "Kommentar," 30).

Both manuscripts also use a hierarchical liturgical ordering in the presentation of chants (indicated in Table 10.1) that extends the ordering found in any standard Common of Saints section of an antiphonal, which would include chants first for apostles, then evangelists, martyrs, confessors (indicating heroic virtue) who were popes or bishops, confessors who were not popes or bishops, and finally virgins. Most antiphonals have three sections: a Temporale that moves chronologically through the church seasons (Advent, Christmas, Epiphany, etc.) and the Sanctorale that moves chronologically through the calendar of saints (St. Andrew on November 30, St. Nicolas on December 6, Conception of Mary on December 8, etc.). The Common of Saints does not follow a chronological ordering but rather is organized thematically and hierarchically. It provides text and music that can be used for any saint who bears the characteristics identified (apostle, martyr, confessor, etc.) and would be used in a monastic or cathedral setting where a specific saint was being celebrated for whom that institution did not have a complete office. We might have expected Hildegard, or her scribes, to use the chronological organization found in the Temporale and Sanctorale sections of antiphonals since many of her saints or feast days are either named in the rubric or obvious from the text and so would be associated with a specific date.

The decision, however, to follow instead the thematic order found in the Common of Saints makes sense if we consider how Hildegard's music would have been used liturgically. A complete office, for example, for a particular saint requires somewhere between twenty-five and forty different chants depending on whether or not certain antiphons or responsories are repeated over the course of the day. Hildegard, however, did not compose any complete offices or a complete set of proper chants for a Mass (as the numbers indicated in the genre columns of Tables 10.2 and 10.3 illustrate). All of her chants would have been used as substitute chants for either a corresponding Mass or for a Feast in the Sanctorale (Trinity Sunday, any Marian Feast, Feast of the Patriarchs, any Feast for angels) or a corresponding common office from the Common of Saints found in the cathedral's or monastery's liturgical books. Ordering her chants hierarchically made that matching process easier.

The comparison in Table 10.1 of the order of feasts in the two main manuscripts does reveal a few interesting differences, as indicated by the emboldened items. The placing of Mary before the Trinity in Dendermonde does not fit the standard hierarchical order of the Father, the Son, and the Holy Spirit. Instead, as Barbara Newman suggests, since there are no liturgical chants for Christ, Mary takes his place in the

Table 10.1 *Comparison of the order of feasts in Dendermonde and the Riesencodex*

Dendermonde		Riesencodex	
153r	God the Father (Feast of Trinity)	God the Father (Feast of Trinity)	466r
153r–156v	**Mary**	Trinity	466r–466v
157r–158r	Trinity	**Mary**	466v–468r
159r–157v	Angels	Angels	468r–468v
159v–160v	Patriarchs	Patriarchs	468v–469r
160v–161v	Common of the Apostles	Common of the Apostles	469r–469v
161v–162r	John the Evangelist	John the Evangelist	469v
162r–162v	**Disibod (Bishop/Confessor)**	Common of several martyrs	470r
163r	Common of several martyrs	Common of several confessors	470r
163v–164r	Common of several confessors	**Disibod (Bishop/Confessor)**	470v
164v–missing folio	Rupert of Bingen	Rupert of Bingen	471r
165r–165v	Common of virgins	Common of virgins	471r–471v
166r	**Widows**	Ursula and the 11,000 virgins	471v–472r
166v–167r	**Holy Innocents**	**Holy Innocents**	472r
167r–169r	Ursula and the 11,000 virgins	Dedication of a church	472r–472v
170r	Dedication of a church	Mass ordinary (Kyrie)	472v
		Trinity	473r
		Mary	473v–474v
		Matthias (Apostle)	474v
		Boniface (Archbishop/Confessor and martyr)	475r
		Disibod (Bishop/Confessor)	475v
		Eucharius (Bishop/Confessor, 1st Bishop of Trier)	475v–476r
		Maximin (Bishop/Confessor, 5th Bishop of Trier)	476r
		Rupert of Bingen	476v
		Ursula and the 11,000 virgins	477r–477v
		Common of virgins	478r
		Widows	478v
		Ordo virtutum	478v–481v

Table 10.2 *Organization in the Dendermonde manuscript by feast and genre*

Folio	Feast	Genre
153r	God the Father (Trinity)	2 antiphons
153r–156v (missing folio in middle)	Mary	2 responsories 7 antiphons hymn (beginning only) missing folio sequence (end only) responsory
157r–158r	Trinity	3 antiphons hymn sequence
159r–157v	Angels	antiphon responsory
159v–160v	Patriarchs	antiphon antiphon + verse (responsory?)
160v–161v	Common of the Apostles	antiphon responsory
161v–162r	John the Evangelist	antiphon responsory
162r–162v	Disibod	antiphon responsory sequence
163r	Common of several martyrs	antiphon responsory
163v–164r	Common of several confessors	responsory antiphon
164v–missing folio	Rupert of Bingen	2 antiphons sequence (beginning only)
165r–165v	Common of virgins	antiphon responsory simphonia
166r	Common of widows	simphonia
166v–167r	Holy Innocents	responsory
167r–169r	Ursula and the 11,000 virgins	responsory antiphon responsory 8 antiphons sequence hymn
170r	Dedication of a church	2 antiphons

Table 10.3 *Organization in the* Riesencodex *by feast and genre*

Cycle 1

Folio	Feast	Genre
466r	God the Father (Trinity)	responsory
		2 antiphons
466r–466v	Trinity	6 antiphons
466v–468r	Mary	7 antiphons
		4 responsories
468r–468v	Angels	antiphon
		responsory
468v–469r	Patriarchs	antiphon
		responsory
469r–469v	Common of the Apostles	antiphon
		responsory
469v	John the Evangelist	antiphon
		responsory
470r	Common of several martyrs	antiphon
		responsory
470r	Common of several confessors	responsory
		antiphon
470v	Disibod (Bishop/Confessor)	2 responsories
		antiphon
471r	Rupert of Bingen (Confessor)	3 antiphons
471r–471v	Common of virgins	antiphon
		responsory
471v–472r	Ursula and the 11,000 virgins	2 responsories
		9 antiphons
472r	Holy Innocents	responsory
472r–472v	Dedication of a church	4 antiphons

Cycle 2

Folio	Feast	Genre
472v	Mass ordinary (Kyrie)	Kyrie
473r	Trinity	sequence
		hymn
473v–474v	Mary	Alleluia
		sequence
		sequence? symphonia?
		hymn
474v	Matthias (Apostle)	hymn (sequence?)
475r	Boniface (Archbishop/Confessor and martyr, Archbishop of Mainz)	antiphon?
475v	Disibod (Bishop/Confessor)	sequence
475v–476r	Eucharius (Bishop/Confessor, 1st Bishop of Trier)	responsory (labelled sequence)
		sequence

Table 10.3 *(cont.)*

Folio	Feast	Genre
476r	Maximin (Bishop/Confessor, 5th Bishop of Trier)	sequence
476v	Rupert of Bingen (Confessor)	sequence
477r–477v	Ursula and the 11,000 virgins	sequence hymn
478r	Common of virgins	symphonia
478v	Common of widows	symphonia
478v–481v	*Ordo virtutum*	liturgical drama

hierarchical ordering, since "only through her can Christ and then the Spirit be revealed."[10] The compilers of the music section of the *Riesencodex* who prepared it as part of the process of seeking Hildegard's canonization rectified that problem by placing Mary in her theologically correct position hierarchically after the Trinity. Similarly, Disibod in the Dendermonde manuscript really should have been placed next to the confessors, not before the martyrs: confessors have heroically confessed their faith, perhaps even suffering torture or exile, but they have not died for their faith as martyrs have, and Disibod, although exiled, was not a martyr. The reversal of the Holy Innocents and Ursula and the 11,000 virgins perhaps has no particular theological significance, and the shifting place for Widows is not theological but rather a different discrepancy in ordering: the Dendermonde manuscript goes through the cycle of feasts only once, while the *Riesencodex* goes through the cycle twice, and in the *Riesencodex* the chant for widows is in the second cycle.

Why does Dendermonde use only one cycle, while the *Riesencodex* uses two? In Dendermonde, as outlined in Table 10.2, all of the genres are kept together for a particular feast, but in the *Riesencodex*, as outlined in Table 10.3, the first cycle through the feasts includes only antiphons and responsories, while the second cycle has a mix of genres. Honey Meconi has suggested that the *Riesencodex* puts all of the shorter chants in the first cycle and the longer chants in the second cycle, but the division is more likely to be liturgical: the responsories and antiphons in the first cycle are genres used in

---

[10] Barbara Newman, *Sister of Wisdom: St. Hildegard's Theology of the Feminine* (Berkeley: University of California Press, 1987), 162.

the Office, while the second cycle contains sequences, the Alleluia, and the Kyrie, genres used in the Mass.[11] The second cycle also contains hymns, which can be found in both Antiphonals (for the Office) and Graduals (for the Mass) and frequently occur in a hymnary section of a book rather than within the regular liturgical organization. The second cycle also includes six chants with some ambiguity in relation to their genres, two of which appear only in the *Riesencodex* and have no genre rubrics. *O viridissima virga* (O greenest branch) has the layout of a sequence or a hymn because of the decorated letters at the beginning of phrases throughout but not the musical structure.[12] *O Bonifaci lux vivens vidit te* (O Boniface, the living light saw you) has the general appearance of an antiphon (it is short and has no internal divisions), but it does not have a psalm tone formula following it, which may or may not mean anything since neither manuscript is consistent with the psalm tone formulae for antiphons.[13] *O Euchari columba* (O Eucharius, the dove) appears only in the *Riesencodex* as well, where it is erroneously labeled a sequence, when it in fact has the structure of a responsory and so should really be in the first cycle of chants.[14] Similarly, Margot Fassler has shown that Hildegard's *Matthias Sanctus* while labeled a hymn in the *Riesencodex* really has the structure of a sequence.[15] The other two ambiguous chants are in both the *Riesencodex* and the Dendermonde manuscript and in either one or both are given the rubric "Symphonia" (in the *Riesencodex*) or "Simphonia" (in Dendermonde): *O dulcissime amator* (O sweetest lover) designated as a "Symphonia/Simphonia virginum" (of virgins),[16] and *O pater omnium* (O Father of all) designated "Simphonia viduarum" (of widows) in Dendermonde only, appearing with no rubric in the *Riesencodex* manuscript.[17] While "Symphonia/Simphonia" is not a genre designation that appears in any other known liturgical book, both chants have some internal divisions, resembling sequences or hymns, although again without the musical structure of either.

When studying a liturgical manuscript, the first thing scholars do is work out which feast days appear in the book and then consider why certain feasts are included and others are not. What becomes clear from even a cursory glance at Tables 10.2 and 10.3 is that Hildegard favored

[11] Honey Meconi, *Hildegard of Bingen* (Urbana: University of Illinois Press, 2018), 48–49.
[12] Wiesbaden, fols. 474r–474v.   [13] Wiesbaden, fols. 475r–475v.   [14] Wiesbaden, fols. 475v–476r.
[15] Wiesbaden, fols. 474v–475r. Margot Fassler, "Volmar, Hildegard, and St. Matthias," in Judith Peraino, ed., *Medieval Music in Practice: Studies in Honour of Richard Crocker* (Middleton, WI: American Institute of Musicology, 2013), 85–109.
[16] Wiesbaden, fols. 478r–478v and Leuven, fols. 165v–166r.
[17] Wiesbaden, fol. 478v and Leuven, fols. 166r–166v.

virgin saints, composing more for Mary and for Ursula and the 11,000 virgins than for any other occasion. As well, for Hildegard many of the saints for whom she composed had local significance. Ursula and the 11,000 virgins were associated with Cologne further up the Rhine, and Hildegard's contemporary, Elisabeth of Schönau, contributed to Ursula's veneration in the twelfth century through her visionary activity. St. Disibod was the patron of Hildegard's first monastic home at Disibodenberg, and St. Rupert the patron of the priory she established at Rupertsberg. Saints Eucharius and Maximin had both been bishops of Trier, and Hildegard corresponded with the monks in Trier of the monastery named for Eucharius, an establishment that was reconsecrated to St. Matthias in 1148.[18] St. Boniface was an eighth-century archbishop of nearby Mainz, and he was a patron of the Benedictines.[19] All of these saints had special meaning for Hildegard.

Hildegard Writing About Music

In addition to the manuscript evidence of Hildegard's musical activity, there are also statements that Hildegard herself made in a couple of places to her compositional output as well as the recurrence of a number of her chant texts in other written works. In the *Vita sanctae Hildegardis* (Life of Saint Hildegard), for example, some parts of which were written by Hildegard herself, she describes the experience of her first vision in 1141 and declares that, when she received that vision, she "also composed and sang chant with melody, to the praise of God and his saints."[20] In the opening of her *Liber vitae meritorum*, the second of her three large theological and visionary treatises, Hildegard makes reference to her own musical activity, when a vision showed her "the symphony of the harmony of heavenly revelations."[21] She provides the full texts of twenty-nine of seventy-seven of her chants in other writings, as indicated in Table 10.4,

[18] Letters 209–220, in *The Letters of Hildegard of Bingen*, Vols. 2–3, trans. Joseph L. Baird and Radd K. Ehrman (New York: Oxford University Press, 1998–2004), 2:190–199 and 3:9–14. On the reconsecration, see Barbara Newman, "Commentary," in Hildegard of Bingen, *Symphonia: A Critical Edition of the Symphonia Armonie Celestium Revelationum*, ed. and trans. Barbara Newman, 2nd ed. (Ithaca, NY: Cornell University Press, 1998), 300.

[19] Newman, "Commentary," 300.

[20] Anna Silvas, ed. and trans., *Jutta and Hildegard: The Biographical Sources* (University Park, PA: Pennsylvania State University Press, 1999), 160. See Embach, Chapter 1, this volume, for further discussion of the biographical materials relating to Hildegard.

[21] Hildegard of Bingen, *Liber uite meritorum*, ed. Angela Carlevaris, Corpus Christianorum Continuatio Mediaevalis (CCCM) 90 (Turnhout: Brepols, 1995), p. 8, ll. 4–10; *The Book of the Rewards of Life (Liber Vitae Meritorum)*, trans. Bruce W. Hozeski, (New York: Garland, 1994), 9.

Table 10.4 *Textual references by Hildegard to specific chants in other written sources*

Date	Source	Specific chant cited	Feast	Genre
1151/2	Scivias, book 3, vision 13	O splendidissima gemma	Virgin Mary	antiphon
		O tu suavissima virga	Heavenly Spirits	responsory
		O gloriosissimi lux	Patriarchs and Prophets	antiphon
		O vos angeli	Apostles	responsory
		O spectabiles viri	Martyrs	antiphon
		O vos felices radices	Confessors	responsory
		O cohors milicie	Virgins	antiphon
		O lucidissima	Dedication of a church?	responsory
		O victoriosissimi		antiphon
		Vos flores rosarum		responsory
		O successores		antiphon
		O vos imitatores		responsory
		O pulcre facies		antiphon
		O nobilissima viriditas		responsory
		Ordo virtutum		liturgical drama
1152	Life of St. Rupert	O Jerusalem	Rupert of Bingen	sequence
		O felix apparitio		antiphon
		O beatissime Ruperte		antiphon
before 1153	Letter 192, Hildegard to the Congregation of Nuns (book 2, 159–164)	**O viridissima virga**		sequence?
		Alleluia, O virga mediatrix	Virgin Mary	Alleluia
		O quam magnum miraculum		antiphon
		O tu illustrata		antiphon
		Ave Maria, o auctrix vite		responsory
		O clarissima mater		responsory
		Hodie aperuit / Nunc aperuit		antiphon
		Quia ergo femina		antiphon
		O quam preciosa		responsory
before 1155	Letter 74, Hildegard to Abbot Kuno	O mirum admirandum	Disibod	antiphon
		O viriditas digiti Dei		responsory
		O presul vere civitatis		sequence

including in *Scivias*, in the *Vita sancti Ruperti confessoris* (Life of St. Rupert, Confessor), and in two letters; all of these texts are included as musical works in the *Riesencodex*, and all but those in bold are included in Dendermonde as well.

Both direct and indirect textual evidence can also tell us something about the centrality of music to Hildegard and the value she ascribed to music in monastic life and in Christian theology. The available direct evidence comes in the form of an oft-cited letter from Hildegard to the prelates of Mainz, very late in her life. In 1178, a year before she died, Hildegard was ordered by the prelates to exhume the body of a nobleman from the convent cemetery because they claimed that he was an excommunicant at the time of his death. When Hildegard refused, the prelates imposed sanctions on the community of nuns, forbidding them from singing and intoning the Divine Office, the daily cycle of prayers, readings, and chants that structured the lives of all monastic communities. Hildegard responded at length in an attempt to have the sanctions lifted, asserting that the man had been "buried without any objection, with his own priest officiating" and that further he "had confessed his sins, had received extreme unction and communion."[22] Moreover, when she looked "to the True Light," she saw in a vision that if he were disinterred that "a terrible and lamentable danger" would come upon the community.[23]

To strengthen her case further, Hildegard invokes two ancients to stress the importance of music in salvation, with an explicit reference to the Prophets and an implicit reference to Boethius, celebrated in the Middle Ages as an authority on music, among other things. She explains that, before Adam's disobedience, his voice "blended fully with the voices of the angels in their praise of God," but he lost his "angelic voice" along with his residence in Paradise.[24] She writes that, infused with the Holy Spirit, the Holy Prophets composed psalms and canticles – that form the core of the Divine Office – to "recall to mind that divine melody of praise which Adam, in company with the angels, enjoyed in God before his fall."[25] She asserts that it is the Devil (now acting through the prelates) who tries to interfere with humankind's praise of God through singing.[26]

Hildegard grounds her next argument in the very definition of music provided by Boethius in *De institutione musica* (The Principles of Music), invoked and repeated by music theorists throughout the Middle Ages and into the early modern era. In book 1, chapter 2, Boethius divides music into

---

[22] Letter 23, *Letters*, trans. Baird and Ehrman, 1:176.   [23] Ibid.   [24] Ibid., 77–78.   [25] Ibid., 78.
[26] Ibid.

three types: *musica mundana,* the celestial music controlling the spheres; *musica humana,* which brings the body and soul in harmony with each other; and *musica instrumentalis,* actual sounding music.[27] For this last category, Boethius himself only describes music produced by instruments, but later writers, including the twelfth-century author Dominicus Gundissalinus, divide *musica instrumentalis* further into two subtypes: natural, that is music produced by the body (singing), and artificial music, produced through musical instruments.[28] Hildegard invokes Boethius' trifold definition of music when she writes the following to the prelates of Mainz:

> Consider, too, that just as the body of Jesus Christ was born of the purity of the Virgin Mary through the operation of the Holy Spirit, so too, the canticle of praise, reflecting celestial harmony [*musica mundana*], is rooted in the Church through the Holy Spirit. The body is the vestment of the soul, which has a living voice, and so it is proper for the body, in harmony with the soul [*musica humana*], to use its voice to sing praises to God [*musica instrumentalis*].[29]
>
> Pensate itaque quoniam, sicut corpus Iesu Christi de Spiritu Sancto ex integritate Virginis Marie natum est, sic etiam canticum laudum secundum *celestem harmoniam* per Spiritum Sanctum in Ecclesia radicatum est. Corpus vero indumentum est anime, que vivam vocem habet, ideoque decet ut *corpus cum anima per vocem Deo laudes decantet.*[30]

For Hildegard, the singing of the liturgy is not just pleasing to God but necessary for salvation, and she suggests further that the salvation of those imposing the interdict is in jeopardy:

> Therefore, those who, without just cause, impose silence on a church and prohibit the singing of God's praises and those who have on earth unjustly despoiled God of His honor and glory will lose their place among the chorus of angels, unless they have amended their lives through true penitence and humble restitution.[31]

---

[27] Anicius Manlius Severinus Boethius, *De institutione musica, liber primus,* ed. Jacques Paul Migne, *Patrologia latina* 63 (Paris: 1847), 1171–1172, accessed through *Thesaurus Musicarum Latinarum,* electronic version prepared by Stephen E. Hayes, Peter M. Lefferts, Bradley Jon Tucker, and Thomas J. Mathiesen, 1994 (www.chmtl.indiana.edu/tml).

[28] Dominicus Gundissalinus, *De divisione philosophiae,* ed. Ludwig Baur, Beiträge zur Geschichte der Philosophie des Mittelalters IV/2–3 (Münster: Aschendorff, 1903), 99, accessed through *Thesaurus Musicarum Latinarum,* electronic version prepared by C. Matthew Balensuela, Andreas Giger, and Thomas J. Mathiesen, 1996 (www.chmtl.indiana.edu/tml).

[29] *Letters,* trans. Baird and Ehrman, 1:79.

[30] Hildegard of Bingen, *Epistolarium: Pars Prima,* ed. Lieven Van Acker, CCCM 91 (Turnhout: Brepols, 1991), 64.

[31] *Letters,* trans. Baird and Ehrman, 1:79.

This view of the significance of liturgical singing and its association with the heavenly choir of angels is a theme that comes through as well in the final three visions of Hildegard's first theological and visionary text, *Scivias*, completed in 1151 or 1152.

Hildegard's *Scivias* is a large work in three books tracing the creation and the fall of humankind to the salvation of a postapocalyptic world in which heavenly music appears at the moment of salvation. Book 1 describes the Creator and creation, book 2 the Redeemer and redemption, and book 3 the virtues and the history of salvation. The last three visions of book 3 were what circulated the most in the Middle Ages through a compilation put together by Gebeno of Eberbach in 1220.[32] The three final visions (11, 12, and 13) cover the last days and the fall of the Antichrist, the Last Judgment and the new heaven and new earth, and finally a symphony of praise, in which Hildegard hears music and poetry together. In *Scivias*, and in her other two visionary works, *Liber vitae meritorum* and *Liber divinorum operum* (Book of Divine Works), Hildegard's visionary style follows a very clear pattern of describing her entire vision, and then moving sentence by sentence through the vision, interpreting each element, a style reminiscent of biblical exegesis. She describes each vision in visual and aural terms, using phrases like "I looked," "I saw," and "I heard." In her interpretive commentary, she states frequently that it is the voice of God who has explained the meaning to her – a frail human – what it is that she is seeing. Her final two visions in *Scivias* give a good sense of this style.

In vision 12, on the Last Judgment, Hildegard describes a ferocious scene of natural disaster followed by the raising of the dead and final judgment. The description in this vision is far more extensive than can be quoted here, but extracts will provide a sense of the style of explication:

> After this I looked, and behold, all the elements and creatures were shaken by dire convulsions; fire and air and water burst forth, and the earth was made to move, lightning and thunder crashed and mountains and forests fell, and all that was mortal expired . . .
> And behold, all the human bones in whatever place in the earth they lay were brought together in one moment and covered with their flesh . . .
> And some of them had been sealed with the sign of faith, but some had not; and some of those signed had a gold radiance about their faces, but others a shadow, which was their sign . . .[33]

---

[32] See Hayton, Chapter 8, this volume.
[33] Hildegard of Bingen, *Scivias*, trans. Mother Columba Hart and Jane Bishop (New York: Paulist Press, 1990), 515.

After presenting the entire vision and then offering further elucidation on the opening, she returns to the idea of those who had been "sealed with the sign of faith":

> And those who are signed are taken up to meet the Just Judge not with difficulty but with great speed, so that in them, who had faith in God, the works of faith may clearly be seen. And, as was shown you, the good are separated from the bad, for their works are dissimilar. For here it is apparent how both the bad and the good have sought God, in infancy and childhood and youth and old age.[34]

Note that she does not use the earlier language exactly (even in the original Latin) but clearly refers back to the vision and that group of the dead, elaborating further on what the "sign of faith" means. Hildegard continues in vision 12 with a description of what she sees of the new heaven and earth and presents the new earth as embodying stasis: the sun, moon, and stars stand still, there are no waves in the ocean, no heat in the fire, and no night. If there is no night, then the new heaven and earth are instead filled with light.

In vision 13, Hildegard's emphasis is on this light-filled new heaven and new earth, in which, significantly, she hears music:

> Then I saw the lucent sky, in which I heard different kinds of music, marvellously embodying all the meaning I had heard before … And this sound, like the voice of a multitude, making music in harmony praising the ranks of Heaven, had these words …[35]

Hildegard is very specific about the music that she hears, listing the full texts of fourteen of her own liturgical chants (provided in Table 10.5) but without musical notation. They are presented in a thematic organization, following the same hierarchy found in the organization of Hildegard's musical repertory in the two main manuscripts transmitting her musical corpus, with Mary first, then the angels, the patriarchs, apostles, martyrs, confessors, and virgins. All of these fourteen texts, moreover, return with musical notation in the two large collections of her musical works (the *Riesencodex* and Dendermonde), there identified as the liturgical genres of antiphons and responsories. Immediately following the fourteen texts are two laments from her liturgical play, *Ordo virtutum* (*O plangens vox* [O

---

[34] Ibid., 518.
[35] Ibid., 525 and Hildegard of Bingen, *Scivias*, ed. Adelgundis Führkötter and Angela Carlevaris, CCCM 43 and 43A (Turnhout: Brepols, 1978), 615. Hart and Bishop translate "Et sonus ille" as "And this song" rather than "And this sound."

Table 10.5 *Order of antiphon/responsory pairs in* Scivias, *book 3, vision 13, with location provided for the musical versions of these works in Dendermonde and the* Riesencodex

Theme	Genre	Incipit	D	R
Mary	Antiphon	*O splendissima gemma*	154r	466v
	Responsory	*O tu suavissima virga*	156v	468r
Nine orders of heavenly spirits	Antiphon	*O gloriosissimi lux*	159r	468r
	Responsory	*O vos angeli*	159r	468v
Patriarchs and prophets	Antiphon	*O spectabiles viri*	159v	468v
	Responsory	*O vos felices radices*	160r	469r
Apostles	Antiphon	*O cohors milicie*	160v	469r
	Responsory	*O lucidissima*	161r	469r
Martyrs	Antiphon	*O victoriosissimi*	163r	470r
	Responsory	*Vos flores rosarum*	163v	470r
Confessors	Antiphon	*O successores*	164r	470v
	Responsory	*O vos imitatores*	163v	470r
Virgins	Antiphon	*O pulcre facies*	165r	471r
	Responsory	*O nobilissima viriditas*	165r	471r

lamenting voice] and *O vivens fons* [O living fountain]) as well as a shorter, unnotated version of the *Ordo virtutum*, of which she heard a multitude of voices "proclaim in harmony" (*in harmonia sic clamabat*).[36] Hildegard ties the heavenly voices directly to salvation in her explication of the vision, stating that "the human intellect has great power to resound in living voices, and arouse sluggish souls to vigilance by the song," and that there is exultation "in the concord of those who are resurrected from their fall out of the path of justice, and are at last uplifted to true beatitude, for the Good Shepherd has brought back to the fold with joy the sheep that was lost."[37]

In addition to outlining the function of liturgical music in salvation, this culminating final vision in *Scivias* also summarizes in numerous ways Hildegard's approach to intertextuality, her style of returning to and reworking earlier ideas. These fourteen musical texts appear here in *Scivias* and then appear again in the musical section of both Dendermonde and the *Riesencodex*. The text of the *Ordo virtutum* also appears in *Scivias* and then appears again in the musical section of the *Riesencodex* not only with musical notation but also in an expanded form. Beyond the *Scivias* vision, Hildegard writes the lives of two saints, Rupert and Disibod, and composes chants for

---

[36] *Scivias*, ed. Führkötter and Carlevaris, 621.   [37] *Scivias*, ed. Hart and Bishop, 533.

their feast days as well, drawing on themes in her own *Vita sancti Ruperti* and *Vita sancti Disibodi episcopi* (Life of St. Disibod, Bishop). The virtues appear throughout *Scivias* and are the central focus of the sung *Ordo virtutum*. Hildegard returns repeatedly to the theme of virginity, composing more music for Mary and for Ursula and the 11,000 virgins than for any other Feast Day, and returns to the Marian chants by including nine of their texts in a letter to her congregation of nuns. In her letter to the prelates of Mainz, Hildegard makes reference to the book of Genesis, and to the prophets of the Old Testament, and also alludes to Boethius, turning his definition of music into a description of salvation. For Hildegard, composing and singing liturgical music were at the core of her monastic life, but these activities were not separate from any of her other work; they were interwoven with all the ways in which she expressed her spiritual and theological understanding of the world. A closer examination of her chant repertory will demonstrate this interweaving from a musical perspective, focusing on musical intertextuality.

Hildegard's Musical Style in Context

Numerous scholars have described Hildegard's Latin chant as standing outside the standard repertory in terms of musical style. John Stevens refers to the style of Hildegard's texts and music as "generally in themselves so peculiar, having neither scriptural texts nor Gregorian-type melodies."[38] In the major and standard English-language music encyclopedia, *Grove Music Online*, the authors of the article on Hildegard's music (Ian D. Bent and Marianne Pfau) similarly, but in a more understated way, claim that her "music is not drawn from plainchant and is in some respects highly individual."[39] Stevens refers to "Gregorian" melodies, which generally means earlier chant, copied already in books of the tenth and early eleventh centuries, while Bent and Pfau use the term "plainchant," which is a general term that can refer to many different styles of chant. Andrew Hughes takes this position further, describing Hildegard's music as a collection that was "truly isolated, with no apparent direct or obvious musical relatives."[40]

---

[38] John Stevens, "The Musical Individuality of Hildegard's Songs," in Charles Burnett and Peter Dronke, eds., *Hildegard of Bingen: The Context of Her Thought and Art* (London: The Warburg Institute, 1998), 167.

[39] Ian D. Bent and Marianne Pfau, "Hildegard of Bingen," *Grove Music Online* (2001). https://doi.org /10.1093/gmo/9781561592630.article.13016.

[40] Andrew Hughes, *Style and Symbol, Medieval Music: 800–1453* (Ottawa: Institute of Mediaeval Music, 1989), 30.

This description from Andrew Hughes is odd given that he had published an article the year before on rhymed offices for Thomas of Canterbury in which he describes a number of musical features that he could have also applied to Hildegard's musical output as well as the eleventh-century offices composed by Hermannus Contractus:[41] the chants tend to be longer; they use larger ranges than in the standard repertory, occasionally incorporating "both plagal and authentic ranges"; and they distinguish different ranges, "the lower 5th of the octave ... contrasted sharply with the higher 4th,"[42] described in another way by David Hiley as an emphasis on particular modal nodes: the final, the fifth, and the octave.[43] Hildegard does have a penchant for long melismas but includes them mostly in the genres where we might expect to find them in the general repertory as well: in the responsories, the Alleluia, and the Kyrie. In terms of formal structure, Hildegard generally follows the stylistic norms of the twelfth century, although she does have an idiosyncratic and flexible poetic and musical approach to sequences and hymns, both genres of which normally feature strict syllable counts and musical repetition.[44]

Another feature of Hildegard's musical style is the use of melodic borrowing, a kind of musical intertextuality. It was not unusual at all to reuse individual chants, both texts and melody, particularly when there were multiple offices for a specific saint, like the Virgin Mary. The antiphon, *Haec est regina virginum* (This is the queen of virgins), for example, appears in manuscript sources for either Lauds or Vespers in offices celebrating her Nativity, her Conception, her Assumption, and the Annunciation, as well as in a less-known office, Saint Mary of the Snows.[45] Composers also borrowed melodies and set new texts to them, with the new chant known as a contrafact of the old one; if monks or nuns knew both versions of the chant, they might hear one as they sang the other and new meanings would be understood from considering both simultaneously.

---

[41] See Pfau and Morent, *Hildegard von Bingen*, 293–309 and Jennifer Bain, "Hildegard, Hermannus and Late Chant Style," *Journal of Music Theory* 52, no. 1 (2008): 123–149.

[42] Andrew Hughes, "Chants in the Rhymed Office of St Thomas of Canterbury," *Early Music* 16, no. 2 (1988): 189.

[43] David Hiley, "Das Wolfgang-Offizium des Hermannus Contractus—Zum Wechselspiel von Modustheorie und Gesangspraxis in der Mitte des XI. Jahrhunderts," in Walter Berschin and David Hiley, eds., *Die Offizien des Mittelalters: Dichtung und Musik*, Regensburger Studien zur Musikgeschichte 1 (Tutzing: Schneider, 1999), 129–142.

[44] Jennifer Bain, "Varied Repetition in Hildegard's Sequence for St. Rupert: *O Ierusalem aurea civitas*," in Brenda Ravenscroft and Laurel Parsons, eds, *Analytical Essays on Music by Women Composers: Secular and Sacred Music to 1900* (New York: Oxford University Press, 2018), 11–46.

[45] The Cantus Database retrieved thirty-three results for this chant on November 15, 2018, in the offices listed. *Cantus: A Database for Latin Ecclesiastical Chant – Inventories of Chant Sources*, directed by Debra Lacoste (2011–), Terence Bailey (1997–2010), and Ruth Steiner (1987–1996), web developer, Jan Koláček (2011–), cantus.uwaterloo.ca.

Sometimes liturgical composers borrowed only the first phrase or two of another chant, as perhaps a way of drawing associations between different saints. A search for the melody from a rare antiphon for St. Roch, for example, yields the same opening musical phrase in ninety-one other chants catalogued in the Cantus Database.[46] A cursory analysis of the other texts that use this opening musical phrase shows that it is reused primarily for other male saints rather than female, including Nicholas, Benedict, Simperti (Bishop of Augsburg), and Maurice and his companions, and significantly for other saints associated with northern France and/or the Low Countries where Roch was popular, including St. Lambert (Bishop of Maastricht), St. Willibrord (Bishop of Utrecht), St. Babolenus (Abbot of St. Peter's near Paris), and St. Eligius (Bishop of Noyon and Tournai).

Following this broader practice, Hildegard sometimes quotes herself musically, setting new texts to her own melodies. Scholars have long known that her *Kyrie* is a contrafact of the first half of her responsory for apostles, *O lucidissima apostolorum turba* (O most luminous band of apostles), or vice versa,[47] but there are others as well. As demonstrated in Example 10.1, two of Hildegard's antiphons, *O spectabiles viri* for Patriarchs (O you clear-sighted men) and *O gloriosissimi lux vivens angeli* for Angels (O most glorious living-light angels), share first phrases, while Example 10.2 features a much longer shared opening. (Note that "Q" above the staff in the musical examples marks the

Example 10.1 Hildegard's antiphons *O spectabiles* (for Patriarchs) and *O gloriosissimi* (for Angels) from the *Riesencodex* (Hochschul- und Landesbibliothek RheinMain in Wiesbaden, MS 2)

[46] *Confessor dei venerande obtinuit* on fol. 197v in the Salzinnes Antiphonal, Halifax, Saint Mary's University, Patrick Power Library, M2149.L4 1554. *Cantus: A Database.*
[47] Barbara Stühlmeyer, *Die Gesänge der Hildegard von Bingen: Eine musikologische, theologische und kulturhistorische Untersuchung* (Hildesheim: Georg Olms, 2003), 162.

Example 10.2 Hildegard's *Tu nescis nec vides* (OV 15) and the first phrase of *Quia ergo femina* (antiphon). *Tu nescis nec vides* is transcribed from the *Riesencodex* (Hochschul- und Landesbibliothek RheinMain in Wiesbaden, MS 2) and *Quia ergo femina* from Leuven, Katholieke Universiteit, no shelf number (formerly housed in the St.-Pieters en Paulusabdij in Dendermonde, Belgium, MS 9)

special *quilisma* neume and that the small note heads indicate *liquescents*.) The whole of *Tu nescis nec vides* (You do not know or see), sung by the virtue Knowledge of God in the *Ordo virtutum* (OV 15), shares a melody with the opening phrase of one of Hildegard's Marian antiphons, *Quia ergo femina* (Therefore because a woman). The only differences between the melodies in the opening of the phrase are in repetitions of pitches and in the placement of syllables, since *Tu nescis* opens with nine syllables and *Quia ergo* with seven. The phrases continue similarly, with some small elaborations in *Quia ergo*. While both phrases end on E, they have rather different approaches to the final. The final gesture of *Tu nescis*, though, is found in a later phrase of *Quia ergo femina*, as shown in Example 10.3. Again, the *Quia ergo* version is more elaborated, providing embellishments of the fifth on B, and then adding a flourish just before the final pitch on E.

As well, contrary to the earlier portrayals of Hildegard's music as standing outside of the plainchant tradition, a number of other scholars have demonstrated that Hildegard's texts and melodies come out of a deep grounding in scriptural texts and liturgical music. Barbara Newman, in her edition and translation of Hildegard's poetic texts, provides extensive commentary on Hildegard's scriptural allusions.[48] In 1998, Margot Fassler convincingly presents Hildegard's *O nobilissima viriditas* (O most noble verdure) as a reworking of a standard chant for Mary, *Ave regina celorum* (Hail O queen of heaven).[49] In 2013, Luca Ricossa found that *Qui*

---

[48] Newman, "Commentary," 267–319.
[49] Margot Fassler, "Composer and Dramatist: 'Melodious Singing and the Freshness of Remorse,'" in Barbara Newman, ed., *Voice of the Living Light: Hildegard of Bingen and Her World* (Berkeley: University of California Press, 1998), 152–154 and 166–168.

Example 10.3 End of *Tu nescis nec vides* (OV 15) and later phrase from *Quia ergo femina*
(antiphon), both from the *Riesencodex* (Hochschul- und Landesbibliothek RheinMain
in Wiesbaden, MS 2)

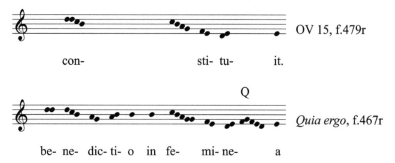

OV 15, f.479r

con-   sti- tu-   it.

Q

Quia ergo, f.467r

be- ne- dic- ti- o in fe-   mi- ne-   a

sunt hi qui ut nubes (Who are these who [fly] like clouds), the very first
chant in Hildegard's *Ordo virtutum*, quotes directly both text and music, of
the opening of a responsory found in offices of the Evangelists and
Apostles, suggesting that the liturgical drama would have been sung on
that Feast Day.[50] I agree completely with Ricossa's identification of the
responsory but suggest the Feast of All Saints, for which it also appears, as
a far more likely liturgical occasion for the *Ordo virtutum*, since the Feast of
All Saints had special significance for Hildegard as the anniversary of
the day that she was enclosed at Disibodenberg (November 1, 1112).[51]
    Intrigued by these examples, I set up a project with research assistants to
search digitally for other possible borrowings by Hildegard and we found
further examples of Hildegard borrowing from other chants in the plainchant repertory.[52] Hildegard, for example, in a chant from the *Ordo
virtutum* sung by the Patriarchs and Prophets, *Nos sumus radices* (We are
the roots), borrows from the opening of an antiphon for the Conception of
Mary, *Gratulare et letare* (Rejoice and be glad), reproduced in Example 10.4
from a twelfth-century Klosterneuburg manuscript. Both phrases have the
same number of syllables, but Hildegard distributes them differently and
elaborates the melody through a technique I have called varied repetition,

[50] Luca Ricossa, "Préface," in Hildegard von Bingen, *Ordo virtutum*, ed. and French trans.
Luca Ricossa (Geneva: Lulu), 2.
[51] Jennifer Bain, "The Music of Hildegard of Bingen," *Church Music Quarterly* (June 2019): 15. See also
Margot Fassler, "History and Practice: The Opening of Hildegard's Scivias in a Liturgical
Frame Work," *Religion and Literature* 42 no.1/2 (2010): 211–227.
[52] Martha Culshaw (MA 2020) and Lucia Denk (MA 2021), both MA Musicology students at
Dalhousie University.

Example 10.4 Hildegard of Bingen, *Nos sumus radices* (OV 3) and *Gratulare et letare* (antiphon, Conception of Mary). *Nos sumus* from the *Riesencodex* (Hochschul- und Landesbibliothek RheinMain in Wiesbaden, MS 2) and *Gratulare et letare* from Klosterneuburg, Augustiner-Chorherrenstift Bibliothek, MS 1012

which Hildegard uses as well in her approach to the paired melodies in her sequences.[53]

A much more substantial borrowing, closer to Fassler's *O nobilissima viriditas* and *Ave regina caelorum* example, is Hildegard's reworking of the first few phrases of the standard repertory responsory, *Gloriosa dicta constant* (Glorious things are said [about you] that establish), for the Conception of Mary, for her Trinity antiphon, *O quam mirabilis est* (O how marvelous it is). Example 10.5 includes the MS pitch level on the bottom with a transposed version of the twelfth-century *Gloriosa dicta constant* from Klosterneuburg, so the relationships will be easier to see. *Gloriosa dicta constant* begins with an opening gesture that is repeated twice, while Hildegard repeats it only once in a varied form. As the antiphon and responsory continue, however, we see further relationships between the two chants in the same order, although Hildegard interpolates an additional gesture taking the phrase melodically up to fill out the octave.

The earlier known examples as well as these two quotations from the plainchant repertory demonstrate Hildegard's deep engagement with the medieval liturgy. They also show her familiarity with the compositional practice of melodic borrowing, itself rooted in the intertextuality that permeated medieval literary culture.

Singing the liturgy was central to Hildegard's monastic life, just as it was for all nuns and monks in the Middle Ages, and writing and composing her own plainchant was an extension of this liturgical practice. Grounded in

---

[53] Bain, "Varied Repetition."

Example 10.5 Hildegard of Bingen, *O quam mirabilis est* (antiphon) and *Gloriosa dicta constant* (responsory, Conception of Mary). *O quam mirabilis est* from the *Riesencodex* (Hochschul- und Landesbibliothek RheinMain in Wiesbaden, MS 2) and *Gloriosa dicta constant* from Klosterneuburg, Augustiner-Chorherrenstift Bibliothek, MS 1012

(a)

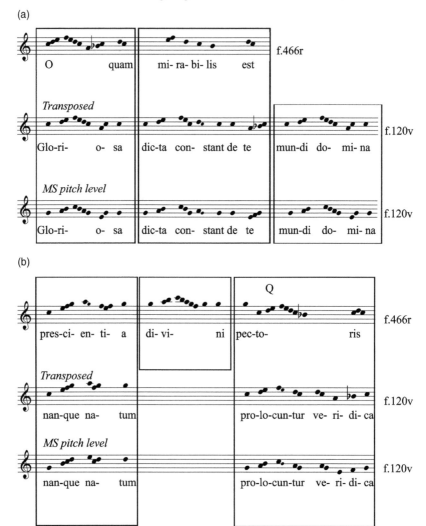

(b)

the practice she knew so well through her many decades as a nun, her plainchant would have played a liturgical role in her own community to celebrate numerous local saints and the patron saints of regional institutions as well as the institutions with which she was directly associated (at Disibodenberg and Rupertsberg). Her chant texts appear in letters, complement her hagiographical writings, and take on a climactic role in the culminating vision of her theological and visionary text, *Scivias*. Just as participation in the liturgy structured every day of her Benedictine life, Hildegard's expressive musical output was deeply integrated with her other activities as a spiritual leader and educator of a community of women, and as a visionary writer and a theologian.

Further Reading

Latin and Music Editions and English Translations

Hildegard of Bingen. *Lieder: Faksimile Riesencodex (Hs.2) der Hessischen Landesbibliothek Wiesbaden, fol. 466-481v*, ed. Lorenz Welker. Commentary by Michael Klaper. Elementa musicae 1. Wiesbaden: Ludwig Reichert Verlag, 1998.

Symphonia armonie celestium revelationum, ed. and trans. Marianne Richert. 8 vols. Bryn Mawr, PA: Hildegard Publishing Company, 1997.

Symphonia harmoniae caelestium revelationum: Dendermonde: St.-Pieters & Paulusabdij, Ms. Cod. 9, ed. Peter van Poucke. Peer: Alamire, 1991.

Symphonia: A Comparative Edition, ed. Vincent Corrigan. Lion's Bay, BC: Institute of Mediaeval Music, 2016.

Symphonia: A Critical Edition of the Symphonia armonie celestium revelationum, ed. and trans. Barbara Newman, 2nd ed. Ithaca, NY: Cornell University Press, 1988.

Secondary Literature

Bain, Jennifer. *Hildegard of Bingen and Musical Reception: The Modern Revival of a Medieval Composer*. Cambridge: Cambridge University Press, 2015.

Bain, Jennifer. "Varied Repetition in Hildegard's sequence for St. Rupert: *O Ierusalem aurea civitas*." In Laurel Parsons and Brenda Ravenscroft, eds., *Analytical Essays on Music by Women Composers: Secular and Sacred Music to 1900*. New York: Oxford University Press, 2018, 11–46.

Choate, Tova Leigh, William T. Flynn, and Margot Fassler. "Hearing the Heavenly Symphony: An Overview of Hildegard's Musical Oeuvre with Case Studies." In Beverly Mayne Kienzle, Debra L. Stoudt, and George Ferzoco, eds., *A Companion to Hildegard of Bingen*. Leiden: Brill, 2014, 163–192.

Fassler, Margot. "Composer and Dramatist: 'Melodious Singing and the Freshness of Remorse.'" In Barbara Newman, ed., *Voice of the Living Light: Hildegard of Bingen and Her World*. Berkeley: University of California Press, 1998, 149–175.

Meconi, Honey. *Hildegard of Bingen*. Urbana: University of Illinois Press, 2018.

Pfau, Marianne Richert and Stefan Morent. *Hildegard von Bingen: Der Klang des Himmels*. Cologne: Böhlau Verlag, 2005.

Roberge, Pierre-F. *Hildegard von Bingen (1098–1179): A Discography*. Updates by Todd McComb. www.medieval.org/emfaq/composers/hildegard.html

Stühlmeyer, Barbara. *Die Gesänge der Hildegard von Bingen: Eine musikologische, theologische und kulturhistorische Untersuchung*. Hildesheim: Georg Olms, 2003.

CHAPTER II

The Ordo virtutum *and Benedictine Monasticism*

Alison Altstatt

The *Ordo virtutum* (the Order of the Virtues) is a sung Latin drama that Hildegard completed circa 1152 for her newly founded community at Rupertsberg. The drama depicts the struggle between the Devil and a chorus of personified virtues for the control of the wayward *Anima* (the soul). It is the only surviving notated sung drama from the Middle Ages whose authorship is certain. Unique in style, scope, and ambition, the *Ordo* has invited a multitude of modern responses. Contributing factors to this diversity of interpretation are the striking originality of its language and imagery and the many possible comparisons to Hildegard's own visionary and theological writing. Further, as an allegorical work that must be relevant to all who witness it, the *Ordo* is arguably open-ended by design: this may be seen in the fact that the Soul's sins are never named. Yet Hildegard's work is firmly grounded in the theology and liturgy of the medieval Benedictine convent. This chapter examines how Hildegard draws on the Benedictine rule, the rite of the Consecration of Virgins, and the processional and dramatic rituals of the convent to create an embodied theology of the soul's salvation that is original, vivid, and specific to the female monastic experience.

Overview

The *Ordo* is transmitted in Wiesbaden, Hochschul- und Landesbibliothek RheinMain, MS 2 (the so-called *Riesencodex* or giant codex), a posthumous collection of Hildegard's works copied by the Rupertsberg community.[1] A shorter version without musical notation also concludes Hildegard's

---

[1] Hildegard von Bingen. *Lieder: Faksimile Riesencodex (Hs. 2) der Hessischen Landesbibliothek Wiesbaden*, fols. 466–481v, ed. Lorenz Welker, with commentary by Michael Klaper (Wiesbaden: L. Reichert Verlag, 1998). A complete digitized version of the manuscript is viewable at: http://hlbrm .digitale-sammlungen.hebis.de/handschriften-hlbrm/content/titleinfo/449618.

visionary and theological treatise, *Scivias*,[2] and the play exists as well in a fifteenth-century copy made by Johannes Trithemius, abbot of Sponheim.[3] The *Ordo* consists of monophonic chant and takes up to an hour to perform. Its singing roles include *Anima* (the Soul), a chorus of patriarchs and prophets, a chorus of souls imprisoned in bodies, and sixteen personified virtues led by Humility, their Queen (see the list of virtues in Table 11.1). The Devil has the sole speaking role, reflecting Hildegard's view of liturgical singing as a sacred act and the responsibility of the incarnate soul.[4] The play's female roles approximate the number of the founding community of Rupertsberg. Presumably, the convent's clerics, possibly including Volmar, Hildegard's editor and scribe, played the male roles. While the inaugural performance context of the *Ordo virtutum* is unknown, arguments have been made for the Dedication of Hildegard's convent at Rupertsberg on May 1, 1152, or on the occasion of the Consecration of Virgins, the rite in which nuns took their vows.[5]

The *Ordo* comprises four scenes, bookended by a prologue in which a chorus of patriarchs and prophets introduce the virtues, and a concluding chant that meditates on the meaning of Christ's incarnation. In the first scene, the lament of a chorus of souls imprisoned in bodies contrasts with the joyful, if somewhat naïve, proclamations of the Happy Soul (*felix Anima*). Soon, she, too, wearies of incarnation and complains that she can no longer bear wearing the garment in which she is clothed – that is, the body – and succumbs to the Devil's temptations of worldly honor and pleasure. The Soul is absent from the second scene, in which each virtue introduces herself and her powers and is affirmed in turn by the chorus of virtues. The Devil interjects occasionally in an attempt to undermine their confidence. In the third scene, the wounded Soul returns, repentant and seeking the help of the virtues. Together, the Soul and virtues triumph in the fourth scene, vanquishing the Devil and praising God. A final chorus addresses God the Father in the voice of Christ, who displays his wounds from the crucifixion and prays for the salvation of humankind.

[2] Tova Leigh Choate, William T. Flynn, and Margot Fassler, "Hearing the Heavenly Symphony: An Overview of Hildegard's Musical Oeuvre with Case Studies," in Beverly Kienzle, Debra L. Stoudt, and George Ferzoco, eds., *A Companion to Hildegard of Bingen* (Leiden: Brill Publishing, 2014), 164.
[3] London, British Library, Add. MS 15102. See Hildegard of Bingen, *Ordo Virtutum: A Comparative Edition*, ed. Vincent Corrigan (Lions Bay, BC: Institute of Mediaeval Music, 2013).
[4] Audrey Ekdahl Davidson, "Music and Performance: Hildegard of Bingen's Ordo Virtutum," in Audrey Ekdahl Davidson, ed., *The* Ordo Virtutum *of Hildegard of Bingen: Critical Studies*, Early Drama, Art, and Music Monographs 18 (Kalamazoo, MI: Medieval Institute Publications, 1992), 12.
[5] See Pamela Sheingorn, "The Virtues of Hildegard's Ordo Virtutum, or, It Was a Woman's World," in Davidson, *The* Ordo Virtutum *of Hildegard of Bingen*, 52–53; Peter Dronke, *Nine Medieval Plays* (Cambridge: Cambridge University Press, 1994), 152.

Table 11.1 List of virtues

	Hildegard, Ordo Virtutum	Prudentius, Psychomachia	Benedictine Rule	Aldhelm, Carmen de Virginitate	Speculum virginum	R. Benedic domine domus istam et omnes	Consecration of Virgins, 12th century, Mainz
1	Knowledge of God (*Scientia Dei*)	*					*
2	Humility (*Humilitas*)	*	*	*	*	*	*
3	Charity (*Caritas*)		*	*	*	*	*
4	Fear of the Lord (*Timor domini*)		*		*		**
5	Obedience (*Obedientia*)		*		*	*	*
6	Faith (*Fides*)	*	*		*	*	*
7	Hope (*Spes*)	*	*			*	*
8	Chastity (*Castitas*)	*	*				*
9	Innocence (*Innocentia*)						*
10	Contempt of the World (*Contemptus mundi*)						*
11	Heavenly love (*Amor caelestis*)		1				1
12	Discipline (*Disciplina*) +		*		*	2	
13	Modesty (*Verecundia*)		*		*		3
14	Mercy (*Misericordia*)	*	*				
15	Victory (*Victoria*)					*	
16	Discernment (*Discretio*)		*		*		
17	Patience (*Patientia*)	*	*	*	*	*	*

* Virtue present
+ Erasure
1 Love (*Amor*)
2 Spiritual discipline (*Spiritualis disciplina*)
3 Modesty (*Modestia; Pudicitia*)

The Music of the *Ordo*

The text of the *Ordo* is unmetered, having no regular syllable count, accent pattern, or rhyme. The music responds to this irregular organization, setting lines as sense units of unequal length. As is typical of Hildegard's composition, the chants of the *Ordo* are wide ranging, exceeding the typical modal registers of Gregorian chant. Their emphasis on the final, fifth, and octave of the mode, incorporation of large upward leaps and long downward runs, and repeating melodic formulae are characteristic of the late chant style.[6] The *Ordo* is distinguished by a coherent overall tonal plan in which D-Dorian represents the spiritual salvation of the Soul, while E-Phrygian expresses the pain of the Soul's separation from God.[7] Hildegard also uses range, texture, melodic formulae, and quotations of Gregorian chant to characterize the virtues, further the plot, and enhance the dramatic action.[8]

The *Ordo virtutum* As Drama

A long tradition of religious drama underlies the *Ordo*, beginning with the *Visitatio sepulchri* (Visitation of the Tomb) recorded from the tenth century, which dramatized the three Marys' visit to the sepulcher of Christ.[9] By the late eleventh and twelfth centuries, new, expanded forms of the *Visitatio* were recorded, along with plays of expanded subject matter and new styles of versification.[10] The performance of the *Visitatio sepulchri* in women's communities is implied in the tenth-century English *Regularis Concordia* (a rule of monastic practice), while the hagiographic plays of Hrosvitha of Gandersheim (ca. 935–973) bear witness to an interest in literary dramas in Ottonian women's houses. The *Visitatio sepulchri* may have been particular meaningful to women religious as it emphasizes the

---

[6] See Jennifer Bain, "Hildegard, Hermannus and Late Chant Style," *Journal of Music Theory* 52, no. 1, *Essays in Honor of Sarah Fuller* (Spring 2008): 123–149. A comprehensive review of the secondary literature on Hildegard's music, as well as editions and recordings, may be found in Choate, Flynn, and Fassler, "Hearing the Heavenly Symphony," 184–192, Davidson, "Music and Performance," and Margot E. Fassler, "Allegorical Architecture in Scivias: Hildegard's Setting for the Ordo Virtutum," *Journal of the American Musicological Society* 67, no. 2 (2014): 334–364.

[7] See Davidson, "Musical Performance," 11; Fassler, "Allegorical Architecture," 334–337, Choate, Flynn, and Fassler, "Hearing the Heavenly Symphony," 186–189.

[8] See Davidson, "Musical Performance," Fassler, "Allegorical Architecture;" Choate, Flynn and Fassler, "Hearing the Heavenly Symphony."

[9] See Susan Rankin, "Liturgical Drama," in Richard Crocker and David Hiley, eds., *The New Oxford History of Music, Vol. 2: The Early Middle Ages to 1300* (Oxford: Oxford University Press, 1990), 310–320.

[10] See Rankin, "Liturgical Drama," 310–327.

Marys' apostolic role as the first witnesses to the resurrection. Moreover, the Marys' singing mirrored the convent's own experience of shared female devotion. The performance of drama for a mixed religious and lay audience furthermore challenged the principle of female enclosure. Importantly, drama represented an area of convent ritual that women had the authority to influence or even determine.[11] While the *Visitatio sepulchri* transmitted in the antiphoner Engelberg Stiftsbibliothek codex 103 from the nearby Benedictine house of Sponheim is quite modest, examples from somewhat later manuscripts reflect a rich dramatic tradition in women's houses that expanded the roles of the Marys, especially that of Mary Magdalene, to create a highly affective performance.[12]

Nils Holger Petersen has argued that in the context of eleventh- to twelfth-century debates on the nature of the eucharist, drama can be considered sacramental because, like the eucharist, it had the power to make visible the body of Christ. Petersen suggests that in accordance with Peter Abelard's definition of a sacrament as "a visible sign of the grace of God," the physical act of drama served as a figurative representation of an invisible spiritual reality.[13] This concept of the sacramentality is particularly relevant to the medieval convent, as drama represented an area in which women could exercise spiritual authority and artistic creativity. In the *Ordo*, which is about the problem of incarnation, drama makes visible the invisible: not the body of Christ but the soul and its Christlike qualities – the virtues – through the devices of personification and physical embodiment.

The term "liturgical drama," often used to describe the *Ordo*, has been critiqued for its tendency to obscure a spectrum of representational

---

[11] See Margaret Aziza Pappano, "Sister Acts: Conventual Performance and the *Visitatio Sepulchri* in England and France," in Theodolinda Barolini, ed., *Medieval Constructions in Gender and Identity: Essays in Honor of Joan M. Ferrante* (Tempe: Arizona Center for Medieval and Renaissance Studies, 2005), 43–67; Anne Bagnall Yardley, *Performing Piety: Musical Culture in Medieval English Nunneries* (New York: Palgrave Macmillan, 2006), 153–155.

[12] On the origin of Engelberg Stiftsbibliothek Cod. 103, see Tova Choate, William T. Flynn, and Margot Fassler, "Hildegard As Musical Hagiographer and Her Songs for Saints Disibod and Ursula," in Kienzle, Stoudt, and Ferzoco, *A Companion to Hildegard of Bingen*, 194–199. For early examples of convent drama, see Augustiner-Chorherrenstift, Bibliothek, Klosterneuberg 1013; Národní knihovna České republiky, Praha VI.E.13 (Prague, St. George 12th-century breviary); Herzog August Bibliothek, Wolfenbüttel 309 Novi (Marienberg bei Helmstedt 12th–13th-century antiphoner). See further discussion in Rankin, "Liturgical Drama," 335–337; Pappano, "Sister Acts," 44–45; Yardley, *Performing Piety*, 146–155.

[13] See Nils Holger Petersen, "Biblical Reception, Representational Ritual, and the Question of 'Liturgical Drama,'" in Gunilla Iverson and Nicholas Bell, eds., *Sapientia et Eloquentia: Meaning and Function in Liturgical Poetry, Music Drama, and Biblical Commentary in the Middle Ages* (Turnhout: Brepols, 2009), 179 and 182.

practices ranging from liturgical dialogues to Latin didactic plays.[14] The musicologist Michael Norton has recently proposed the term "representational rite" for those sung dialogues with a clear liturgical context and "religious representation" to describe those "where evidence of liturgical use is scant," stressing that "there is no single noun that can adequately stand for all instances."[15] Because the intended context and audience of the *Ordo virtutum* are unknown, its liturgical placement remains uncertain. This does not, however, preclude that the play was part of the broader ritual of the convent. The distinction between representational rite and religious representation rests on the definition of "rite," and how one defines this term has profound implications for understanding convent ritual. A definition of rite limited to the Mass, canonical office, and clerically officiated ceremony excludes those local and individualized practices over which religious women had the greatest amount of authority and creative autonomy. A broader notion of "rite" that encompasses all of the corporate prayer of a community includes more observances over which religious women exercised authority, such as stational liturgies, devotional and votive offices, the ritual of the chapter house, and table readings.[16] Even if the *Ordo* was not used in the liturgy narrowly defined, it was likely part of the broader ritual of the convent in which local practices could develop.

Hildegard's Virtues

The virtues are prominent in the *Rule of St. Benedict* and later Benedictine literature as powers that support the soul's journey toward salvation. For Hildegard, the virtues were magnified in Christ's incarnation, or his having "put on flesh," in order to bring salvation to humanity.[17] In *Scivias*, book 1, vision 2:31, she states:

> after Man's ruin many shining virtues were lifted up in Heaven, like Humility, the queen of virtues, which flowered in the virgin birth, and other virtues, which lead God's elect to the heavenly places. For when a field

---

[14] See Michael Norton, *Liturgical Drama and the Reimagining of Medieval Theater: Early Drama, Art, and Music* (Kalamazoo, MI: Medieval Institute Publications, 2017), 1–18, and Petersen, "Biblical Reception," 169–172.

[15] Norton, *Liturgical Drama*, 7.

[16] See Alison Altstatt, "The Music and Liturgy of Kloster Preetz: Anna von Buchwald's *Buch im Chor* in its Fifteenth-century Context" (PhD diss., University of Oregon, 2011), 24–33.

[17] Hildegard of Bingen, *Scivias*, trans. Mother Columba Hart and Jane Bishop (New York: Paulist Press, 1990), 87.

with great labor is cultivated, it brings forth much fruit, and the same is shown in the human race, for after humanity's ruin many virtues arose to raise it up again.[18]

Yet, paradoxically, she explains, the state of incarnation prevents the individual soul from appreciating God's justice: "[but] you, o humans, oppressed by the heaviness of the flesh, do not see that great glory God's full justice has prepared for you."[19] It is from this state of incarnate oppression that the Soul must be saved by the virtues. The Soul's struggle to bear the burden of the body mirrors that of Christ's incarnation, passion, and triumph over the power of evil, as recounted in scripture and memorialized in liturgy.

Precedents for the Virtues

In literary concept, the *Ordo* draws on the fourth-century *Psychomachia*, a Latin epic poem by Prudentius that narrates an allegorical battle between the personified Christian virtues and the Pagan vices.[20] While Hildegard was doubtless familiar with this widely circulated and studied text, the plot, language, and characterization of the *Ordo* are distinct from those of the *Psychomachia*, and its virtues are more specific to those of the Benedictine tradition (see Table 11.1).[21] The virtues of Humility, Obedience, and the Fear of the Lord are central to the *Rule of St. Benedict*. The prologue to the *Rule* quotes from Revelation 2:7 and Psalm 33:12 to introduce the important virtue of the Fear of the Lord:

> *Et iterum: qui habet aures audiendi audiat quid spiritus dicat ecclesiis.*
> *Et quid dicit? Venite filii, audite me; timorem domini docebo vos.*

> And again: you that have ears to hear, listen to what the Spirit says to the churches.
> And what does he say? Come and listen to me, sons; I will teach you the fear of the Lord.[22]

Later, the *Rule* describes Fear of the Lord as essential to cultivating Humility, whom Hildegard calls the Queen of the Virtues. The *Rule*

---

[18] Ibid., 87–88.   [19] Ibid., 88.
[20] See Bruce Hozeski, "Parallel Patterns in Prudentius's Psychomachia and Hildegard of Bingen's *Ordo Virtutum*," *Fourteenth-Century English Mystics Newsletter* 8, no. 1 (March 1982): 8–20; Davidson, "Music and Performance," 7–8.
[21] See Peter Dronke, *Poetic Individuality in the Middle Ages: New Departures in Poetry, 1000–1150* (Oxford: Clarendon Press, 1970), 169; Fassler, "Allegorical Architecture," 326–332.
[22] Benedict of Nursia. *RB 1980: The Rule of St. Benedict in English*, ed. and trans. Timothy Fry (Collegeville, MN: Liturgical Press, 1981), 15.

quotes Luke 14:11, that "whoever exalts himself shall be humbled, and whoever humbles himself shall be exalted," and likens this principle to the image of the ladder from the dream of Jacob. The *Rule* explains that humankind descends the heavenly ladder through exaltation and ascends it through Humility. The ladder represents life, its two sides, the body and the soul, and its rungs, the virtues of Humility and Discipline:

> Now the ladder erected is our life on earth, and if we humble our hearts the Lord will raise it to Heaven. We may call our body and soul the sides of this ladder, into which our divine vocation has fitted the various steps of humility and discipline as we ascend.[23]

Thus the soul and the body are both essential parts of the ladder: Humility and Discipline depend on both the soul and the body and mediate between them to create the means to ascend to Heaven. This point is critical to understanding the *Ordo*, which concerns the soul's pursuit of God while in its incarnate state.

The *Rule* sets out a twelve-step path to Humility, the first of which "is that a man keeps the fear of God always before his eyes and never forgets it."[24] Obedience is the third step to Humility, in imitation of "the Lord, of whom the Apostle says: He became obedient even to death."[25] Thus the Fear of the Lord and Obedience are essential to achieving Humility. At the twelfth and final step, the monk must "manifest humility in his bearing no less that in his heart."[26] Humility having become habitual and effortless, the monk is no longer motivated by Fear, but by the Love of God:

> the monk will quickly arrive at that perfect love of God (*caritas Dei*) which casts out fear (*timor*). Through his love, all that he once performed with dread, he will now begin to observe without effort, as though naturally, from habit, no longer out of fear of Hell, but out of love of Christ (*amor Christi*), good habit and delight in virtue. All this the Lord will by the Holy Spirit graciously manifest in his workman now cleansed of vices and sins.[27]

At its essence, the *Ordo* dramatizes this progression through Humility to an effortless Love of Christ (Amor Christi), which Hildegard calls Celestial Love (*Amor Caelestis*).

The Virtues in Convent Liturgy

While the Benedictine path through Humility to the love of Christ was shared by religious men and women alike, the personified virtues are

---

[23] Ibid., 32.   [24] Ibid.   [25] Ibid., 34.   [26] Ibid., 37.   [27] Adapted from Ibid., 37.

particularly important in several texts specific to female religious: the *Carmen de virginitate* (Song on Virginity) written by Aldhelm of Malmesbury (ca. 639–709) for the women's house of Barking Abbey, and the *Speculum virginum* (Mirror for Virgins), a theological work for nuns attributed to Conrad of Hirsau (ca. 1130) that circulated in reformed communities such as Hildegard's.[28]

The virtues also held a prominent place in the convent liturgy of Hildegard's time as may be seen in the rite of the Consecration of Virgins from twelfth-century Mainz and in the weekly Sunday procession that blessed the convent and invited the virtues to dwell within it. To describe the Soul's temptation and triumph over the Devil, Hildegard draws on textual and liturgical tradition of the harrowing of Hell, in which Christ descends into Hell to vanquish the Devil and save humanity. Hildegard creatively reworks these texts and rituals from the Benedictine convent to create an embodied theology of salvation. Each of these liturgies provides important background to understanding the dramatic situation and poetic language of the *Ordo virtutum*.

The Consecration of Virgins in Twelfth-Century Mainz

Hildegard weaves the Benedictine path toward God through the virtue of Humility together with the language of the Consecration of Virgins in which girls took monastic vows. The Consecration ceremony expresses the soul's union with God in gendered terms of the mystical marriage of the *Song of Songs*, casting the consecrand as the beloved and Christ as the lover. The consecrand ritually weds Christ in the person of the bishop, from whom she accepts the tokens of marriage.[29] This narrative is enhanced with the moral dimensions of the parable of the wise and foolish virgins who await the coming of the bridegroom. The ceremony also borrows antiphons from the office of the virgin martyr St. Agnes, who declared her

---

[28] See, for example, the *Carmen virginitate* transmitted in Österreichische Nationalbibliothek, Cod. 969, 9th–10th c., (Mainz?). On the *Speculum virginum*, see Fassler, "Allegorical Architecture," 327–329, 347; Constant J. Mews, "Hildegard of Bingen and the Hirsau Reform in Germany 1080–1180," in Kienzle, Stoudt, and Ferzoco, *A Companion to Hildegard of Bingen*, 70–72.

[29] On the rite of Consecration, see Sheingorn, "The Virtues of Hildegard's Ordo Virtutum," 53–57; Anne Bagnell Yardley, "The Marriage of Heaven and Earth: A Late Medieval Source of the Consecratio Virginum," in Peter M. Lefferts and Brian Seirup, eds., *Studies in Medieval Music: Festschrift for Ernest Sanders, Current Musicology* 45–47 (New York: Columbia University, 1990), 305–324; James Borders, "Gender, Performativity, and Allusion in Medieval Services from the Consecration of Virgins," in Jane F. Fulcher, ed., *The Oxford Handbook of the New Cultural History of Music* (2012), *Oxford Handbooks Online*, www.oxfordhandbooks.com; Anne Bagnall Yardley, *Performing Piety*, 159–177.

mystical marriage to Christ: these are sung by the consecrands as they receive the symbols of their vows from the bishop: the veil, crown, and the ring. As James Borders has described, these antiphons form "a self-standing narrative of devotion, earthly trial, and spiritual union with Christ in Heaven."[30] In the *Ordo*, Hildegard transforms this narrative: while Agnes suffered martyrdom in order to maintain her chastity and her marriage vow to Christ, the Soul's trial in the *Ordo* is to pursue God while continuing to live in the body, with all of its temptations and imperfections.

By Hildegard's time, new elements appeared in the Consecration rite which emphasize specific monastic virtues, as witnessed in the pontifical of her bishop Christian I, from 1165 to 1183 the archbishop of Mainz, where Hildegard's brother Hugo also served as cantor.[31] These additions enhance the Benedictine character of the rite by their focus on achieving the love of God through the cultivation of Humility. They moreover emphasize Contempt of the World as a virtue of particular importance to the enclosed convent. This version of the rite, which expanded the musical roles of both consecrand and convent, profoundly influenced Hildegard's *Ordo*. The sum of the virtues invoked in the twelfth-century Consecration appears in Table 11.1.

The rite of twelfth-century Mainz opens with a threefold exchange between the bishop and the consecrands centering on the virtue of *Timor Dei* (Fear of God), using an antiphon drawn from the rite of the Reconciliation of Penitents.[32] The antiphon's text is adapted from Psalm 33:12, the same verse quoted in the prologue to the Benedictine rule:

> *Venite, venite, venite filii audite me. Timorem domini docebo vos.*

> Come, come, come, children, and hear me. I shall teach you the Fear of the Lord.

The consecrands stand facing the bishop, their heads uncovered and hair loose, holding burning candles in their hands, with the abbess and entire convent standing behind them.[33] The bishop summons them to the altar to be veiled, singing:

---

[30] Borders, "Gender, Performativity, and Allusion," 11.

[31] *Ordo ad virgines velandas*, Bibliothèque nationale de France, Latin 946, fols. 51–58. For more on the expansion of the rite, see Yardley, *Performing Piety*, 168–172. Regarding Hugo (d. 1177), see Anna Silvas, ed. and trans., *Hildegard and Jutta: The Biographical Sources* (University Park: Pennsylvania State University Press, 1999), 240–245, 278–279.

[32] Bibliothèque nationale de France, Latin 946, fol. 51v, fol. 92. See another transcription at: http://musmed.fr/CMN/FC98.pdf.

[33] Bibliothèque nationale de France, Latin 946, fol. 51v.

Venite filie!

Come daughters!

They advance partway toward the bishop, responding with the prayer of Azariah from Daniel 1:18:

> *Et nunc sequamur in toto corde, et timemus te.*
> *Et querimus faciem tuam domine.*
> *Non confundas nos, sed fac nobis iuxta mansuetudinem tuam*
> *et secundum multitudinem misericordiae tuae*

> And now let us follow you with our whole hearts and fear you.
> And we shall seek out your face, O Lord.
> Do not confound us, but do unto us according to your clemency
> and according to your great mercies.

This exchange takes place three times, each time with an additional repetition of the word *Venite!* (Come!). Through this dialogue, the girls express their devotion and acceptance of the Fear of the Lord as necessary to receiving the habit, the outward manifestation of their vows.[34] The bishop's repeated urging and the girls' gradual approach convey a sense of the weightiness of this virtue, necessary to seeking out the face of God.

Similarly, in the *Ordo*, Hildegard presents *Timor Dei* (the Fear of God) as the virtue which prepares the Soul to look into the face of God:

> *Ego, Timor Dei, vos felicimas filias preparo, ut inspiciatis in Deum vivum et non pereatis*

> I, Fear of God, prepare you, most happy daughters, that you might look upon the living God and not perish.

In the *Ordo*, as in the Consecration, the virtue of the Fear of God prepares the Soul to approach Christ. The virtues' repeated calls of *Venite!* (Come!) in the *Ordo* echo those of the Consecration, inviting the Soul to turn toward God. For example, the virtue of Obedience sings:

> *Venite ad me, pulcherime filie, et reducam vos ad patriam et ad osculum regis.*[35]

> Come to me, most beautiful daughter, and I will lead you back to the homeland and to the kiss of the king.

---

[34] See Yardley, *Performing Piety*, 169–174.
[35] Hildegard von Bingen, *Ordo virtutum*, ed. Audrey Ekdahl Davidson (Kalamazoo, MI: Medieval Institute Publications, 1985), line 31.

In the *Rule*, the virtue of Obedience was essential to cultivating Humility, a virtue necessary to developing an effortless love of God. Obedience's line in the *Ordo* expresses this love of God in terms of the kiss of the king and the beloved from *Song of Songs*, verses 1:1 *Osculetur me osculo oris sui* (Let him kiss me with the kiss of his mouth), 1:3: *introduxit me **rex** in cellaria sua* (the king has lead me into his cellar), and 1:14/15 *Ecce tu **pulchra** es amica mea / Ecce tu **pulcher** es dilecte mi* (Behold, thou art beautiful, my love). Thus Hildegard expressed the Benedictine virtue of Obedience in terms of the mystical marriage of the *Song of Songs*.[36]

In the twelfth-century Mainz Consecration, the Secret, read quietly by the bishop, similarly describes the love of God as the entrance to the heaven, though which the consecrands "might deserve to joyfully enter through the open door into the embrace of the King of Heaven."[37] This prayer describes the soul's love of God from the *Rule* as the ***amplexus*** (embrace) of *Song of Songs* 2:6. Hildegard likewise expresses the virtue of Celestial Love (*Celestis amor*) as the *aurea porta* (the golden doorway) to Heaven, where the Soul will be embraced by God, to which the Virtues respond:

> *O filia regis tu semper es in amplexibus quos mundus fugit.*
> *O quam suavis est tua dilectio in summo deo.*

> O daughter of the king, you are always in the embraces which the world flees.
> O how pleasing is your love in the highest God.

The effortless love of God, which is the goal of the twelve steps of Humility in the Benedictine rule, in both the *Ordo* and the Consecration is expressed in the language of the mystical marriage of the *Song of Songs*.

The emphasis on the virtue of Contempt of the World shows a further link between the twelfth-century Mainz Consecration of Virgins and Hildegard's *Ordo virtutum*. The Mainz Consecration borrows two further antiphons from the Office of St. Agnes sung by the consecrands as they accept symbols of their marriage, emphasizing Christ's adornment of his bride. As they accept the veil, the consecrands sing St. Agnes's antiphon:

> *Christus circumdederit me vernantibus atque coruscantibus gemmis preciosis.*[38]

> Christ has encircled me with flowering and shining precious gems.

As they accept the ring, they sing the other Agnes antiphon:

---

[36] For further discussion of Hildegard's use of the *Song of Songs*, see Margot Fassler, "Music for the Love Feast: Hildegard of Bingen and the Song of Songs," in Jane A. Bernstein, ed., *Women's Voices across Musical Worlds* (Boston: Northeastern University Press, 2004), 92–117.

[37] Bibliothèque nationale de France, Latin 946, fol. 58v.   [38] Cantus 001790.

Dexteram meam et collum meam cinxit lapidibus preciosis
Tradidit auribus meis inestimantibus margaritas[39]

He has encircled my right hand and neck with precious stones,
and has given to my ears inestimable pearls.

The convent and consecrands answer with the responsory *Regnum mundi,*
borrowed from the Common of Virgins, which makes clear the spiritual
nature of these adornments: its text shuns worldly ornament, embracing
instead the central virtue of the enclosed convent, *Contemptus mundi,* or
Contempt of the World:

RESPOND: *Regnum mundi et omnem ornatum saeculi contempsi propter amorem domini*
mei Jesu Christi. Quem vidi quem amavi in quem credidi quem dilexi.[40]
VERSE: *Eructavit cor meum verbum bonum dico ego opera mea regi. Quem vidi quem*
amavi in quem credidi quem dilexi.

R. I disdain the Kingdom of the World and every worldly ornament for the love of
my Lord Jesus Christ. Whom I have seen, whom I have loved, in whom
I have believed, and in whom I delighted.
V. My heart has rejoiced in the good word, and I proclaim the works of my king.
Whom I have seen, whom I have loved, in whom I have believed, and in
whom I delighted.

Through singing this responsory, the consecrands and convent together praise
the virtue of Contempt for the World, affirming their abandonment of the
secular world for a marriage to Christ with the enclosure of the convent.

Contempt of the World is also central to the *Ordo,* in which the Soul's
first temptation is the desire to embrace the world:

Deus creavit mundum, non facio illi iniuriam, sed volo uti illo.

God made the world, I do no harm to him, but I do wish to enjoy it.

Later, Contempt for the World introduces herself as the savior of incarnate
souls on earth who long for heavenly union with Christ:

Ego Contemptus Mundi, sum candor vite.
O misera terre peregrinatio, in multis laboris, te dimitto.
O virtutes, venite ad me, et ascendamus ad fontem vito.

I am Contempt for the World, I am the pure radiance of life.
O, poor pilgrim on earth, in much labor, I send you forth.
O virtues, come to me and we shall ascend to the living fountain.

---

[39] Cantus 002186.   [40] Cantus 007524.

Yet this promise of heavenly transcendence must not be mistaken for contempt for the incarnate state or the physical body. As *Scientia Dei* (Knowledge of God) reminds the Soul, the body was created by God:

> *Vide quid illud sit quod es induta, filia salvationis, et esto stabili, et nunquam cades*
>
> Behold what you are clothed in, daughter of salvation, be firm, and you will never fall.

The principal challenge of the Soul in the *Ordo* is not to die (cast off the garment) as did the Virgin Martyr Agnes, but rather to continue to inhabit it while overcoming the trials of embodiment.

In sum, the Consecration of Virgins from twelfth-century Mainz weds the mystical union between the soul and Christ to the Benedictine path through Humility to the Love of God. The virtues invoked in the rite of Consecration anticipate the principal virtues of the *Ordo*, as does the language of mystical marriage. Hildegard offers a creative response to the Consecration rite: the language of the mystical marriage, the penitential dialogue between the Soul and the virtues, and the appeal to the virtues for help all recur in the *Ordo virtutum* but in a transformed manner. Profoundly different in the *Ordo* is the relationship to the body; instead of rejecting the body, the *Ordo* reaffirms the need for incarnation of the soul for the purpose of praising God in song.

The Virtues in Procession

The virtues were also present in the processional activity of the convent. An important liturgical precedent for Hildegard's virtues is the processional responsory, *Benedic domine domus iste et omnes*, sung during the Sunday procession which blessed the convent and its inhabitants.[41] This responsory was first recorded in the late eleventh or early twelfth century as an addition to older liturgies for the Dedication of a Church.[42] It prays for

[41] Cantus 600280. This responsory should not be confused with Cantus 006235 with which it shares an incipit.

[42] Added to Universitätsbibliothek Erlangen-Nürnberg, Hauptbibliothek H62 MS. 10[1, (fol. 13r), Bayerische Staatsbibliothek Clm 14124 (fol. 151), and Bayerische Staatsbibliothek Clm 6264, Freising (back flyleaf) without liturgical assignment; assigned to the Dedication in Österreichische Nationalbibliothek, Cod.1830 (Salzburg, 11th–12th c.) (fol. 71v), and Bibliothèque nationale de France, Latin 946 (Mainz, fol. 64v), Bischöfliches Ordinariat der Diözese Basel, Diözesanarchiv des Bistrums Basel s.n. ("Codex Gressley"), and in Stiftsbibliothek, St. Gallen 380 and 390–391 (St. Gall.) In some twelfth-century sources, it appears in a set of three responsories, possibly used to expand the shorter secular office cursus to the longer monastic one.

God's blessing and invites the virtues to dwell within the community (see Table 11.1.)

RESPOND: *Benedic domine domum istam et omnes habitantes in illa sitque in ea sanitas humilitas sanctitas castitas virtus victoria fides spes et caritas benignitas temperancia patientia spiritualis disciplina et obedentia per infinita secula*
VERSE: *Conserva domine in ea timentes te pusillos cum majoribus*

R. Bless, o Lord, this house and all who dwell in it. And let there be in it Cleanliness, Humility, Holiness, and Chastity, Virtue, Victory, Faith, Hope, and Charity, Goodness, Temperance, Patience, Spiritual Discipline, and Obedience for the infinite ages.
V. Keep safe in it, o Lord, those who fear you, the young ones together with the elders.

This piece is assigned to the Dedication of a Church in the same pontifical of Christian I of Mainz in which the expanded Consecration of Virgins is found and is sung as the procession circles the church thrice, blessing it with holy water.[43] It is conceivable that the responsory was sung in this manner for the dedication of Rupertsberg in 1152, though the pontifical was copied some two decades later.

Another regional manuscript, the aforementioned antiphonal possibly from Sponheim, assigns *Benedic domine domum istam et omnes* instead to the Sunday procession beginning after the Feast of the Epiphany, resulting in its weekly performance for much of the liturgical year.[44] Often referred to in German sources as the procession *per claustrum* or *curiam* (through the cloister or court), the Sunday procession exited the church after the office of Terce and processed around the cloister ambulatory, blessing the convent and its inhabitants prior to Mass. This responsory is an important precedent for the architectural allegory of the virtues found in Hildegard's *Scivias* in both content and performance practice. Margot Fassler has suggested that Hildegard's *Ordo* was intended to be read together with her *Scivias*, which is organized around this architectural allegory of the soul's salvation.[45] As Fassler has pointed out, Hildegard completed her theological treatise *Scivias* and composed the *Ordo* while she was constructing the monastic buildings of Rupertsberg, and ideas involving sacred architecture permeate her work.[46] In *Scivias*, the virtues are grouped in

---

[43] Bibliothèque nationale de France, Latin 946, fol. 64v.
[44] Engelberg Stiftsbibliothek Cod. 103, fol. 93r. This assignment was also used at Kloster Preetz, a convent in Schleswig Holstein whose liturgy transmits some typically Rhenish attributes. See Altstatt, "The Music and Liturgy of Kloster Preetz," 131–141.
[45] Fassler, "Allegorical Architecture," 319.   [46] Ibid., 318–319.

specific locations in the Edifice of Salvation; these groupings offer a more complex characterization, illuminating both the organization and the meaning of the Virtues in the *Ordo*.[47] I propose that the practice of singing while processing was a type of communal *ars memoria*, in which one mentally places things to be recalled in specific loci in an imaginary architectural framework. Through the Sunday procession *per claustrum*, the virtues were thus placed along the ambulatory of the cloister through which the convent processed, becoming associated in the memory with edifice of the cloister and inhabiting the building as the text invites. Thus this responsory, sung in weekly procession as it circles the cloister ambulatory, offers an important context for Hildegard's architectural allegory of the Virtues.

The Harrowing of the Soul

The plot of the *Ordo* can be seen as a microcosmic retelling of salvation history, in which the Soul's journey parallels events in the life of Christ. An important model for Hildegard was the *Descensus Christi ad Infernos* (Christ's Descent into Hell) a fourth-century addition to the apocryphal *Gospel of Nicodemus* and the liturgical commemorations of its central event: Christ's descent into, or harrowing, of Hell. According to this widely circulated text, Jesus, having died on the cross, descended into Hell, breaking open its gates, vanquishing the Devil, and freeing the Old Testament patriarchs, prophets, and all the worthy souls who had languished in Hell since the time of Adam.[48] Hildegard describes the harrowing in *Scivias*, book 2, vision 1:13:

> [h]e poured out his beautiful blood and knew in his body the darkness of death. And thus conquering the Devil, he delivered from Hell his elect, who were held prostrate there, and by His redeeming touch brought them back to the inheritance they had lost in Adam. As they were returning to their inheritance, timbrels and harps and all kinds of music burst forth, because Man, who had lain in perdition but now stood upright in blessedness, had been freed by heavenly power and escaped from death.[49]

The narrative of the harrowing gives context to the chorus of patriarchs and prophets who appear in the prologue to the *Ordo*. They greet the virtues,

[47] Ibid., 318–329.
[48] *The Gospel of Nicodemus: Gesta Salvatoris*, ed. H. C. Kim (Toronto: Pontifical Institute of Medieval Studies, 1973), 36–47.
[49] *Scivias*, trans. Hart and Bishop, 154–155.

singing: *"Qui sunt hi, qui ut nubes?"* (Who are these, who [come] like clouds?). The virtues reply, introducing themselves as concomitant to the incarnation of Christ and teachers of his body (the church):

> *O antique sancti, quid admiramini in nobis?*
> *Verbum Dei clarescit in forma hominis,*
> *Et ideo fulgemus cum illo, edificantes membra sui pulchri corporis.*
>
> O ancient and holy ones, what makes you wonder at us?
> The word of God becomes clear in the form of a man, and therefore,
> We shine with him, edifying the members of his beautiful body.

The patriarchs and prophets answer, greeting the virtues as the heirs of their authority:

> *Nos sumus radices, et vos rami, fructus viventis oculi, et nos umbra in illo fuimus.*
>
> We are the roots, and you the branches, the fruit of the living bud [eye], and we were the shadow in him.

As Luca Ricossa has shown, the antiphon *Qui sunt hi qui ut nubes* quotes both textually and musically from the responsory used in the Common of Evangelists and of Apostles (used as well for the Feast of All Saints, as Jennifer Bain has identified), thus suggesting, by association, that the Virtues were on a par with these biblical and holy figures.[50] The antiphon further recalls the Lauds canticle antiphon for the Feast of the Assumption, itself adapted from the *Song of Songs* 6:9:

> *Quae est ista quae ascendit quasi aurora consurgens,*
> *Pulchra ut luna, electa ut sol, et terribilis ut acies ordinata?*[51]
>
> Who is she who ascends like the dawn?
> As beautiful as the moon, as shining as the sun, and as terrible
>   as an army with banners?

The likening of the beloved's (here, the Virgin's) beauty to that of mighty army further recalls Isaiah 63:1:

> *Quis est ista, qui venit de Edom, tinctis vestibus de Bosra?*
> *Iste formosus in stola sua, gradiens in multitudine fortitudinis suae?*
> *Ego qui loquor justitiam, et propugnator sum ad salvandum.*

---

[50] Luca Ricossa, "Préface," in Hildegard von Bingen, *Ordo Virtutum*, 2. Jennifer Bain, "The Music of Hildegard of Bingen," *Church Music Quarterly* (June 2019): 15.
[51] Engelberg Stiftsbibliothek Cod. 103, f. 143r.

Who is this, who comes from Edom, from Bozrah in garments died crimson?
Who is this, so splendidly robed, marching in his great might?
It is I, who speak of justice, defender of salvation.

These intertextual relationships lend the virtues a sense of beauty and might, and of prophetic and liturgical authority. Significant as well is the presence of the patriarchs and prophets, who in the *Descensus* hail the arrival of Christ their salvation. In the *Ordo*, they instead herald the virtues, the Christlike qualities of the Soul who are her salvation in her own harrowing.

The *Ordo*'s prologue further resonates with Psalm 23:7–9, read as a prophecy of Christ as king and warrior. This dialogue is assigned throughout the liturgical year to commemorate formal entries, including the Dedication of a Church. In the *Descensus*, it heralds the arrival of the warrior Christ into Hell in the form of a dialogue between a voice of thunder, a personified Hell, and the chorus of patriarchs and prophets. When Thunder announces the King of Glory, Hell asks, in the words of Psalm 23:

> *Quis est iste rex gloriae?*
>
> Who is this king of glory?

To which King David responds:

> *Dominus fortis et potens, Dominus potens in bello, ipse est rex Gloria*
>
> The Lord strong and mighty, the Lord mighty in battle, he is the king of Glory

David goes on to describe the coming of Christ and the Virtues to those who languished in sin and darkness:

> invictae **virtutis** auxilium visitavit nos sedentes in tenebris delictorum et umbra mortis peccatorum.[52]
>
> with the help of his invincible host **(virtues)**, visited us sitting in the darkness of wrong-doing and in the deathly shadow of sin.

This imagery of the harrowing provides the basis for the personified virtues of the *Ordo*, who pledge to fight with the King, recalling David's description of the invincible host (the virtues).

Hell's question, "Who is this king of glory?," and its variations ("Who is this, so powerful that he does not fear death?"; "Who is this Jesus who by his words, draws the dead away from me, without a price?"; etc.) anticipate the Devil's question in the *Ordo*:

---

[52] *Gospel of Nicodemus*, ed. Kim, 41.

Quid est tantus timor? Est quid est tantus amor?
Ubi est pugnator et ubi est remunerator?

Who is this great fear? And who is this great love?
Where is the fighter, and where is the rewarder?

The parallels persist in scene 2, when each of the Virtues introduces herself and her power to help the Soul, a scene that others have noted resembles the *Ordo prophetarum* (Procession of the Prophets) performed at Matins of Christmas.[53] Both *Ordos*, I suggest, are indebted to the *Descensus Christi*, in which each of the patriarchs and prophets introduces himself, quoting lines from scripture that prophesy the coming of Christ their salvation. In the *Descensus*, following his defeat of the Devil, Christ leads the patriarchs and prophets out of Hell, calling "Come to me (*venite ad me*), all of my saints, who possess my image and likeness (*imaginem et similtudinem meam*)."[54] This text resonates in the repeated command of "*Venite ad me!*" uttered by the virtues of Humility, Obedience, Faith, and Contempt of the World in scene 2 of the *Ordo*.[55]

Hildegard would have known not only the *Descensus Christi ad Infernos* but also the liturgical commemorations of the harrowing from Holy Saturday. The Matins antiphon *Elevamini portae aeternales* repeats the dialogue from the abovementioned Psalm 23:7–9, while the responsory *Recessit pastor noster* narrates the events of the harrowing:[56]

RESPOND: *Recessit pastor noster fons aquae vivae ad cujus transitum sol obscuratus est, nam et ille captus est, qui captivum tenebat primum hominem. Hodie portas et seras pariter salvator noster destruxit.*
VERSE: *Destruxit quidam claustra inferni et subvertit potentiam diabolus.*

R. Our shepherd withdrew, the font of the living life, at whose passing the sun darkened. And even he was captured, who held captive the first man. Today, our savior had destroyed both the gates and their locks!
V. For he has destroyed the darkness of Hell and subverted the power of the Devil!

Perhaps the most vivid liturgical account of the harrowing is found in the processional antiphon *Cum rex gloriae*, which paraphrases the lament of the imprisoned patriarchs and prophets from the *Descensus Christi*:[57]

---

[53] See Karl Young, *The Drama of the Medieval Church*, vol. 2 (Oxford: Clarendon Press, 1933), 125–171; Rankin, "Liturgical Drama," 348–349; Fassler "Allegorical Architecture," 365 n. 56.
[54] *Gospel of Nicodemus*, ed. Kim, 44.   [55] Nos. 22, 24, 30, 32, 41.
[56] Engelberg Stiftsbibliothek Cod.103, fol. 122v; Cantus ID 002631 and 007509.
[57] Young, *Drama of the Medieval Church*, 151.

Cum rex gloriae Christus infernum debellaturus intraret, et chorus angelicus ante faciem ejus portas principum tolli praeciperet, sanctorum populus qui tenebatur in morte captivus, voce lacrimabili clamaverat: Advenisti desiderabilis, quem expectabamus in tenebris, ut educeres hac nocte vinculatos de claustris. Te nostra vocabant suspiria; te larga requirebant tormenta. Tu factus est spes desperatis, magna consolatio in tormentis, Alleluia.

When Christ, the king of glory, entered Hell to do battle, and the angelic chorus before him commanded the prince to lift the gates, the holy people who had been held captive in death, cried out in a tearful voice: "You have come, the one we wished for, whom we awaited in darkness, so that on this night, you might lead the enchained out of captivity. Our sighs called out to you, our great laments pined for you. You are the hope of the desperate [and] a great consolation in torment, alleluia."

At Mainz, as elsewhere, the antiphon *Cum rex gloriae* and the dialogue from Psalm 23 were part of the *Elevatio crucis* (elevation of the cross), a ritual celebrated on Holy Saturday in which the cross, buried in the sepulcher on Good Friday, was restored to the altar to signify the resurrection.[58] By the late Middle Ages, this dramatization of the harrowing of Hell ranged from simple dialogues to the fully acted-out plays transmitted in sources from Dublin, Barking, and Gertrudenberg.[59] Anne Bagnall Yardley writes that in the *Elevatio crucis* at Barking "the abbess and nuns were clearly intended to represent the patriarchs and prophets."[60] How Hildegard's congregation celebrated the *Elevatio* is unknown, but it was likely similar to that of Mainz in content and dramatic potential.

The language of the *Descensus Christi* and its liturgical celebration in Matins and the *Elevatio crucis* recurs in the *Ordo*. The *Descensus* refers to Christ in militant terms as the fighter (*praeliator*) who fights (*pugnare*) the Devil, trampling (*conculcare*) Death.[61] Hildegard describes the actions of the virtues and Soul as they combat the Devil in similar terms. Modesty cries, "I trample (*conculco*) all the filth of the Devil," while the Soul declares, "I fight (*pugno*) against you!"[62] Victory calls herself the "the swift and strong fighter (*pugnatrix*) ... I trample (*conculco*) the old serpent!"[63] Responding to the

---

[58] See Österreichische Nationalbibliothek, Cod. 1888, fol. 103. For further discussion of the *Elevatio crucis*, see Young, *Drama of the Medieval Church*, 149–177.

[59] See Oxford Bodleian MS Rawlinson liturgy. D.4 (Dublin); University College, Oxford MS 169 (Barking); Diözesanarchiv, Osnabrück GE 01 (Gertrudenberg).

[60] Yardley, *Performing Piety*, 146.   [61] *Gospel of Nicodemus*, ed. Kim, 40, 43.

[62] Hildegard of Bingen, *Ordo virtutum*, ed. Davidson, lines 47, 73.   [63] Ibid., line 51.

Devil's taunt, Chastity retorts, "in the mind of the most high, O Satan, I have trampled (*conculcavi*) your head."[64]

Thus Hildegard draws on the dramatic situation and language of Christ's harrowing of Hell to describe the Soul's own harrowing and triumph over evil. Importantly, however, in the *Ordo* it is not Christ who saves the languishing Soul but rather the virtues – the Christlike aspects of the Soul that dwell within her; and unlike the souls of the patriarchs and prophets, who are led by Christ out of Hell and into heaven, the Soul must continue to live in her incarnate state to achieve her salvation.

Conclusion

Hildegard's *Ordo virtutum*, while highly original and imaginative in expression, must be understood as grounded in twelfth-century women's Benedictine monasticism. In the *Ordo*, Hildegard weaves together elements of the Benedictine progression through the virtue of Humility with the mystical marriage of Christ and the soul from the twelfth-century Consecration of Virgins. The *Ordo* further builds on the responsory *Benedic nos domine . . . et omnes,* sung for the dedication of the church and on a weekly basis in procession to bless the house. These ideas are emplotted in a narrative that borrows elements from the *Descensus Christi ad Infernos* and liturgical retellings of the harrowing of Hell to create an embodied drama of the salvation of the soul. Each of these liturgies provides important background to understanding the dramatic situation and poetic language of the *Ordo virtutum*. As an embodied ritual, the *Ordo* uses the devices of impersonation and personification to make visible the invisible: the soul and its Christlike aspects, the virtues. The use of the embodied medium of drama is important because the entire premise of the *Ordo* is about the difficulties of the soul's embodiment or incarnation. As the *Rule* makes clear, the body is necessary for human salvation, forming one side of the ladder of Humility opposite the soul through which the soul may ascend to heaven.

Further Reading

Latin and Music Editions and English Translations

Hildegard of Bingen. *Lieder: Faksimile Riesencodex (Hs.2) der Hessischen Landesbibliothek Wiesbaden, fol. 466–481v,* ed. Lorenz Welker. Commentary

---

[64] Ibid., line 82.

by Michael Klaper. Elementa musicae 1. Wiesbaden: Ludwig Reichert Verlag, 1998. [Facsimile]

Ordo virtutum. In *Hildegardis Bingensis: Opera minora*, ed. Peter Dronke. Corpus Christianorum Continuatio Mediaevalis 226. Turnhout: Brepols, 2007, 505–521.

Ordo virtutum, ed. Audrey Ekdahl Davidson. Kalamazoo, MI: Medieval Institute Publications, 1985.

Ordo virtutum, ed. and French trans. Luca Ricossa. Geneva: Lulu, 2013.

Ordo Virtutum: A Comparative Edition, ed. Vincent Corrigan. Lion's Bay, BC: Institute of Mediaeval Music, 2013.

Audio and Video Recordings

For a complete list of recordings of the Ordo virtutum, see the online discography of Hildegard's music: Roberge, Pierre-F. *Hildegard von Bingen (1098–1179): A Discography*. Updates by Todd McComb. www.medieval.org/emfaq/composers/hildegard.html

Hildegard von Bingen in Portrait: Ordo Virtutum, directed by Michael Fields and Evelyn Tubb. DVD. BBC/Opus Arte OA 0874 D, 2003.

Sequentia. *Ordo virtutum*. LP and CD. Deutsche Harmonia Mundi 77051-2-RG, 1982.

Secondary Literature

Davidson, Audrey Ekdahl, ed. *The Ordo Virtutum of Hildegard of Bingen: Critical Studies*. Early Drama, Art, and Music Monograph Series, 18. Kalamazoo, MI: Medieval Institute Publications, 1992.

Dronke, Peter. *Nine Medieval Plays*. Cambridge: Cambridge University Press, 1994.

Fassler, Margot E. "Allegorical Architecture in Scivias: Hildegard's Setting for the *Ordo Virtutum*." *Journal of the American Musicological* Society 67, no. 2 (2014): 317–378.

Norton, Michael. *Liturgical Drama and the Reimagining of Medieval Theater: Early Drama, Art, and Music*. Kalamazoo, MI: Medieval Institute Publications, 2017.

Rankin, Susan. "Liturgical Drama." In Richard Crocker and David Hiley, eds., *The New Oxford History of Music, Vol. 2: The Early Middle Ages to 1300*. Oxford: Oxford University Press, 1990, 310–352.

Yardley, Ann Bagnall. *Performing Piety: Musical Culture in Medieval English Nunneries*. New York: Palgrave Macmillan, 2006.

CHAPTER 12

Picturing Hildegard of Bingen's Sight: Illuminating Her Visions

Nathaniel M. Campbell

Of the eighteen known manuscript copies of Hildegard of Bingen's visionary trilogy, two stand out in particular because of their distinctive illustrations, so often reproduced in countless books, journals, and magazines, as
well as in many and diverse online sites. With their arresting images and
gleaming fields of silver and gold, the illustrations found in the
Rupertsberg copies of Hildegard's *Scivias* (Know the Ways) produced
during her lifetime and *Liber divinorum operum* (Book of Divine Works)
produced some forty years after her death are among the more popular
elements of the visionary's work today. Together with her music, they lend
themselves to our multimedia sensibilities; indeed, Margot Fassler has
developed a digitally animated planetarium projection of Hildegard's
"Cosmic Egg" from the *Scivias* manuscript (in Figure 12.1), accompanied
by her music, to showcase Hildegard's ideas about the creation and
structure of the cosmos.[1] This image highlights for us the illustration's
enigmatic power: the egg's outer layer bristles uncontrollably with golden
tongues of fire, their edges lined with red and stippled with little white dots
to fool the eye into seeing them move. Contained within are its successive
membranes (*pelles*): a black band set with clusters of red-striking stones;
a deep blue field studded with gold stars and white starbursts; a layer of
green waves held within green clouds; a circle of watery blue; and at last,
a central round with the four elements in a simple landscape: a tongue of
blue water lapping at green hills of earth, with golden air above and black
fire below. Meanwhile, four strange, triple-headed groupings are stationed
throughout the layers, blowing all around the rest of the instrument.

Cosmological diagrams were quite common in twelfth-century manuscripts, and an eye familiar with such imagery would recognize the basic

---

[1] Fassler previewed the project in her 2014 plenary lecture to the American Musicological Society,
"Hildegard's Cosmos and Its Music: Making a Digital Model for the Modern Planetarium": https://
youtu.be/qx2oTsm7XB4.

Figure 12.1 *Scivias* 1.3, The Cosmos as an Egg; Wiesbaden, Hochschul- und
Landesbibliothek RheinMain, MS 1 (missing since 1945), fol. 14r. © Rheinisches
Bildarchiv Köln, rba_013324.

concept. Yet this ovoid's transgressive undulations set it apart from the traditional regularity of such imagery, begging the viewer to investigate its peculiarities further. So we must turn the page, to engage with Hildegard's text and discover what this image is supposed to mean. Only then do we hear from "the voice from Heaven" that this model of the cosmos shows "not just the things that are visible and temporal, but also the things that are invisible and eternal" (*Scivias* 1.3.1). The firmament itself becomes a map for the history of salvation, with the great star at its peak representing the Son of God himself, "the sun of justice" (*Scivias* 1.3.4). The successive layers, meanwhile – of fire both bright and dark, of purest ether and watery air, as well as the four winds scattered throughout them – signify the constant tension between the dark forces of the devil and the light of the faith contending against him.[2]

The *Scivias* illustrations thus invite you into a deeper engagement with the text of Hildegard's visions and their meaning. Much of their popular reception today, however, cuts off that engagement by springing the images from their original context and turning them almost into talismans. Often referred to as "mandalas," their composition is treated as practically ahistorical. Yet the power of the *Scivias* illustrations is not so much mystical as communicative. Hildegard designed them as part of a larger apparatus to make the ideas in her visions more accessible. They are neither literal records of her original visionary experiences (though some visual elements may correspond to those experiences) nor designed for the cultivation of visionary or contemplative experiences. Instead, their purpose is primarily didactic. They are carefully crafted to combine specific details of Hildegard's visions with other visual vocabularies of twelfth-century Christian Europe familiar to readers of the manuscript. In this way, the images serve to orient before one plunges into the often bewildering world of Hildegard's visions.[3]

Unfortunately, the original Rupertsberg *Scivias* manuscript (Wiesbaden, Hochschul- und Landesbibliothek RheinMain, MS 1) has been lost since 1945, after evacuation to Dresden for "safekeeping" during the war – though the other major Wiesbaden Hildegard manuscript (MS 2, the *Riesencodex*) had been kept in the same bank vault and was later smuggled out of East Germany

---

[2] Hildegard of Bingen, *Scivias*, trans. Mother Columba Hart and Jane Bishop (New York: Paulist Press, 1990), 93–105.

[3] I first laid out this thesis, along with an historiographical review, in Nathaniel M. Campbell, "*Imago expandit splendorem suum*: Hildegard of Bingen's Visio-Theological Designs in the Rupertsberg *Scivias* Manuscript," *Eikón/Imago* 2, no. 2 (2013): 1–68.

in 1948, so hope springs eternal that the *Scivias* will someday turn up, too.[4] Fortunately, black-and-white photographs of the original were made in the 1920s, concurrently with a facsimile hand-painted by the nuns of the Abbey of St. Hildegard in Eibingen. Although the facsimile's color images are more widely known,[5] the photographs will be used here, with color information corroborated against the image catalogue of Hiltgart Keller's 1933 study of the original manuscript.[6] At the end of this chapter, we will also look briefly at the equally famous illustrations for Hildegard's third great visionary volume, the *Liber divinorum operum* (Lucca, Biblioteca Statale, MS 1942). That manuscript was also likely made in the Rupertsberg scriptorium but a generation after Hildegard's death, perhaps in the 1220s as part of a (failed) bid for the visionary's canonization. It allows us to see how the nuns of Hildegard's monastery followed their holy mother's late impulse to use visual elements as part of a wider program to make her work more accessible. Its cosmological vision (part I, vision 2) also explicitly revises the *Scivias*'s Egg, thus highlighting the evolution (and regularization) of that image. Both manuscripts – one designed by Hildegard, the other inspired by her – reveal a mission not only to celebrate and cement her visionary authority but also to integrate her originality into the wider traditions of medieval Christianity.

The Visionary and the Visual

As a category of experience, Hildegard's visions were, in fact, rather commonplace in medieval Christianity, as Wendy Love Anderson's chapter in this volume elucidates.[7] With ample scriptural precedents, it was taken for granted that God would reveal himself and his messages in prophetic visions. The most common experiences included otherworldly journeys, glimpses of one's or others' eternal fate, and, increasingly in the

---

[4] Jennifer Bain, "History of a Book: Hildegard of Bingen's 'Riesencodex' and World War II," *Plainsong and Medieval Music* 27, no. 2 (2018): 143–170.

[5] A link to an online gallery is given in the manuscript section of the bibliography; the reproductions have also been printed at full size and color, together with detailed schematics of their visual elements, in Sara Salvadori, *Hildegard von Bingen: A Journey into the Images*, trans. Sarah Elizabeth Cree and Susan Ann White (Milan: Skira, 2019).

[6] Hiltgart L. Keller, *Mittelrheinische Buchmalereien in Handschriften aus dem Kreise der Hiltgart von Bingen* (Stuttgart: Surkamp, 1933).

[7] See Anderson, Chapter 9, this volume. Barbara Newman, "What Did It Mean to Say 'I Saw'? The Clash between Theory and Practice in Medieval Visionary Culture," *Speculum* 80 (2005): 1–43; Bernard McGinn, "Hildegard of Bingen As Visionary and Exegete," in Alfred Haverkamp, ed., *Hildegard von Bingen in ihrem historischen Umfeld* (Mainz: Trierer Historische Forschungen, 2000), 321–350, at 321–326.

later Middle Ages, interactions with the human Jesus or his mother, Mary. Moreover, the monastic prayer practices of *lectio divina* – the meditative reading of scripture – cultivated a predisposition to such imaginative experiences of the divine. St. Augustine's definition of three modes of vision – physical, spiritual, and intellectual – in book 12 of his *De Genesi ad litteram* (Literal Commentary on Genesis) provided a framework for understanding human access to divine truths in the second and third modes. Spiritual vision, he argued, was the inner sight of the mind and imagination, while intellectual vision was a direct understanding of divine truth, the imageless vision of the angels.[8]

Hildegard's own descriptions of her visionary experiences fit broadly within these Augustinian categories.[9] The main body of her work was spiritual vision, though her interior senses of sight and hearing were often synaesthetically fused. As she explains in a letter written near the end of her life to her admirer and final secretary, Guibert of Gembloux:

> But even in my infancy, before my bones, muscles, and veins had reached their full strength, I was possessed of this visionary gift in my soul, and it abides with me still up to the present day. In these visions my spirit rises, as God wills, to the heights of heaven and into the shifting winds, and it ranges among various peoples, even those very far away. And since I see in such a fashion, my perception of things depends on the shifting of the clouds and other elements of creation. Still, I do not hear these things with bodily ears, nor do I perceive them with the cogitations of my heart or the evidence of my five senses. I see them only in my sight, with my eyes wide open, and thus I never suffer the defect of ecstasy in these visions . . .
>
> The light that I see is not local and confined. It is far brighter than a lucent cloud through which the sun shines. And I can discern neither its height nor its length nor its breadth. This light I have named "the shadow of the Living Light," and just as the sun and moon and stars are reflected in water, so too are writings, words, virtues, and deeds of men reflected back to me from it . . . Moreover, the words I see and hear in the vision are not like the words of human speech, but are like a blazing flame and a cloud that moves through clear air.[10]

This inner light seems to have been Hildegard's near constant companion, and it is within its *umbra*, its shadow or reflection (or, as Bernard McGinn

---

[8] St. Augustine, *The Literal Meaning of Genesis, Books 7–12*, trans. J. H. Taylor (New York: Paulist Press, 1982), 178–222.

[9] See esp. Peter Dronke, *Women Writers of the Middle Ages: A Critical Study of Texts from Perpetua (†203) to Marguerite Porete (†1310)* (Cambridge: Cambridge University Press, 1984), 145–147; and McGinn, "Hildegard of Bingen As Visionary and Exegete," 326–337.

[10] Letter 103r, in *The Letters of Hildegard of Bingen*, trans. Joseph L. Baird and Radd K. Ehrman, 3 vols. (Oxford: Oxford University Press, 1998), 2:23.

suggests, upon its movie screen), that Hildegard sees and hears all that would form her voluminous writings.[11] On a few occasions, however, she experienced something much deeper and more delightful – the Living Light itself. Though it likely corresponds to Augustine's intellectual vision, Hildegard speaks of it with sensuality: its warmth consumed her heart and brain in 1141 to commission the *Scivias*;[12] and it distilled "drops of sweet rain into [her] soul's knowing" in the 1160s to spark the *Liber divinorum operum*.[13]

Despite fitting into standard medieval typologies, however, those visionary experiences also stand apart in several ways. Hildegard's time saw the development of devotional practices in western Europe intensely focused on Christ's humanity that would become the matrix for most later medieval visionary experiences.[14] Visual representation was often an essential element in such devotion.[15] Certain later medieval books that might seem to recall the striking qualities of Hildegard's *Scivias*, such as the Rothschild Canticles (ca. 1300),[16] were specifically designed to provoke visionary experiences in the meditational practices of their privileged users. Hildegard, however, did not participate in most of the devotional practices that came to characterize medieval women religious. She counseled moderation and discretion rather than the extreme ascetic practices common in later centuries; and she showed little interest in the physical suffering of Christ, focusing instead on the cosmic dimensions of the creative, incarnate, and redemptive Word.

Her writings, moreover, are not mystical, for their focus is not union with the Godhead but the communication of divine truths.[17] On the few occasions when she records losing consciousness in the flood of the Living Light, the result was not mystical union but inspired understanding of

---

[11] McGinn, "Hildegard of Bingen As Visionary and Exegete," 328.

[12] *Scivias*, "Declaration" (*Protestificatio*), trans. Hart and Bishop, 59.

[13] Recounted in an autobiographical passage in the *Vita S. Hildegardis* 2.16, Anna Silvas, ed. and trans., *Jutta and Hildegard: The Biographical Sources* (Turnhout: Brepols, 1998; rprt., University Park, PA: Pennsylvania State University Press, 1999), 179; on the dating of this experience, see further Embach, Chapter 1, this volume.

[14] Rachel Fulton, *From Judgment to Passion: Devotion to Christ and the Virgin Mary, 800–1200* (New York: Columbia University Press, 2002); and Caroline Walker Bynum, *Holy Feast and Holy Fast: The Religious Significance of Food to Medieval Women* (Berkeley: University of California Press, 1988).

[15] Newman, "What Did It Mean to Say 'I Saw'?," 14–33; Jeffrey Hamburger, *The Visual and the Visionary: Art and Female Spirituality in Late Medieval Germany* (New York: Zone Books, 1998).

[16] Yale University, Beinecke MS 404: https://brbl-dl.library.yale.edu/vufind/Record/3432521; see Barbara Newman, "Contemplating the Trinity: Text, Image, and the Origins of the Rothschild Canticles," *Gesta* 52, no. 2 (2013): 133–159.

[17] Caroline Walker Bynum, "Preface" to *Scivias*, trans. Hart and Bishop, 2–3; but see Bernard McGinn's nuanced assessment in *The Growth of Mysticism: Gregory the Great through the 12th Century* (New York: Crossroad, 1994), 333–336.

God's Word. She repeatedly stresses that her common visionary mode was wakeful rather than in ecstasy, because what she saw was ordered not for her own delight but toward the instruction of the faithful. Her visionary gift came with a prophetic mission, to speak and to write "in such a way that the hearer, receiving the words of his instructor, may expound them in those words, according to that will, vision and instruction."[18] The visionary experiences that Hildegard described in words are teaching tools, illuminated frameworks that "the voice from heaven" fills with verbal meaning.

The uncompromisingly prophetic and therefore didactic mission of Hildegard's visions provides a unity to her life's work not found in many other medieval visionaries. As Barbara Newman has noted, Hildegard's visions are uncommonly visually detailed, and Kathryn Kerby-Fulton has compared their descriptions to the practice of modern art historians of cataloguing the visual features of a work of art before assessing its iconography, or visual meaning.[19] This is because every intricate detail of Hildegard's visions – their shapes, colors, placements, movements, and even the speeches of visionary figures – becomes the starting point for the exegesis that forms the bulk of her theological writing. Her fundamental method is to treat her verbal descriptions of her visions as one would treat the biblical text. To be sure, it is God's voice, and not her own, she insists, that explicates her vision texts. But the allegorical logic by which her visions, which at the literal level are often obscure, bordering sometimes on incoherent, unfold into lavish landscapes rich with theological meaning, is inherited from the traditions of scriptural exegesis. It is only in that interpretive stage that the underlying unity of meaning becomes apparent among a disjointed collection of images.[20]

The Rupertsberg *Scivias* Manuscript

The illustrations in the Rupertsberg *Scivias* operate in a similar way, as "visual exegesis" of Hildegard's visions.[21] When the aged visionary set her

---

[18] *Scivias*, "Declaration," trans. Hart and Bishop, 59.

[19] Barbara Newman, "The Visionary Texts and Visual Worlds of Religious Women," in Jeffrey Hamburger and Susan Marti, eds. *Crown and Veil: Female Monasticism from the Fifth to the Fifteenth Centuries* (New York: Columbia University Press, 2008), 151–171, at 156–157; Kathryn Kerby-Fulton, "Hildegard of Bingen," in Alastair Minnis and Rosalynn Voaden, eds., *Medieval Holy Women in the Christian Tradition, c. 1100–c.1500* (Turnhout: Brepols, 2010), 343–369, at 359–360.

[20] Christel Meier, "Zwei Modelle von Allegorie im 12. Jahrhundert: Das allegorische Verfahren Hildegards von Bingen und Alans von Lille," in Walter Haug, ed., *Formen und Funktionen der Allegorie* (Stuttgart: Metzler, 1979), 70–89, at 77–79.

[21] I follow generally the approaches of Christel Meier and Lieselotte Saurma-Jeltsch, with one important difference: while they deny Hildegard's hand in designing the illustrations, I affirm it. See Meier, "Zum Verhältnis von Text und Illustration im überlieferten Werk Hildegards von

scriptorium to work on this deluxe illuminated manuscript in the last decade of her life (i.e. the late 1160s and 1170s), she very carefully designed its layout and structure in order to make the work more accessible.[22] Each of its twenty-six visions begins with a list of *capitula*, or chapter summaries, followed by the illustration(s). Then comes the vision text itself, followed by its explication in Hildegard's visionary voice, with each chapter summary repeated in rubrics (red ink) before its respective chapter.[23] With its thirty-five illustrations and doubled distribution of chapter summaries, this *Scivias* manuscript departs from the format used by all the other manuscripts of Hildegard's works produced in her scriptorium during her lifetime. Its elaborate framework is designed to guide the reader, using both textual summaries and a visual vocabulary that situates Hildegard's unique images within the theological traditions from which she speaks, as well as the communal practices of her monastery. It should, moreover, be understood as part of a larger project of her final decade to shape her "public persona" and strengthen the legacy of her prophetic teachings.[24]

Rather than always reproducing Hildegard's visions literally, the illustrations sometimes draw on other visual vocabularies to help one understand what they mean. As I will show, we can glimpse Hildegard's hand in designing the illustrations as orientation tools for the nuns who would read the manuscript when the images intentionally diverge from the text or provide information not found there. Many of these divergences come through the adoption of traditional Christian iconography in place of the more unusual images described in Hildegard's visions. Despite the

Bingen," in Anton Ph. Brück, ed., *Hildegard von Bingen, 1179–1979. Festschrift zum 800. Todestag der Heiligen* (Mainz: Selbstverlag der Gesellschaft für mittelrheinische Kirchengeschichte, 1979), 159–169; Meier, "Calcare caput draconis: Prophetische Bildkonfiguration in Visionstext und Illustration: zur Vision 'Scivias' II, 7," in Edeltraud Forster, ed., *Hildegard von Bingen: Prophetin durch die Zeiten* (Freiburg im Breisgau: Herder, 1997), 340–358; and Saurma-Jeltsch, *Die Miniaturen im "Liber Scivias" der Hildegard von Bingen: Die Wucht der Vision und die Ordnung der Bilder* (Wiesbaden: Reichert, 1998).

[22] For dating, I follow Albert Derolez, "The Manuscript Transmission of Hildegard of Bingen's Writings: The State of the Problem," in Burnett and Dronke, *Hildegard of Bingen: The Context of Her Thought and Art*, 17–28, at 24; see also Campbell, "*Imago expandit splendorem suum*," 10–19.

[23] José Carlos Santos Paz, "Modo de percepción y modo de representación: Las *tabulae* del *Scivias*," in Claudio Leonardi, Marcello Morelli, and Francesco Santi, eds., *Fabula in tabula: Una storia degli indici dal manoscritto al testo elettronico*, Quaderni di cultura mediolatina 13 (Spoleto: Centro italiano di studi sull'alto medioevo, 1995), 79–97.

[24] Barbara Newman, "Hildegard and Her Hagiographers: The Remaking of Female Sainthood," in Catherine M. Mooney, ed., *Gendered Voices: Medieval Saints and Their Interpreters* (Philadelphia: University of Pennsylvania Press, 1999), 16–34; and John Van Engen, "Letters and the Public Persona of Hildegard," in Alfred Haverkamp, ed., *Hildegard von Bingen in ihrem historischen Umfeld* (Mainz: Trierer Historische Forschungen, 2000), 375–418.

peculiarities of the visions themselves, the overarching structure of the *Scivias* is on par with contemporary illustrated twelfth-century projects aimed at telling the encyclopedic breadth of salvation history, such as Lambert of St. Omer's *Liber floridus* (Book of Flowers) or Herrad of Hohenbourg's *Hortus deliciarum* (Garden of Delights), like Hildegard's *Scivias*, a manuscript made by women. More explicitly visionary aspects of the illustrations draw on the rich traditions of illustrating the Revelation of St. John, while quite a few of the *Scivias* images pull details and compositions from the pictorial repertoire related to the creation accounts in Genesis. Hildegard also likely looked to the visual vocabulary developed in liturgical volumes like Gospel books, missals, and psalters, to illustrate the major events of salvation history.[25] Such books would have been intimately familiar to the women of her monastery, and so Hildegard could draw on them to design illustrations for her own manuscript that would provide them with visual reference points while venturing through the challenging text. She may also have incorporated designs associated with the special crowns and veils used in her monastery, thus linking the illuminated manuscript directly into the life of the community that produced it.

Let us look at illustrations from the first two visions of the second part of *Scivias*, to see the various sources Hildegard used and the resulting dynamic between the images and the text. The image of the Trinity in *Scivias* 2.2 (Figure 12.2) is one of the visual keystones of the manuscript. Its concentric circles and triadic color scheme of gold, blue, and silver reappear in the illustrations for the preceding and following visions (*Scivias* 2.1 and 2.3, fols. 41v and 51r), making it an icon for the Trinity's work in the history of creation and redemption. Sprung from their circles, the colors also appear together in other images of the manuscript to denote the divine presence, such as in the background of the heavenly symphony in *Scivias* 3.13 (fol. 229r). Yet Hildegard's text itself does not specify the circular schema, and although the Son's sapphire blue is as described, the metallic pigments are not strictly congruent with the vision's words:

> Then I saw a bright, calm light [*serenissima lux*], and in this light a human figure the color of sapphire, which was all blazing with a gentle, red-glowing fire [*rutilans ignis*]. And that bright, calm light bathed the whole of the red-glowing fire, and the red-glowing fire bathed the bright, calm light; and the

---

[25] For comparison, see the detailed studies of Keller, *Mittelrheinische Buchmalereien*; and Saurma-Jeltsch, *Die Miniaturen*; and the suggestions in Kerby-Fulton, "Hildegard of Bingen," 358–362.

Figure 12.2 *Scivias* 2.2, The Trinity; Wiesbaden, Hochschul- und Landesbibliothek RheinMain, MS 1 (missing since 1945), fol. 47r. © Rheinisches Bildarchiv Köln, rba_013331.

bright, calm light and the red-glowing fire poured over the whole human figure, so that the three were one light in one power of potential.[26]

The Father's *serenissima lux* has been depicted in gold overlaid with concentric lines of red or brown lacquer, while the Spirit's red-glowing fire (*rutilans ignis*) has been crafted in silver overlaid with concentric lines of yellow. Although the manuscript color scheme for this Trinity does not intuitively flow from the vision text, we can find evidence from other of Hildegard's writings from her last decade to show that she developed it herself. In her treatise on the Trinitarian theology of the Athanasian Creed, written in the early 1170s as part of a series of shorter works meant to distill her ideas for the benefit of her community of nuns, she revisits the fire imagery used for God in *Scivias* 2.1. Distinguishing the fire (the Father), the flame (the Son), and a powerful breeze (the Spirit), she notes, "Material and visible fire is the color of gold."[27] Gold and silver come together, moreover, in the alloy of electrum that appears among the elaborate allegorical adornments crafted by the apostles for Lady Justice in the sweeping final vision of the *Liber divinorum operum*, completed in 1173. There, the apostle Bartholomew's gift is a set of electrum plating for Justice's forearms, divided into three sections connected with gold chains, to represent "the true Trinity – three persons in one God, invisibly and ineffably connected to one another."[28] Put together, these indicate that Hildegard could translate her Trinitarian imagery from fire into metal, casting the Father's fire in gold and combining it with silver.

The circular schema of the *Scivias* Trinity image, meanwhile, may reflect another piece of elaborate jewelry that Hildegard describes – not merely an allegorical fiction this time but the real coronets that her nuns were said to have worn upon their heads for high feast days. These "crowns of gold filigree," along with long, white silk veils and gold rings, were notorious enough to be criticized in a letter from Tengswich, the superior of a congregation of reformed canonesses at Andernach, around 1150.[29] Such criticism, however, did not deter Hildegard from giving the liturgical

---

[26] *Scivias* 2.2, trans. adapted from Hart and Bishop, 161.

[27] *Explanatio Symboli Sancti Athanasii*, ed. C. P. Evans, in *Hildegardis Bingensis, Opera Minora* (Turnhout: Brepols, 2007), 116, lines 206–209.

[28] Hildegard of Bingen, *The Book of Divine Works*, trans. Nathaniel M. Campbell (Washington, DC: The Catholic University of America Press, 2018), 3.5.9: 438.

[29] Letter 53, in *Letters*, trans. Baird and Ehrman, 1:127; see Dronke, *Women Writers*, 165–169; Alfred Haverkamp, "Tenxwind von Andernach und Hildegard von Bingen: Zwei "Weltanschauungen" in der Mitte des 12. Jahrhunderts," in *Institutionen, Kultur und Gesellschaft im Mittelalter: Festschrift für Josef Fleckenstein*, ed. Lutz Fenske, Werner Rösener, and Thomas Zotz (Sigmaringen: Jan Thorbecke Verlag, 1984), 515–548.

headgear divine sanction in her vision of the throng of virgins held at the Church's breast in *Scivias* 2.5:

> Some of these had their heads veiled in white, adorned with a gold circlet; and above them, as if sculpted on the veils, was the likeness of the glorious and ineffable Trinity as it was represented to me earlier [i.e. in *Scivias* 2.2], and on their foreheads the Lamb of God, and on their necks a human figure, and on the right ear cherubim, and on the left ear the other kinds of angels; and from the likeness of the glorious and supernal Trinity golden rays extended to these other images.[30]

In a letter to Guibert of Gembloux of about 1175, Hildegard provides an additional, crucial detail: to signify the Trinity, these circlets are "of three colors joined into one."[31] The Trinitarian triple color was not mentioned in Tengswich's early description of the crowns and likely corresponds to the *Scivias* Trinity illustrations that Hildegard later designed: silver and gold, perhaps "joined into one" as the alloy electrum; and blue, which was one of the most common colors of enamel used in twelfth-century metalwork in the Rhineland and the famous workshops of Limoges. Kathryn Kerby-Fulton has proposed the influence of such enamelwork as an alternative to the migraine hypothesis that was put forward by Charles Singer and championed by Madeline Caviness to explain the brilliant light effects of the Rupertsberg manuscript's images.[32] This revives a suggestion made in the 1930s by one of the last scholars to work with the original manuscript, Hiltgart Keller, who noted that strongly contoured figures against fields of gold, or conversely, golden figures amid fields of blue, are features shared between the manuscript and contemporary enamelwork.[33]

When younger nuns in Hildegard's monastery would open the illuminated *Scivias* for the first time, their experiences wearing their distinctive crowns would have helped them to recognize the meaning of the golden and blue circles at the top of the illustration for the first vision of part 2 (Figure 12.3). This vision retells the story of creation and fall (explained once already in *Scivias* 1.2) and then pushes forward into the story of redemption, the focus of the work's second part. As with the following

---

[30] *Scivias* 2.5, trans. Hart and Bishop, 201.
[31] Letter 103r, in *Letters*, trans. Baird and Ehrman, 2:24.
[32] Kerby-Fulton, "Hildegard of Bingen," 362–363; for Caviness's contributions, see the list of her works in the bibliography; but note also the important critique in Katherine Foxhall, "Making Modern Migraine Medieval: Men of Science, Hildegard of Bingen and the Life of a Retrospective Diagnosis," *Medical History* 58, no. 3 (2014): 354–374, at 371–372.
[33] Keller, *Mittelrheinische Buchmalereien*, 137; see also Keller's discussion of the similarities in frames and border motifs on 25 and 29.

Figure 12.3 *Scivias* 2.1, Creation, Fall, and Redemption; Wiesbaden, Hochschul-
und Landesbibliothek RheinMain, MS 1 (missing since 1945), fol. 41v. Photo credit:
© Rheinisches Bildarchiv Köln, rba_013330.

vision, this one opens with a Trinitarian light show, "a blazing fire . . . with a flame in it the color of the sky, which burned ardently as with a gentle breath." Immediately, however, text and illustration begin to diverge. The text describes the Word's sky-colored flame blazing forth to strike blows upon the atmosphere, "a dark sphere of great magnitude," slowly hammering it like a blacksmith into the created universe.[34] The flame then "extended itself to a little clod of mud which lay at the bottom of the atmosphere, and warmed it so that it was made flesh and blood, and blew upon it until it rose up a living human."[35]

Yet rather than the Son's sky-blue, it is the Spirit's silver finger that descends from the Trinitarian circles at the top of the illustration, down through the darkness to rouse Adam's head from the red earth. The discrepancy is, however, didactic. The text gives no concrete role in creation to the "gentle breath" of the Spirit that "was borne over the waters" (Genesis 1:2), so Hildegard has used the illustration to clarify the Spirit's presence, first brooding as the background silver of the top and bottom registers, and then sweeping down to breathe the breath of life into Adam's face (Genesis 2:7). Moreover, instead of a smith's forge in the central band of mottled brown and black threads, there appears a standard set of roundels depicting the six days of creation from the first chapter of Genesis (known as the Hexaemeron). Hildegard has invoked here traditional Christian iconography in place of the more unusual image of the vision text, precisely in order to make the image easier to understand. At the same time that she was designing the illustrations for this manuscript, Hildegard was also writing a full-fledged commentary on the Hexaemeron, in the second part of her *Liber divinorum operum* – the only medieval woman known to do so.[36] The concurrence of her design of the *Scivias* images and her work on Genesis subtly appears in the painter's simile she uses early in that commentary to describe God's planning of the cosmos: "he did as one does who is planning out certain forms, for first one marks out each part with one's compass, and then afterwards paints each one with colors."[37] With the works of the six days of creation in the front of her mind, Hildegard similarly planned out the *Scivias* illustrations with a more traditional image than she had once seen in her vision.

When first looking at the illustration for *Scivias* 2.1, one's eye moves from the Trinitarian circles at the top down along the silver finger into the circle of creation. There is, however, a countervailing movement arising

---

[34] See also *Vita S. Hildegardis* 2.16, in Silvas, *Jutta and Hildegard*, 179.
[35] *Scivias* 2.1, trans. Hart and Bishop, 149.
[36] *The Book of Divine Works* 2.1.17–49, trans. Campbell, 287–347.
[37] *The Book of Divine Works* 2.1.17, trans. Campbell, 288.

from the swell of blue and gold at the bottom of the image (echoing the Trinitarian circles above), with a brilliant golden figure bursting up with flames into the muddied middle. With his flowing hair and beard and hand raised in blessing, the figure is easily recognizable as Christ, the Redeemer. Yet there is again an apparent divergence from the text, which describes the Word's flame being "miraculously absorbed" into "a radiance like the dawn . . . without being separated from the blazing fire," and then emerging again from that dawn as "a serene Man . . . Who poured out His brightness into the darkness."[38] The explication of this vision text refers to "the great and venerable counsel" that was fulfilled "in the bright and roseate serenity" of this dawn – an explanation nearly as obscure as the vision text itself.[39]

By aligning this dawn light with her own Trinitarian icon, however, Hildegard allows the movement of the visual image to clarify what words alone struggle to convey: the dynamic of creative movement out from the divine source above, and of recreative and redemptive movement back to it from below. Salvation history is, for Hildegard, a continual series of creative emanations from the divine foreknowledge, of falling away therefrom, and of returning thereto. At the heart of this classically Neoplatonic cycle is the Incarnation, which for Hildegard was eternally planned, the core of God's "great and venerable counsel" for all creation. Here is how she explained this in a prayer at the opening of *Scivias* 3.1:

> Grant me to make known the divine counsel, which was ordained of old, as I can and should: how You willed Your Son to become incarnate and become a human being within Time; which You willed before creation in Your rectitude and the fire of the Dove, the Holy Spirit, so that Your Son might rise from a Virgin in the splendid beauty of the sun and be clothed with true humanity, a man's form assumed for Man's sake.[40]

The dawn light of the Incarnation was thus also a favorite of Hildegard's images for the Virgin Mary (especially in the poetic texts of her musical compositions), whose elliptical presence in the illustration of *Scivias* 2.1 is perhaps the most intriguing. When Christel Meier attempted to interpret this image without recourse to the text, the only element that she could not derive from the repertoire of traditional Christian motifs was the appearance of a man in the upper right, emerging from the darkness to smell a white flower.[41] Although some interpreters have astutely noted that the

---

[38] *Scivias* 2.1, trans. Hart and Bishop, 149.   [39] *Scivias* 2.1.11, trans. Hart and Bishop, 154.
[40] *Scivias* 3.1, trans. Hart and Bishop, 309–310.
[41] Meier, "Zum Verhältnis von Text und Illustration," 161–165.

flower echoes the white lily that was a common companion of the Virgin Mary in scenes of the Annunciation,[42] it is also possible that Hildegard intentionally chose to illustrate this element of her vision literally, without any visually exegetical support, in order to focus the viewer-reader's attention upon it as she turned the page to begin reading the text. For when one of her nuns would reach chapter 8, she would learn that God had offered to Adam "the sweet precept of obedience" but that he did "not taste it with his mouth or touch it with his hands" and so "sank into the gaping mouth of death."[43] This startling inversion of the Fall transforms the biblical image of Eve picking and tasting the fruit of the knowledge of good and evil into Adam's failure to pick and taste the flower of obedience. Moreover, it highlights for Hildegard's nuns the act of obedience to God that gave the Virgin Mary's body the power to bear the God-Man, to rescue humankind from those jaws of death. This power, too, they share by participation in her holy virginity, to be Brides of Christ adorned with crowns to honor him, bearing the gleaming gold, blue, and silver of the life-giving Trinity. Hildegard's illustrations for this *Scivias* manuscript were thus designed specifically to speak to the nuns of her monastery, to aid them in understanding her teachings.

The Lucca *Liber divinorum operum* Manuscript

In the decades after Hildegard's death in 1179, those nuns dedicated themselves to affirming their holy mother's sanctity and prophetic authority. In addition to the completion of her saintly *vita* (biography), the composition of liturgical materials to commemorate her feast (September 17), and efforts to encourage pilgrimage to her shrine and collect miracle reports as a result, they undertook artistic projects to put her holy power on display. For example, they produced a massive embroidered altar cloth (called an "antependium") in the 1220s that showed Hildegard with a saint's nimbus or halo and her characteristic white silk veil, standing before Christ with Saints Rupert and Martin.[44] At the same time, they commissioned a deluxe edition of the *Liber divinorum operum*,

---

[42] Barbara Newman, *Sister of Wisdom: St. Hildegard's Theology of the Feminine* (Berkeley: University of California Press, 1987; 2nd ed., 1997), 168; and Rebecca L. Garber, "Where Is the Body? Images of Eve and Mary in the *Scivias*," in Maud Burnett McInerney, ed., *Hildegard of Bingen: A Book of Essays* (New York: Garland Publishing, 1998), 103–132, at 110.

[43] *Scivias* 2.1.8, trans. Hart and Bishop, 153.

[44] Newman, "Hildegard and Her Hagiographers," 30; see also Margot Fassler's arguments on the Rupertsberg's embroidery workshop in her forthcoming *Cosmos, Liturgy, and the Arts in the Twelfth Century: Hildegard's Illuminated Scivias* (Philadelphia: University of Pennsylvania, forthcoming).

replete with full-page illustrations for each of its ten visions. This manuscript, now housed in the Biblioteca Statale di Lucca (MS 1942), took its inspiration from the *Scivias* manuscript produced in the Rupertsberg scriptorium a half-century before.[45] Like that manuscript, it distributes the *capitula* (chapter summaries) throughout the text, copied in rubrics before each chapter, to give the work a didactic superstructure.[46] Its illustrations, moreover, enhance Hildegard's visionary authority by repeating her author portrait with every image. Based on a similar image at the beginning of the *Scivias* manuscript, these show Hildegard gazing up at the vision while writing down the words she hears from heaven upon wax tablets; in the more elaborate version accompanying the first vision (fol. IV), her head is also touched by streams of illuminating fire.

The work's second vision introduces a vast cosmological scheme that occupies the next two visions as well, to explain the intertwined physical and spiritual structure of the universe (the macrocosm) and its interplay with the physical and spiritual constitution of the human person (the microcosm). The regularity of its illustrative diagram (reproduced in Figure 12.4) sets it apart from the corresponding Cosmic Egg in the *Scivias*, and that difference is intentional. The later vision explicitly revises the egg image, which was sufficient only to show the universe's layers. This new, much more detailed cosmic wheel more precisely describes "the circumference and correct proportion of the elements," though only a spinning three-dimensional globe would be truly sufficient to model the universe.[47] The Lucca illustration portrays these proportions with the compassed precision missing from the *Scivias* Egg. Based on the ratios given in the vision text, the diameter of the central globe is one-fifth that of the total instrument; the next fifth on either side corresponds to the thin air full of clouds, in white and light blue; while the final fifth on either side can be subdivided into three sections of equal width: the combined circles of strong, bright white air and watery air; the circle of ether, in blue studded with red stars; and the combined circles of black and bright (red) fire.

The whole cosmos, meanwhile, is held within the embrace of the red, curving arms of a composite figure, revealed in the first vision to be Divine Love (*Caritas*), surmounted by the gray-haired head of divinity, the Ancient of Days. Because red is used in this manuscript in the same way that silver was

---

[45] Madeline Caviness, "Hildegard As Designer of the Illustrations to Her Works," in Burnett and Dronke, *Hildegard of Bingen: The Context of Her Thought and Art*, 29–62, at 34–41.

[46] Nathaniel M. Campbell, "The Authorship and Function of the Chapter Summaries to Hildegard of Bingen's *Liber diuinorum operum*," *The Journal of Medieval Latin* 27 (2017): 69–106, at 102–105.

[47] *The Book of Divine Works* 1.2.3, trans. Campbell, 55.

Figure 12.4 *Liber divinorum operum* 1.2, The Cosmic Spheres and Human Being; Biblioteca Statale di Lucca, MS 1942, fol. 9r, thirteenth century. Courtesy of the Ministry of Heritage, Cultural Activities and Tourism.

employed in the Rupertsberg *Scivias*,[48] this figure plays the same role as the Holy Spirit's silver ground in the Creation scene of *Scivias* 2.1 (in Figure 12.3).[49] Love gives the cosmos its origins and direction, while the whole instrument is joined together within by the superimposed figure of a human being, arms and legs outstretched like Leonardo Da Vinci's "Vitruvian Man" (a drawing still several centuries in the future). Meanwhile, nearly every element of this cosmos finds itself connected to another. Distributed throughout the outer ring of bright (red) fire, for example, are sixteen gold stars, four evenly spaced in each quadrant, their rays piercing down into the sphere of thin air: "Like the nails that hold together the wall in which they are fixed," Hildegard writes, "these cannot be moved from their places, but orbit with the firmament, keeping it solidly fixed together."[50]

The most complicated network in the image, though, is the beams that connect the seven celestial bodies above the head of the human image and the series of twelve winds distributed around the cosmos, figured as animal heads: the leopard in the east, the wolf in the west, the lion in the south, and the bear in the north; and with each principal wind, two subordinate winds, either a crab, a stag, a serpent, or a lamb. The physical interdependencies of every element are, for Hildegard, the essential means by which the universe is kept in proper balance: each part restrains another from excess and succors it against privation. However, this physically interconnected cosmos also has a moral meaning inextricably bound with it. Each celestial body and wind corresponds to a particular virtue, and the virtues support one another as do the physical elements in order to sustain the human person, who is called to "mount from virtue unto virtue" (Psalm 84:7, in a phrase ubiquitous in the *Liber divinorum operum*).[51]

Unfortunately, the designer of the Lucca illustration misunderstood the perspectives from which Hildegard described these elements and thus reversed the placement of north and south, with their respective winds and beams, as well as the southern course of the sun (a golden star) through the black fire. The problem for the illustrator is that the vision text itself uses only spatial relationships of right and left, above and below. Only

---

[48] Caviness, "Hildegard As Designer of the Illustrations to Her Works," 35.
[49] Bernard McGinn, "Theologians As Trinitarian Iconographers," in Jeffrey F. Hamburger and Anne-Marie Bouché, eds., *The Mind's Eye: Art and Theological Argument in the Middle Ages* (Princeton: Princeton University Press, 2006), 186–207, at 189–192.
[50] *The Book of Divine Works* 1.2.39, trans. Campbell, 98.
[51] For a diagram of the winds and their corresponding virtues, see Bertha Widmer, "Moralische Grundbegriffe Hildegards in ihrem Rad der Winde," in Forster, *Hildegard von Bingen. Prophetin durch die Zeiten*, 211–222, at 217.

later, in the vision's explication by the heavenly voice, are the vision elements assigned compass directions. The orientation of the image is provided by the identification of the leopard's head above the human image as the east wind (east was usually oriented at the top in medieval maps). When Hildegard's text says that the lion's head (the south wind) appears in the bright fire "to the right" of the human image, she must mean "right" from *her* perspective looking at the image; however, the designer interpreted it from the perspective of the figure looking out at us from the page, which means the lion's head appears at the left edge of the illustration. Likewise, the bear's head (the north wind) is described as "to the left" of the human image but appears on the right side of the illustration, at the figure's left hand. Moreover, when Hildegard's text describes the subordinate winds, her perspective shifts, as she imagines herself standing in the middle of the circles, turning to face each principal wind in turn. Thus, when she describes the crab's head to the leopard's right and the stag's head to its left, that puts the crab to the south side and the stag to the north.[52] The illustrator, however, has instead interpreted the text to put the crab at the leopard's right side (our left, or north) and the stag at its left (our right, or south). The illustrator tried to depict the vision text literally, without recourse to its later explication – but without the compass directions, the initial visual perspective remains unclear. When we saw discrepancies between text and image in the *Scivias* manuscript, we found that they communicated additional meaning that clarified the vision text, indicating Hildegard's hand in their design. The discrepancies in the *Liber divinorum operum* image, however, result from the ambiguity in the text; had Hildegard designed the illustration as she did for the *Scivias* manuscript, it would have clarified the orientation rather than misinterpreting it.

Hildegard's Visual Legacy

Despite their efforts, the canonization campaign of the Rupertsberg's women for their spiritual mother floundered, as detailed in Michael Embach's contribution to this volume.[53] Sporadic interventions over the next few centuries, including the issuing of indulgences, indicate a local assumption of Hildegard's holiness, but her universal appeal in the later Middle Ages proved much narrower than the rich breadth of imagery contained in the *Scivias* and *Liber divinorum operum*

---

[52] *The Book of Divine Works* 1.2.17, trans. Campbell, 64.   [53] See Embach, Chapter 1, this volume.

manuscripts. Most popular were her prophecies of the end times, rather than her intricate cosmology and accounts of the full breadth of salvation history.[54]

In part, this is because the role of visionary experience and the place of painted images in expressing it had changed, rendering Hildegard's prophetic teaching mission and its visual instruments out of date. Despite the planning that went into these two illustrated manuscripts – one designed by Hildegard herself, the other by her spiritual heirs – their imagery remained, it would seem, almost entirely unknown to the wider world, inconsequential to the Christian society Hildegard was divinely commissioned to teach. The only other illustrated manuscript of Hildegard's works to survive is a late twelfth- or early thirteenth-century copy of *Scivias* from the Cistercian abbey at Salem.[55] Its dozen understudied illustrations were designed independently of the Rupertsberg manuscript, though in drawing on a standard repertoire of Christian art (particularly other illustrated books in the Salem abbey's library), it unknowingly followed Hildegard's own didactic impulse.

There is, however, one tantalizing story of the influence of the Rupertsberg *Scivias* images outside their home monastery – but it illustrates precisely how much things had changed. In 1339, in a sermon to the nuns of St. Gertrude in Cologne, the mystical Dominican preacher Johannes Tauler spoke about the image for the first vision in the Rupertsberg *Scivias* (fol. 2r).[56] Showing two figures, representing Fear of God and Poverty of Spirit, at the foot of an iron mountain, with the golden Godhead enthroned above, it was an image known to the nuns because they had a copy of it in their refectory – a wall painting, perhaps, or a tapestry. For Hildegard, this vision was her prophetic commission, to "cry out and speak of the origin of pure salvation" to those "who, though they see the inmost contents of the Scriptures, do not wish to tell or preach them."[57] In her visionary mode, images were as much the vehicles for that teaching as words. The interiority of Tauler's brand of contemplative mysticism, however, prized the negation of imagery in the journey to be

---

[54] Kathryn Kerby-Fulton, "Hildegard and the Male Reader," in *Prophets Abroad: The Reception of Continental Holy Women in Late-Medieval England,* ed. Rosalynn Voaden (Cambridge: D. S. Brewer, 1996), 1–18.

[55] Heidelberg, Universitätsbibliothek, cod. Salem X, 16: https://digi.ub.uni-heidelberg.de/diglit/salX16

[56] Jeffrey F. Hamburger, "The 'Various Writings of Humanity': Johannes Tauler on Hildegard of Bingen's *Liber Scivias,*" in Kathryn Starkey and Horst Wenzel, eds., *Visual Culture and the German Middle Ages* (New York: Palgrave Macmillan, 2005), 161–205.

[57] *Scivias* 1.1, trans. Hart and Bishop, 67.

united with God. Departing subtly from the *Scivias* text, Tauler took his cue from the visual image itself and shifted the allegorical figures to fit his own theological moment, turning the Fear of God's ever-watchful gaze into the self-forgetting blindness of abandonment, and Poverty's humble imitation of Christ into the nakedness of complete inner detachment. Hildegard's sanctity authorized the image, but the outward and didactic charge of her prophetic mission in the twelfth century was turned inward and released by the devotional practices of the fourteenth. The liability of Hildegard's visual images to such reinterpretation, whether in Tauler's day or our own, demonstrates perhaps more than anything else the necessity (at least from Hildegard's perspective) of the heavenly voice's definitive explanation of them.

Further Reading

Latin Editions and English Translations

Hildegard of Bingen. *The Book of Divine Works*, trans. Nathaniel M. Campbell. Washington, DC: The Catholic University of America Press, 2018.
Liber divinorum operum, ed. Albert Derolez and Peter Dronke. Corpus Christianorum Continuatio Mediaevalis 92. Turnhout: Brepols, 1996.
Scivias., ed. Adelgundis Führkötter and Angela Carlevaris. 2 vols. Corpus Christianorum Continuatio Mediaevalis 43 and 43A. Turnhout: Brepols, 1978.
Scivias, trans. Mother Columba Hart and Jane Bishop. New York: Paulist Press, 1990.

Manuscript Images Online

Scivias

Black-and-white photographs of the original, Wiesbaden, Hochschul- und Landesbibliothek RheinMain, MS 1: www.kulturelles-erbe-koeln.de/docu ments/obj/00043147
Modern facsimile of the Rupertsberg manuscript at the Abbey of St. Hildegard, Eibingen, Germany: www.abtei-st-hildegard.de/die-scivias-miniaturen/
Salem Codex (Heidelberg, Universitätsbibliothek, cod. Salem X, 16): http://digi .ub.uni-heidelberg.de/diglit/salX16

Liber divinorum operum

Biblioteca Statale di Lucca, MS 1942, fully digitized: www.wdl.org/en/item/21658/
Lucca illustrations, together with an English translation of the *capitula* (chapter summaries): www.hildegard-society.org/p/liber-divinorum-operum.html

Secondary Literature

Campbell, Nathaniel M. "*Imago expandit splendorem suum*: Hildegard of Bingen's Visio-Theological Designs in the Rupertsberg *Scivias* Manuscript." *Eikón/ Imago* 2, no. 2 (2013): 1–68.

Caviness, Madeline H. "Artist: 'To See, Hear, and Know All at Once.'" In Barbara Newman, ed., *Voice of the Living Light: Hildegard of Bingen and Her World*. Berkeley: University of California Press, 1998, 110–124.

Caviness, Madeline H. "Gender Symbolism and Text Image Relationships: Hildegard of Bingen's *Scivias*." In Jeanette Beer, ed., *Translation Theory and Practice in the Middle Ages*. Kalamazoo, MI: Medieval Institute Publications, 1997, 71–111.

Caviness, Madeline H. "Hildegard As Designer of the Illustrations to Her Works." In Charles Burnett and Peter Dronke, eds., *Hildegard of Bingen: The Context of Her Thought and Art*. London: The Warburg Institute, 1998, 29–62.

Hamburger, Jeffrey F. *Nuns As Artists: The Visual Culture of a Medieval Convent*. Berkeley: University of California Press, 1997.

Hamburger, Jeffrey F. *The Visual and the Visionary: Art and Female Spirituality in Late Medieval Germany*. New York: Zone Books, 1998.

Hamburger, Jeffrey F. and Bouché, Anne-Marie, eds. *The Mind's Eye: Art and Theological Argument in the Middle Ages*. Princeton: Princeton University Press, 2006.

Salvadori, Sara. *Hildegard von Bingen: A Journey into the Images*, trans. Sarah Elizabeth Cree and Susan Ann White. Milan: Skira, 2019.

CHAPTER 13

Hildegard of Bingen and Her Scribes

Margot Fassler

Hildegard of Bingen's scriptorium on the Rupertsberg and the nature of the work and of scribal practices during her lifetime are areas of study foundational for understanding her life and her writings. The first scholars to prove beyond a doubt both that there was a designated scriptorium on the Rupertsberg, with its own set of surviving manuscripts, and a distinctive style of script practiced by multiple scribes were Marianna Schrader and Adelgundis Führkötter.[1] The publication of their book in 1956 was the beginning of the serious study of manuscript production on the Rupertsberg in the lifetime of Hildegard, and to read their work today remains an exciting exercise.[2] Their close work with the manuscripts has also proved crucial for establishing the authenticity of Hildegard's writings and the major role she played in securing their survival; it was not so long ago that it was fairly common to dismiss her own role in the writing of the treatises that are now securely attributable. Schrader and Führkötter suggest a probable setup of the scriptorium on the Rupertsberg, with one room in the cloister and another outside on the edge of the complex, where male religious could work or even laypeople, with manuscripts passing freely

---

[1] The most essential writings on Hildegard's manuscripts as copied on the Rupertsberg are Marianna Schrader and Adelgundis Führkötter, *Die Echtheit des Schrifttums der Heiligen Hildegard von Bingen* (Cologne: Böhlau, 1956); Albert Derolez, "The Genesis of Hildegard of Bingen's *Liber divinorum operum*: The Codicological Evidence," in J. P. Gumbert and M. J. M. de Haan, eds., *Essays Presented to G.I. Lieftinck*, vol. 2 (Amsterdam: Van Gendt, 1972), 23–33; Derolez, "Deux notes concernant Hildegarde de Bingen," *Scriptorium* 27 (1973): 291–295; Derolez, "Neue Beobachtungen zu den Handschriften der visionären Werke Hildegards von Bingen," in Alfred Haverkamp, ed., *Hildegard von Bingen in Ihrem historischen Umfeld* (Mainz: P. von Zabern, 2000) 461–488; and the notes to the critical editions of Hildegard's trilogy, most especially those for the *Liber divinorum operum* (Book of Divine Works; *LDO*) provided by editors Albert Derolez and Peter Dronke, Corpus Christianorum Continuatio Mediaevalis (CCCM) 92 (Turnhout: Brepols, 1996).

[2] It would be a boon to paleographic studies of the Hildegard manuscripts to have an English translation of Schrader and Führkötter; the work has long been out of print, and the highly technical language used for paleographical and codicological study is not readily understood by many non-specialist English-reading students.

between the two workrooms as was necessary. With such a setup, it would have been easy for both Volmar (Hildegard's secretary and confidante) and Hildegard to play active roles in the supervision of scribal activity. In Guibert of Gembloux's description of Hildegard's monastery, he mentions the importance of work to the lives of these Benedictine nuns, most of whom were high-born, including the work of copying: "On ordinary days they obey the Apostle who says 'Whoever will not work shall not eat' (2 Thess. 3:10), and apply themselves in well-fitted workshops to the writing of books, the weaving of robes or other manual crafts."[3]

The foundational work of Schrader and Führkötter has provided an excellent beginning in understanding Hildegard's scribes and her relationships to them. Yet, although work on the manuscripts is presently ongoing, many unanswered questions remain, and clearly much paleographical and codicological study remains. This chapter provides an overview of scribal activity and manuscript production on the Rupertsberg during the lifetime of Hildegard of Bingen, helping to understand the role of production of manuscripts, especially of Hildegard's writings, in Hildegard's own monastery, and by nuns who were under her direct supervision. Through this work, we come to know yet another vitally important aspect of Hildegard's genius, and one that has been somewhat neglected, that is, the energy she expended to make sure her massive *oeuvre* was both disseminated in her lifetime and also preserved for posterity.

Following a brief introduction, I discuss the Zwiefalten letter collection (Stuttgart, Württembergische Landesbibliothek, Cod.theol.et.phil.qt.253, hereafter Z), a compendium of letters copied by scribes from the Disibodenberg, the Rupertsberg, and Zwiefalten. This collection, available online, provides a fascinating array of scribal activity from the time the nuns arrived at the Rupertsberg until around 1170 and provides insight into the numbers of scribes involved in the letter collections and the nature of their work.[4] Moving to later activity on the Rupertsberg during the final decade or so of Hildegard's lifetime, the chapter focuses on the production

---

[3] Guibert of Gembloux's letter to the monk of Gembloux, Bovo, is discussed in some detail in Anna Silvas, ed. and trans., *Jutta and Hildegard: The Biographical Sources* (University Park, PA: Pennsylvania State University Press, 1999), 89–98, the preface to her English translation of the document, Letter 38, 99–117, here at 101. Silvas follows the critical edition of Guibert's letters, *Guiberti Gemblacensis Epistolae*, ed. Albert Derolez, CCCM 66a (Turnhout: Brepols, 1989), letter 38, 366–379. Hildegard's *Lingua Ignota* contains a set of words for the implements of the scriptorium: see Sarah Higley, *Hildegard of Bingen's Unknown Language: An Edition, Translation and Discussion* (New York: Palgrave Macmillan, 2007).

[4] Stuttgart, Württembergische Landesbibliothek, Cod.theol.et.phil.qt.253, http://digital.wlb-stuttgart.de/start/.

of her three major theological treatises, all the surviving Rupertsbergian copies of which were made in the late 1160s and 1170s. From this copying activity, we learn much about the interrelationships of the three treatises and can begin to have a clearer picture of that last final scramble to get the copies finished before Hildegard's death in 1179. In the final part of the chapter, I introduce one of the main Rupertsberg scribes, a person who was involved in the apparent copying of at least four manuscripts during this later timeframe. Features of the scribe's hand are useful for underscoring the chief characteristics of the Rupertsberg scriptorium more generally. This last part of the chapter depends especially upon the paleographical studies of Albert Derolez and upon the foundation of understanding laid earlier by Schrader and Führkötter. The main manuscripts are listed in Appendix 13.1, along with their sigla and links to online digitized copies.

From the Disibodenberg to the Rupertsberg

Hildegard, Volmar, the Rupertsberg scribes, and the few surviving twelfth-century manuscripts produced in the final campaign need to be positioned within the larger framework of Hildegard's and Volmar's activities. It is clear that, by the last decade or so of her life, there was an ongoing and even rather feverish amount of scribal production which had many components and which involved several people; all of the surviving Rupertsberg manuscripts are the work of more than one scribe, with the possible exception of the Vatican *Scivias* (Know the Ways). There was a purpose behind this activity, both to commemorate Hildegard and to ensure the preservation of her writings and reputation, but also to lay down a foundation for the continued fame and influence of the monastery she had founded.[5] Death intervened in 1173, when Volmar, who was the probable head of the scriptorium, died before the final major treatise, the *Liber divinorum operum* (Book of Divine Works), was completed. The massive *Riesencodex* (Wiesbaden, Hochschul- und Landesbibliothek RheinMein, MS 2), the large "critical edition" of her works (minus the scientific treatises) was for the most part produced after the death of Volmar.

There has been a great deal of speculation about the ways in which the production of Hildegard's manuscripts fit into a larger strategy of validating her visionary writings, a process that was surely initiated by Volmar and

---

[5] See my "Volmar, Hildegard, and St. Matthias," in Judith A. Peraino, ed., *Medieval Music in Practice, Studies in Honor of Richard Crocker*, Miscellanea 7 (Middleton, WI and Münster: American Institute of Musicology, 2013), 85–109; and John Van Engen, "Letters and the Public *Persona* of Hildegard of Bingen," in Haverkamp, *Hildegard von Bingen in Ihrem historischen Umfeld*, 375–418.

with Hildegard's knowledge and consent. In describing the close relationship between them and their common goals, Barbara Newman underscores the term *"symmista,"* a "fellow initiate in God's mysteries," a word that Volmar used for Hildegard and that was also applied to Volmar in Hildegard's *Vita*.[6] Both wrote about the importance of each other to the work that is represented in the scribal activities on the Rupertsberg, although Hildegard was always clear that the contents of the works were her own and that corrections made by others were merely of surface details.[7] Hildegard says of Volmar in the preface to her first major treatise *Scivias* (speaking through the Voice of the Living Light who describes Hildegard and Volmar in the first person):

> Hence in My love she searched in her mind as to where she could find someone who would run in the path of salvation. And she found such a one and loved him, knowing that he was a faithful man, working like herself on another part of the work that leads to Me. And, holding fast to him, she worked with him in great zeal so that My hidden miracles might be revealed.[8]

And Volmar says of Hildegard in a letter to the community (Letter 195), when she was very ill and believed to be near death:

> Who then will give answers to all who seek to understand their condition? Who will provide fresh interpretations of the Scriptures? Who then will utter songs never heard before and give voice to that unheard language? Who will deliver new and unheard-of sermons on feast days? Who then will give revelations about the spirits of the departed? Who will offer revelations of things past, present, and future? Who will expound the nature of creation in all its diversity?[9]

Although no securely attributable writings of Volmar (besides this letter) survive in copies from the Rupertsberg, it has been suggested by Anna

---

[6] Barbara Newman, "Liminalities: Literate Women in the Long Twelfth Century," in Thomas F. X. Noble and John Van Engen, eds., *European Transformations: The Long Twelfth Century* (Notre Dame: University of Notre Dame Press, 2012), 401–454, at 418.

[7] I. Herwegen, "Les collaborateurs de sainte Hildegarde," *Revue Bénédictine* 21 (1904): 192–203; 302–315; 381–403, at 194–195; Schrader and Führkötter, *Die Echtheit*, 182; and Albert Derolez, "The Manuscript Transmission of Hildegard of Bingen's Writings: The State of the Problem," in Charles Burnett and Peter Dronke, eds., *Hildegard of Bingen: The Context of Her Thought and Art* (London: Warburg Institute, 1998), 17–28, see 18 especially.

[8] Vnde in amore meo scrutatus est in animo suo, ubi illum inueniret, qui uiam salutis curreret. Et quendam inuenit et eum amauit, agnoscens quod fidelis homo esset et similis sibi in aliqua parte laboris illius qui ad me tendit. Tenensque eum simul cum illo in omnibus his per supernum studium contendit, ut absconsa miracula mea reuelarentur. *Scivias* 1.pref., 69–75; 5; 60.

[9] Volmar to Hildegard, Ep. 195 in *Hildegardis Bingensis Epistolarium*, ed. Lieven Van Acker, CCCM 91a (Turnhout: Brepols, 1993), 2: 443; Letter 195, *The Letters of Hildegard of Bingen*, vol. 2, trans. Joseph L. Baird and Radd K. Ehrman (Oxford: Oxford University Press, 1998), 168–169.

Silvas that he may have been responsible both for the chronicle of the Disibodenberg, a work that mentions Hildegard, and for the *Life of the Lady Jutta the Anchoress* (hereafter the *Life of Jutta*).[10] G. W. Waitz, the editor of the chronicle, believed that the work was compiled in 1146–1147 and by a monk of the Disibodenberg from a variety of sources. Hildegard figures in the chronicle, and as it was compiled soon before Volmar and Hildegard left this establishment and struck out on their own, the timing is right for it to have been the work of Volmar. The *Life of Jutta*, too, is especially important for understanding the later activities of Volmar and Hildegard, for it suggests that their initial goal was to promote the Disibodenberg with Jutta as a major figure of importance.[11] Already in the *Life of Jutta*, Hildegard is shown receiving a mystical revelation which God also commands her to preserve in writing. In their interactions at the Disibodenberg, it seems that Volmar may have been the author and Hildegard the consultant. When they moved to the Rupertsberg, as far as we know, this relationship reversed, although they seemingly had intentions even early on for committing her visions to writing, as may be seen in descriptions of Hildegard in the *Life of Jutta*. A person (or persons) in the company that departed the Benedictine monastery of the Disibodenberg for the new priory in Bingen, must have been a well-trained scribe both of text and of music, and it surely fell to that person to establish the new scriptorium on the Rupertsberg. We can only imagine, although it cannot yet be proved, that Volmar was this person.

The Zwiefalten Letter Collection

The letters are the most important single genre available for the study of scribal activity in the 1150s through around 1170: a variety of copies remain,

---

[10] A supposition with which I presently concur, although further consideration of the matter is necessary: see my "Volmar, Hildegard, and St. Matthias," and Silvas, *Jutta and Hildegard*, 3, and 46–50. The manuscript containing the chronicle is Universitätsbibliothek Johann Christian Senckenberg, Frankfurt am Main, MS Barth. 104.

[11] The two surviving sources of the *Life of Jutta* date from the late fourteenth or early fifteenth and the mid fifteenth century, and the younger of these is a fragmentary lectionary, today found in Paderborn (see Silvas, *Jutta and Hildegard*, 46, for full descriptions of these sources). An English translation of the *Life of Jutta* is in Silvas, *Jutta and Hildegard*, 65–84. Silvas prepared her translation from the edition made by Franz Staab: *Reform und Reformgruppen im Erzbistum Mainz. Vom 'Libellus de Willigisi consuetudinibus' zur 'Vita domnae Juttae inclusae'*, appendix II, in *Quellen und Abhandlungen zur mittelrheinischen Kirchengeschichte, Vol. 68: Reformidee und Reformpolitik im spätsalisch-frühstaufischen Reich*, ed. Stefan Weinfurter (Mainz, 1992). For her critique of the edition and a discussion of her translation and the importance of the work, see Silvas, *Jutta and Hildegard*, 46–63.

although none of the actual originals or the Rupertsberg copybooks containing the letters survive.[12] The fundamental work on the letters was, like so much else, done by Schrader and Führkötter, and much that has since been written on the extant manuscripts builds on the foundation they established. The extant material falls into chronological stages. The earliest stage is represented by three manuscripts: (1) the so-called Zwiefalten collection now in Stuttgart, which contains many folios copied by scribes from the Disibodenberg and the Rupertsberg; (2) Vienna, Österreichische Nationalbibliothek, Cod. 881, from the third quarter of the twelfth century and copied on the Rupertsberg, which parallels the collection now in Stuttgart in many ways;[13] and (3) Berlin, Staatsbibliothek Preußischer Kulturbesitz, Cod. Theol. Lat. Fol. 699, a book that belonged to the Cistercian abbey of Maizières and select folios of which are online.

The second stage in preserving Hildegard's letters was apparently part of vigorous copying activity on the Rupertsberg, undertaken at first under the probable direction of Volmar but ongoing after his death in 1173. In this second stage, as Christopher D. Fletcher's chapter in this volume elucidates,[14] the letters found in stage one were rearranged by Volmar, undoubtedly in consultation with Hildegard. In addition, copies of the originals were paired with copies of Hildegard's responses; the letters also were arranged by the rank of the person writing to Hildegard, the most prestigious correspondents coming first. At this point, then, the letters were not only dramatically rearranged to make a kind of cohesive treatise, a *Liber epistolarum*, but also organized to demonstrate Hildegard's highly respected reputation as a seer. Comparison with the letters in stage one also demonstrates that many additions and subtractions were made at this point. Van Engen points out that nearly all of the incoming letters survive as originals only in this second stage, and this raises many questions about authenticity. This second stage is preserved in a thirteenth-century codex: Vienna, Österreichische Nationalbibliothek, Cod. 963, presumed to have been copied from Volmar's original.[15] Stages one and two are the most

---

[12] John Van Engen's clear analysis of Volmar's work on the various collections of Hildegard's letters and Volmar's apparent editorial strategies is fundamental for beginning to understand Volmar's and Hildegard's ultimate relationship regarding copying and transmission. See Van Engen, "Letters and the Public *Persona*."

[13] This manuscript is not yet online, and so readers cannot easily reference it at present; I have not seen it and do not own a microfilm or other copy. However, the contents are tabulated in both Schrade and Führkötter (*Die Echtheit des Schrifttums*) and in Hildegard of Bingen, *Epistolarium*, ed. Lieven Van Acker and Monika Klaes-Hachmöller, 3 vols., CCCM 91, 91A, and 91B (Turnhout: Brepols, 1991–2001).

[14] See Fletcher, Chapter 5, this volume. [15] This book is presently not available online.

important, but a kind of third stage is found in the letters collected in the *Riesencodex*. This third stage follows the arrangement of stage two, which represents Volmar's work. In this third stage, however, the letters reveal the editorial overview of Hildegard and her newer secretary, Guibert (or Wibert) of Gembloux, who worked with Hildegard in the last two years of her life, during the time when the giant codex was brought together.[16]

The most varied collection of scribes from a chronological point of view is that found in the letter manuscript from Zwiefalten, presently in Stuttgart (Stuttgart, Württembergische Landesbibliothek, Cod.theol.et. phil.qt.253), and known in the literature as MS Z. This varied collection is dated to the period 1153–1170 by Schrader and Führkötter as well as Lieven van Acker and Monika Klaes-Hachmöller.[17] Estimations of the numbers of hands it contains vary slightly, with the most recent estimate by Klaes-Hachmöller standing at twenty-two hands, fifteen in part 1 and six in part 2, with a rubricator rounding out the number.[18] The scribes' work represents three different scriptoria: the Disibodenberg, the Rupertsberg, and Zwiefalten.[19] Building on Schrader and Führkötter, van Acker and Klaes-Hachmöller provide a table that identifies all the scribes in the manuscript, letter by letter, and associates each scribe with a particular scriptorium; in another column each letter, is dated, if possible, or, when possible, linked to a range of probable dates.[20] The earliest date or the range of dates of letters copied by a given scribe can provide a *terminus a quo* for that person's copying activity. Using the table to number how many of these scribes can be identified with the Rupertsberg scriptorium, it seems that the Stuttgart collection (which is connected with Zwiefalten) contains the work of at least seven scribes working in Hildegard's monastery, and several of these appear in the other early letter collection found in Vienna. One thing is for sure, then: there were several people copying letters in the Rupertsberg scriptorium in the early 1150s through around 1170. When the hands can be found in other manuscripts associated with

[16] Wiesbaden, Hochschul- und Landesbibliothek RheinMain, MS 2, http://hlbrm.digitale-sammlungen.hebis.de/handschriften-hlbrm/content/titleinfo/449618

[17] As the manuscript is digitized and online (http://digital.wlb-stuttgart.de/start/), I have been able to reference it here (although I have not yet been able to see it in person).

[18] See Schrade and Führkötter, *Die Echtheit des Schrifttums*, van Acker, *Epistolarium* 91, part 1, XXII–XXIII, and L. van Acker and M. Klaes-Hachmöller, *Epistolarium* 91B, X–XIII.

[19] A useful introduction to the Abbey of Zwiefalten in the twelfth century, part of the Hirsau reform, is found in Felix Heinzer, "'Scalam ad coelos.' Poésie liturgique et image programmatique. Lire une miniature du livre du chapitre de l'abbaye de Zwiefalten," *Cahiers de Civilisation Médiévale* 44, no. 176 (2001): 329–348.

[20] The table of scribes in Z is found in the third volume of Hildegard's letters as edited by L. van Acker and M. Klaes-Hachmöller, CCCM 91B, 212–226.

Rupertsberg, and scholars say that several of them can be, this collection of letters provides a tentative tool for suggesting a range of dates for scribal activity. The letter collections offer the most interesting and complicated groups of scribes from the Rupertsberg and the closely related scriptoria of the Disibodenberg and Zwiefalten.[21] Hildegard was always surrounded by scribes and the activities of manuscript production, and copying was an apparent expectation, at least for a number of the women, which accounts for the numerous distinct hands, all very near to each other, and yet – in toto – recognizable as representing one scriptorium.

As has long been recognized, the transfer of Hildegard's community from the Disibodenberg apparently required a new scriptorium to be founded on the Rupertsberg itself. The Stuttgart letter collection suggests that it seems to have been staffed by at least one scribe originally trained at the Disibodenberg and who subsequently left, moving with Hildegard's community to the Rupertsberg. This scribe, Scribe 6 in MS Z in the table of van Acker and Klaes-Hachmöller, most likely would have been a nun.

Scribe 6 (MS Z), the so-called Disibodenberg scribe, began in the first fascicle on folio 29r and copied 10 letters, one of which is corrected by a hand from Zwiefalten (Z, Scribe 4, active from the dating of the letters from 1153/4 to ca. 1165). These letters are found from folios 29r to 34v. Scribe 6 also copied some letters in fascicles 4 and 5 of the codex (fols. 47r–48v; and 51r–56v). All the letters copied by this Disibodenberg scribe are relatively early, dating from 1147/8 to circa 1153. After this time, Scribe 6 apparently was no longer copying letters for the collection. Schrader and Führkötter have studied this hand and suggest that it also copied the *Rule of St. Benedict* at the Disibodenberg in 1143.[22] A few of the features of this scribe's work could be explored to develop the argument that the Rupertsberg style developed out of scribal work carried on at the Disibodenberg, which, of course, would make perfectly good sense.[23] Also Z, Scribe 6, from the Disibodenberg, changes in some of its features from fascicle 1 to the work in fascicles 4–5. This change might be accounted for by date, or by copying from an exemplar with different features, or by both sets of circumstances.

---

[21] The stylistic differences between Hildegard's letters produced with the help of Volmar as opposed to those written with the aid of Guibert of Gembloux are significant according to Mike Kestemont, Sara Moens, and Jeroen Deploige, "Collaborative Authorship in the Twelfth Century: A Stylometric Study of Hildegard of Bingen and Guibert of Gembloux," *Digital Scholarship in the Humanities* 30 (2015): 199–224 (https://doi.org/10.1093/llc/fqt063).

[22] See Schrader and Führkötter, *Die Echtheit des Schrifttums.*

[23] Study of the Disibodenberg scriptorium remains difficult because of a dearth of sources.

The model of Zwiefalten, with a male as well as a female scriptorium, would have been well known to them.[24] This seems the best hypothesis for explaining the fact that several scribes were already copying letters seemingly in fascicles that contained works from a given period, and some of these are quite early. Thus there were trained scribes in the community from the beginning. The nun Richardis was known for her help to Hildegard during the time *Scivias* was written; perhaps she made copies in this hypothetical "independent copying room" for women at the Disibodenberg. As she left Hildegard in 1151, and then died in 1152, there are no known examples of her work surviving. Another unnamed nun who worked later in the Rupertsberg scriptorium is mentioned by Hildegard in both the *Liber vitae meritorum* (Book of Life's Merits) and the *Liber divinorum operum* (Book of Divine Works).[25] Yet there were more women than these two copying on the Rupertsberg.

The Disibodenberg and Rupertsberg scribes cannot presently be known by name, or by gender, although it is surely likely that the hand of Volmar is among them. No one has argued for the possibility that one of the many Rupertsberg hands may be that of Hildegard herself. She apparently wrote exclusively on wax tablets rather than on parchment; still the possibility that her hand is present among the scribes cannot be utterly denied. We can assume that Hildegard and Volmar were roughly contemporaries in age, and that they may have copied or supervised the copying of manuscripts in the course of the 1150s before the codices containing Hildegard's treatises were made. Surely there were liturgical books among them – these were a necessity for any new religious establishment – but no known liturgical books survive from the Rupertsberg.[26] The identifiable Rupertsberg style may have developed out of practices at the Disibodenberg before the nuns moved, and we can hypothesize, then,

---

[24] Zwiefalten was a dual-sex Benedictine monastery, and each "side" apparently had its own scriptorium. See Alison I. Beach, "'Mathild de Niphin' and the Female Scribes of Twelfth-Century Zwiefelten," in Virginia Blanton, Veronica O'Mara, and Patricia Stoop, eds., *Nuns' Literacies in Medieval Europe: The Hull Dialogue* (Turnhout: Brepols, 2013), 33–50, a study of scribes from the first half of the twelfth century at Zwiefalten, and so slightly before this letter codex was copied.

[25] For example in the prologue to the *LDO*, Hildegard mentions both Volmar and the girl: "This [writing] is witnessed by that person whom I had sought and found in secret, as I have related in my previous visions; it is also witnessed by that girl of whom I made mention in my most recent visions." Hildegard of Bingen, *The Book of Divine Works*, trans. Nathanial M. Campbell (Washington, DC: Catholic University of America, 2018), 30.

[26] A study of surviving fragments from the region by Jennifer Bain and myself is forthcoming. My book *Cosmos, Liturgy, and the Arts in the Twelfth Century: Hildegard's Illuminated Scivias* (Philadelphia: University of Pennsylvania Press, forthcoming) has a chapter on scribal activities on the Rupertsberg, with an emphasis on the now missing Wiesbaden, Hochschul- und Landesbibliothek RheinMain, MS 1.

that they may have had their own group of working scribes before making the change to a new place. It would have been there that their distinctive style began to develop, and so was in practice even before the move in around 1150. Otherwise how can these scribes be already copying in this style in the first decade or so of the establishment of the new community, as apparently witnessed to by the Rupertsberg necrology and by the Stuttgart letter collection?

The several Rupertsberg scribes who copied letters found in the Stuttgart collection are not studied in this overview. Yet just from the study of the numbers of scribes, and the characteristics of some of them, we can draw some conclusions about scribal activity on the Rupertsberg in the first decades after the move from one place to another. We can tell that there was some continuity across the years, and we know that at least one scribe copied in both places. It seems as well that there were enough practiced scribes early on at the Rupertsberg to suggest a continuity of practice, and perhaps even that the women had their own copying room on the Disibodenberg. From the apparent number of hands at work copying Hildegard's letters and other manuscripts, we can also assume that learning to copy was an expectation for nuns, and this may help to explain why there are so many different hands involved in the copying. The relationship of Hildegard to "her" scribes further defines the powerful relationship of Hildegard to the community, and to her hopes for their theological education and establishment in the monastic life. Surely to copy her works was another way to "know" them. Scribal practices in the letter collections lead directly from the copying of the earlier decades to the production of Hildegard's trilogy and finally to the collected works in the *Riesencodex*, a book that came together in the very last years of her life. Careful tracing of scribal hands from these three stages of work remains to be done; but for the most important work to date on the final stages of scribal production, I turn now to the analyses of Albert Derolez as applied to the surviving Rupertsbergian manuscripts of Hildegard's theological treatises, with concentration on one scribe.

Copying Hildegard's Trilogy on the Rupertsberg

At the present time, the work of the Rupertsberg scribes must be evaluated through the surviving Hildegard sources, and study is at a relatively early stage. Comparing the ideas of the major scholars who have done the analysis reveals points of disagreement about details, and previous work on the letter manuscripts is presently being reexamined by a team of

German scholars. Future large-scale studies of the manuscripts, especially
of the codicological and paleographical dimensions of this *oeuvre*, will
include of necessity more detailed analysis than has been produced to
date on the *Riesencodex*.[27] The only Rupertsberg manuscript that has
received careful paleographical and codicological analysis since the time
of Schrader and Führkötter more than sixty years ago is manuscript
G (Ghent, Universiteitsbibliotheek, MS 241), work carried out by
Derolez, especially in the introduction to the critical edition of the *Liber
divinorum operum* in Corpus Christianorum. As Derolez points out,
however, much remains to be done even with this book, including
a systematic study of its numerous additions and corrections. In his
analysis, Derolez suggests that the main scribe of G (Hand 2 in the
book) may be Volmar, but this cannot at present be confirmed.[28]

Although there has been substantial analysis of the Rupertsberg scribes,
scholars remain in disagreement about some of the most basic relationships
between the scribes and their identifications for a number of reasons,
foremost of which is that the scribes, for the most part, were trained
from an early age by one master and encouraged to copy in a particular
style, down to the very last detail. Distinguishing one hand from another
remains exceedingly difficult in many cases because this is a closely knit
scribal community.[29] Several minor scribes have been distinguished by
scholars as well, and as they sometimes added only a few lines of correction
to particular manuscripts, establishing more about these scribes is especially difficult. There are also scribes involved who copied parts of several
codices, who do not have Rupertsberg features to their styles of writing,
and who are otherwise unknown within the major corpus (which may
change once there is more work completed on the letter manuscripts).
Another difficult aspect seems to be that a scribe who worked over several
years might change key features of letter production, this too making
distinguishing hands nearly impossible in some cases.[30] Finally, a lack of
a consistent nomenclature to identify the scribes is one of the problems for
sorting out the arguments. We proceed, then, with exceeding caution.

In his table presenting the Rupertsberg scribes of Hildegard's three
major theological treatises, Derolez makes several points about the

---

[27] See Van Engen, "Letters and the Public *Persona*," and Sr. Maura Zátonyi, *Hildegard von Bingen*
(Munster: Aschendorff, 2017), 55–58, who provides a concise discussion of the present state of affairs.
[28] Dronke and Derolez, notes to the critical edition of *Liber Divinorum Operum*, XCII. In my
forthcoming *Cosmos, Liturgy, and the Arts*, I suggest a different hypothesis.
[29] Derolez, "Neue Beobachtungen," 468.
[30] In my more detailed study of Scribe A (in progress), I provide a trajectory of development.

numbers of scribes and their interrelationships.[31] It is clear that the major treatises and the *Symphonia* were copied by a number of scribes, some of them appearing multiple times. One of the most important scribes on the Rupertsberg is the person (if it is one person) known in Schrader and Führkötter as Scribe A. According to Derolez, Scribe A can be found at work in four Rupertsberg copies of Hildegard's trilogy: W, Den, T, and V.[32] She or he has telling ways of making letters and using abbreviations, and getting to know them is a fascinating exercise in training the eye for making comparisons of all Hildegard's scribes. Careful study of all four manuscripts could lead to some doubt about the claim that this is indeed one hand. Analysis provided here of this hand, which also forms a useful introduction to the chief characteristics of the Rupertsberg scriptorium during Hildegard's lifetime, is of two manuscripts: W (which survives in photos only) and V (which is online and so can be readily used for comparison). I have chosen folio 181r here from Wiesbaden 1 (W) for reproduction, with comparisons sometimes to the same passage as it appears in V, folio 158v, column 1, line 11 to folio 159r, column 1, line 12. As these two pages are reproduced in Appendix 13.2, many of the examples can be put in context. Scribe A worked on this copy of *Scivias* (W) in tandem with another scribe from whom she or he took over much of the copying from folio 58 forward. There is also a third scribe involved in the copying of W, but her or his work is minimal by comparison. According to Derolez this hand can be found in two other books, T and R, and so she or he copied the texts for the *Symphonia* and the *Ordo Virtutum* in the *Riesencodex*. Paleographic observations support the understanding that the surviving manuscripts of the trilogy were copied in a fairly narrow band of time, including the texts for the chant texts in D and R.

Unless otherwise designated, the following examples are found in: W – Wiesbaden 1, folio 181r (*Scivias* 3.8.8, 277–319; 485–486; 429–430); and in V – Vatican MS Pal. Lat. 311, folios 158v, column 1, line 11 to 159r column 1, line 12 (the folios designated above for *Scivias*). Photos of the two pages are provided in Appendix 13.2 in full, and a block of the text is transcribed and translated there as well (W col. A, line 1 to col. B, line 16, which compares to V, col. A, line 11, to col. B, line 27). These materials could be useful for a number of classroom exercises, as the same text is written in two different sources, and so there are many avenues of comparison for the habits of this scribe.

---

[31] Derolez, "Neue Beobachtungen," 483.
[32] See Appendix 13.1 for expansions of these abbreviations.

Some Details of Scribal Features

Scribe A – if this is one and the same scribe – is a highly practiced and careful copyist, whose letter forms are somewhat consistent throughout the manuscripts on which she or he probably worked. This book hand, dating from the third quarter of the twelfth century, is commonly in use for liturgical books of the period as well as for letters and treatises for the schoolroom (as reproduced here, all examples are magnified). This script is what Derolez would call "littera Praegothica," and although some features of Gothic are present from time to time, they do not appear regularly enough or frequently enough to make this a Gothic book hand. Derolez says of Praegothica: "It is in fact a Carolingian script that displays to a greater or lesser extent one or more of the new features. These features would only be present all together in the fully developed Gothic Textualis."[33] Some useful letters for distinguishing Scribe A are illustrated in Figures 13.1–13.12 and generally by the texts in Appendix 13.2. The letter "a" has a short back and a simple, oval-shaped bow that ends in a hairline stroke. The uncial d is rarely used by this scribe, who normally uses Caroline d, as in Figure 13.1. The d has a forked ascender (as does b), and this is more pronounced in V than in W because the scribe was working more quickly and with a pen that had a thinner nib. Consistently, the feet of letters are slightly more extended in V than in W, which was copied more slowly and with greater care, being a deluxe manuscript.

A close comparison of the script in two of the several manuscripts on which scholars think this scribe worked shows Rupertsbergian practice as well as distinctive features of Scribe A's style. There are, however, some differences in the execution of particular letter forms, abbreviations, or ligatures when comparing the two passages in just two of the manuscripts (here W and V), which make it difficult to determine if it really is the same scribe whose style perhaps evolved over time or if Scribe A is really two or more scribes. The only way to be sure is through much more painstaking comparative study of the manuscripts themselves, and given the number of scribal hands already distinguished, this work remains a monumental task. For this discussion, I am assuming that Scribe A copied both the passages in W and V under discussion, but readers can keep sharp eyes for details and perhaps come to different conclusions.

---

[33] Albert Derolez, *The Palaeography of Gothic Manuscript Books from the Twelfth to the Early Sixteenth Century* (Cambridge: Cambridge University Press, 2003), 57.

(a)

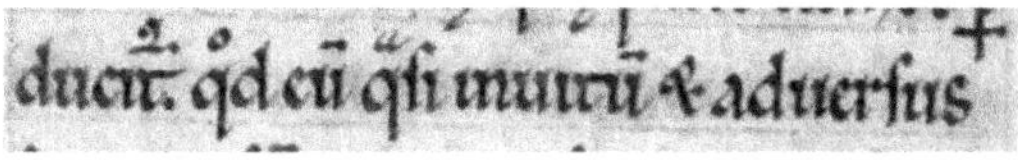

(b)

Figure 13.1 The letters a, s, and d: (a) W (aduersus), fol. 181r; (b) V (aduersus), fol. 158v

(a)

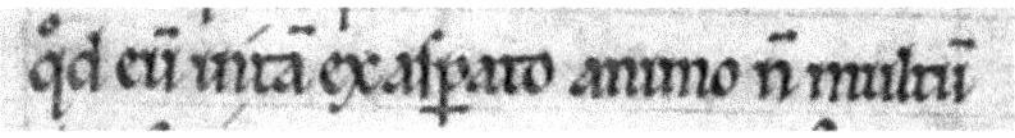

(b)

Figure 13.2 The letter x: (a) W (in tam exasperato), fol. 181r; (b) V (exasperato), fol. 158v

Scribe A occasionally used round s at the ends of words, as can be seen in Figure 13.1. (Please note that the extracts from W of the now lost *Scivias* manuscript are necessarily taken from black-and-white photographs that predate World War II and the resolution is not as sharp.)

Note the way "x" is made in W in Figure 13.2, with a hairline cross bar that ends in a small blob of ink at the very bottom left and extends quite far below the neighboring letter.

The letter g in Figure 13.3 has an oval-shaped lower bow, and it is sometimes even wider than the top half of the letter. The question mark can be seen in this example too, and that sign is made in a slightly different way in V. These are the kinds of details that occasionally make one suspect the hands are different. The forked top of "l" in this example is also typical of

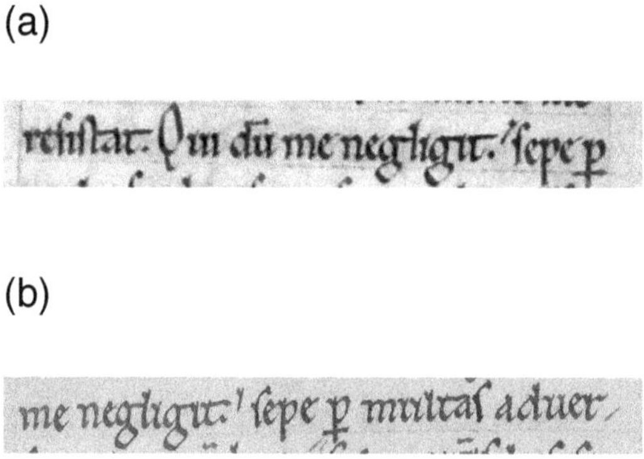

(a)

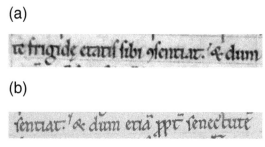

(b)

Figure 13.3 The letters g and e: (a) W (me negligit?), fol. 181r; (b) V (me negligit?), fol. 158v

(a)

(b)

Figure 13.4 The ampersand: (a) W, fol. 181r; (b) V, fol. 158v

many ascenders in W, whereas ascenders in V have thinner forked tops. The hairline tongue of e is readily observable in examples found in Figure 13.3.

The abbreviations are telling in identifying Rupertsberg scribes, and Scribe A in particular, beginning with those for "et," the ampersand and the tironian "et." The ampersand in Figure 13.4 shows the slight differences in this hand from MS to MS, making it always very difficult to be sure the scribes are the same. For example, the shaft of the ampersand is generally more vertical in W than in V; it would be unusual to have such a predominance of the ampersand this late in the twelfth century, but this is a monastic scriptorium and change came more slowly to this "house style."

Although tironian "et" is rare by comparison in Scribe A, when it does appear, it is very simple, with a wavy-line top. As there is no example on folio 181r, Figure 13.5 comes from folio 63v (*quoniam deus iustus est? et quia*

(a)

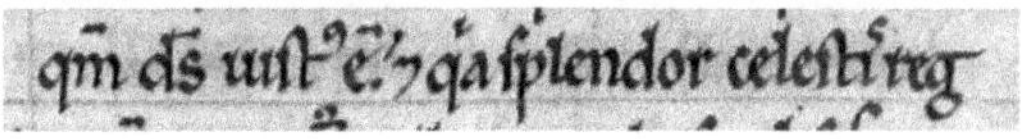

(b)

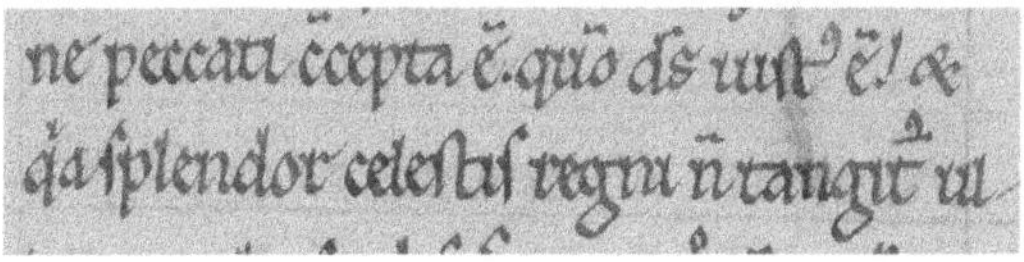

Figure 13.5 Tironian "et" and further examples of differences between W and V: (a) W, fol. 63v; (b) V, fol. 52v

spendor celestis) (*Scivias* 2.4.12). I have also included this passage as found in V for sake of comparison (52v). Continuing discussion of the differences between the way Scribe A copied in W and in V, one can compare the slightly longer hairline strokes in V to those of W. Note the top of the r of "splendor," and the feet of several minims, and the short hairline foot on the descender of p in V of Figure 13.5. If these are copied by the same scribe, they may have been copied at a space of time from each other and under different circumstances, when habits had evolved. The little dip on round s, seen here on deus, is characteristic of V, but not found in W.

The "tur" abbreviation used in W and V is formed quite high on the text line and consists of a straight bar with a comma-like stroke above the bar. It can be seen in V in Figure 13.5 (tangi*tur*) and in Figure 13.6 in both W and V.

The "per" abbreviation is cross-like for Scribe A. As can be seen in both examples in Figure 13.7, the cross bar of "per" fits neatly onto the lead line. Figure 13.7 also provides a good example of the st ligature in W, which is curved at the top.

The "con" abbreviation in Figure 13.8 has a tall, curved shape in W resembling the "us" abbreviation, but merely taller. The st ligature in the word constituit in Figure 13.8 is more rounded in W than in V.

The "orum" and "arum" abbreviations are an important distinguishing figure not only of this hand but of the Rupertsberg scriptorium in general, as the word *aliorum* in Figure 13.9 indicates.

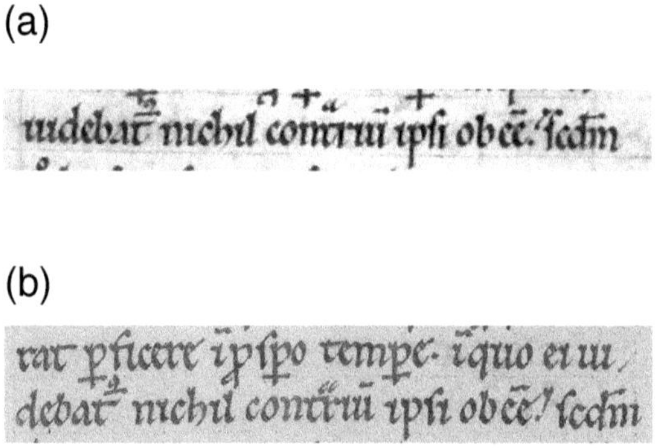

(a)

(b)

Figure 13.6 The "tur" abbreviation: (a) W (uidebatur), fol. 181r; (b) V (uidebatur), fol. 158v

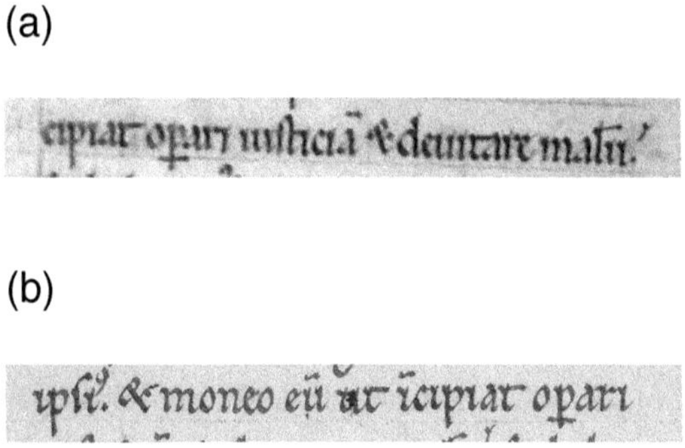

(a)

(b)

Figure 13.7 The "per" abbreviation and the st ligature: (a) W (operari iusticiam), fol. 181r; (b) V (operari), fol. 158v

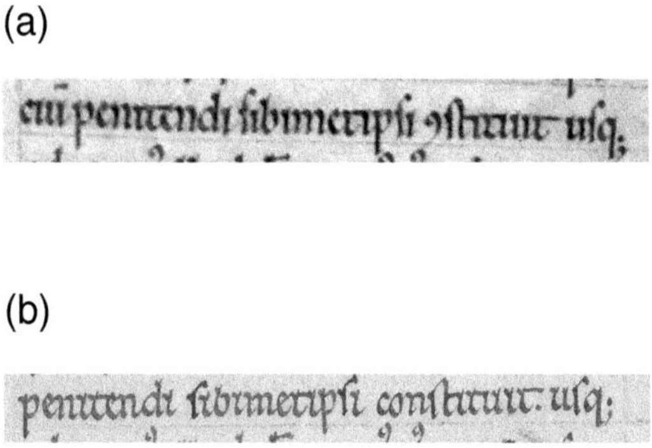

(a)

(b)

Figure 13.8 The "con" abbreviation: (a) W (constituit), fol. 181r; (b) V (constituit), fol. 158v

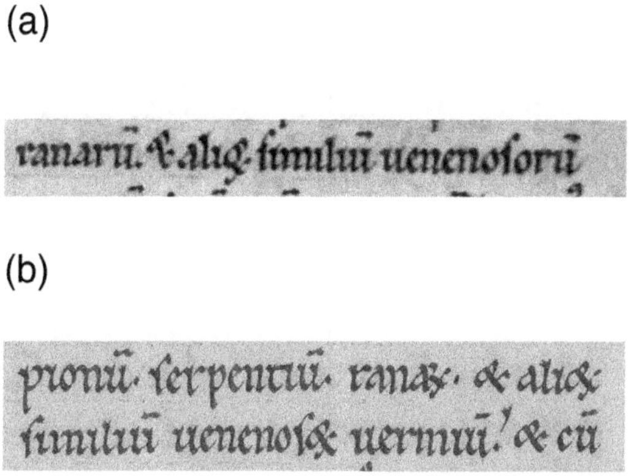

(a)

(b)

Figure 13.9 The "orum" abbreviation: (a) W (et aliorum similium), fol. 181r; (b) V (et aliorum similium), fol. 158v

(a)

(b)

Figure 13.10 The cedilla: (a) W (que = quae), fol. 181r; (b) V (que = quae), fol. 158v

The bar to indicate m or n is made from one stroke, as in "similium" found in V (in Figure 13.9); the bar in W is somewhat different but difficult to see clearly as examples are only as found in early photographs. It is interesting to compare these two examples for the tall s, that of V being somewhat more angular.

Cedilla indicates the abbreviated "ae." In general, the cedilla is thinner with a longer tail in W than in V, where the body of the stroke is thicker, as in Figure 13.10.

Some ligatures are characteristic of Scribe A, but there is variation here, too, as seen in Figure 13.11. The "ct" is broken and sometimes marked with a little blob of ink in the connector, more typical of W than of V, which has

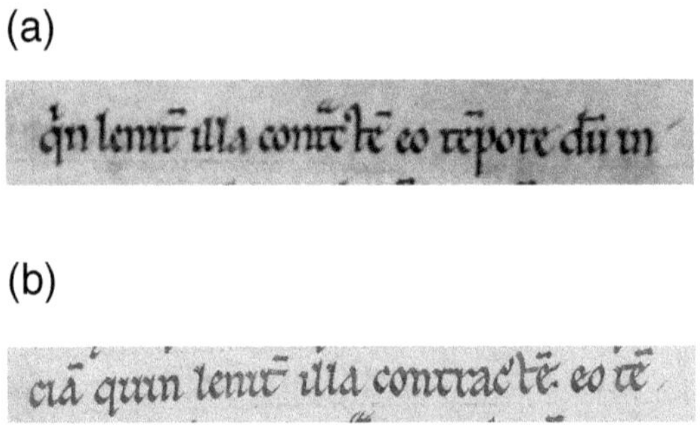

(a)

(b)

Figure 13.11 The ct ligature: (a) W (contractem), fol. 181r; (b) V (contractem), fol. 158v

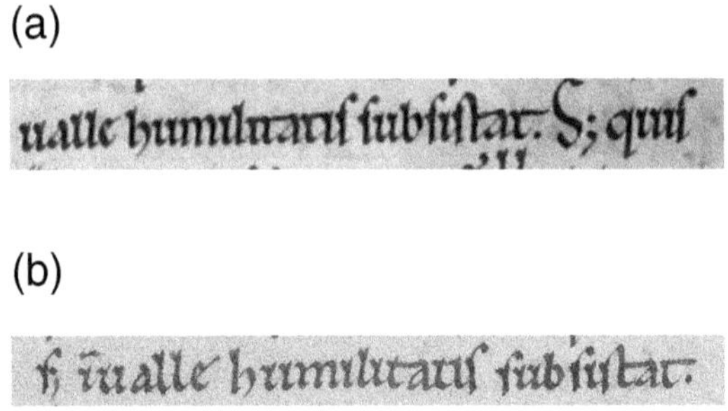

(a)

(b)

Figure 13.12 The st ligature: (a) W (subsistat), fol. 234r; (b) V (subsistat), fol. 204v

a somewhat different ct ligature at some points. This ligature is used as a major defining feature by scholars in trying to distinguish one Rupertsberg hand from another.

The curved "st" ligature continues through the copying of W as can be seen in this example from folio 234r in Figure 13.12, near the end of the manuscript, compared to the same word in V at 204v, where the st ligature has a more "pointed" appearance. This final example concludes our brief summary of some characteristic features of Hand A.

* * * * * * *

This overview of scribal activity on the Rupertsberg during the lifetime of Hildegard of Bingen demonstrates some of the ideas that are now in circulation among scholars concerning her scriptorium and the nature of the copying that took place there. I have put forward some ideas that the state of the manuscripts suggest: (1) The nuns may have already been producing manuscripts on the Disibodenberg, and this helps account for the fact that they were able to have an up and running scriptorium quite soon after the move to the Rupertsberg. (2) The large number of probable scribal hands copying on the Rupertsberg reveals a great deal about the importance of copying and scribal activity in Hildegard's community, including the idea that copying was seen as a worthy craft, and one which was an expectation for many of the women. (3) Because so many nuns were probable scribes, this means that their knowledge of Hildegard's writings was of a particularly intimate character. The scriptorium may have provided a kind of school of study for women, a place where craft and theological understanding could meet. (4) If the nuns worked on the designs for the illuminated *Scivias* under Hildegard's guidance, the craft of embroidery and theological understanding might have been entwined in their other work rooms, too, one of which was designated for weaving and embroidery and another for copying.[34]

There remains much to be done on the manuscripts and on the work of the Rupertsberg scribes, and many questions remain unanswered. Still, the codices are relatively plentiful and often available in digitized copies online (see Appendix 13.1). The time is ripe for teachers in classrooms and scholars alike to investigate these intriguing materials with ever closer attention to detail. It is hoped that this chapter will suggest some ways of working and inspire students to engage in a range of further scholarly projects, from simple classroom exercises to advanced paleographical and codicological study. The task of attempting to match scribes in the letter manuscripts to those who worked on the main treatises is ongoing and of great importance. Some of the main scribes working on the trilogy can be examined more closely; as I mentioned, I have a forthcoming study of the so-called Scribe A, who also features in a major way in my forthcoming book, *Cosmos, Liturgy, and the Arts*, but what about the others? They too provide exciting opportunities to draw ever closer to ways Hildegard and her scribes were engaged with the actual production of books. The difficulties involved in working with a particular monastic scriptorium are only matched by the rich rewards that can come from study of this group of scribes. The activities of the Rupertsberg scribes offer a fairly unique set of circumstances, but one that can tell scholars ever more about how Hildegard worked not only as a writer and thinker but also as the leader of a community whose scriptorium formed a central feature of shared life.

---

[34] For a review of arguments concerning the possibility that the paintings were first designed and expressed as embroideries, see my forthcoming monograph: *Cosmos, Creation, and the Arts*.

APPENDIX 13.1

Copies of the Trilogy Made on the Rupertsberg

The three treatises and the dates during which Hildegard worked on them:

Sciv. = *Scivias* (1141–1151)
LVM = *Liber vitae meritorum* (1158–1163)
LDO = *Liber divinorum operum* (1163–1174)

Manuscript Sources of Hildegard's Trilogy Copied on the Rupertsberg

1. This manuscript contains all three major theological treatises and the *Symphonia* and *Ordo virtutum*
   • **R** Wiesbaden, Hochschul und Landesbibliothek RheinMein, MS 2 [Rupertsberg, 1175–1179] http://hlbrm.digitale-sammlungen.hebis.de /handschriften-hlbrm/content/titleinfo/449618
2. Other manuscripts besides R containing *Scivias*:
   • **W** Wiesbaden, Hochschul- und Landesbibliothek RheinMein, MS 1 [Rupertsberg 1170–1179]. Presumed lost, but black-and-white photos exist (seen), and a color copy of the original survives at the Abbey of Hildegard, Eibingen, this latter available in facsimile.[35]
   • **V** Vatican, Biblioteca Vaticana, MS Pal. Lat. 311 [Rupertsberg, 1170–1179] https://digi.ub.uni-heidelberg.de/diglit/bav_pal_lat_311/0146
3. Other sources besides R containing *Liber vitae meritorum* (1158–1163):
   • **Den** Dendermonde, Abteilbibliothek, MS 9 [Rupertsberg, 1170–1176] http://depot.lias.be/delivery/DeliveryManagerServlet?dps_p id=IE9129581 https://www.idemdatabase.org/
   • **T** Trier, Seminarbibliothek, MS 68 [Rupertsberg, 1170–1179] http://d fg-viewer.de/show/?set[mets]=http%3A%2 F%2Fzimks68.uni-trier.de %2Fstmatthias%2FS0068%2FS0068-digitalisat.xml
   • **Ber** Berlin, Staatsbibliothek, Preußischer Kulturbesitz, MS Theol. lat. fol. 727 [Rupertsberg, 1170–1179]
4. Other sources besides R containing *Liber divinorum operum* (1163–1174):
   • **G** Ghent, Universiteitsbibliotheek, MS 241 [Rupertsberg, 1170–1179] https://lib.ugent.be/en/catalog/rug01:000821881TS: Link
   • **Cit** Troyes, Médiathèque du Grand Troyes MS 683 [Rupertsberg, 1170–1179] https://portail.mediatheque.grand-troyes.fr/iguana/ww w.main.cls?surl=search&p=*#recordId=2.615&srchDb=2

---

[35] Hildegard of Bingen, *Liber scivias: Rüdesheimer Codex: aus der Benediktinerinnenabtei St. Hildegard. Vollständige Faksimile-Ausg. im Originalformat* (Graz: Akademische Druck- u. Verlagsanstalt, 2013).

Reproductions of W, Folio 181r, and V, Folio 158v, with Latin texts
transcribed and an English translation provided

**Latin from the Critical Edition, Excerpted from *Scivias* 3.8.8,
277–319; 485–86; English, 429–430**

(homi)nem in animo ipsius et moneo eum ut incipiat operari iustitiam et
deuitare malum; sed dedignatur me et putat quod possibile sibi sit
quidquid facere uoluerit, ac spatium paenitendi sibimetipsi constituit

usque ad tempus illud, dum corpus eius in simplicitate frigidae aetatis sibi consentiat et dum etiam propter senectutem sibi fastidio sit amplius peccare. Tunc iterum admoneo atque hortor eum ad bonum et ut animo suo resistat. Qui dum me negligit saepe per multas aduersitates ut in diuitiis et in ceteris his similibus quae patitur ad hoc perducitur, quod eum quasi inuitum et aduersus semitipsum oportet facere bonum et quod eum in tam exasperato animo non multum delectat ea adimplere quae prius proposuerat perficere in prospero tempore, in quo ei uidebatur nihil contrarium ipsi obesse, secundum quod ipse in semetipso ordinauerat tanto tempore illa agere ut sibi placuisset. Hic homo dubie suscepit me: nolo tamen eum derelinquere, quia quamuis sic susciperet me, tamen non omnino despixit me. Unde et ego non laboraui frustra in ipso.

Taedio enim mihi non est tangere ulcerata uulnera, quae circumdata sunt sorde comedentium uermium in innumerositate uitiorum et foetore mali rumoris et infamiae et languore inueteratae iniquitatis peccatorum, nec despiciam quin leniter illa contractem eo tempore dum incipio extrahere edacem liuorem malitiae, hoc est cum intueor et tango eadem uulnera blando calore expirationis Spiritus sancti. Sed saepe cum huiusmodi dolor ueteri fomento inueteratur, ita quod peccatum incipit calere ardens in animo hominis et cum etiam sic orientur in dolore uulnera peccatorum, ita quod erunt in coagulatum opus huius immunditate quasi globus et aceruus se erigens de magna sorde uermium et fomentatione inuoluti luti de quo nascuntur mortifera uenena scorpionum, serpentium, ranarum et aliorum similium uenenosorum uermium; . . ..

English Translation

And sometimes I touch a person's mind to warn him/her to begin to work justice and avoid evil, but s/he disdains me and thinks s/he can do what s/he wants. S/he postpones the time of repentance until the body is reduced to old age enough to obey, and s/he is old and tired of sinning. And then I admonish and urge the person again to do good and resist in his/her mind. If s/he ignores me, s/he is often brought to the pass of doing good as it were unwillingly and in spite of himself, by monetary and other troubles that come upon the person. And, the mind thus troubled, s/he has little delight in doing what s/he planned to do when prosperous and unopposed, when s/he thought s/he could act as and when s/he pleased. And such a person receives me in doubt; but yet I choose not to forsake her or him, for although it was thus that s/he received me, s/he did not wholly despise me. And so I do not labor vainly in him or her.

For I do not find it loathsome to touch ulcerated wounds surrounded by the filthy, gnawing worms that are innumerable vices, stinking with evil report and infamy, and stagnating in habitual wickedness. I do not refuse to close them gently up, drawing forth from them the devouring poison of malice, by touching them with the mild fire of the breath of the Holy Spirit. But often such a wound grows hardened by old irritation, so that sin grows hot and burning in the person's mind; and in the clotted mass of the filth new wounds of sin appear, swelling and rising from the defilement of worms and the application of dark muck, from which come the deadly venoms of scorpions, frogs and other poisonous vermin.

Further Reading

Latin Editions and English Translations

Higley, Sarah. *Hildegard of Bingen's Unknown Language: An Edition, Translation and Discussion*. New York: Palgrave Macmillan, 2007.
Silvas, Anna, ed. and trans. *Jutta and Hildegard: The Biographical Sources*. University Park, PA: Pennsylvania State University Press, 1999.

Scivias Manuscript Images Online

Vatican, Biblioteca Vaticana, MS Pal. Lat. 311 [Rupertsberg, 1170–1179]. https:// digi.ub.uni-heidelberg.de/diglit/bav_pal_lat_311/0001
Wiesbaden, Hochschul- und Landesbibliothek RheinMein, MS 2 [Rupertsberg, 1175–1179]. http://hlbrm.digitale-sammlungen.hebis.de/handschriften-hlbrm/content/titleinfo/449618

Secondary Literature

Beach, Alison I. "'Mathild de Niphin' and the Female Scribes of Twelfth-Century Zwiefalten." In Virginia Blanton, Veronica O'Mara, and Patricia Stoop, eds, *Nuns' Literacies in Medieval Europe: The Hull Dialogue*. Turnhout: Brepols, 2013, 33–50.
Derolez, Albert. "The Manuscript Transmission of Hildegard of Bingen's Writings: The State of the Problem." In Charles Burnett and Peter Dronke, eds., *Hildegard of Bingen: The Context of Her Thought and Art*. London: Warburg Institute, 1998, 17-28.

Derolez, Albert. *The Palaeography of Gothic Manuscript Books: From the Twelfth to the Early Sixteenth Century.* Cambridge: Cambridge University Press, 2003.

Fassler, Margot. *Cosmos, Liturgy, and the Arts in the Twelfth Century: Hildegard's Illuminated Scivias.* Philadelphia: University of Pennsylvania, forthcoming.

Fassler, Margot. "Volmar, Hildegard, and St. Matthias." In Judith A. Peraino, ed., *Medieval Music in Practice, Studies in Honor of Richard Crocker.* Miscellanea 7. Middleton, WI and Münster: American Institute of Musicology, 2013, 85–109.

Kestemont, Mike, Sara Moens, and Jeroen Deploige. "Collaborative Authorship in the Twelfth Century: A Stylometric Study of Hildegard of Bingen and Guibert of Gembloux." *Digital Scholarship in the Humanities* 30 (2015): 199–224. https://doi.org/10.1093/llc/fqto63.

Schrader, Marianne and Adelgundis Führkötter. *Die Echtheit des Schrifttums der heiligen Hildegard von Bingen. Quellenkritische Untersuchungen.* Beihefte zum Archiv für Kulturgeschichte 6. Cologne and Graz: Böhlau, 1956.

Van Engen, John. "Letters and the Public *Persona* of Hildegard." In A. Haverkamp, ed., *Hildegard von Bingen in ihrem historischen Umfeld: Internationaler wissenschaftlicher Kongreβ zum 900 jährigen Jubiläum, 13.–19. September 1998, Bingen am Rhein.* Mainz: Verlag Philipp von Zabern, 2000, 375–418.

Select Bibliography

Latin Editions and English Translations of Hildegard's works

Scivias

Hildegard of Bingen. *Liber scivias: Rüdesheimer Codex: aus der Benediktinerinnenabtei St. Hildegard. Vollständige Faksimile-Ausg. im Originalformat.* Graz: Akademische Druck- u. Verlagsanstalt, 2013.

Scivias, ed. Adelgundis Führkötter and Angela Carlevaris. 2 vols. Corpus Christianorum Continuatio Mediaevalis 43 and 43A. Turnhout: Brepols, 1978.

Scivias, trans. Mother Columba Hart and Jane Bishop. New York: Paulist Press, 1990.

Liber vitae meritorum

Hildegard of Bingen. *The Book of the Rewards of Life (Liber Vitae Meritorum)*, trans. Bruce W. Hozeski. New York: Garland, 1994.

Liber uite meritorum, ed. Angela Carlevaris. Corpus Christianorum Continuatio Mediaevalis 90. Turnhout: Brepols, 1995.

Liber divinorum operum

Hildegard of Bingen. *The Book of Divine Works*, trans. Nathaniel M. Campbell. Washington, DC: The Catholic University of America Press, 2018.

Liber divinorum operum, ed. Albert Derolez and Peter Dronke. Corpus Christianorum Continuatio Mediaevalis 92. Turnhout: Brepols, 1996.

Letters

Hildegard of Bingen. *Epistolarium*, ed. Lieven Van Acker and Monika Klaes-Hachmöller. 3 vols. Corpus Christianorum Continuatio Mediaevalis 91, 91A, and 91B. Turnhout: Brepols, 1991–2001.

The Letters of Hildegard of Bingen, ed. Joseph L. Baird and Radd K. Ehrman. 3 vols. New York and Oxford: Oxford University Press, 1994–2004.

306

Sanctae Hildegardis abbatissae in Monte S. Roberti apud Naam fluuium, prope Bingam, sanctissimae uirginis et prophetissae. *Epistolarum Liber,* ed. Justus Blanckwald. Cologne: Johannis Quentel & Geruuinum Calenium, 1566.

Music *(*Symphonia *and* Ordo virtutum*)*

Hildegard of Bingen. *Lieder: Faksimile Riesencodex (Hs.2) der Hessischen Landesbibliothek Wiesbaden, fol. 466-481 v,* ed. Lorenz Welker. Commentary by Michael Klaper. Elementa musicae 1. Wiesbaden: Ludwig Reichert Verlag, 1998. [Facsimile]
Lieder nach den Handschriften, ed. Pudentiana Barth, OSB, M. Immaculata Ritscher, OSB, and Joseph Schmidt-Görg. Salzburg: Otto Müller Verlag, 1969.
Lieder: Symphoniae, ed. Abtei St. Hildegard, Eibingen; trans. Barbara Stühlmeyer. Beuroner Kunstverlag, 2012.
Ordo virtutum. In *Hildegardis Bingensis: Opera minora,* ed. Peter Dronke. Corpus Christianorum Continuatio Mediaevalis 226. Turnhout: Brepols, 2007, 505–521.
Ordo virtutum, ed. Audrey Ekdahl Davidson. Kalamazoo, MI: Medieval Institute Publications, 1985.
Ordo virtutum, ed. Audrey Ekdahl Davidson; trans. Marianne Richert Pfau. Bryn Mawr, PA: Hildegard Publishing Company, 2002.
Ordo virtutum, ed. and French trans. Luca Ricossa. Geneva: Lulu, 2013.
Ordo virtutum: A Comparative Edition, ed. Vincent Corrigan. Lion's Bay, BC: Institute of Mediaeval Music, 2013.
Symphonia: A Comparative Edition, ed. Vincent Corrigan. Lion's Bay, BC: Institute of Mediaeval Music, 2016.
Symphonia: A Critical Edition of the Symphonia armonie celestium revelationum, ed. and trans. Barbara Newman. Ithaca, NY: Cornell University Press, 1998. [Text only]
Symphonia armonie celestium revelationum. In *Hildegardis Bingensis: Opera minora,* ed. Barbara Newman. Corpus Christianorum Continuatio Mediaevalis 226. Turnhout: Brepols, 2007, 373–477.
Symphonia armonie celestium revelationum, ed. and trans. Marianne Richert Pfau. 8 vols. Bryn Mawr, PA: Hildegard Publishing Company, 1997.
Symphonia harmoniae caelestium revelationum: Dendermonde: St.-Pieters & Paulusabdij, Ms. Cod. 9, ed. Peter van Poucke. Peer: Alamire, 1991. [Facsimile]

Medical and Scientific

Hildegard of Bingen. *Beate Hildegardis Cause et cure,* ed. Laurence Moulinier. Berlin: Akademie-Verlag, 2003.
Experimentarius medicinae continens Trotulae curandarum aegritudinem mulieb-rium ante, in, et post partum librum unicum … Libros item quatuor

Hildegardis, de elementorum, fluminum aliquot Germaniae, metallorum, legu-minum, fruticum, herbarum, arborum, arbustorum, piscium, volatilium et animantium terrae naturis et operationibus. Strasbourg: Johannes Schott, 1544.

Hildegard of Bingen: On Natural Philosophy and Medicine, trans. Margaret Berger. Cambridge: D. S. Brewer, 1999.

Hildegard von Bingen's Physica: The Complete English Translation of Her Classic Work on Health and Healing, trans. Priscilla Throop. Illustrations by Mary Elder Jacobsen. Rochester, VT: Healing Arts Press, 1998.

Physica. Edition der Florentiner Handschrift (Cod. Laur. Ashb. 1323, ca. 1300) im Vergleich mit der Textkonstitution der Patrologia Latina (Migne), ed. Irmgard Müller and Christian Schulze. Hildesheim: Olms-Weidmann, 2008.

Physica s. Hildegardis. Elementorum, Fluminum aliquot Germaniae, Metallorum, Leguminum, Fructuum et Herbarum: Arborum et Arbustorum: Piscium denique, Volatilium et Animantium terrae naturas et operationes. IV. Libris mirabili experientia posteritati tradens. Strasbourg: Johannes Schott, 1533.

Physica. Liber Subtilitatum diversarum naturarum creaturarum, ed. Reiner Hildebrandt and Thomas Gloning. Berlin: De Gruyter, 2010.

Subtilitatum diuersarum naturarum creaturarum libri nouem, ed. Charles Daremberg and F. A. Reuss. In *Patrologia Latina* 197, ed. Jacques Paul Migne. Turnhout: Brepols, 1855, 1117–1352.

Homilies on the Gospels

Hildegard of Bingen. *Expositiones Evangeliorum.* In *Hildegardis Bingensis: Opera minora,* ed. Beverly Mayne Kienzle and Carolyn A. Muessig. Corpus Christianorum Continuatio Mediaevalis 226. Turnhout: Brepols, 2007, 187–333.

Homilies on the Gospels, trans. Beverly Mayne Kienzle. Cistercian Studies 241. Collegeville, MN: Liturgical Press, 2011.

Lives of Saints Disibod and Rupert

Hildegard of Bingen. *Vita sancti Disibodi episcopi, Vita sancti Ruperti confessoris.* In *Hildegardis Bingensis, Opera minora II,* ed. Jeroen Deploige, Michael Embach, Christopher P. Evans, Kurt Gärtner, and Sara Moens. Corpus Christianorum Continuatio Mediaevalis 226A. Turnhout: Brepols, 2016, 15–108.

Two hagiographies: Vita sancti Rupperti confessoris. Vita sancti Dysibodi episcopi, ed. and English trans. Hugh Feiss; Latin ed. Christopher P. Evans. Dallas Medieval Texts and Translations 11. Paris: Peeters, 2010.

Explanation of the Rule of St. Benedict

Hildegard of Bingen. *De Regula sancti Benedicti.* In *Hildegardis Bingensis: Opera minora,* ed. Hugh Feiss. Corpus Christianorum Continuatio Mediaevalis 226. Turnhout: Brepols, 2007, 23–97.

Explanation of the Rule of Benedict, trans. Hugh Feiss. Eugene, OR: Wipf & Stock, 2005.

Explanation of the Athanasian Creed

Hildegard of Bingen. *Explanatio Symboli Sancti Athanasii*. In *Hildegardis Bingensis Opera Minora*, ed. Christopher P. Evans. Turnhout: Brepols, 2007, 109–133.
Explanation of the Athanasian Creed, trans. Thomas M. Izbicki. Toronto: Peregrina, 2001.

Solutions to Thirty-Eight Questions

Hildegard of Bingen. *Triginta octo quaestionum solutiones*. In *Hildegardis Bingensis Opera Minora II*, ed. Christopher P. Evans. Corpus Christianorum Continuatio Mediaevalis 226A. Turnhout: Brepols, 2016, 42–44 and 109–129.
Solutions to Thirty-Eight Questions, trans. Beverly Mayne Kienzle, Jenny C. Bledsoe, and Stephen H. Belmke. Collegeville, MN: Liturgical Press, 2014.

Lingua ignota

Higley, Sarah. *Hildegard of Bingen's Unknown Language: An Edition, Translation and Discussion*. New York: Palgrave Macmillan, 2007.
Hildegard of Bingen. *Lingua ignota*. In *Hildegardis Bingensis Opera Minora II*, ed. Kurt Gärtner and Michael Embach. Corpus Christianorum Continuatio Mediaevalis 226A. Turnhout: Brepols, 2016, 237–366.

Anthologies

Gebeno of Eberbach. *La Obra de Gebenón de Eberbach*, ed. José Carlos Santos Paz. Florence: SISMEL – Edizioni del Galluzzo, 2004. [*Pentachronon* or *Speculum futurorum temporum*]
Hildegard of Bingen. *Analecta Sanctae Hildegardis Opera*, ed. J. B. Pitra. Analecta sacra spicilegio solesmensi parata 8. Paris: A. Jouby & Roger, 1882.

Biographies of Hildegard of Bingen

Bruder, Petrus, ed. "*Acta Inquisitionis de virtutibus et miraculis S. Hildegardis, magistrae sororum ord. S. Benedicti in Monte S. Ruperti iuxta Bingium ad Rhenum.*" *Analecta Bollandiana* 2 (1883): 116–129.
Flanagan, Sabina. *Hildegard of Bingen: A Visionary Life*. 2nd ed. London: Routledge, 1998.
Gottfried of Disibodenberg and Theodoric of Echternach. *The Life of the Saintly Hildegard*, trans. Hugh Feiss. Toronto: Peregrina Publications, 1996.

Maddocks, Fiona. *Hildegard of Bingen: The Woman of Her Age*. London: Headline, 2001.

Meconi, Honey. *Hildegard of Bingen*. Urbana: University of Illinois Press, 2018.

Silvas, Anna, ed. and trans. *Jutta and Hildegard: The Biographical Sources*. University Park, PA: The Pennsylvania State University Press, 1999.

Stilting, J. "De S. Hildegarde virgine, magistra sororum ord. S. Benedicti in monte S. Ruperti juxta Bingium in Dioecesi Moguntina." In *Acta sanctorum* 168 (1755): 629–701.

Vita sanctae Hildegardis, ed. Monika Klaes, Corpus Christianorum Continuatio Mediaevalis 126. Turnhout: Brepols, 1993.

Zátonyi, Sr. Maura, OSB. *Hildegard von Bingen*. Munster: Aschendorff, 2017. [In German]

Additional Resources for the Study of Hildegard of Bingen

1877 Bibliography on the Life and Works of Hildegard of Bingen (1098–1179), directed by Jennifer Bain. Dalhousie University, 2003–. http://hildegard.music.dal.ca /index.php.

Annales sancti Disibodi, ed. Georg Waitz. Monumenta Germaniae Historica 17. Hannover: Hanhnsche Buchhandlung, 1861.

Aris, Marc-Aeilko, Michael Embach, Werner Lauter, Irmgard Müller, Franz Staab, and Scholastica Steinle, OSB, eds. *Hildegard von Bingen: Internationale Wissenschaftliche Bibliographie*. Mainz: Gesellschaft für Mittelrheinische Kirchengeschichte, 1998.

Benedict XVI, Pope. "Decrees of the Congregation for the Causes of Saints." May 10, 2012. VIS. Vatican Information Service. Holy See Press Office.

Benedict XVI, Pope. "Apostolic Letter Proclaiming Saint Hildegard of Bingen, Professed Nun of the Order of Saint Benedict, a Doctor of the Universal Church." October 7, 2012.

Cantus: A Database for Latin Ecclesiastical Chant – Inventories of Chant Sources. Directed by Debra Lacoste (2011–), Terence Bailey (1997–2010), and Ruth Steiner (1987–1996), web developer, Jan Koláček (2011–). https://cantus .uwaterloo.ca/

Embach, Michael and Martina Wallner. *Conspectus der Handschriften Hildegards von Bingen*. Münster: Aschendorff, 2013.

Haverkamp, Alfred, ed. *Hildegard von Bingen in ihrem historischen Umfeld: Internationaler wissenschaftlicher Kongreß zum 900järhigen Jubiläum, 13.–19. September 1998, Bingen am Rhein*. Mainz: Verlag Philipp von Zabern, 2000.

Hildegard von Bingen (1098–1179): A Discography. Pierre-F. Roberge (ca. 1998–2013) and Todd McComb (2013–). www.medieval.org/emfaq/composers/ hildegard.html.

Kienzle, Beverly Mayne, Debra L. Stoudt, and George Ferzoco, eds. *A Companion to Hildegard of Bingen*. Leiden: Brill, 2014.

Kotzur, Hans-Jürgen, ed. *Hildegard von Bingen, 1098–1179.* Mainz: P. von Zabern, 1998.

Mainzer Urkundenbuch 2. Die Urkunden seit dem Tode Erzbischof Adalberts I. (1137) bis zum Tode Erzbischof Konrads (1200), ed. Peter Acht. Darmstadt: Historischer Verein für Hessen, 1968.

Newman, Barbara, ed. *Voice of the Living Light: Hildegard of Bingen and Her World.* Berkeley: University of California Press, 1998.

Patrologia Latina, ed. Jacques Paul Migne, 221 vols. Paris: 1841–1855; 1862–1864. http://patristica.net/latina/

Patrologia Latina Database (PLD). Chadwyck-Healey, Inc. ProQuest, LLC, 1996–. http://pld.chadwyck.co.uk/.

Benedict of Nursia. *RB 1980: The Rule of St. Benedict in Latin and English*, ed. and trans. Timothy Fry. Collegeville, MN: Liturgical Press, 1981.

Benedict of Nursia. *The Rule of Saint Benedict*, ed. and trans. Bruce L. Venarde. Dumbarton Oaks Medieval Library. Cambridge, MA: Harvard University Press, 2011.

Thesaurus Musicarum Latinarum (TML): Online Archive of Music Theory in Latin. The Center for the History of Music Theory and Literature: Indiana University Jacobs School of Music, 1990–. www.chmtl.indiana.edu/tml.

Selected Manuscripts of Hildegard's works

For a complete list and detailed descriptions of the 363 known manuscripts transmitting works of Hildegard, see: Michael Embach and Martina Wallner. *Conspectus der Handschriften Hildegards von Bingen.* Münster: Aschendorff, 2013.

Copenhagen, Kongelige Bibliothek, Ny kgl. saml. 90b fol. [*Cause et cure*]

Dendermonde, St.-Pieters & Paulusabdij, MS Cod. 9. Now held in Leuven, Katholieke Universiteit, no shelf number. [*Symphonia armonie celestium revelationum* and *Liber vitae meritorum*]: www.idemdatabase.org/

Florence, Biblioteca Medicae Laurenziana, Ashburnham 1323. [*Liber simplicis medicinae* or *Physica*]

Ghent, Universiteitsbibliotheek, MS 241 [*Liber divinorum operum*]: https://lib .ugent.be/en/catalog/rug01:000821881

Heidelberg, Universitätsbibliothek, cod. Salem X, 16. [*Scivias*]: https://digi .ub.uni-heidelberg.de/diglit/salX16

London, British Library, Add. MS 15102. [*Ordo virtutum*]

Lucca, Biblioteca Statale di Lucca, MS. 1942 [*Liber divinorum operum*]: www .wdl.org/en/item/21658/. Illustrations, together with English translations of the chapter summaries, by Nathaniel M. Campbell: www.hildegard-society.org/p/liber-divinorum-operum.html

Munich, Bayerische Staatsbibliothek, clm. 2619 [*Pentachronon*]

Stuttgart, Württembergische Landesbibliothek Stuttgart, Cod.theol.et.phil.qt.253 [*Epistolarium*]: http://digital.wlb-stuttgart.de/start/

Trier, Seminarbibliothek, MS 68 [*Liber vitae meritorum*]: http://dfg-viewer.de/s
    how/?set[mets]=http%3A%2F%2Fzimks68.uni-trier.de%2Fstmatthias%2F
    S0068%2FS0068-digitalisat.xml
Troyes, Médiathèque du Grand Troyes MS 683 [*Liber divinorum operum*]: https://
    portail.mediatheque.grand-troyes.fr/iguana/www.main.cls?surl=search&
    p=*#recordId=2.615&srchDb=2
Vatican, Biblioteca Vaticana, MS Pal. Lat. 311 [*Scivias*]: https://digi.ub.uni-
    heidelberg.de/diglit/bav_pal_lat_311/0001
Wiesbaden, Hochschul- und Landesbibliothek RheinMain, HS 1. [Illuminated
    Rupertsberg *Scivias* manuscript, lost since 1945]. Black-and-white images of
    the illuminations from the original manuscript: www.kulturelles-erbe-
    koeln.de/documents/obj/40049358/rba_013349. Color images from the mod-
    ern copy made by hand from 1927 to 1933 at the Abbey of St. Hildegard
    (Eibingen, Germany): www.abtei-st-hildegard.de/die-scivias-miniaturen/.
Wiesbaden, Hochschul- und Landesbibliothek RheinMain, HS 2. [Riesencodex,
    including: *Scivias, Liber vitae meritorum, Liber divinorum operum, Vita
    Hildegardis, Epistolarium, Expositio Evangeliorum, Lingua ignota,
    Symphonia, Ordo virtutum*]: http://hlbrm.digitale-sammlungen.hebis.de/
    handschriften-hlbrm/content/titleinfo/449618.

Index

abbots and abbesses, 20, 117, 118–119
Abelard, Peter, 239
Acker, Lieven van, 286, 287
Acta inquisitionis (Act of Inquisition), 29, 32
Adam, 30, 98, 159, 221, 270, 272
Adam of Ebrach, abbot, 133–134
Adelaide of Turin, countess, 108
Adelbert of Disibodenberg, prior, 52
Adelheid of Vilich, abbess, 67, 69
Admont, nuns and *magistra* of, 65, 67, 70, 75–76
Albero of Verdun, bishop, 22
Aldhelm of Malmsbury, *Carmen de virginitate* (Song on Virginity), 237, 243
Alexander III, pope, 26
All Saints, feast of, 19, 230, 251
Alleluia, O virga mediatrix (Hildegard), 220
  manuscript sources, 211, 212
altar cloth (antependium) of Rupertsberg, 43, 272
Ambrose, saint, 127, 129, 133, 139, 140
Amor. See love
Amorbach, monks of, 119
amulets, 150, 151, 157–158
Andrew of Averbode, provost, 134–138
angels, 261
  choirs of, 223
  feasts of, 211, 214, 215, 216
Anima (soul) in *Ordo virtutum*, 235, 236–238, 239, 244, 245, 247–248, 252, 254–255
animals, living creatures, 155, 156–157
  images, iconography of, 275, 276
  representative of five ages, 177–179, 180
Anna of Klingnau, 67
Anne of Ramschwag, 71
Anselm, 75–76, 108, 117
Antichrist, 137–138, 171–172, 179, 180, 184
Antidotarium Nicolai, 148
Antony, saint, 191
Apocalypse, book of, 174–175, 198, 265
apocalypticism, 171–173, 176–182, 196–197, 198
architectural imagery, 19, 93, 100–101, 249–250
ariditas. See dryness

Arnold I of Trier, archbishop, 15
Arnold of Selenhofen, archbishop of Mainz, 25
ascetic, asceticism, 19, 20, 64
Assumption, feast of, 251
astrology, 149, 159
Auffahrtabend (Ascension Eve), 197
Augustine, saint, 127, 132, 139, 140, 261
Aurelian of Arles, *Regula ad virgines*, 60
authenticity of authorship, 115–116, 280, 285
Ave Maria, o auctrix vite (Hildegard), 220
Ave regina caelorum, antiphon
  intertextuality, musical borrowing, 229

Bain, Jennifer, 251
Beach, Alison, 75, 77
Bede, 158
Beli of Winterthur, 64
Benedic domine domus, responsory,
  248–249
Benedict XVI, pope, 1, 35, 203
Benedictine ideals, 20, 24, 235, 241–248, 255
Benediktinerinnenabtei Sankt Hildegard, 28,
  260, 300
Bent, Ian, 226
Berlin, Staatsbibliothek Preußischer Kulturbesitz
  Cod. Theol. Lat. Fol. 699: 285
  Lat. qu. 674: 147
  MS Theol. lat. fol. 727: 300
Bermersheim, 16
Bernard of Clairvaux, saint, 21–23, 28,
  108, 117
Bertha of Bingen, saint, 95, 103
Berthold of Henneberg, archbishop of Mainz, 34
Birgitta of Sweden, saint, 196
Blanckwald, Justus, 200
Böckelheim, 16
body
  as microcosm, 154–155, 158–159
  Cathar contempt of, 102
  conditions, diseases of, 159–164
  goodness, sanctity of, 101–102, 222, 236

313

Index

Cambridge Companions To ...

AUTHORS

Edward Albee edited by Stephen J. Bottoms
Margaret Atwood edited by Coral Ann Howells (second edition)
W. H. Auden edited by Stan Smith
Jane Austen edited by Edward Copeland and Juliet McMaster (second edition)
Balzac edited by Owen Heathcote and Andrew Watts
Beckett edited by John Pilling
Bede edited by Scott Degregorio
Aphra Behn edited by Derek Hughes and Janet Todd
Saul Bellow edited by Victoria Aarons
Walter Benjamin edited by David S. Ferris
William Blake edited by Morris Eaves
James Baldwin edited by Michele Elam
Boccaccio edited by Guyda Armstrong, Rhiannon Daniels, and Stephen J. Milner
Jorge Luis Borges edited by Edwin Williamson
Brecht edited by Peter Thomson and Glendyr Sacks (second edition)
The Brontës edited by Heather Glen
Bunyan edited by Anne Dunan-Page
Frances Burney edited by Peter Sabor
Byron edited by Drummond Bone
Albert Camus edited by Edward J. Hughes
Willa Cather edited by Marilee Lindemann
Cervantes edited by Anthony J. Cascardi
Chaucer edited by Piero Boitani and Jill Mann (second edition)
Chekhov edited by Vera Gottlieb and Paul Allain
Kate Chopin edited by Janet Beer
Caryl Churchill edited by Elaine Aston and Elin Diamond
Cicero edited by Catherine Steel
J. M. Coetzee edited by Jarad Zimbler
Coleridge edited by Lucy Newlyn
Wilkie Collins edited by Jenny Bourne Taylor
Joseph Conrad edited by J. H. Stape
H. D. edited by Nephie J. Christodoulides and Polina Mackay
Dante edited by Rachel Jacoff (second edition)
Daniel Defoe edited by John Richetti
Don DeLillo edited by John N. Duvall
Charles Dickens edited by John O. Jordan
Emily Dickinson edited by Wendy Martin
John Donne edited by Achsah Guibbory
Dostoevskii edited by W. J. Leatherbarrow
Theodore Dreiser edited by Leonard Cassuto and Claire Virginia Eby
John Dryden edited by Steven N. Zwicker

Mario Vargas Llosa edited by Efrain Kristal and John King
Virgil edited by Fiachra Mac Góráin and Charles Martindale (second edition)
Voltaire edited by Nicholas Cronk
David Foster Wallace edited by Ralph Clare
Edith Wharton edited by Millicent Bell
Walt Whitman edited by Ezra Greenspan
Oscar Wilde edited by Peter Raby
Tennessee Williams edited by Matthew C. Roudané
William Carlos Williams edited by Christopher MacGowan
August Wilson edited by Christopher Bigsby
Mary Wollstonecraft edited by Claudia L. Johnson
Virginia Woolf edited by Susan Sellers (second edition)
Wordsworth edited by Stephen Gill
Richard Wright edited by Glenda R. Carpio
W. B. Yeats edited by Marjorie Howes and John Kelly
Xenophon edited by Michael A. Flower
Zola edited by Brian Nelson

TOPICS

The Actress edited by Maggie B. Gale and John Stokes
The African American Novel edited by Maryemma Graham
The African American Slave Narrative edited by Audrey A. Fisch
African American Theatre by Harvey Young
Allegory edited by Rita Copeland and Peter Struck
American Crime Fiction edited by Catherine Ross Nickerson
American Gothic edited by Jeffrey Andrew Weinstock
American Literature of the 1930s edited by William Solomon
American Modernism edited by Walter Kalaidjian
American Poetry since 1945 edited by Jennifer Ashton
American Realism and Naturalism edited by Donald Pizer
American Travel Writing edited by Alfred Bendixen and Judith Hamera
American Women Playwrights edited by Brenda Murphy
Ancient Rhetoric edited by Erik Gunderson
Arthurian Legend edited by Elizabeth Archibald and Ad Putter
Australian Literature edited by Elizabeth Webby
The Beats edited by Stephen Belletto
Boxing edited by Gerald Early
British Black and Asian Literature (1945–2010) edited by Deirdre Osborne
British Fiction: 1980–2018 edited by Peter Boxall
British Fiction since 1945 edited by David James
British Literature of the 1930s edited by James Smith
British Literature of the French Revolution edited by Pamela Clemit
British Romantic Poetry edited by James Chandler and Maureen N. McLane
British Romanticism edited by Stuart Curran (second edition)
British Romanticism and Religion edited by Jeffrey Barbeau